From the creators of BABY BARGAINS

Baby 411

Clear Answers &
Smart Advice for Your
Baby's First Year

Ari Brown, M.D. and Denise Fields

Copyright Page and Low-Impact Pilates Workout

Saxophone, lead guitar by Denise Fields
Drums, rhythm guitar and interior layout by Alan Fields
Cover/interior design and keyboard solo by Epicenter Creative
Catering by Mark Brown and the Salt Lick
Backing harmony vocals and keyboards by Andy and Julia Brown
Percussion and additional guitar by Ben and Jack Fields
Index by New West Indexing
Band photography by Jim Lincoln

Distribution to the book trade by Publisher's Group West, Berkeley, CA (800) 788-3123. Thanks to the entire staff of PGW for their support.

To order this book, call 1-800-888-0385. Or send $11.95 plus $3 shipping (or, in Canada, $19.95 plus $4 shipping) to Windsor Peak Press, 436 Pine Street, Boulder, CO 80302. Questions or comments? Please call the authors at (303) 442-8792. Or fax them a note at (303) 442-3744. Or write to them at the above address in Boulder, Colorado. E-mail us at authors@ baby411.com.

Updates to this book are on the web at www.Baby411.com

Library Cataloging in Publication Data

Brown, Ari, M.D.
Fields, Denise
    Baby 411: Clear Answers & Smart Advice for Your Baby's First Year/
Ari Brown, M.D. and Denise Fields
    480 pages.
    Includes index.
    ISBN 1-889392-15-4
    1. Infants. 2. Child rearing. 3. Infants—Care.

Child Care—Handbooks, manuals, etc. 2. Infants' supplies—Purchasing—United States, Canada, Directories. 3. Children's paraphernalia—Purchasing—Handbooks, manuals. 4. Product Safety—Handbooks, manuals. 5. Consumer education.
    649'.122'0296—dc20. 2003.

Version 1.0

Do you have an old copy of this book? Check our web site at Baby411.com make sure you have the most current version (click on "which version?").

OVERVIEW

What decisions do you have to make before your baby is born? This section explores finding a pediatrician, the latest news on newborn screening and other timely topics. Next, let's talk about your baby's doctor—what are the insider tips to scheduling appointments and what to do on weekends and holidays. Finally, it's Labor Day. Your baby is here! We'll talk about your baby's first few days . . . plus how to survive the first two weeks.

How do you care for your newborn? The first part of this section explores cleaning your newborn, diaper rash and other hygiene issues. Next, let's talk nutrition and growth—what do growth charts mean? What nutrition does your baby need for the first year? We've got the low-down on your baby's nutrition, including tips on vitamin supplements, avoiding obesity and getting enough calcium, fiber and iron. Finally, we'll break down nutrition into separate chapters that focus on liquids and solids. We'll discuss breastfeeding, formula and other liquids like when you should start milk. Next, we'll discuss how to tell when your baby is ready for solid foods, including advice on avoiding food allergies. The last chapter in this section is titled "The other end"—everything you wanted to know about baby poop and more!

Let's talk sleep—this section will give you the scoop on your baby's sleep (or lack thereof). We'll talk about setting up good habits and look at the different sleep "gurus" that haunt the bookstore aisles. Next, we'll look at how your baby will develop, including milestones and social/emotional growth. Finally, it's a topic every parent must deal with: discipline. We'll give you advice on how to soothe a newborn, how to develop a good discipline style and dealing with temper tantrums.

Here, we'll discuss vaccinations—what's required and what's optional. We'll hit the vaccines controversies head on, including the autism debate and thimerisol. A special section will highlight smallpox. This section also covers the most common infections and diseases, with separate chapters devoted to such topics as the common cold, bacterial infections and more.

What should you do when your baby gets sick? This section will give you advice on taking your baby's vital signs and what to have in a first aid kit. We'll hit the Top 12 problems and solutions for newborns, including fever, rashes, trauma and more.

This section includes detailed information on medicines, alternative therapies, lab tests, more info on infections, the glossary, references and footnotes.

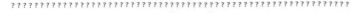

ACKNOWLEDGEMENTS

This book has been my third baby. It has been a labor of love (without the labor pains). And, I am as sleep deprived as when I had a newborn in the house! I am grateful for the help and encouragement of family, friends, and colleagues. If you aren't mentioned by name here, it's because my editors have only allowed 200 words!

Mark, Andy, and Julia—I love you. You have sacrificed a lot to make this book happen. I'm reading tonight! Mom—My hero. How did you manage to have four of us? Daddy—Hope I make you proud. Mom and Dad Brown—Thanks for making me part of the family, even though I eat corn on the cob the wrong way. Ashly and the whole Fontenot clan—WE are so lucky!

Editorial review board: Sidney Seidman, M.D., Thomas Hughes, M.D., Lewis R. First, M.D., Ed Peters, M.D., Julie Boom, M.D., Mark Brown, M.D., Arlinda Michael, R.N., B.S.N., CIMI, IBCLC, Mark Zamutt, RPh., Corinne Frank, Esq., Joyce Jordan, L.V.N.

Other special people: Capital Pediatric Group (my home away from home), St. David's Hospital Parent Education/Lactation Services, Seton Hospital Nurses, Austin Area OB/Gyn, Boston Children's Hospital, University of Texas at Austin Child Development Department, Baylor College of Medicine.

Special thanks: Aiden Thompson, Sadie Engelmann, and Ava Kizer. Hair by Sean Hayes.

And finally, thank you to my patients and their families. You are my inspiration.

— Ari Brown, M.D.

TABLE OF CONENTS

SECTION ONE: 3-2-1 BABY! PREPARING FOR THE NEW ONE

Chapter 1

DECISIONS

Chapter 2

YOU & YOUR BABY'S DOC: INSIDER TIPS & ADVICE

Chapter 3

LABOR DAY

Section Two: Care & Feeding

Chapter 4

Hygiene: The Spa Treatment

Chapter 5

Nutrition & Growth

Chapter 6

Liquids

Chapter 7

SOLIDS

Chapter 8

THE OTHER END

SECTION THREE: SLEEP, DEVELOPMENT & DISCIPLINE

Chapter 9

SLEEP

Chapter 10

DEVELOPMENT

Chapter 11

DISCIPLINE & TEMPERAMENT

Section Four: Sickness & How To Avoid It!

Chapter 12

Vaccinations

Chapter 13

Common Infections

Chapter 14

Common Diseases

SECTION FIVE: FIRST AID—TOP 12 PROBLEMS & SOLUTIONS

Chapter 15

FIRST AID

SECTION SIX: THE REFERENCE LIBRARY

Icons

 Helpful Hint

 Reality Check

 Bottom Line

 Red Flags

 Feedback from the Real World

 Old Wives Tale

 Insider Secrets

 New Parent 411

Introduction

Why read this book?

Welcome to the world of parenthood. Yes, having a baby is both exciting . . . and terrifying.

Soon, you'll be responsible for taking care of this little urchin 24/7, with no time off for good behavior. We've been there—and know what it feels to stand on the edge of the new parent abyss wondering just the what the heck we were doing.

Once your baby is born, your thoughts will be swimming with dozens of questions . . . from the mundane (what's THAT in my baby's diaper?) to the serious (why won't my baby stop crying? Does he have a fever? Should I call the doctor?).

That's why we are here. Think of us as your sherpa guide as you climb Mt. Everest Baby. You need detailed, up-to-date info about taking care of your baby—we've got it. You want straight answers on controversial topics like vaccines, circumcision and newborn screening—again, we're there.

Yes, we realize there are many other baby books out there, all promising to reveal the secrets to taking care of your baby. So, does the world really need another baby book? Let's put that into bold type.

Does the world need another baby book?

Well, darn it, we think so. Yes, if you stand in the parenting aisle of your local bookstore, you'll be assaulted by an avalanche of baby books with titles like YOUR BABY'S FIRST YEAR—SECOND BY SECOND . . . and our personal favorite, WE KNOW MORE THAN YOU: WHAT CELEBRITIES AND SUPERMODELS CAN TEACH YOU ABOUT BEING A PARENT.

All that is well and good, but we found that MOST baby books miss the mark when it comes to nuts and bolts issues—like how do you clean a baby? And feed it? And what happens when something goes wrong, like God forbid, your baby gets sick?

And let's not forget about the new addition to your family—no, not your baby. We're talking about your baby's *doctor*. How do you pick a pediatrician? And how do you get along with this person? Can you call your doc at 2am and ask a question about diaper rash? (Short answer: yes, but don't expect the doc to be real cheery on the phone).

When it comes to offering advice about medical issues with newborns, most baby books fail because, well, they aren't written by someone who's actually been to medical school. Yes, there are guidebooks written by "girl-friends" and other so-called experts . . . but if we want actual medical advice, we'd prefer that to come from someone who knows more about medicine than you can learn from watching ER.

Okay, to be honest, there are a few baby books written by doctors and nurses. But we found many so boring and dry, they are listed as FDA-approved cures for insomnia. (Not that new parents will ever have that problem, of course).

And other good books on babies by respected docs haven't been updated since the Reagan administration. Sorry, the world of baby care moves at Internet speed these days, so a book published ten years ago isn't going to cut it when it comes to a topic like cord blood banking. We're proud that this book contains the very latest recommendations and controversies swirling around the world of babies. And we are one of the few baby books with a detailed web site that offers the latest updates and news on baby's health.

Finally, let's talk about our biggest pet peeve when it comes to baby books: generic advice. Too many books on babies are marred by a lack of specifics and detail.

We get the feeling that authors water down their advice and opinions so as not to offend any reader. While that's nice, it doesn't help when you want a specific answer to a question you have at 3am with your baby. As new parents, we wanted detailed, specific answers to our questions about our newborn—not bland generic platitudes.

Yes, despite all the resources available to new parents (books, magazines, the web), it is amazing how we all end up asking all the same questions as new parents: will we ever sleep through the night again? How come this breastfeeding thing is so difficult? How do I take my baby's temperature? And another 337 questions like that.

That's why we wrote this book—think of it as an FAQ for new parents.

Meet the new authors, same as the old authors

This book was created by the same team that brought you Baby Bargains—Denise & Alan Fields. This time, we've added a new twist: a co-author, Dr. Ari Brown.

Actually, Dr. Brown has written the majority of this book . . . especially the detailed medical advice. An award-winning pediatrician in private practice in Austin, TX, Dr. Brown graduated from the Baylor School of Medicine. She did her pediatric residency at the renowned Children's Hospital in Boston, under the auspices of legendary pediatrician T. Berry Brazelton. In short, Dr. Brown knows her stuff.

Denise Fields brings her 15 years of experience as a consumer advocate to Baby 411—as the co-author of *Baby Bargains* and *Toddler Bargains*, Fields has been featured on Oprah, The Today Show and Good Morning America as well as in articles in the *Wall Street Journal* and *New York Times*. For Baby 411, Denise adds in her experience as both a mom and author— many of the questions we get on our message boards hit the same hot button issues you'll see here.

As always, the secret sauce to our books is reader feedback. First, you'll notice readers of our previous books contributed to several sections of this book—you'll see their "Real World Feedback" when it comes to topics like child care, feeding and more. Second, look at the questions we list in each chapter. These are the frequent questions asked by patients of Dr. Brown and the readers of *Baby Bargains* . . . and the same questions that most first-time parents ponder.

Yes, both of the authors of this book are also mommies. They have four children between them. Best of all, the authors are from your generation—we know you want detailed info, the latest research and trends, plus handy web resources. We know you want to go online to get the latest updates, so we've created a special web site for this book (Baby411.com). There you can read any breaking news, swap stories with other parents on our message boards and sign up for a free newsletter that will provide even more insight.

How to Use this Book

Instructions: Open cover. Start reading.

Just kidding! We realize you know how to read a book, but let's go over a few details on how to get the most out of Baby 411.

First, let's talk about BIG UGLY LATIN WORDS. You can't discuss baby's health without whipping out the Latin. To keep the jargon from over-whelming you, we have a handy glossary at the end of this book. When you see a **BIG UGLY LATIN WORD** in bold small caps, turn to the back to get a quick definition.

Second, if you flip through the chapters, you'll note boxes with Dr. B's opinion. As it sounds, these are her *opinions* on several hot button issues. Feel free to disagree with these thoughts, but they are based on years of seeing real-world patients and talking with parents.

Finally, let's talk footnotes—we've tried to footnote the sources used throughout this book. These references start on page 427.

No ads? No plugs?

Yes, that's true—as with all our books, this guide contains ZERO ads, spam and commercial plugs. No pharmaceutical or formula company has paid the authors to plug their products in this book. Dr. Brown does NOT go on all-expense paid junkets to Aruba to learn about the latest drug or medical research (although she could use a beach vacation after writing this book). The opinions in this book are those of Denise Fields and Dr. Brown—in the latter case, based on her training and experience in the practice of pediatric medicine.

Show us the science!

The goal of Baby 411 is to provide you with the most up-to-date medical info on your baby. We're talking state-of-the-art when it comes to your baby's health and nutrition.

So, in the age of Internet rumors and 24/7 cable news, let's take a moment to talk SCIENCE.

When it comes to your baby's health, our mantra is SHOW US THE SCIENCE! Before we recommend a particular treatment, parenting method or medicine, we expect there to be good science behind it.

What is good science? Good scientific research is conducted by reputable researchers and published in a major medical journal, like the *New England Journal of Medicine*. Good science is based on a large enough sample to be statistically significant—and verified by peers before it is published.

Contrast this to junk science. Much of what you see online is, unfortunately, junk science—"research" done by questionable individuals who are usually trying to sell a miracle cure along with their theories. Junk science is often based on flawed studies that use too-small samples to be relevant. Just because four of your friends have babies with blue eyes does not mean there is an epidemic of blue-eyed babies on your block.

Much of the junk science you see online or read in the media is there to push a political agenda. Sure, these zealots are well meaning, but they harm their cause by hyping some obscure study from a doctor in Fiji as medical "truth."

Of course, this isn't always so black and white—sometimes good science is "spun" or hyped by groups who want to push their cause.

To put this in perspective, let's look at an example from Canada. In June 2003, the *Financial Post* newspaper in Canada reported that government researchers there found that most cereal-based baby foods contained small amounts of "mycotoxins." What the heck are mycotoxins? These are naturally occurring toxins that are related to molds . . . and are present in most of the world's cereal crops.

The headline in the *Financial Post* read: "Federal study finds toxins in baby food." Yet, this same story was picked up by a U.S. web site and labeled "Scientists find most baby foods toxic." Whoa! Sounds scary, no?

But let's look at what the study *really* said. The Health Canada researchers found "low levels" of toxins in baby food cereal. And the word "low" was an understatement. The Canadian scientists found a level of 32 parts *per billion* of one mycotoxin in oat-based baby cereal. That's more than "low" folks—that's infinitesimally small.

And let's face it—humans have been eating these tiny amounts of fungus in grains for centuries without ill effect. There are toxins, molds and other nasty stuff that occurs naturally in our environment.

Fortunately, there was no panic among parents that was set off by the Canadian study—perhaps CNN was too busy with the latest J. Lo news to report on this "baby food crisis." But this is an example of how "science" often gets distorted and warped as it winds its way through the meatgrinder of the web and media these days.

As your guides in Baby Health Land, we hope to steer you toward the good science when making decisions for your baby.

The Six Ground Rules for Being a Good Parent

1 **THERE ARE NO GROUND RULES.** Well, what we mean is there are no absolute truths. Thanks to that quirky thing called DNA, every baby is different. Yes, there are "general" guidelines that will help you be a good parent (and we'll spend the next 400+ pages giving you those guidelines), but there are no absolute truths. Your baby will consistently amaze, surprise, frustrate and confound you. Did we mention surprise?

2 **CHECK YOUR PRIORITIES AT THE DOOR.** Make a list of all things that are important in your life—your hobbies, house, friends, etc. Now, crunch that list up into a little ball and throw it out the window. Your baby is now priorities #1 through #17. Example: your house. Don't expect it to be clean again until 2022.

3 **GO WITH YOUR GUT.** Well-meaning people—friends, your parents, book authors, complete strangers—are going to try to advise you as to what's best for you and your baby. That's nice, but after a while you are just going to have figure out this parent thing on your own. Think of it like flying a plane . . . you can sit in a flight simulator all you want, but taking the controls in a 747 zipping along at 500 MPH at 30,000 feet is more like what if feels like to be a real parent.

4 **SCHEDULE TIME FOR YOURSELF.** Want to take a shower after your baby is born? You've got to schedule that 15 minutes. After the first couple of months (or sooner), take time OFF from being mommy and daddy. Have a friend or babysitter watch the baby and go out to dinner and a movie. Give your spouse a break once a week for an hour of "hobby time."

5 **CALLING ALL FAVORS.** Don't be afraid to ask for help—and free feel to lean on your friends and relatives to help you through the first few weeks.

6 **BELIEVE IN YOUR CHOICES.** No matter what you decide for your family (breast feeding, work, child care, etc), you're going to hear sniping from others. Often, that's guilt-driven—folks feel defensive about what they decided for their own kids . . . so, they take it out on you. Nice, eh? The best advice: surround yourself with supportive friends who can counter any negativism.

Major Legal Disclaimer

Yes, no medical book about babies is complete without that ubiquitous legal disclaimer . . . so here's ours:

The information we provide in this book is intended to help families understand their baby's medical issues. It is NOT intended to replace the advice of your doctor. Before you start any medical treatment, always check in with your baby's doctor who can counsel you on the specific needs of your baby.

We have made a tremendous effort to give you the most up to date medical info available. However, medical research is constantly providing new insight to pediatric healthcare. That's why we have an accompanying website at Baby411.com to give you the latest breaking updates (and why you should also discuss your baby's medical care with your baby's doc).

Baby 411

3-2-1 Baby!
Preparing for the New One

Chapter 1

Decisions

"When choosing between two evils, always choose the one you haven't tried yet."
~ Mae West

Yes, your job as a parent begins the moment your baby is conceived. You will find yourself instinctively making decisions from a parent's viewpoint. Maybe it's the hormones. Or, maybe for the first time in your life, you have a sense of responsibility to a helpless little urchin inside of you. Yes, YOU are now a GROWN-UP.

This sense of responsibility will cause you to ponder the questions that all parents ponder.

1. **Will I be a good parent?** (Babysitting and pet ownership are helpful job experiences.)

2. **Can I be as good a parent as my parents were?** (Yes. You've learned from their mistakes!)

3. **Will I handle discipline dilemmas better than my friends do?** (Maybe. It's very easy to be critical when you aren't yet a parent.)

4. **Will I make the right decisions for my child's health?** (That's why we're here—to help point the way to the best choices for you and your child).

This chapter will address the decisions you will need to make before your baby is born. First, we'll discuss parenting styles—yep, you have to pick one BEFORE the baby is born. Then let's talk about finding the baby's doctor. Unlike most experiences you've had with doctors, this one you actually pick before you need her. Next, it's on to a couple of controversial topics: circumcision and optional newborn metabolic screenings. Should you bank your newborn's cord blood? Yes, another decision faced by today's parents that your parents never had to deal with.

Finally, let's talk about childcare options. Again, you must at least mull this issue before baby is born—that's because other expectant parents are already putting their names on waiting lists for the hottest day care options in your community now.

If you are adopting a baby, we'll discuss the decisions you'll face in this chapter as well.

With all these decisions that need to be made, let's get rolling. In order to make some sense of this, let's start with a timeline of what you should decide and when.

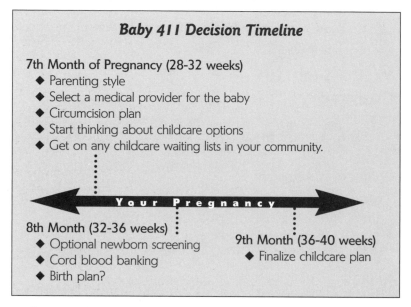

Baby 411 Decision Timeline

7th Month of Pregnancy (28-32 weeks)
- ◆ Parenting style
- ◆ Select a medical provider for the baby
- ◆ Circumcision plan
- ◆ Start thinking about childcare options
- ◆ Get on any childcare waiting lists in your community.

Your Pregnancy

8th Month (32-36 weeks)
- ◆ Optional newborn screening
- ◆ Cord blood banking
- ◆ Birth plan?

9th Month (36-40 weeks)
- ◆ Finalize childcare plan

Once you have reached your seventh month, it's time to make some decisions. No, we're not talking about choosing names or wallpaper designs. Now you'll have to make choices that will affect how you raise your child together as a team (that includes moms, dads, grandparents, etc.). First and foremost is determining your team's parenting style.

Picking a Parenting Style

Q. How do I pick a parenting style?

Remember Dorothy in the Wizard of Oz? She always wore the shoes she needed to take her home, but didn't realize it. You, New Parent, are wearing the shoes. You have the skills and instincts to be a great parent. TRUST YOURSELF.

Your style reflects your approach to certain situations. This includes food (breast vs. formula), sleep (family bed vs. crib), and discipline of your newest family member.

You and your significant other will need to discuss these issues and come to terms that are agreeable to both. Remember when you had to agree on a china pattern for your wedding registry? (Hopefully there will be fewer arguments). You *both* need to be happy about your strategy. This can be modified once you really have a baby to care for, but it helps to have some of the ground rules in place. Here are some ways to get started:

1. **Remember your own parents' style.** Besides nit-picking all the mistakes they made, consider what worked—and use it. Yes, you will hear yourself saying what your parents once said . . . and cringe!

2. **Watch other parents.** See how they respond to stressful situations with their kids (grocery store, restaurant, airplane flight). Think about what you would do. Ask your spouse how he/she would respond.

3. **Read some more books.** The parenting aisle of your bookstore is stuffed with all sorts of books on how to be a parent. Including these authors. How do you find the best books? Read reviews of books on Amazon.com, talk to your pediatrician, and ask other parents what books worked for them. There are lots out there! Some prominent child development authors include: T. Berry Brazelton, Penelope Leach, William Sears, and Benjamin Spock. I am a Brazelton groupie, but you can decide for yourself.

Be flexible—sometimes the best parenting style is a combination of approaches, mixing a bit of this and some of that. Your style may change over time as well.

Selecting a Doctor

Q. Do I need to select a pediatrician before the baby is born? If so, why?

Yes. It's helpful to meet a pediatrician (at a prenatal consultation) before the baby is born. Here are three reasons:

1. **It gives the pediatrician a chance to review any medical problems** during your pregnancy or with your family members that could affect the baby. (The doctor appreciates being prepared.)

2. **You can get advice** regarding medical decisions you'll be making in the first few days of your baby's life. (You'll appreciate being prepared.)

3. **You will be more relaxed** knowing who is examining and advising you in the hospital—yes, your pediatrician will come to visit both you and baby right there in the maternity ward. (More details in the Labor Day chapter.)

Q. So, how do I pick a pediatrician?

Ask your OB-GYN for a recommendation or consult with friends, relatives or other parents. Then, schedule a "prenatal consultation" with each candidate (keep the list short to maintain your sanity). While doctors consider this meeting a "consultation," it's really a job interview—you are considering hiring this doctor to take care of your baby, from birth to college. Consider your prenatal consultation as parent-doctor bonding time.

Q. When should I schedule a prenatal consultation?

Schedule a consult as you begin your third trimester. Don't wait any later than your 36th week. Why so early? Two reasons: first, to get some help making the medical decisions you need to make about your newborn. Second, because your pregnancy and due date are unpredictable—your baby could be early. You don't want to be shopping for a pediatrician while you are recovering from labor!

Q. Do pediatricians charge a fee for prenatal consultations?

Some do, some don't.

Pediatricians are about the only physician specialists who routinely schedule "meet the doctor" visits. Such visits aren't just for the parent's benefit—it helps give the doctor a heads up about any potential medical problems the baby may have. Don't be offended if you get a bill—it is perfectly kosher. Pediatricians are offering their time to answer parenting questions—and some parents come in with *lots* of questions! I had one couple come in with their questions on dual laptops. While I endured 45 minutes of interrogation, I thought to myself, "Why is it that I don't charge for prenatal visits?" A smart move: when you schedule the appointment, ask if there is a charge for the prenatal visit.

Q. What general questions should I ask at a prenatal consultation?

If you've read any pregnancy book, you've seen a list of questions to ask at your prenatal visit. Here is some advice: ignore those cookie-cutter lists and make your own, based on the issues that are important to you. This could include:

1. **Ask questions about topics you are wondering about.** You may be so overwhelmed, you can't come up with specifics and that's okay—just pick the topic and we can fill in the details. Example: allergies. You might discuss how to avoid food allergies or the history of allergies in your family.
2. **Ask questions that help you get to know the doctor.** Pretend you are on the "Dating Game," and not on the "Weakest Link."
3. **Ask questions about how the practice flows.** There is more to your office experience than your doctor. You need to be an informed consumer. Medical care has changed dramatically since you were a kid. We'll discuss more details on this next.

BOTTOM LINE: You don't have to ask *every* question that you have in your first meeting with your pediatrician.

Q. Okay, what smart questions SHOULD parents ask of a pediatrician?

Let us walk you through a typical prenatal visit and tell you what parents USUALLY ask . . . and what questions parents SHOULD ask instead. (Note: at the end of this section, we'll list all these questions you should ask in one handy list).

Parent asks: What is your training?
A better question: How did you decide on pediatrics?

All pediatricians have about the same training. Just look on the wall. We spent a lot of time and money to get all those degrees. Our parents would kill us if we didn't get them framed and hung up in our office. Pediatricians complete four years of medical school and then three more years of a residency program focused only on children's medical care. Family Practitioners complete four years of medical school and then three to four years of residency that includes child and adult health care. Regardless of where a doctor trained, we will take a Board Certification Exam to prove we learned our stuff. Look for the letters F.A.A.P. or F.A.A.F.P. after our names. The "F" stands for Fellow, a distinguished title doctors get for passing our boards in either pediatrics or family practice. All pediatricians take continuing medical education courses annually and recertification exams every seven years to make sure we are keeping up with current trends in medicine.

Ask why the doctor chose pediatrics for a career, instead of say, urology. It's a more open-ended question. You'll likely hear her credentials in the answer, but you'll get a better idea of whom this person is.

Parent asks: Do you divide the sick and well waiting rooms?
A better question: How long will I be sitting in your waiting room?

Even if the practice's waiting room is divided into sick and well areas, the *patient/exam* rooms are not. Don't expect the entire doctor's office to be germ free. View your trip to the doctor like a trip anywhere else—where there are kids, there will be germs. One tip: bring your own toys and wash your hands after the visit.

I'd rather know how long I have to entertain my child before the doctor sees us. You'll get an idea by how late the doctor is for the prenatal visit. We all try to be as punctual as possible, but unexpected things happen. A

NEW PARENT 411: WELL-CHILD VERSUS SICK VISITS

Doctors divide their visits with your baby into two categories: well-child and sick visits. Well-child visits are what you might think of as a regular check-up—these are scheduled at regular intervals to check your child's general health, do vaccinations, etc. Sick child visits are when your child is, well, sick. FYI: Each of these visits is scheduled differently by most doctors. We'll discuss this on page 9.

practice that flows well should get you and the doctor face to face within 30 minutes of your scheduled appointment.

Real world mom advice: first, call BEFORE you leave home and make sure the doctor is on schedule. If your doctor is running behind, you can prepare. Bring extra entertainment for you and your child and even snacks. Another tip: if you are sitting in the office and are not called within 20 minutes of your appointment time, it's time to find out what's going on—ask the front desk for an update on the doctor's situation. Finally, don't add to your stress—never schedule another appointment or meeting immediately after your doctor appointment. Doing so (and then running late) will only add to the frustration.

Let's talk about acceptable wait times to see your baby's doctor. On the message board for our other book, *Baby Bargains*, when discussing how to select a pediatrician, we were shocked that some parents were left waiting for up to three hours! Obviously, that was the extreme . . . we found "average" wait times to be all over the board. Some parents wait as little as ten or 15 minutes while others reported average wait times of an hour or more. In our opinion, acceptable average wait times should be about ten to 15 minutes during non-flu season. When doctors get slammed with sick patients at the height of flu season, it is understandable that wait times can slip to 30 minutes or more. Bottom line, waiting longer than an hour to see your doctor for a scheduled visit is not acceptable—you need to shop for another pediatrician.

So, what are doctors doing back there while you cool your heels in the waiting room? Are they watching CNN? Shooting the breeze over a latte with other doctors? No, there are several things that usually conspire to make a doctor run late. See the following box for more on this.

BEHIND THE SCENES: WHY IS MY DOCTOR SO LATE?

Do you ever wonder why your doctor is late? I'll let you in on the secrets behind the waiting room door. Let's look at a typical morning at my practice:

◆ "Dr. Brown, your 8:00am well child appointment is stuck in traffic, can you see them at 8:20am?" (Answer—"Yes.") That patient actually arrives at 8:25am and is brought to an exam room at 8:30am.

◆ My 8:15am well child appointment is brought back to a room at 8:35am because they had new insurance that needed to be verified first (this takes my business office about 20 minutes on the phone).

◆ My 8:30am sick child with the flu also has asthma and needs a breathing treatment. I need to go back and examine him a second time after my nurse administers a treatment.

◆ "Dr. Brown, your 8:45am sick visit has a sister who is sick, too. Do you have time to see her?" (Answer—"Yes," . . . but now I am double booked at 8:45am.)

So, at 8:35am, I have five patients in four exam rooms that all need to be seen. By 9:00am, I'm already 20 minutes behind and will need to play catch up. It's about this time I'm dreaming of sitting on a

Parent asks: How do I schedule well child visits/sick visits?
A better question: How does your daily schedule flow? How much time is allotted for visits?

Most practices schedule well child checks in advance. A smart tip: in a busy practice, schedule the *next* well child visit when you are in the office having one. The doctor's nurse or secretary will always advise you when another well child visit is needed.

Sick visits are usually scheduled on the same day you call. Obviously, you can't predict when your child will get sick and you won't settle for waiting until tomorrow to be seen. This is probably different than what you are used to with your own doctor. I once tried to see my doctor for a sick visit and was told I could have an appointment a week later. I told the receptionist, "Thank you. I could be dead by then." But I digress.

What you really want to know is how much time you will spend with the pediatrician. Every practice varies, but well checks usually get more time than sick visits. A typical well check may be a 15-minute appointment. A sick visit may be ten minutes. If there is a chronic problem (e.g. headaches, constipation, school problem, behavior problem), we may schedule consultation appointments which are 30 minutes or longer. You'll note these time guidelines are never published or posted in a doctor's office. Why? Because doctors will take as long as needed to address the issues at hand— even if this means making other patients wait (which leads us back to the earlier discussion of why it takes so long to see a doctor). Remember appointment slots are just a framework for a doctor's day.

If you keep up with the news, you know that the U.S. health care sys-

beach somewhere with a drink adorned with a cute umbrella.

All hope is not lost. Some sick visits are simple and will take less time than the appointment slot (i.e. rashes, ear infection rechecks). Some days, there are only sick kids that are "sicker than billed" and parents that need extra handholding. I will be behind all morning.

Reality check: doctors are notoriously behind schedule because we try to address the needs of each patient, no matter how long it takes. It helps if we can anticipate what those needs are. If you want to discuss your child's school problems during an appointment for a sore throat, tell the appointments person. Otherwise, it's likely your doctor will ask you to schedule another appointment so there is more time to talk.

For more tips on when is the best time to schedule your baby's check ups, see Chapter 3, "Labor Day."

Finally, another point to remember: some doctors now have amazing office hours. A few are even open until 9pm each night and on Saturdays and Sundays! What a concept. Yes, these are typically larger practices in bigger cities, but they do exist. And if a practice has longer "operating hours" and more doctors, odds are the waits will be less. Again, the key is to shop around and see what is available in your community.

tem is under intense scrutiny. The costs of medical care and prescription drugs are on the rise. Your insurance premiums are on the rise. The CEO's salary of your health insurance company is on the rise, too. But, insurance companies have steadily *decreased* reimbursements to doctors for office visits and procedures. Yet, doctors need to keep up with our bills (overhead costs, malpractice insurance, student loans—yep, I'm still paying those off). The result? We have to schedule more patients each day.

BOTTOM LINE

Sick visits are "problem oriented." Be prepared to ask all your questions up front. If you have numerous issues or chronic issues to discuss, schedule a separate consultation. Doctors expect your list of burning questions at *well check* appointments, not sick visits. You can always call too.

Parent asks: What is your philosophy? (This one must be in some parenting book because everyone asks it.)
Better questions to ask: How do you approach the doctor-parent relationship? How do you feel about alternative therapies?

Doctor-parent relationships have changed since you were a child. When you went to the doctor, he told your mother what she needed to do to make you feel better. Your mother said "thank you" and did what she was told. There was no debate . . . and no "alternative therapies" mom could look up on the Internet. Doctors still wistfully reminisce about these days like a retired hall of famer recalls the '64 World Series.

When some parents ask about "philosophy," they really want to know about what type of medicine the doctor practices. An M.D. (medical doctor) educated in the United States is trained in traditional medicine. She is a scientist who learns how the body works and malfunctions and how to fix the body with medicine or surgery. Doctors also learn how scientific research is done and how to read medical studies critically. As a rule, doc-

DR B'S OPINION:
ALTERNATIVE MEDICINE

In today's world, I tell the parent what their child's diagnosis is, explain the diagnosis, and explain the therapy that I would advise. Then the parent often quotes recent information about alternative therapies that they found on the Internet (sometimes accurate and sometimes not) and asks what I think of it. I don't mind these interactions—I find them stimulating. They keep me on my toes. As you can tell by now, I like educating parents. But, not every physician is enthusiastic about this style of practicing medicine.

As we discussed in the introduction to this book, our mantra on alternative medicine and therapies for your baby is SHOW US THE SCIENCE. If an alternative therapy is shown to be effective in a reputable scientific study, then we are happy to recommend it. But if it is just snake oil or an Internet myth, we won't hesitate to say so. See Appendix B, Alternative Medicine for more details.

tors are skeptical of new therapies unless they see data and good science to support the treatment. As a result, traditional doctors generally do not embrace the philosophies of herbalists or chiropractors.

Parent asks: Do you accept our health insurance?
A better question: Do you have a list of health insurance plans you accept?

Both big and small businesses switch insurance plans as frequently as the weather changes. The result: doctors lose patients when they change insurance. There is a reasonable chance that the doctor you select now may not perform your baby's college physical. Watching your child grow is one of the most rewarding parts of any doctor's job. So, losing a family to another practice due to insurance change is something most doctors try hard to avoid. A good practice will have a smart office administrator at the helm that negotiates reasonable contracts with *many* insurance plans.

Parent asks: What hospitals do you have privileges at?
Better questions to ask: Do you have privileges at the hospital where I am delivering? Who cares for my child in an emergency hospital visit, or hospitalization?

The answers to these questions will vary significantly depending on where you live. Gone are the days of the "Do It All Doctor" unless you live in a rural area.

Although continuity of patient care is important, doctors are starting to realize they are better at some things than others. The current trend in medicine is to divide outpatient care (office-based practice) and in-patient care (hospital-based practice). Our patients get more specialized care and our spouses are happier with us. So, this is how some practices work:

1. **A pediatrician goes to a select number of area hospitals to see newborns.** If there is a problem with the baby at the time of delivery, there is likely to be an "in-house" pediatrician or neonatologist in the hospital to handle emergencies. If you deliver at a hospital that your pediatrician does not go to, a staff pediatrician may care for the baby until he goes home.
2. **In emergencies, your pediatrician is available by phone.** If an emergency room visit is warranted, an emergency room physician may evaluate and treat your child. That doctor will call your doctor to discuss a plan.
3. **If your child needs to stay in the hospital overnight** (an admission), a staff pediatrician (hospitalist) may be responsible for care. That doctor will call your doctor to make discharge and follow up plans.

BOTTOM LINE: You may not see your own doctor if you have an emergency or a hospital stay.

Parent asks: How are phone calls handled?
Better questions to ask:

1. Who answers your patient calls during the day?
2. Who answers emergency calls at night?
3. What is the expected waiting time for a phone call to be returned?

Phone calls during office hours are handled in a variety of ways. On one extreme, a nurse will screen and answer all phone calls. On the other extreme, the doctor will answer all calls (a rarity now, as most doctors are busy seeing patients). Most practices fall somewhere in the middle. Some practices offer a "call in hour" each day where patients can speak directly to the doctor. I'm not fond of this approach. I'd compare it to calling a radio station to win tickets for something. If you don't have auto-redial, forget it. Some high tech practices have e-mail or voicemail accessibility to the doctor. In general, most practices will have a nurse who can answer routine calls efficiently and hand the more complicated calls over to the doctor.

After office hours, practices usually have an answering service that dispatches emergency calls to the physician "on-call." The on-call doctor is usually (but not always) an associate in the practice. You will likely see or speak to all of your doctor's partners at some point in your child's life. Some practices utilize a nurse call center after hours to handle routine calls. Call centers use strict protocols to manage every type of emergency imaginable. Even with a call center, the on call doctor is still available for questions.

Here are more questions to ask about phone calls:

1. What is the name of the nurse who handles phone calls? You two will be on a first name basis soon, so ask now.

2. If you want to speak to the doctor, can you? You should never feel that there is a fortress built around your doctor. You have every right to talk to your doctor directly. If it's not an urgent call, it may take until the end of the business day to get back with you . . . but it should be an option.

3. How long does it take for the nurse or doctor to return calls? You'll want to know how long to sit by the phone (you can also leave a cell phone number). If you don't hear from us in a "reasonable" amount of time you should call us back.

4. Do you charge for phone call consultations? Yes, this does happen. It is becoming more common for doctors to charge a nominal fee for phone calls. It used to be taken for granted that phone advice was a freebie. With the current status of health care, doctors are more likely to bill for services that were previously 'part of the package.'

BEHIND THE SCENES: CALLING YOUR DOC AT 3AM

When doctors are on call at night, we are not sitting by the phone in our offices waiting for your call. We go to sleep at home with our beepers at our bedside table. So if you talk to us at 3am and we sound sleepy . . . we are. In our residency training (the medical equivalent of boot camp), doctors became experts at answering questions while sleep deprived. Don't expect us to have any information from your child's chart, schedule appointments, or be excited about discussing diaper rash creams at 3am. Be a friend and save those calls for office hours.

BOTTOM LINE: THE 12 QUESTIONS YOU SHOULD ASK

Okay, let's sum it up again. Here are the 12 questions we suggest you ask any potential pediatrician. (See earlier in this chapter for an explanation of why we think these questions are important—and some good answers you should hear from the doctor).

1. How did you decide on pediatrics?
2. How long will I be sitting in your waiting room?
3. How does your daily schedule flow?
4. How much time is allotted for visits?
5. How do you approach the doctor-parent relationship?
6. How do you feel about alternative therapies?
7. Do you have a list of health insurance plans you accept?
8. Do you have privileges at the hospital where I am delivering?
9. Who cares for my child in an emergency hospital visit, or hospitalization?
10. Who answers your patient calls during the day?
11. Who answers emergency calls at night?
12. What is the expected waiting time for a phone call to be returned?

Q. How do I decide which doctor is right for my child?

Go with your gut instincts. Think to yourself, "Will I feel comfortable asking this person some really embarrassing questions?" If the answer is yes, go for it.

Pediatricians develop a relationship with you and your child. Doctors enjoy being a part of your family and watching your child grow with you. Unless you move or change insurance, your doctor will see your child until he moves out of your house. That means you will probably see him more than any other medical provider until you get your AARP card and senior discounts at the movies.

So now that you have discussed how you will parent with your partner and chosen your child's doctor it's time to move onto some more controversial topics. If you're having (or think you're having) a son, congratulations!

With three boys between us, we authors are pretty on top of the boy thing. And one of your first decisions when you have a boy will be: circumcision or not?

Circumcision

Q. Is circumcision right for my son?

Before your son is born, you should decide whether or not you want to have him circumcised. If you feel weird thinking about the future of your son's penis, join the club.

The practice of circumcision (surgical removal of foreskin) became common in the United States in the late 1800's for hygienic reasons. It has continued to be the "mainstream" choice for most American boys . . . and the subject of much controversy because today's parents want to do the "right" thing for their sons.

The problem? No one in the medical community will tell you what is "best," including the American Academy of Pediatrics, the American Urological Association, and the American College of Obstetrics and Gynecology (you'll understand why they are interested in your son's penis as you read on). Why? That's because there is no right or wrong answer to the question of circumcision. *You* have to make the call.

Circumcisions are done more for social, cultural, and religious reasons than for medical necessity.

Q. What are the advantages of circumcision?

In a nutshell, fewer hygiene problems, infections, and risk of cancer.

1. **Hygiene.** It is easier to keep a circumcised penis clean. The foreskin can harbor germs (see **HUMAN PAPILLOMAVIRUS**-HPV) and dead skin. When a boy is uncircumcised, the penis can get infected and swell (see **BALANITIS**). Although it doesn't occur often, it hurts as much as it looks like it does. The foreskin can also get stuck in a pulled back position (see **PARAPHIMOSIS**)—OUCH!

2. **Bladder infections.** Bladder infections (see **URINARY TRACT INFECTION-UTI**) occur more frequently in girls. However, boys who are uncircumcised have a ten to 20 times greater risk of infection than their circumcised friends. This again is due to hygiene reasons. In general, boys have about a 1% risk of getting a bladder infection.

3. **Penile Cancer.** Cancer of the penis is rare. A man's lifetime risk of getting penile cancer is 1 in 100,000. Compared to breast cancer (1 in 8 women) and skin cancer (1 in 75 people), it's almost not worth worrying about. But, yes, you guessed it, it happens more frequently in uncircumcised men.

4. **HIV.** It is well documented that uncircumcised men are more likely to have the HIV virus and infect their partners. Why? Because the area under the foreskin makes a nice spot for the virus to set up housekeeping.

5. **Cervical Cancer.** This is where our gynecology colleagues get involved. A recent study published in the *New England Journal of Medicine* has intrigued the medical community.[1] It showed that women involved with uncircumcised "high risk" partners (more than six previous sexual partners) had a five-times greater risk of getting cancer of the cervix compared to women whose sex partners were circumcised. The reason? **HUMAN PAPILLOMAVIRUS—HPV** (a sexually transmitted virus) loves to live under the foreskin. HPV is a known cause of cervical cancer. So, your decision to circumcise your son may affect your daughter-in-law's health someday.

Q. What are the disadvantages of circumcision?

Like any surgical procedure, circumcision has risks:

1. **The risk of surgery.** Circumcision involves cutting the foreskin away from the head of the penis. As with any surgical procedure, there is a small chance of bleeding (1 in 3000 risk) or infection (1 in 1000 risk).

2. **Penile Adhesions.** Occasionally, the skin between the shaft and

the head of the penis will get stuck together due to a collection of sticky, cream cheesy stuff called smegma. The penis will look like it is uncircumcised. Your pediatrician can pull the skin back if necessary (For more details, see Chapter 4, Hygiene, and **PENILE ADHESIONS**).

3. **The Hidden Penis.** It sounds like a concealed weapon, doesn't it? Chubby baby boys have a fat roll above their genitals. It causes the circumcised penis to get sucked inwards. The penis looks normal as the boys grow up, but it's always concerning to parents.

4. **Sexual Pleasure.** Those who advocate for leaving the penis intact will tell you that men who are uncircumcised have greater sexual pleasure. See the box below for more discussion on this.

BOTTOM LINE

There are certainly medical benefits to having a circumcised penis. The benefits are just not clear cut enough for any medical group to strongly advocate for the procedure. If you are truly having trouble making a decision about circumcision, I suggest you consider what Dad's penis looks like. It certainly will raise fewer questions when your son starts comparing his body parts to Dad's.

Q. Who performs the circumcision?

In most large cities, your obstetrician performs the circumcision procedure just before your baby leaves the hospital.

Why the obstetrician? Many pediatricians do not perform any surgical procedures—for good reason. You wouldn't want to see the way I slice my Thanksgiving turkey! Obstetricians have surgical training and are at the hospital already taking care of Mommy. But you need to check with your OB to be sure. Urologists can also perform a circumcision on your baby. This requires special arrangements, however. Urologists do not generally come to the hospital to perform routine circumcisions. You'll need to do some homework if you choose this option.

In smaller towns and rural areas, other physicians (family practitioners or pediatricians) will perform circumcisions because there is limited access to specialty care. As long as the person has been trained to do the procedure, it does not matter what the doctor's specialty is.

What if you decide to circumcise your son after they leave the hospital? That's fine, but there is one caveat: some insurance providers will NOT cover the cost of the procedure once baby leaves the hospital.

DR B'S OPINION:
SEXUAL PLEASURE & CIRCUMCISION

Addressing the sexual pleasure question: How do you compare orgasms in a scientific way? Think about it. Most American men are circumcised and seem quite capable of having really great sex. I personally wouldn't use this as a deciding factor. Also: there are some fringe groups who care very deeply about what you do with your son's penis. I'm not really sure what their motivation is, but I'd avoid their websites.

Circumcision is performed as a religious ritual for some families. The person performing the procedure is called a mohel. Most families pay out of pocket for this service. Some savvy families have attempted to have their insurance company pick up the tab. It may be worth checking into.

Q. Is any pain medication used during the circumcision?

Most of the time, yes. Every doctor has her own approach. You can ask your doctor what she feels comfortable doing. Here are the options:

1. Injecting numbing medicine directly into the area (nerve block).
2. Applying topical numbing cream one hour before the procedure.
3. Giving the baby sugar water just prior to the procedure.

BOTTOM LINE: The whole procedure takes about 60 seconds. Yes, it hurts. But most babies go to sleep for a few hours and wake up happy to see you. For more information on circumcision, check out these web sites: medicirc.org, circinfo.net and circumsicion.cjb.net.

Optional Newborn Metabolic Screening: What To Know

Once your baby is born, you'll notice that he is whisked away to get cleaned up and tested. No not an IQ test, a blood test. Your state requires some tests and others are optional. Recently parents have become more interested in the optional tests available. Here's an idea of what's out there and how newborn screening works.

Q. Do all babies get tested for metabolic diseases?

Yes. Every state in the U.S. performs a panel of blood tests on every newborn. This can vary from 3 to 8 tests, depending on the state. (For details on this, see Chapter 3, "Labor Day.")

Q. Are there more screening tests available other than those required by the state?

Yes. Many academic medical centers offer low cost newborn screening for 25 to 60 metabolic disorders.

Metabolic diseases are disorders in which the body fails to break down (metabolize) certain products. If these products are not broken down, they start to get stored up in the body and that creates problems, including heart enlargement, mental retardation, and even death.

So, how do these tests work? When blood is drawn for the state-mandated tests, additional blood can be used for these optional tests. You can get more information from either your obstetrician or pediatrician. The cost varies, but it is usually about $25. You probably spent more money on your Diaper Genie.

Keep in mind that disorders tested for in the optional screen are quite rare (about 1 in 56,000), which is why optional tests aren't on the required screen.

Our opinion: Optional Newborn Screening is a bargain and well worth it especially if you have a family history of these diseas

BEHIND THE SCENES: MORE ON OPTIONAL SCREENS

Although most metabolic diseases are rare, early detection is critical to the health of an affected baby. There are groups, such as the March of Dimes, who advocate for expanding the panel of required state metabolic screening tests. This is a very expensive proposal, given how tight state budgets are these days. So for now, the tests are available only if parents choose to pay for it. FYI: If you choose to bank your baby's cord blood (see more below), you may get a "free" supplemental newborn screen to go with it. For more information, here are some groups you can contact:

1. Baylor Univ. Medical Ctr.
Web: baylorhealth.com
(800)-4-BAYLOR

2. Neo Gen
Web: neogenscreeing.com
(866)-4-NEOGEN toll free

3. CBR Newscreen
Web: newscreentest.com
(888) 267-3256

4. March of Dimes
Web: marchofdimes.com

5. Mayo Clinic
Web: mayoclinic.com

6. University of Colorado Health Sciences Center
(303) 315-7301

7. National Coalition for PKU and Allied Health Disorders
Web: pku-allieddisorders.org
(877) 996-2723

To see which states require what screens, you can visit the web site for the National Newborn Screening and Genetics Resource Center (web: http://genes-r-us.uthscsa.edu). We also have a state by state list of required screens on our web site at Baby411.com (click on "bonus material").

Another amazing new option available to parents today: cord blood banking. Only recently has there been an option for parents to "bank" their baby's cord blood in case of an emergency illness in the future. So here's one more decision for parents to make.

Cord Blood Banking

Q. What exactly is cord blood banking anyway?

The era of modern medicine has given us the opportunity to store the blood from your baby's umbilical cord.

Why is this a cool idea? Well, that blood is loaded with the 'seeds' (hematopoietic stem cells) that later grow into white and red blood cells. These very special cells are also found in the bone marrow of all humans. The umbilical cord blood can be used like a bone marrow transplant. These cells are used to treat genetic and blood disorders and certain types of cancer.

Keep in mind the Food and Drug Administration does not regulate cord blood banking as of this writing. Most, if not all companies are accredited by the American Association of Blood Banks (AABB) or licensed by the state where they're located. But it's still up to parents to research companies carefully. The cost of cord blood banking is high (starting at $300 plus annual storage fees averaging about $100), so parents should be well educated about the options before investing.

Q. Is it worth the money to store cord blood?

And you thought selecting a crib was a major decision…

Here's some information to help you decide if you want to open an account at the local blood bank:

◆ Your baby's risk of ever needing his own cord blood later is uncertain, but estimates vary from 1 in 1000 to 1 in 200,000.[2] If you have a family member who has leukemia, your baby's risk of needing it goes up. The cells can also be used for *anyone* in your family, if they match.

◆ The stem cells may have great potential use if "gene therapy" becomes mainstream medical treatment for genetic disorders, but that is still several years in the future. At this moment, it is being tested in the research labs of academic medical centers and pharmaceutical companies. If your family has a genetic disorder, banking might be worth it for you.

◆ If you choose to bank the cord blood, there are 16 companies in the U.S. that offer this service. The set up cost varies between $300 and $2000. Then, you'll need to pay annual premiums of $50-$100 per year to save it.

◆ Be sure to use a company that processes and stores cord blood in their own facility. Why does that matter? Because some companies subcontract the storage to another company.

◆ If a company you're interested in does other lab work besides cord blood banking, make sure their storage facilities are intended for long-term use. Special cryogenic techniques are required to make sure the blood is stored properly.

◆ Be sure your obstetrician is experienced in cord blood collection. It is imperative that the blood be collected quickly (within ten minutes) and that enough blood is collected. Most companies offer training resources for doctors. Obstetricians will charge a fee to collect the cord blood–be sure to find out this cost in advance.

◆ For more information, check out the following non-profit sites: National Marrow Donor Program (web: marrow.org/NMDP/cord.bloodbank.list. html), and A Parent's Guide to Private Cord Blood Banks (web: parents-guidecordblood.com. See picture on next page). Private companies are accessible if you do an Internet search under "cord blood banks." Here is a partial list of what's out there: lifebankusa.com, cordblood.com, viacord.com, cordbloodbank.com, and cryobank.com.

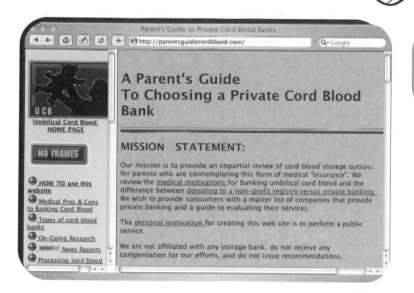

This fabulous site, run by an astrophysicist who lost her own daughter to leukemia, includes a terrific sample questionnaire for parents to use when they interview cord blood banks. Web: parentsguidecordblood.com

CORD BLOOD OPTIONS

BANK	ENROLLMENT FEE	ANNUAL FEE	# OF CORDS BANKED*	COMMENTS
American Red Cross redcross.org	Free	Free	6,000	Difficult to find info on the web site–search for cord blood. Blood donated is available to anyone who needs it.
California Cryobank cryobank.com	$700	$50-80	3,000	All processing & storage are done in-house
Cord Blood Registry Systems cordblood.com	$1290	$95	40,000	Excellent FAQ online. Affiliated with Univ. of Arizona. One of the first to bank cord blood.
CorCell corcell.com	$1350	$95	5,900	Too many clicks to find info. Works with some insurance companies.
Life Bank USA lifebankusa.com	$1295	$95	10,000	Special prices for multiples. Licensed in New York.
ViaCell viacord.com	$1550	$95	20,000	Materials and training provided for those col lecting the blood.

Wall Street Journal article, April 24, 2002.

DECISIONS

? ?

BEHIND THE SCENES: DONATING CORD BLOOD

If you decide that banking is not for you, you can donate your baby's cord blood so that someone who needs a bone marrow transplant can benefit. What an incredible way to share the gift of life—a baby is born AND a life is saved. The American Red Cross and the National Marrow Donor Program accept donations. They have particular trouble finding bone marrow matches for ethnic and racial minorities. Keep that in mind as an option.

Okay, we realize you're a bit overwhelmed with all these decisions, but here's just one more to consider before your child is born: childcare. Bet you didn't expect to see a discussion of this topic in a book on the medical care of infants. But not surprisingly, there are medical consequences to consider when choosing a childcare option as well as lifestyle and economic concerns. Let's look at this topic next.

Childcare

Q. When do I need to start thinking about childcare?

Now.

I know you don't even have a baby yet, but this is something you need to think about now. Why? Because all of your buddies in your baby care class already have. Yes, it IS that competitive. The best daycares and preschools in town will have your baby's due date (instead of birth date) listed on the waiting list application.

Q. Why is my selection for childcare so important?

That seems like an obvious one—your baby is the most precious gift in the world to you. And you want to give your baby the best childcare you can find. Here are some things you should think about:

Studies have consistently shown that the first three years of life are critical times in your child's development. This is when your baby learns to trust others, function independently, problem solve, and learn the boundaries of acceptable behavior. The person/people you choose to care for your baby are incredibly important.

There are economic decisions as well. Consider what your family can afford. In tallying the cost of childcare, add the expense of a sick child. We'll explain how that issue will crop up in each scenario.

BOTTOM LINE: Your child's illness may cost you a lost workday, and the price of co-payments and deductibles when you visit the doctor.

We'll discuss the types of child care in a second; first let's talk about juggling work, family and your sanity.

Feedback from the Real World

If you plan on returning to work after your baby is born, be prepared for a fine balancing act. I suggest you strongly consider how your life will 'work'. For an accurate depiction of how just how stressful it is to balance career and family obligations, rent the movie *One Fine Day* with Michelle Pfeiffer and George Clooney. It was supposed to be a comedy. I didn't think it was funny at all—I felt like I was watching my life!

Just getting out the door in the morning may be more stressful than any board meeting you've attended. Getting yourself ready is the easy part. If you use out-of-the-home childcare, you will have to get your baby ready, fed, and packed with food for the day. This can take awhile because your baby has no idea what your schedule is for the day, nor does he care. He also won't care if he spits up on your silk blouse or suit jacket.

Another point: be prepared for that phone call from childcare telling you that your baby is sick and needs to be sent home.

Balancing Act: Juggling work and family

How do you balance family, career—and your sanity? While the ideal situation would be to be at home for your baby 24/7, some parents find they want to work outside the home at least some of the time. For others, it is a necessity.

So, let's take a look at how moms and dads do the seemingly impossible—juggling baby, career, marriage and more. How do they do it all? To get the answers, we asked the readers of our books to share their wisdom.

First, check out Six Commandments for Balancing Work & Baby. Next, we'll look at this issue day to day, with 15 tips and tricks for juggling family and a career.

Six Commandments for Balancing Work & Baby

1 **FORGET BALANCE.** When we say "balance" work and family, this implies some kind of happy equilibrium. Forget it—the best you can hope for is OCCASIONAL peaceful coexistence between your family and job. Something will always be working to upset the balance, however . . . from a childcare situation, sickness, job demands, etc.

2 **DO THE MATH.** Sit down with a piece of paper and do a serious cost/benefit analysis before returning to work. Kelly Anderson of San Diego, CA emailed her advice to moms: "Most people would be shocked to see that after including many hidden costs of working outside the home (dry cleaning, taxes, eating out, gas, plus the fact that someone else will be essentially raising your child for you). For many people, the benefits just don't outweigh the costs." Good point: even if you have a good job with excellent pay, the cost of childcare and other hidden expenses may wipe out a good part of the earnings.

3 **DUAL CAREERS, DUAL SACRIFICE.** Both you and your spouse must make sacrifices for this to work. While nothing in life or marriage is always 50/50, both parents must help to make the schedule work.

4 **MEET THE NEW BOSS—YOUR BABY.** That means your old boss at work must adjust to your new life. "You don't want to work for a boss who does not put family first," says reader Tricia Gagnon. She's right—if your

boss doesn't understand why you need to take a day off to care for a sick child, you need to find a new job.

5 **AVOID THE GUILT TRIPS.** Whatever you decide for your baby, get ready for second-guessing from friends, relatives and complete strangers. E. Moeller, Boulder, CO, wrote in to stress this important point: A happy mommy (and daddy) makes for a happy baby. "If you are fulfilled and enjoying your work and have made good childcare choices, your baby will thrive."

6 **WILL IT MATTER NEXT MONTH? OR NEXT YEAR?** When you have to decide whether to work late or another weekend, ask yourself: "How important is my job as a _____ compared to my job as a father or mother. Will this project matter next month, year or in five years?" Your child will.

Day-to-Day: Tips & Tricks for Juggling Family & Career

Sometimes it is the small details that make the difference—here are our readers' tips and tricks for balancing work and family in their daily routines:

◆ **The routine is KING.** Reader Wendy Stough emailed: "Create one that works for you and do your best to stick to it, to some degree. It cuts down on the chaos of little things like lost keys and forgotten diaper bags and allows us, as parents, to take advantage of those special moments when our children need us most. Even when chaos reigns, you'll still know where the keys are!"

◆ **Make up snacks in advance.** Reader MK Krum of Toledo, Ohio makes up snacks and even sippy cups for snack-time a week in advance. "In the morning, just grab what you need and stick it in the diaper bag and go!"

◆ **Organize your baby's closet.** One reader uses a hanging organizer marked with the days of the week. "On Sunday, we load it up with the clothes for each day and any diaper bag refills." Of course, as your baby gets older, she may want a say in what she wears, but that's another story.

◆ **Don't be afraid to ask for help.** When you feel overwhelmed, ask friends and relatives to pitch in.

◆ **Look for a local "Moms Day Out" program** to get a break once in a while. Laurie Galbreath of San Antonio emailed us this tip: "Many churches offer this and you don't have to be a member! It is also very reasonable."

◆ **Create shortcuts to make your life easier.** Example: use white boards in each room of your house to write down needed supplies. This tip was sent in by Debby Moro of Cumming, GA. She emailed: "I stuck a small write on/wipe off board on the back of every door in the house. When I was in a particular room and noticed I was getting low on some supply, I jotted it down then and there. Before I hit the store, I walked through the house, made out the list, and avoided forgetting something."

◆ **Use the web.** You have one advantage that previous generations of parents didn't—the Internet. The web is your friend . . . use it to shop for everything. Reader Area Madaras uses the web to order groceries. "It's cheaper for me to pay $10 for Albertsons.com or Vons.com to delivery my groceries than it is for me to pay a babysitter." And always consider the value of your time—it may be better to shop online and save a car trip.

◆ **Pack the car the night before.** Avoid forgetting something during morning rush by packing that diaper bag, wallet and cell in the car the night before (assuming you have a secure garage).

◆ **When you cook, double the quantity**—then freeze the extra portion for a quick meal later in the week.

◆ **Get up a bit earlier.** This will give you a jump-start on the day—many moms and dads find they can get some chores done in the 30 minutes or so before baby wakes up.

◆ **Have a "two stop" rule.** We found our children would get very cranky/hungry/(fill in blank) when we tried to do more than two errand stops. While it is tempting to try to sync errands together by stopping at X, Y and Z after work, we found there was a limit to our children's patience— usually more than two stops would make life less than pleasant for all.

◆ **Know your employer's sick leave policy.** The Family Medical Leave Act (FMLA) allows parents to stay at home with a sick child without penalty (except for lost wages).

◆ **Schedule fun time.** One mom takes ten minutes out of every morning to jump on the bed or read stories with her toddler. A few stolen moments like that can make the difference.

◆ **Cook on the weekend for the rest of the week.** "That way we always have home-cooked meals that are healthy and tasty ready to pack for lunches or to re-heat at dinner time," emailed Lori Lankey of Woodbury MN. "It saves time and energy during the week, not to mention calories and money if we ended up eating out instead."

◆ **Have a backup sitter plan.** And then get a backup for the backup. That way, if an emergency strikes, you have a plan B. And plan C.

So, let's sum it up. Here are the Top Tips to Balancing Work & Family:

1. Be organized.
2. Trust your instincts.
3. Prioritize.
4. Stick to the routine.
5. But be flexible too.
6. Ask for help when you need it.
7. Lower your expectations.
8. Control freaks need not apply.
9. Laugh! Keeping a sense of humor about EVERYTHING is key.

Q. So what are my options for childcare?

Your baby stays at home with someone, goes to someone else's home, or goes to a licensed childcare facility. Let's go over these options so you can get moving on this one.

1 **PARENT AT HOME.** This is not just an option for moms anymore. More dads are staying at home these days. This is the childcare choice any child development expert would recommend. But, your childcare cost is the loss of one parent's salary—which may be significant unless you already have a single-earner household. Think of your parenting job as a career change. Full time parenting is hard work, and an admirable profession. (I have great respect for stay at home parents! My job at work is much easier than my job at home.)

DR B'S OPINION

"Having a parent at home is the best childcare option because you have complete control over caring and nurturing your child. You will never regret being there to watch your baby grow."

 Reality Check

First babies in the household rarely get sick from birth to one year. They spend their days playing on the living room floor with their own toys. When playgroups get together (a good sanity break), the infants play independently of each other. When children start playing with each other and sharing toys (12 to 24 months), they start sharing germs. Firstborn babies who stay at home don't get sick that often.

However, your second child will get *much* sicker in his first year of life. Why? Big brother or sister brings illnesses home from preschool, Mother's Day Out, Gymboree, etc. Second babies also gets dragged around to more family activities. It's almost guaranteed that you'll have more trips to the doctor with each subsequent child.

2 **FAMILY CARETAKER.** This is when a grandparent or some other willing family member cares for your baby while you go to work.

It is a great alternative if you have someone who is able and willing. It lets you pay the bills while your baby is at home with someone you can trust. Not only is family childcare free, but your child develops a special relationship with a family member.

Your child's frequency of illness is the same as if a parent stays at home.

 Reality Check

Be sure you have a healthy grandparent! Infants require lots of lifting and time on the floor to play.

DR B'S OPINION

"You won't be able to call all the shots on childrearing. It's difficult to tell your mother-in-law what to do! Set up a consistent parenting plan with your caretaker before differences in parenting styles arise. Otherwise, it could get ugly!"

3 **NANNY/AU PAIR.** You hire someone to parent your child in your home. This may be a professional, or someone who just enjoys taking care of kids.

This is a great way to have a consistent caregiver. Your child will have a special relationship with another caring adult. Because you are paying her and she isn't your mother-in-law, you can set up the parenting guidelines you have in mind. If your child gets sick, you don't need to miss work. You'll only have a problem if your *provider* gets sick, needs to take a vacation or (yes, it happens) quits.

And, it is the most expensive form of childcare. Some parents fear that they cannot trust someone (other than a family member) alone with their child. This option requires good instincts of both the parents and the provider.

Reality Check

You won't need a home surveillance system to check on your nanny. An infant will tell you if he is uncomfortable with someone—he won't be happy to see that person. Obviously, you need to do an extensive background check on a nanny BEFORE you hire them. See Chapter 11 of our other book, *Baby Bargains* (see the back of this book for details), for tips and advice on how to do a background check on potential nannies.

> ### DR B'S OPINION
>
> *"Take it from a full time working mom with two young kids...there is no way I could make my day work without a nanny. It is the priciest form of childcare, but well worth it for my children and my career schedule. I could tell you stories about what happens when my nanny calls in sick, but you can just rent One Fine Day instead."*

Tips for finding a nanny

There are various ways to find a childcare provider who will come to your home. If you put an ad in the paper or on a bulletin board in the education building of your local college, you'll need to rely on your first impression to make a decision. If you go through a nanny or au pair placement service, you can pay huge sums of money to them to screen candidates for you. (They will do a police, credit, and reference background check.) Our advice: we'd recommend a trial day with your prospective provider to see how it goes before hiring her/him.

4 **IN HOME DAY CARE.** A parent has a license to care for a few children (in addition to their own kids) in her home.

This is a way to hire a mother for your child. It can be great. Your child will be around different ages of children. Often, older kids enjoy playing with the little ones. Your child may get lots of love and attention. He may also see these kids as role models. Sick child policies with in-home daycare tend to be less rigid than those in licensed daycare facilities. So, you can go to work occasionally, even if your child is ill. The cost is moderate but if your child gets sick, you may need to take off work.

Reality Check

As discussed in the stay-at-home scenario, second kids always get more illnesses. You will be adding your child to an existing household of children, so expect the same result. Also, those older kids may not be great role models. You might want to interview both the provider *and* the children she cares for before you make any decisions.

Tips for finding in-home daycare

To find these hidden gems, you'll need to start asking friends, neighbors, and co-workers for possible leads of in-home daycare providers. It's definitely a word-of-mouth kind of option.

5 **LICENSED DAY CARE FACILITY (CENTER CARE).** This is a popular option for many parents. So, I'll spend a bit more time talking about it. If you plan to have your child in daycare, you should already have done some homework. If not, put this book down right now and start!

Tips for finding a good daycare facility

Here are some quick tips on finding a good center care facility:

◆ *Look for a program that is NAEYC (National Association for the Education of Young Children; web: www.naeyc.org) approved.* This organization sets the strictest guidelines for childcare facilities. If a program has been accredited, you are more likely to be in good hands. You'll be able to do a search on their site based on your zip code.

◆ *Talk to parents whose kids are in the program.*

◆ *Find out how approachable the teachers and director are.* Are modifications made if there is a problem?

◆ *Spend some time observing in the classroom.*

◆ *How do the teachers manage discipline?*

◆ *Do the teachers get down on the floor and play with the kids?*

◆ *Are both the children and the adults having fun?*

◆ *What are the program's policies regarding infection control (sick child policy)?* Some programs are so strict that they require a doctor's note for your child to get back in.

Center care is the most popular form of childcare in the United States. Parents have a sense of security knowing that the providers are licensed professionals. You can always check up on them. Also good news—many daycares are trending towards a "preschool" format. Translated, they emphasize a more structured environment and learning through play.

Center daycare is relatively inexpensive as far as childcare goes. But there are hidden costs: you will have to factor in several missed workdays and doctor bills into the price tag.

Reality Check

Hopefully, you are sitting down for the following statistic: *young children have an average of eight to ten viral infections per year.*[3] Your child will be asked to leave daycare every time he gets sick and asked not to return until he is fever free for 24 hours. With each illness, expect your child to be contagious for the first two to four days of the illness.

The Monster Virus from Venus

As parents of a new baby, we got a quick lesson on daycare sickness—and it wasn't pretty. Our oldest son, Ben, was about two years old when he started a part-time program at a local daycare center. When the MONSTER VIRUS FROM VENUS struck, we didn't see it coming.

See, as parents who worked at home, the most human contact we had was with the UPS guy. And as long as he wasn't coughing on us when he made a package delivery, we were fine. Then our son started at the day care center. About a month into the adventure, he came home with a new friend—we called it the monster virus. Sure, he had a slight fever and stuffy nose—one day later, he was fine. But not Mom and Dad. Somehow, this little virus mutated and by the time it hit us it had become a cross between Ebola and the Black Plague. We were so sick, we couldn't get out of bed for three days and had to call in the emergency parent response team (that is, grandma).

The lesson: be prepare to be struck by all sorts of bizarre diseases if your baby starts daycare. And it won't only be your baby that will suffer . . . everyone in your family is going to have to deal with this!

Feedback from the Real World

There's nothing more vexing than searching for the right childcare for your child. And the "answer" is always a moving target—your childcare needs will change as your child grows. We asked our readers how they made sense of all the childcare options out there. And here are their tips on finding the best childcare:

◆ *Look for a referral service.* MK Krum of Toledo, Ohio emailed that the YMCA in her area "offers a referral service for about $25 per year. You tell them what kind of daycare you are interested in (center, provider's home, your home, etc) and they match it up to you by zip code." Each year the providers are required to resubmit their info along with letters of recommendation. "It gave us several options both close to work and home."

◆ *Evaluate your commute.* You may find it makes more sense to use a day care close to your home or work, depending on the circumstance.

BEHIND THE SCENES: IS DAYCARE SICKNESS GOOD?

From a health standpoint, it's not all bad that your child gets exposed to infections. A recent study in showed that children who were in daycare/center care from birth to at least one year of age had fewer allergies at age two than their "sterile" stay-at-home peers. It's called the "Hygiene Hypothesis." [4]

◆ **Look for red flags when you visit a childcare facility.** Do children seem unattached to their caregivers? Or vice versa?

◆ **Consider going slow to ease the transition.** Instead of dropping your child in to a new childcare situation cold turkey, take it slow. "Bring her for a few hours one day while you're with her," said one mom we interviewed. Or do a new program part-time for a week or more to ease the transition.

◆ **Get on those waitlists early.** It's a fact of life—the best childcare in your town will probably have a wait list. A word to the wise: get on the waitlist NOW, while you are still pregnant. Waiting to arrange childcare usually means having to go with your third or fourth choice—or worse.

◆ **Don't make any firm decisions about childcare until AFTER your baby is born.** Now that sounds like a contradiction with the previous tip, but it isn't—getting on a waiting list for a popular childcare alternative in your town does NOT mean you have to take the spot. Meanwhile, many parents advise waiting until after baby is born before you make your decision about whether to go back to work. Deb Steenhagen, Muskegon, MI emailed her advice: "You may feel completely differently once the baby is born. Give yourself as much time for maternity leave as possible, it helps to bond with the baby strongly before you go back to work and then you'll have those memories to hold onto after you do go back."

◆ **"If you can find one, go with an in-home provider,"** emailed E. White of Maple Grove, MN. "They are much cheaper. The different centers I looked at cost twice as much as in home daycares."

◆ **"Talk to friends and co-workers about what they did.** You might stumble upon a great nanny referral or a nanny share option. My co-worker turned me on to a great service (non-profit organization) in our area that links parents to home daycare providers. While I was leery of home daycare providers (because they have no standards governing their behavior), these particular providers are subject to rules and regulations set by the non-profit organization. Now our son is being watched after by a wonderful woman and we could not be happier!" T. Ross, Arlington, Virginia.

◆ **"In Texas, some of the best center care to be found is provided by churches, which don't advertise heavily like private day care centers.** Ask around, visit lots of places, and ask the tough questions." L. Alvarado, Houston, TX.

◆ **Consider an au pair.** Au pairs are authorized cultural exchanges—a young woman in her 20's comes to live with you to do childcare. Pros: you have one person who takes care of your baby in your home and the au pair becomes part of your family instead of just hired help. Downsides: you have to have a separate bedroom because you have a new family member and they must leave after one year. For more info, go to AuPairAmerica.com.

◆ **Accept the fact that your babysitter or nanny will do things differently than you do.** As long as your child is content and healthy, that is just fine. Don't try to micro manage day care.

◆ Laura L. of Hot Springs, AR says *getting some help cleaning your house was critical to her sanity*: "Hiring a housekeeper, even one that comes every two weeks, is worth every penny you pay. Amazing how much more time it gives you with your baby and family to have that help, even if your budget is already strained!"

Having a child is quite an exciting experience, no less so for parents who choose to adopt. In their case, there's more to it than just picking up their new baby and heading on home. Here are some topics for adoptive parents to consider while you're waiting to adopt.

Q. I plan on adopting a baby. Is there anything special I should know?

It depends on the age of the baby at the time of adoption, and from whom you are adopting the baby (for example, international adoption). Here are some considerations:

1. If you are adopting the baby in infancy, adoptive mothers can try to stimulate their breast milk production with a prescription medication. If this is something you are interested in, contact your doctor.

2. It is helpful to know the medical history of the birth parents (if possible). Parental drug use and high-risk sexual activity are important to find out. For all babies, screening tests for HIV, Hepatitis B and syphilis are encouraged.

3. For infants adopted internationally, additional testing is suggested including the following:
   ◆ Stool culture for intestinal parasites.
   ◆ TB (tuberculosis) screening test.
   ◆ Tests routinely done in U.S. on state metabolic screens (thyroid, phenylketonuria, sickle cell disease, etc.).

4. Vision, hearing, nutrition status, anemia testing, and developmental milestones can be assessed when your baby meets the pediatrician.

5. If the baby's immunization status is unknown, he is presumed to be NOT immunized and will start the series at the beginning.[5]

Q. Are there special doctors who care for children who are adopted?

Because adoption is an increasingly common choice for families, most pediatricians and family practice doctors feel comfortable taking care of these children.

However, there are some physicians who have an additional level of expertise in the field. For a listing of these physicians and general info on adoptions, check out the AAP website (www.aap.org/section/adoption/). Another good site is calib.com/naic.

Strangely, the last topic we're going to discuss in this chapter is the birth plan. What, you might wonder, does this have to do with pediatrics? You probably thought the birth plan was just for the nurses and doctors who deliver babies. Not so as you'll see in this section.

The Birth Plan

Q. I am writing a birth plan for my baby's delivery. Do you have any advice? How does my decision regarding pain medication during childbirth affect my baby?

It is currently en vogue for first time parents (notably second-time parents skip this) to create a birth plan. This means that you sit down with your spouse before D-Day (Delivery Day) and discuss how you want to manage the pain of childbirth. This includes interventions you want and don't want at the hospital. This list of demands is posted in your labor room for every medical provider to abide by. Some parents get very detailed about the experience they want—down to what color wallpaper they prefer in the labor room (I'm not kidding—I had someone do this.)

Thoughts on Creating a Birth Plan

◆ *Having a baby is a beautiful, amazing experience.* Medical providers who work in the baby making/caring field chose this profession for a reason—they like to participate in that experience. They also want it to be as wonderful as possible. Doctors and nurses will ask you what you need. Times have changed since the 1950's.

◆ *You don't need written orders* to demand dim lights, music, extra pillows, or just to be left alone for a while.

◆ *For the person giving birth: don't ever let your partner decide for you what pain relief you will have.* You're the one in pain; you decide what you want and when you want it. For the partner: don't be disappointed that your partner chose pain relief. It's easy for well meaning friends, relatives and partners to armchair quarterback when it comes to pain. But until you've been there, you know not of what you speak!

◆ *You can use as many breathing techniques as you want.* When you beg for pain medicine, the staff will give it to you. No one will sneak pain medicine into you—even though you'll be wishing they could. Here's another true story… one family of mine typed up their birth plan. It stated, "No pain medication until we ask for it." During the delivery, that line was crossed out in ink and in bold letters was handwritten, "NOW PLEASE!!"

◆ *Seasoned parents never make birth plans because they know that having a baby is an unpredictable event.* You pray for the best and put yourself in the hands of people you trust. Seasoned parents also know how much childbirth hurts!

DR B'S (AND DENISE'S) OPINION: GIVING BIRTH

I have two children. I never really wanted a "natural childbirth" but ended up having one with my first child. I was afraid to have another child! I wouldn't wish that experience on my worst enemy. It took me three years to get over my fear and do it again. With my second delivery, I had the perfect epidural and it was a cakewalk.

After that experience, if you insist on having a birth plan, I think it should read as follows: "Get this baby out as quickly, painlessly, and safely as possible!"

Denise's opinion: Okay, I've had babies both ways: cesarean section and vaginal. Which was easier? C-section hands down. Why? They definitely give you anesthetic for a c-section. And afterwards, during recovery, you get the self-administering morphine machine. We have one here in the office right now. Just kidding. As for the vaginal birth. . . woah! I almost missed the window for getting an epidural. If I had, I might have bent the bed out of shape. I had irregular contractions that defied all my breathing techniques. So in the end, even though I have great respect for moms who do it naturally, just remember you don't have to. By the way, both my kids were born alert and healthy.

Reality Check

Having a baby is more painful than you can ever imagine. Would you consider having your wisdom teeth taken out without any pain medication? Then why is having a baby any different? Despite urban legends, pain medication does *not* have harmful effects on your baby.

ENJOY the birth of your child, without any guilt.

Notes

Chapter 2

You & Your Baby's Doc
Insider Tips & Advice

"There is no such thing as fun for the whole family."
~ Jerry Seinfeld

WHAT'S IN THIS CHAPTER

- ◆ **THE SCHEDULE OF WELL BABY CHECKUPS.**
- ◆ **HOW AND WHY TO SCHEDULE A SICK VISIT APPOINTMENT.**
- ◆ **THE DIFFERENCE BETWEEN A SICK VISIT AND A CONSULTATION.**
- ◆ **INSIDER TIPS FOR BOOKING APPOINTMENTS.**
- ◆ **WHAT TO DO IN THE EVENING AND ON WEEKENDS.**
- ◆ **GETTING IN TOUCH: PHONE CALLS, VOICEMAIL, EMAIL, AND FAX.**

Welcome to your baby's second home—the doctor's office. Now that you've picked the person you want to be your baby's doctor, it's important to understand how their office works—and the insider tips and tricks to making your time here as smooth as possible. Let's take a walk around.

Q. Does my baby need to be seen by a doctor regularly?

Yes. These appointments are called well child visits or well baby checkups.

Bringing your child in at regular intervals is an important part of his health care. These visits let your doctor evaluate your child's health, growth, and development. It lets you address issues that concern you. Smart advice: make a list of questions to discuss at each appointment. At the first few visits, your list may be quite lengthy (up to several pages!). But by the one-year well check, your list will probably fit on a sticky note. That's when you know you have graduated to professional parenthood.

Q. Is there a standard well child visit schedule?

Yes. Most pediatric practices follow the guidelines of the American Academy of Pediatrics (AAP) for routine well child checks. At every visit, we examine your child head to toe. Some visits involve screening tests and immunizations. Below is a standard well child visit schedule. Note: the immunization schedule has some variability, but this gives you a rough idea of what to expect.

AGE OF VISIT	SCREENING TESTS	IMMUNIZATIONS*
Birth	Metabolic screen, hearing	Hep B
2 weeks	Metabolic screen	
2 months		DTaP, IPV, Hep B, HIB, Prevnar
4 months		DTaP, IPV, HIB, Prevnar
6 months		DTaP, HIB, Prevnar
9 months		IPV, Hep B
12 months	Hematocrit, Lead screen	MMR, Varicella, Prevnar
15 months		DTaP, HIB
2 years	Dental referral	
3 years	Blood pressure	
4-5 years	Hearing, vision, Urinalysis, PPD	DTaP, IPV, MMR
6-18 years	Hematocrit, cholesterol for at risk kids	Tetanus
	(Tetanus booster at age 14-16)	
18-21 years	Annual pap smear for at risk	

*What the heck is a DTaP? IPV? HIB? Yes, the world of immunizations has a language all its own. We'll explore the topic of immunizations (and decipher these codes) in Chapter 12, "Vaccines."

Screening Tests

◆ *Metabolic Screen.* This is a blood test performed at 24 hours of life and repeated at two weeks of age. The number of tests varies by state, but typically includes screens for (big words alert) phenylketonuria, congenital hypothyroidism, galactosemia, sickle cell disease, and adrenal gland insufficiency. (See Chapter 3, "Labor Day" and the glossary.)

◆ *Hearing Screen.* The AAP recommends all newborns have a hearing test before leaving the hospital. This simple test identifies children with congenital deafness (Again, see Chapter 3, "Labor Day" and BAERS in glossary). A hearing screen is often repeated before starting kindergarten.

◆ *Hematocrit.* This is a blood test performed at one year of age to determine if your child is anemic. This test may be repeated as necessary.

◆ *Urinalysis.* A urine sample is obtained at age four to five to evaluate for diabetes and kidney function. This test may also be repeated as needed.

◆ *PPD* (Tuberculosis or TB test). This skin test demonstrates exposure to tuberculosis, an infectious lung disease. Routine testing is performed in high-risk areas, and many schools require one TB test before school entry.

◆ *Vision screen.* A vision test is performed at age four to five and may be repeated as necessary. If your school district screens annually, this may be omitted from your child's physical exam.

◆ *Lead Screen.* This blood test demonstrates exposure to lead. High levels can cause anemia and neurological problems. Routine testing is performed in high-risk areas. If you live in a house built before 1978 that has peeling paint or has been renovated, notify your baby's doctor.

◆ *Cholesterol screen.* This blood test identifies children who have elevated levels of fat that can lead to heart disease. Routine testing is not performed in children. If someone in your family has had problems with high cholesterol, or heart problems before the age of 55, inform your baby's doctor.

◆ *Pap smear.* This lab test is performed annually on sexually active young women for early detection of cervical cancer.

◆ *Immunizations*. This is a whole chapter unto itself, literally. (See Chapter 12, "Vaccines.")

Q. What kind of appointment do I schedule if my baby is sick?

A sick visit. This is a problem-focused appointment. Your child has a

BEHIND THE SCENES: WHO IS THE AMERICAN ACADEMY OF PEDIATRICS (AAP)?

Just who is the AAP? And why are their "policy statements" so important? The AAP is an organization of 50,000+ pediatricians who are "dedicated to the health, safety, and well being of infants, children and adolescents in North, Central, and South America."

This active group makes recommendations (called policy statements) that allow doctors to maintain the highest standard of care for their patients. The policies are reviewed and updated frequently. You can check the AAP's policy statements online at www.aap.org.

Doctors who bear the letters, F.A.A.P. after their names are pediatricians who are Fellows of the American Academy of Pediatrics. Fellowship is granted after passing a standardized board certification exam and learning the secret handshake (just kidding on that last one). Fellows must take recertification exams every seven years to remain board certified. Look for the FAAP designation from your pediatrician. This means your doctor is not only trained in her specialty, but also has proof of her competency.

problem (fever, ear ache, rash) that needs to be evaluated. Your doctor will focus on the issue and likely do a physical exam limited to the problem. We point this out so you can appreciate the difference in appointments.

Reality Check

Your baby can get his vaccinations at his well child visit even if he is sick. Many families cancel a well child visit if their baby wakes up ill on the day of his appointment. This causes delays in getting the baby immunized. Unless your baby has a fever of 102 or greater, he can still get his shots. There are also lots of other things to do at a well baby check besides shots. Bottom line: keep your well child appointments!

Q. What kind of appointment do I schedule if I have several/chronic issues I want to discuss?

See if your doctor schedules consultations.

Many doctors offer longer office visits for patients with chronic medical problems or several involved issues. Typically these concerns are behavioral issues, sleep problems, school problems, or medical problems that have been occurring for more than three or four weeks. If the appointment is scheduled this way, your doctor can provide ample time to assess these problems.

Insider Tips: How To Make Friends With The Office Staff

Bringing cookies is helpful. Just kidding! Seriously, here are five tips to make a nice impression in the doctor's office:

1. **Bring your insurance card.** Most doctors' staffs verify proof of insurance at *every* office visit.
2. **When you come for your first office visit, arrive 30 minutes before your appointment time.** You'll need to fill out a lot of paperwork and the office staff need to verify your insurance (that often takes 20 minutes on the phone with your insurance company). The same is true if you have changed insurance plans.
3. **If you are an established patient, come a few minutes early for well child visits.** You will soon understand why. Your

NEW PARENT 411: WHEN DOES MY CHILD STOP GOING TO THE PEDIATRICIAN?

It depends on the child. Some teenagers wouldn't be caught dead in their pediatrician's waiting room. Other teenagers never want to leave the nest. Most pediatricians feel comfortable seeing their patients until the age of 18-21 years, if they still want to see us. (My pediatrician kicked me out after he performed my physical examination for medical school.)

Family practice physicians are comfortable seeing teenagers. Internal medicine physicians (internists) are not. They often limit their practice to age 18 and up.

DR B'S OPINION: WELL CHECKS

Don't try to squeeze in a well child visit when you come in for a sick visit. Busy families frequently bring their baby in for a sick visit and ask, "So, can't you do a well check today since we are here?" I usually say no, unless my schedule is light. I need time to do a complete exam and evaluation. Doing a quick once-over isn't doing justice to the importance of a well child visit.

your baby's doc

doctor will require you to completely undress your baby to take his measurements. This itself can be an event. Then, inevitably, the baby will either poop or pee on the measuring scale, which then further delays the measurements being taken. Multiply this experience by two if you have twins.

4. **If you have more than one child that needs to be evaluated by the doctor, schedule an appointment for each of them.** It shows that you respect your doctor's time. If everyone would follow this mantra, there's no doubt that wait times to see your doctor would decline.

5. **If you are running late for an appointment, call your doctor.** Most medical offices can modify their schedule if they know when you are coming.

Insider Tips: The Best Time To Schedule Appointments

Let's make an analogy to airports. Your baby's doctor's office is a bit like La Guardia Airport. When is the best time to fly? In the early morning, before delays set later flights back.

When is the worst time to fly? Monday mornings, Friday afternoons, and national holidays.

Now let's look at some trends in the doctor's office. Because many doctors' offices are closed on the weekends, parents tend to bring their sick kids in either before the weekend or after enduring a long weekend with them. Translation: *peak volume days are Mondays and Fridays.*

Seasons also cause volume trends. Cold and flu season (October through April) is the highest patient volume all year. Christmas Eve is always busy because no parent will allow their child to be ill on Christmas. National holidays are popular times to visit because many parents have the day off from work.

In the summer (June through August), our older patients keep us busy with well child visits because they don't have to miss school. They also need camp or sports physicals.

May and September are the slowest months of the year (that's when I usually take a vacation!)

If you want to visit your doctor when the office is quieter (or running less behind) here are some tips:

1. Schedule well baby visits on Tuesdays, Wednesdays, or Thursdays.

2. Try to get the first appointment of the morning or afternoon to avoid delays.

3. *Schedule well baby visits that occur in the winter months far in advance.* There are often fewer well child visits offered to make room for the sick visits.

4. *If you want to avoid the rush for school or camp physicals, consider booking in May or September.*

5. *See if your doctor offers weekend hours. Then you can avoid the Monday/Friday crunch.*

Q. Who will I meet in the doctor's office?

Let me introduce you to the office staff. Practices vary a great deal, but these are the usual folks that you will encounter.

◆ *The medical provider or 'primary care provider':* This is the person responsible for your child's medical care. This may be a pediatrician or family practice doctor, depending on whom you select. Their initial medical school training is through a certified medical school (M.D.) or a school of osteopathic medicine (D.O.). Their specialty training is either in children's healthcare (pediatrics) or a combination of both adult and children's healthcare (family practice). When all is said and done, either type of provider will have at least seven years of training beyond college before they have their own office.

◆ *Midlevel providers:* These people have been popular additions to busy offices. Nurse practitioners (NP's) and physician assistants (PA's) help with straightforward sick visits and well child visits. They can evaluate patients, make decisions, and treat patients with the supervision of a medical provider. Nurse practitioners have at least two years of training beyond their bachelor's degree in nursing (B.S.N.). Physician assistants complete a two-year program after completing at least two years of college.

◆ *Nursing staff:* The staff may have a variety of degrees. The head nurse may have either an R.N.(registered nurse) or L.V.N.(licensed vocational nurse) degree. Many pediatric offices utilize medical assistants who are trained to administer shots and perform screening tests.

Q. What do I do if my baby gets sick in the evening or on the weekend?

It is Murphy's Law that your baby will only get sick when the office is closed. Be prepared for this and have a game plan. Some offices offer limited evening and weekend hours. Find out the specifics for your doctor's office.

If the office is closed, the next option is a minor care center or an emergency department of your local hospital. Ask your office for their recommendation. The most convenient location may not be the best place to go.

BOTTOM LINE: Always call your doctor first before you go running anywhere. What may seem like an emergency to you may not be. Your phone call might save you a trip in the middle of the night.

Q. What is the best way to contact my doctor's office?

The age of technology. So many options—phone, fax, email, voicemail...
The most effective way to contact the office is by picking up the phone. Doctors' offices anticipate numerous calls during office hours and have systems in place to answer the calls efficiently.

Some offices are more progressive and have started accepting questions via fax and email. However, most offices still rely on the telephone to communicate with patients. One reason for the resistance to change is for medical privacy issues. The U.S. Government has recently enacted a program to protect medical information (HIPAA). The act is subject to interpretation by individual medical offices. Thus, some offices now prohibit transmitting medical records via fax or email, or leaving medically sensitive information on answering machines or voicemail. Although this may seem like a hassle, these restrictions are meant to protect you.

Notes

Chapter 3

Labor Day

"Giving birth is like taking your lower lip and forcing it over your head."
~ Carol Burnett

WHAT'S IN THIS CHAPTER

◆ **THE DETAILS OF YOUR BABY'S FIRST PHYSICAL EXAMINATION.**

◆ **SCREENING TESTS, VITAMIN K, AND EYE OINTMENT.**

◆ **THE SIGNIFICANCE OF GROUP B STREP.**

◆ **WHY IS YOUR BABY SHRINKING?**

◆ **WHAT YOU WILL SEE IN YOUR BABY'S DIAPER.**

◆ **JAUNDICE.**

◆ **CARSEATS.**

◆ **SPECIAL SECTION: THE TWO-WEEK SURVIVAL GUIDE.**

Labor Day is finally here—the most incredible day of your life. You have prepared the nursery and taken the birthing class, breast-feeding class, and baby care class. You've bought too many childcare and parenting books. Hopefully, you've also met with your pediatrician (see Chapter 1, "Decisions"). So you're ready, right?

There is no way anyone can prepare you for this, but this chapter will guide you through your baby's first day at the hospital.

Let's leave the giving birth part to other pregnancy books . . . ask your obstetrician if you have any questions on this. Instead, let's focus on what happens once your baby is born. Many people are not aware of this, but pediatricians and family practitioners examine their patients for the first time in the hospital. Why, you may ask? Because entering the world is a big transition. Babies who are still inside the womb may have certain medical problems that do not show themselves until they take their first breath of fresh air. It is very helpful in the world of modern day medicine to have ultrasounds, lab tests, and amniocentesis to get a glimpse of potential problems in your baby—but they don't cover every problem.

When the hospital calls your doctor to notify her of your baby's birth, she will be out to examine her new patient and visit with his mom and dad (that's you—has a nice ring to it) within 24 hours of the birth. If there is an emergency at delivery, or urgent problems with your newborn, the hospital may ask a neonatologist (newborn intensive care specialist) or a pediatrician who is present in the hospital to care for your baby immediately.

Q. Tell me about the baby's first exam. What are you looking for?

Bear with us—this stuff is a little dry, but we think it will help you to understand what your doctor is doing. It will also make you appreciate how fortunate you are to have a baby who makes an A+ on his first exam!

Vital Signs

This includes heart rate (pulse), breathing rate (respiratory rate), body temperature, and weight. Abnormalities can indicate infection, dehydration, and heart/lung abnormalities. These are checked at least every eight hours. Babies are weighed daily. Input (length of breast feeding/amount of formula) and output (number of pees and poops) are also documented.

The Head

◆ Shape of the head. (Your baby will not be a permanent member of the Conehead family—it rounds out after a few weeks).

◆ Bruises from the trauma of delivery caused by forceps, vacuum, pushing on your pelvic bones for 2+ hours). Big bruises can take 6-8 weeks to resolve (see **CEPHALHEMATOMA**)

◆ Soft spot. The soft spot (**FONTANELLE**) in the middle of the skull is open with room for the brain to grow. (see **CRANIOSYNOSTOSIS**)

The Eyes

◆ Red reflex. Doctors use a special light to see the baby's red reflex (the 'red eye' you see in flash photography pictures). **CATARACTS** and eye tumors (see **RETINOBLASTOMA**) are two problems doctors are trying to catch here.

◆ Tear ducts. Many newborns get clogged tear ducts (see **NASO-LACRIMAL DUCT OBSTRUCTION**). The ducts are narrow and cause the tears to get goopy and make the eye look infected. This can come and go for your baby's entire first year of life. We'll cover this issue later in Chapter 15, "First Aid."

Reality Check

Newborns can only see 8 to 12 inches in front of them. They can see you if you bring their face up close to yours. They frequently look cross-eyed for the first two months.

The Ears

◆ Eardrums are checked, as well as abnormal formations of the outer part of the ears (see **PREAURICULAR PITS, SKIN TAGS**).

◆ A hearing test is performed on all newborns. No, we don't ask them to raise their hand when they hear the beep. The baby wears headphones and we measure the electrical activity of the brain when a noise is made. (see **BAERs**)

Reality Check

The American Academy of Pediatrics recommends hearing screening for *all* newborns. Thirty-seven states require the testing by law. However, not all states enforce their legislation by requiring insurance companies to foot the bill for the test. Even if a hearing test is not a coveered benefit, however, you as a parent should insist on such a test. Congenital hearing loss occurs in 3 per 1000 newborns. Early detection can make a considerable difference for a child's language development.[1]

The Nose

◆ Can baby breathe through their nose (see **CHOANAL ATRESIA**)? By the way, all babies have stuffy noses at birth and continue to have nasal congestion for the next four to six weeks (see **NEWBORN NASAL CONGESTION**).

The Mouth

◆ Formation of the mouth. A doctor will check to make sure the roof of the mouth (palate) has formed and the funny thing hanging in the back of the mouth (uvula) is there (see **CLEFT LIP** and **CLEFT PALATE**).

◆ Tongue. Your baby's tongue is checked for a forked tip or any trouble in moving it. This is called a tongue tie (see **ANKYLOGLOSSIA**).

◆ Gums. Some babies are born with white pimples on the gums (see **EPSTEIN'S PEARLS**) that go away on their own. These are not teeth— the first tooth usually comes out between six to 12 months of age.

The Throat

◆ Breathing. Occasionally, babies make unusual noises when breathing. Some babies are born with floppy breathing tubes (see **LARYNGOMALACIA**) that they will outgrow. This sound concerns parents, but is usually of no consequence.

The Neck and Shoulders

◆ These are checked for any unusual lumps, bumps, or cysts (see **BRANCHIAL CLEFT CYST**).

◆ If birth was difficult (big baby, small mommy), the collarbone can break (see **CLAVICLE FRACTURE, SHOULDER DYSTOCIA**).

◆ Can your baby turn its head to each side? Some babies will have a stiff neck muscle that limits head motion (see **TORTICOLLIS**).

The Chest

◆ Doctors look for any signs of difficulty breathing (see **RESPIRATORY DISTRESS**). Adults breathe 12 times per minute at an even rate. Newborns breathe 30 to 40 times per minute and have episodes of **PERIODIC BREATHING**. So, your baby will breathe rapidly several times, p-a-u-s-e, then breathe again. That pause will seem like an eternity to you. It is normal. Signs of respiratory distress are:

1. A pause between breaths that lasts 15 to 20 seconds (see **APNEA**).
2. Baby is consistently breathing over 60 times per minute. (see **TACHYPNEA OF NEWBORN**)
3. Baby's ribs are sucking in at each breath, nostrils are flaring, grunting noises are heard (see **RETRACTIONS, RESPIRATORY DISTRESS**)

The Heart and Circulation

◆ Murmurs (unusual noises), irregular beats, fast or slow heart rate. Doctors listen very carefully to newborns' hearts. Many heart problems, especially severe defects (see **CONGENITAL HEART DISEASE**) are now detected on fetal ultrasounds. However, most doctors still rely on their good old stethoscope to pick up abnormalities.

◆ Baby's pulses are carefully checked, particularly those in the groin area (femoral pulses). The main blood vessel (aorta) supplying oxygen rich blood to the body can have kinks and narrowings (see **COARCTATION OF AORTA**) causing a weakened pulse in the groin.

◆ A normal, benign murmur is heard in the first 24 hours of life as the newborn circulation transitions from its former "fetal" beat. Hence the name, "**TRANSITIONAL MURMUR.**" Transitional murmurs are no longer heard after the few days of life and are not a problem.

◆ Purple hands and feet (see **ACROCYANOSIS**) are due to newborn circulation that's making its first debut out of the womb. This is also normal and can last for a couple of weeks.

The Abdomen

◆ Your doctor will feel your baby's belly to check the size of her liver and spleen. The belly should be soft and not hurt to touch. Abnormally large body organ size can be caused by problems metabolizing foods (see **METABOLIC STORAGE DISEASE**) or poor heart function (see **CONGESTIVE HEART FAILURE**). Abnormal fullness or distention alerts doctors to look for **ABDOMINAL TUMORS**.

◆ Firm or full bellies may be a sign of abnormal intestine formation (see **MALROTATION, DUODENAL ATRESIA**). An abnormal exam and problems feeding—that is, vomiting, especially bile, will be a tip off to investigate things further.

◆ A baby is expected to pass one stool called **MECONIUM** in the first 24 hours of life. A delay in pooping will make us evaluate for abnormal anus formation (see **HIRSCHSPRUNG'S DISEASE, ANAL ATRESIA**) or poor stool formation that can be seen in cystic fibrosis (see **MECONIUM PLUG, CYSTIC FIBROSIS**).

◆ Sometimes the belly button (umbilicus) pops out. This is the extreme form of an "outty" (see **UMBILICAL HERNIA**) and often resolves on its own.

The Genitals
Boys

◆ For boys, your doctor makes sure both testes are in the scrotum. Occasionally, one or both testes will not make the pilgrimage south (see **UNDESCENDED TESTES**).

◆ For boys, the fullness of the scrotum is also checked. Many boys are born with extra fluid in the scrotum that goes away over the first six months of life. (see **HYDROCELE**) The other thing that causes fullness is a hernia—part of the intestine that has pushed into the scrotum. (see **INGUINAL HERNIA**). Cool doctor trick: we can tell the difference by shining a light on the scrotum. Fluid (hydrocele) is light and intestine (hernia) is dark.

◆ For boys, your doctor will make sure the opening (urethra) is at the tip of the penis. The opening can abnormally develop on the undersurface of the penis shaft (see **HYPOSPADIAS**) or on topside (see **EPISPADIAS**). Boys with this problem are not routinely circumcised because the foreskin is needed to surgically correct it around six months of age.

GIRLS

◆ For girls, the vagina and urethra (the holes tucked inside the lips) are checked. The lips (labia minora) can be stuck together (see **LABIAL ADHESION**). Usually, you see some white mucousy fluid (see **VAGINAL DISCHARGE**). This is normal. Occasionally, newborn girls also have some vaginal bleeding (see What's That in My Baby's Diaper? question on page 49). Dads—you need to learn how to clean this area well. (See Chapter 4, "Hygiene" for details.)

BOTH SEXES

◆ When the clitoris looks too large, or the penis looks too small, your doctor will evaluate for problems with the baby's hormones or chromosomes. (see **AMBIGUOUS GENITALIA**)

◆ For both sexes, the breasts can be swollen due to Mom's hormones passing through to baby. It is temporary and they shrink back down on their own.

The Kidneys and Bladder

◆ Expect the baby to pee (urinate) once in the first 24 hours of life. We start investigating if this does not occur.

◆ Abnormal formation of the passageway from the kidneys to the bladder (see **VESICOURETERAL REFLUX**, **POSTERIOR URETHRAL VALVES**) can occur in rare occasions. An evaluation for this is done if a baby develops a bladder or kidney infection. (see **URINARY TRACT INFECTION, PYELONEPHRITIS**)

The Spine and Nervous System

◆ Your doctor will look for dimples or tufts of hair near the buttocks. Abnormalities on the skin can be a clue to a spine abnormality underneath the skin (see **SACRAL DIMPLE, NEURAL TUBE DEFECT, SPINA BIFIDA**).

◆ Also checked: the newborn's unique reflexes that fade over the first six months of life. It tells us their brain and nerves are coordinated. (see **CEREBRAL PALSY**) These reflexes include: *Rooting* (turning the head when the cheek is rubbed), *Sucking* (automatically sucking on objects placed in the mouth), *Palmar Grasp* (closing fingers on object placed on the palm), and *Moro* (body startles when head is dropped back).

The Arms and Legs (Extremities)

◆ Do both arms move? A weakness of the nerves causes a limp arm. (see **ERB'S PALSY**)

◆ Many people are familiar with purebred dogs with hip problems. Humans can have similar problems. We check the hips by rotating them in and out. If there is a concern, we'll order an ultrasound to look at the hips. Breech babies have a slightly increased risk of this disorder. (see **HIP DYSPLASIA**)

- Rarely, babies will have extra fingers and toes, and some that are fused together (see **POLYDACTYLY**, **SYNDACTYLY**).
- A severe deformity (see **CLUB FOOT**) makes the bottoms of the feet face each other and requires casting.

The Skin

- Brown birthmarks: Moles (see **CONGENITAL NEVUS**) and light brown oval shaped areas (see **CAFÉ AU LAIT SPOTS**) are permanent markings and rarely are related to other medical problems.
- Purple birthmarks: These marks (see **PORT WINE STAINS**) are permanent and can be quite large. If they are located on the face, your doctor will look for other medical problems (see **STURGE-WEBER SYNDROME**).
- Red birthmarks: These marks (see **STRAWBERRY HEMANGIOMA**) may be seen at birth, or by the first month of life. They start out flat, grow much larger and become raised. These particular marks shrink and usually go away by the age of three.
- More red birthmarks: Red marks known as stork bites and angel kisses (see **NEVUS FLAMMEUS**, **FLAT ANGIOMATA**) are on the back of the neck or eyelids and fade over the first few months of life. When your baby gets mad at you, you will see them turn even redder.
- Blue, bruise-like marks: These spots (see **MONGOLIAN SPOTS**) are found on the buttocks of dark skinned babies. They fade over several years.
- Yellow skin: This is a whole topic in itself—see section on **JAUNDICE**.

Go to our web site Baby411.com for pictures of all of these common birthmarks. Click on "Bonus Material".

Reality Check

Newborns are really rashy. Most rashes will come and go. You'll have a window of "photo opportunity" from two to three weeks of age when their skin is clearer. Then more rashes crop up at four to eight weeks of age. These are all due to fluctuating hormone levels. No matter what you do, they will go away. A good thing to remember is your baby could care less. The names are listed below. For details, refer to the glossary. (see **ERYTHEMA TOXICUM**, **MILIA**, **MILIARIA**, **NEONATAL ACNE**, **PUSTULAR MELANOSIS**). For pictures of these rashes, check out our web site Baby411.com (click on "Bonus Material.")

Q. What is the PKU/Newborn Screen and why does my baby need to be tested?

This is a test required by all 50 states to check for serious diseases that would otherwise go undetected in the first several weeks to months of life. The number of screening tests varies from state to state but all include: **HYPOTHYROIDISM**, **PHENYLKETONURIA (PKU)**, and **GALACTOSEMIA**. These tests are done once at the hospital, and again at two weeks of age. Some states also test for **SICKLE CELL ANEMIA** and **ADRENAL GLAND INSUFFICIENCY** (see glossary for details of diseases).

Although the risk of any of these diseases is quite low, the benefit of making an early diagnosis is tremendous. Children with undetected

SPECIAL BABIES, EXTRAORDINARY PARENTS

With all of the advances in medicine, many families know before birth that their baby has a genetic abnormality. This information is helpful for families prepare for their baby's special needs. Numerous support groups are available for families via organizations (see reference section) and the Internet.

Meet one special baby, Eliza, and her extraordinary mom, June Richard. Eliza is a nine month old born with Down Syndrome. Eliza's facial features are considered "classic" for a child with Down Syndrome. However, she has no other medical problems that are typically seen in a child with this genetic defect. And, developmentally, she keeps up with her nine month old peers. June describes Eliza as "a gift from God, merely wrapped with an extra chromosome." June organizes a parent support group and chat room on Babycenter.com. She encourages all parents with affected babies to utilize their site for information and support.

hypothyroidism were permanently mentally retarded prior to the era of state newborn screening programs.

FYI: We've posted a list of which states require what screens on our web site Baby411.com (again, click on "Bonus Material").

Q. Why do all babies get a shot of Vitamin K?

Vitamin K is essential for blood clotting. Babies who are born with a Vitamin K deficiency can have significant bleeding into vital organs (such as the brain, see **HEMORRHAGIC DISEASE OF THE NEWBORN**). Since time is of the essence, it makes more sense to give all babies the vitamin K than to test them all and find out too late who needed it.

Q. Why do all babies get eye ointment?

Having a baby is messy. Some mothers carry bacteria that can lead to serious eye infections in the baby. Again, it makes more sense to treat every baby immediately than to test every mother at delivery and figure out which baby needs it. Antibiotic ointment is very benign.

Q. Will my baby's blood type be tested?

Sometimes. Blood types are not routinely tested in the hospital. This

NEW PARENT 411: WHY DO ALL THESE TESTS?

Some parents feel uncomfortable with all the poking and prodding their newborn endures. Trust us—there is a method to the madness. Your doctor wants to make sure you are taking home a healthy baby! Remember the key rule to all these tests: if it wasn't important, we wouldn't be doing it!

might worry some parents, who are concerned that not knowing their baby's blood type immediately is dangerous. You should know that any person with a medical emergency (such as a car accident) that requires a blood transfusion gets type O negative blood regardless of his or her blood type. O negative blood is compatible with ALL blood types. When a blood transfusion is less urgent, a person's blood type is tested and numerous tests are done to find a donor blood match.

Your baby's blood type will be tested if Mommy has O blood type. Blood type incompatibility (i.e. baby is A or B) can lead to problems with jaundice. See Jaundice section (**ABO INCOMPATIBILITY**).

Strep: All You Ever Wanted to Know & More!

Q. What is the significance of the Group B Strep or Beta Strep test?

Mothers are routinely screened at the 35th to 37th week of their pregnancy for the presence of a bacteria that lives harmlessly in the genitals and intestines of some healthy women. This bacteria, called Group B Strep, can infect a newborn as he passes through the birth canal.

If Mom is a carrier for Group B Strep, she is given intravenous (IV) antibiotics during labor to suppress the growth of this bacteria. If Mom goes into labor before 37 weeks, has her water broken for more than 18 hours or has a fever greater than 100.4, she also gets IV antibiotics because of the risk of Group B Strep infection. (Women who have planned C-sections don't have to worry about this stuff).

Doctors get worked up about Group B Strep because it can cause blood infection (bacteremia), pneumonia, and meningitis in newborns. All newborns are watched closely, but those babies with moms who test positive for Group B Strep are watched even more closely.

It is standard protocol to get a complete blood count and blood culture on a newborn *if* mom is Group B Strep positive and: she didn't get: pretreated with antibiotics (which happens with quick labor), the baby is born sooner than 35 weeks gestation or if a baby starts misbehaving (temperature instability, labored breathing, etc.).[2]

Reality Check

Don't be too alarmed if you carry Group B Strep. This does not mean you are Typhoid Mary. Most babies with Group B Strep positive mothers do not get sick—they are just at a slightly higher risk.

Q. Are there any other tests on mom done during pregnancy that the pediatrician needs to know about?

Yes! It is a standard of prenatal care to obtain blood tests looking for previous infections in the mother. This panel of tests includes Hepatitis B exposure (see **TORCH INFECTIONS**). If Mom received prenatal care, her lab work should be on the baby's chart at the hospital.

Getting to Know You: Your Baby's First Few Days

After your baby passes their first exam, the fun is just beginning—it's time for you the parent to get to know your little guy or gal. Let's talk about what you'll experience for the first few hours . . . and days. This section will cover Apgar tests, changing those first diapers and more.

Q. Are there any vaccinations given to the baby at the hospital?

It depends. The Hepatitis B vaccine is recommended for all newborns as part of the universal immunization series. Infants usually get the first of three doses between birth and two months of age. It is ESSENTIAL to get the first dose at birth *if* Mom tests positive for Hepatitis B to prevent infection in the newborn. If Mom does not have the disease, some pediatricians prefer to give the first dose in their office. For more information see Chapter 12, Vaccines.

Q. Does my baby need to study for the Apgar test?

No. He probably won't score a perfect "10" either— those foreign judges are so critical of the dismount. Just kidding. The Apgar test determines which babies need extra help adjusting to life outside the womb. They are given a score from zero to ten. Your baby's **A**ppearance (color), **P**ulse (heart rate), **G**rimace (reaction to stimulation), **A**ctivity (tone), and **R**espiration rate are assessed at one minute of life and again at five minutes. Babies who endure difficult deliveries often have low (less than five) Apgar scores at one minute then perk up (greater than seven) at five minutes. The babies that don't rise in their scores may need observation and assistance by medical staff. Rest assured, low Apgar scores do NOT correlate with low SAT scores and future intelligence.

Q. What's THAT in my baby's diaper?

We've got an entire chapter dedicated to poop (exciting, no?), but let's give you a brief primer on what you'll be seeing in those first few diapers.

- ◆ *Black tar poop.* The official name is **MECONIUM**. Doctors expect one of these poops in the first day of life. If you see more, congratulations—you're on your way to being a diaper changing pro. See Elimination Chapter for details.
- ◆ *Brick dust.* Babies should urinate (pee) at least once in the first day as well. If your baby is hovering around that 10% weight loss (see later box, Why is My Baby Shrinking?), you may see a red-orange brick dust spot in the diaper (see **URIC ACID CRYSTALS**). You'll think it is blood, but take a closer look. Blood gets absorbed into the diaper since it's a liquid. The crystal powder sits on the surface. It just means your baby needs to drink. See Baby411.com's "Bonsu Material" for a great picture.
- ◆ *Blood.* Baby girls will have a "period" thanks to Mom's hormones. Don't worry, they don't get the PMS to go with it! This should only happen in the first month of life and not again until puberty.

◆ **Gel balls.** This did not come out of your baby. It is your super absorbent diaper. When the volume of urine (pee) exceeds the diaper absorbency, the gels rise to the surface. I get this question frequently!

Reality Check: Rooming in with Baby

After the baby is born, the nurses will ask you if you want to keep the baby with you at all times. It is also an option to let the nurses "baby-sit" in the nursery while you get some rest. New parents choose to room in because they think:

◆ Their baby will be stolen or worse—fed formula—in the nursery. Reality: neither of these fears is justified.

◆ They need to learn baby's cues while they are at the hospital. Reality: you'll get LOTS of practice during daylight hours.

◆ They will lose the opportunity to breast feed on baby's demand. Reality: crying babies in the nursery are sent back to mom's room to eat.

Q. My baby sleeps all the time. Were my prayers answered?

Wait until the baby gets home…you will find out then! All babies sleep through their first two days of life. They have been through the same experience as their Mom. Their true colors come out on the day you take them home. It is not the magic of the nursery nurse's touch (although you will feel inadequate when faced with a screaming baby). Newborns don't have the skills to pull it together and settle down. You will need to figure out what soothes your baby. For details, see Chapter 9, "Sleep."

Q. Why is my baby turning yellow? What is jaundice?

Here's the 411 on jaundice. While it sounds scary, there are two types of jaundice when it comes to newborns: NORMAL jaundice and ABNORMAL jaundice. Yes, you read it right—there is a form of jaundice that is NORMAL in newborns.

So what is jaundice? Short answer: it's body garbage that hasn't been eliminated yet. Long answer: humans make body garbage called bilirubin. Bilirubin breaks down in our livers and comes out in our poop. The problem: a newborn's liver is not working at full speed yet, nor are his intestines.

So, for most newborns, the body garbage (bilirubin) will start to collect in the skin. This is normal jaundice. Bilirubin has a yellow pigment, causing

NEW PARENT 411: WHY IS MY BABY SHRINKING?

The shrinking baby phenomenon! No, it's not a headline ripped from the tabloids. Babies travel out of the womb with extra baggage. They have about 10% more fluid than their bodies need. Over the first few days of life, they will lose 10% of their birth weight, then quickly gain about an ounce a day once they start eating (about their third day of life). This is sure to cause you anxiety, particularly if you are breastfeeding. For details, see Chapter 5, "Nutrition."

DR B'S (& DENISE'S) OPINION: ROOMING IN

This is my take on rooming in (where your baby sleeps with you in your hospital room), as both a parent and pediatrician. View your hospital stay as your last opportunity for free babysitting. You will be exhausted and need to rest from giving birth. Keep the baby in your room during the day and let her sleep in the nursery at night (or at least for a few hours). Consider the following:

♦ Mom's body needs rest to produce milk.
♦ Babies are really noisy when they sleep. New parents are alarmed at every snort, snore, and pause in breathing that baby makes. It doesn't allow for the 'deep sleep mode' Mom needs.
♦ The nursery nurses are not part of a conspiracy to foil breast-feeding.
♦ You have the rest of your life to stare at and hold your baby.

Denise's Opinion: Now that we've okayed it for you to keep your baby in the nursery at night, what about Dad? First time parents always plan for Dad to spend the night with Mom. But have you ever tried to sleep on one of those fold out chairs in most maternity wards? Let Dad go home and get some real rest for at least one or two nights before you bring baby home. The nursing staff at the hospital can handle anything that comes up and Dad will be much fresher for the first day home.

the whites of the eyes and skin to yellow. The level of yellow (jaundice) correlates with how far down the yellow gets on the body (increasing from head to toe.) The level will continue to rise until baby is eating and pooping regularly (day four to five). You will notice that the poop changes from black to a yellow/green/brown color at that time.

Again, by day four or five of life, bilirubin *normally* comes out in the poop and no longer collects in the skin.

What about abnormal jaundice? See the following red flags.

RED FLAGS: Abnormal Jaundice.

These are signs for ABNORMAL jaundice (see the previous discussion of normal versus abnormal jaundice):

♦ Jaundice is seen in the first 24 hours of life
♦ Jaundice persists more than five days of life
♦ Level of jaundice descends below the belly button
♦ When Mom and Baby's blood types are different (Mom is O and Baby is A or B). Mom's blood can potentially mount a response that destroys some of Baby's red blood cells. This leaves the baby with even more bilirubin to break down.

Q. How is jaundice treated?

The best way to get rid of bilirubin is to eliminate it in the poop. The more the baby eats, the more he poops. For a majority of babies, the bilirubin level peaks around day four of life. This is precisely the time that mom's milk comes in and babies are interested in eating.

For various reasons, some babies either have a delay in eliminating the bilirubin, or produce higher levels than their bodies can eliminate effectively. They need some help for a few days to get rid of the bilirubin. One or more of the following interventions are used to reduce the bilirubin load:

1. **Supplementation with formula until Mom's milk comes in.**
2. **Phototherapy.** This technique uses UV light to breakdown the bilirubin. Babies either rest with a lighted blanket around them or under a bank of lights similar to a tanning booth.
3. **Intravenous fluid.** Dehydrated babies have more trouble with jaundice.

FYI: It is NOT recommended that you lay out poolside with your newborn, or place him by a sunny window to treat jaundice. It's not that effective and can overheat him.

Q. I am getting a lot of different advice from nurses and lactation specialists—who is right?

Everyone, sort of. You will meet many health care professionals in your baby's first few days. They will all have different approaches to the same child health issues. To avoid frustration and confusion, realize that there are many ways, for example, to position a baby to nurse. Just take it all in, then figure out what works for you and your child. P.S. If you feel like you have NEW PARENT stamped on your forehead, you do!

Q. When will I need to use a car seat?

Every time you take your baby with you in the car! This includes your trip home from the hospital. It's the law, folks. Here's what you need to know:

◆ All 50 states require that infants under one year of age be seated (and strapped in) to a car seat. Laws vary from state to state beyond a year of age. However, the American Academy of Pediatrics advises that children be in a safety restraint (convertible car seat and then a booster seat) until they weigh 80 pounds.

◆ Infants must be facing the rear of the car until they are 20 pounds AND at least one year of age.

◆ Kids under age 12 should be in the back seat of your vehicle. Air bags deploy right at the level of a child's head, which can be fatal.

◆ So, what do you need to buy now? Newborns can sit in either an infant car seat (0-20 pounds) or a convertible car seat (0-40 pounds). You can conceivably use only a convertible car seat and save money. But, most parents choose the more expensive option of getting the infant car seat (knowing they'll have to get the convertible car seat after their baby outgrows the infant seat) because it's portable. When your baby falls asleep in the car, you'll find it's worth the investment. For more details on buying a car seat including reviews and recommendations, see our other book, *Baby Bargains* (for more information see the back of this book).

◆ Practice using the car seat *before* game day so you don't feel foolish. You may need an engineering degree to figure out how your particular car seat works, especially if you bought a fancy Swedish one. The hospital nurses will help you get the baby strapped in, but you'll need to do the rest. Our advice: get your seat safety checked BEFORE the baby is born to make sure it is correctly installed.

◆ Where to get help: The National Highway Transportation Safety Administration is the government entity that regulates car seat restraints. They have a helpful web site at www.nhtsa.gov including info on finding someone to check for proper car seat installation (click on "car seat inspections").

Q. When can I take my baby outside?

Whenever you feel like it. Let's review some Old Wives' Tales…

◆ *The baby will catch pneumonia if he is out in the cold weather.* FALSE!

◆ *The baby will get an ear infection if the wind blows in his ears.* FALSE!

It is perfectly fine to go out for a stroll with your baby at any age. Dress him in the same layers you would wear.

However, I recommend avoiding crowded restaurants, grocery stores, and airplanes in the wintertime until your baby is four weeks old (if possible). This minimizes exposure to cold and flu viruses that are spread from respiratory droplets (coughs and sneezes). For details, see Chapter 13, "Common Infections."

The Baby 411 Two-Week Survival Guide
a.k.a. What Do I do NOW?

Okay, now you are ready to take your baby home. Without the luxury of the nursery nurses right down the hall, you are probably scared to death.

Having this book should be helpful to look up all those questions you have. But remember, your pediatrician or family practitioner is only a phone call away. We've covered the basics in this section, but each chapter in this book has information pertinent to newborns. We'll refer you to those sections for more details.

I **BREATHING.** As adults, we breathe about 12 times per minute at an even rate. As we discussed earlier in this chapter, newborns breathe 30 to 40 times per minute and have episodes of *periodic breathing*. This means that your baby may breathe rapidly several times, p-a-u-s-e, then breathe again. This pause can last several seconds (less than ten seconds). This is normal, but is bound to freak you out.

Nasal congestion is normal in the first several weeks of life. Use saline nose drops to flush the secretions.

RED FLAGS: Breathing

◆ When a pause between breaths lasts 15 to 20 seconds.
◆ If your baby is panting, or breathing over 50 to 60 times per minute.
◆ If your baby's rib cage sucks in (*retractions*), nostrils flare, or he makes grunting noises.

2 **FEEDING.** Whether you breast or bottle-feed, your newborn will be very sleepy for the first few days. The result? He may fall asleep during a feeding, sometimes after only a few minutes. Encourage your baby to stay awake by rubbing his head, playing with his feet, or unwrapping him and placing him away from your warm body.

How often does a newborn eat?

◆ A breast-fed baby usually eats every two to three hours (at least eight times in 24 hours).

◆ A formula-fed baby eats about two to three ounces every three to four hours. (six to eight times in 24 hours)

Either way, your baby should wake up spontaneously and eat frequently. In the first two weeks of life, *do not let your newborn go more than 5 hours without eating*. You need to wake him up to feed him if this occurs. (Note: after two weeks of age, if your baby wants sleeps longer—let him!)

Mom's breast milk usually arrives on the baby's 3rd to 4th day of life. Until then, the baby gets antibody rich (but lower-calorie) colostrum when he nurses. This is all your baby needs right now.

Spitting up some milk is normal. It can look fresh or curdled. Both are normal. Vomiting up large volumes at every feeding is not normal.

RED FLAGS: Feeding

◆ You consistently have to awaken your baby to eat.
◆ Your baby is consistently vomiting large volumes of milk (i.e. the whole feeding)
◆ If nursing, your milk has not come in after three or four days.

For more information on this topic, check out the nutrition and growth, liquids and the "other end" chapters. See the end of this section for a handy guide to keep track of feedings.

3 **ELIMINATION.** Your newborn's body is just learning how things work initially. In the first 24 hours of life, he may pee (urinate) and poop (stool) only once. When he really begins to take food in, things should start to come out. This is a good way to tell if your infant is eating enough, particularly if you are nursing. Your hospital lactation specialist should give you a diary to keep track of intake and output.

Urine: By the third day of life, your baby should pee at least four times a day. By one week of age, six to 12 wet diapers a day is normal.

Stool: The first few poops are called **MECONIUM** and are black and **TARRY** looking.

NEW PARENT 411: DR. BROWN'S STOOL RULES

1. Once your baby starts to eat, his poop will change colors and texture.
2. Breastfed babies often have yellow, watery, seedy poop.
3. Formula fed babies often have green, pasty strained-peas poop.
4. Any shade of yellow, green, or brown is normal.
5. Stool frequency can vary from once every feeding to once a week. The frequency is not an indication of constipation— the texture is.
6. *All* babies turn red and grunt when they poop, not just yours.

RED FLAGS: Elimination
◆ Your baby is not urinating at least every six hours.
◆ Your baby's poop looks red, mucousy, or does not change from the black meconium.
◆ Your baby's poop looks like yours.
For more information, check out Chapter 8, "The Other End."

4 **SLEEP.** Your baby sleeps 17 to 20 hours a day, but rarely more than four to five hours at a time. He may be very hard to console initially and force you to walk with him or rock him to sleep. *You can't spoil a newborn.* Do what it takes to get him to sleep. Bad habits happen AFTER two months of age.

RED FLAGS: Sleep
◆ Your baby consistently needs to be awakened to eat.
◆ Your baby is completely inconsolable for over 3 hours straight.
For more information, check out Chapter 9, "Sleep."

5 **SKIN.** Your newborn may have a few bruises from delivery that will fade with time. He may also have a few rashes—also normal.

As we discussed earlier in this chapter, a yellow appearance to the skin, called *jaundice*, is often normal, but is something that should be followed. Your baby's liver is just starting its job of breaking down a body waste called bilirubin. Until this happens, the skin on the face may be a little yellow as a result of the bilirubin's pigment. That's okay. What is NOT normal: if you see this in the first 24 hours of life, or if the yellow color descends below your baby's waistline.

The umbilical cord takes one to four weeks to fall off. Until then, the stump is gooey. This is normal. If the skin around the cord is getting infected (see **OMPHALITIS**), the area is red, tender, and foul smelling.

RED FLAGS: Skin
◆ Jaundice occurs in the first 24 hours of life or below the waistline once you get home.
◆ Redness of the skin around the umbilical cord, or pus draining from it.
See Chapter 4, Hygiene and the Glossary for more information.

6 **FEVERS.** We'll discuss fevers in-depth in Chapter 15, "First Aid." For now, read the red flags below for the basics.

RED FLAGS: Fever

From birth to three months of age, *any* fever can be a sign of a serious infection. You need to call your doctor immediately if your baby has a temperature greater than 100.3 F taken *rectally*. (See the section how to take a rectal temp in Chapter 15, "First Aid").

Ear thermometers tend to be unreliable and since a fever in an infant is so concerning, these are not recommended for use.

Fever medications should not be used for infants under three months of age unless recommended by your doctor (for example, when your baby is vaccinated).

On the next page, we have a feeding and elimination chart—this will help you track your newborn's pee and poop for the first seven days. After day eight, you'll be an old pro.

BABY BLUES

Here is a newsflash for you...your life will never be the same. I know, everyone has told you this during your entire pregnancy. But reality has hit you like a sledgehammer. Becoming a parent is the most amazing experience of your life—so why are you crying right now?!!

Let's see. Your physical body feels like it was run over by a truck. Your hormone levels are off the charts. You haven't had a good night's sleep since the baby was born. You understand why sleep deprivation is used as a form of torture in POW camps. You find it difficult to make rational decisions, or *any* decisions for that matter.

Here's another newsflash for you...you are normal. No matter how wonderful it is to become a parent, it takes time for your body and mind to adjust to it.

RED FLAGS: When Mom has Postpartum Depression

The Baby Blues are short term feelings of sadness that subside after a few much needed breaks provided by supportive family and friends. Postpartum depression doesn't go away that easily. Here are the clues that professional help is needed:

1. Frequent episodes of crying or weepiness.
2. Flat 'affect' (Mom won't smile).
3. Lack of interest in the family or activities.
4. Loss of appetite.

Mothers who experience postpartum depression often don't recognize the clues. If a family member expresses concerns about you, be smart and let them get you some help!

Handy Feeding & Elimination Table: The First 7 Days

Instructions: Circle the hour your baby nurses.
Circle W for wet diaper (urine). Circle S for soiled diaper (poop).

Day 1   *Goal 6-8 feedings*
             Diapers: 1 wet, 1 soiled

12am 1 2 3 4 5 6 7 8 9 10 11 12pm 1 2 3 4 5 6 7 8 9 10 11

W   S   (black, tarry)

Day 2   *Goal 8-12 feedings*
             2 wet   2 soiled

12m 1a 2 3 4 5 6 7 8 9 10 11 12pm 1 2 3 4 5 6 7 8 9 10 11

W W   S S   (black/brown)

Day 3   *Goal 8-12 feedings*
             2 wet   2 soiled

12m 1a 2 3 4 5 6 7 8 9 10 11 12pm 1 2 3 4 5 6 7 8 9 10 11

W W   S S   (green, yellow)

Day 4   *Goal 8-12 feedings*
             4 wet   3 soiled

12m 1a 2 3 4 5 6 7 8 9 10 11 12pm 1 2 3 4 5 6 7 8 9 10 11

W W W W   S S S (yellow)

Day 5   *Goal 8-12 feedings*
             5 wet   3 soiled

12m 1a 2 3 4 5 6 7 8 9 10 11 12pm 1 2 3 4 5 6 7 8 9 10 11

W W W W W   S S S (yellow)

Day 6   *Goal 8-12 feedings*
             6 wet   4 soiled

12m 1a 2 3 4 5 6 7 8 9 10 11 12pm 1 2 3 4 5 6 7 8 9 10 11

W W W W W W   S S S S

Day 7   *Goal 8-12 feedings*
             6 wet   4 soiled

12m 1a 2 3 4 5 6 7 8 9 10 11 12pm 1 2 3 4 5 6 7 8 9 10 11

W W W W W W   S S S S

LABOR DAY

? ?

Notes

Baby 411

Care & Feeding

Hygiene: The Spa Treatment

"Ray! You take that diaper off your head, you put it back onto your sister!"
~ Raising Arizona

You survived nine months of pregnancy, Labor Day and the hospital food after your baby was born. Now the fun begins—it's time to take baby home.

Due to budget cutbacks at the federal government, babies are no longer sent home with personal butlers or detailed care instructions on cleaning and hygiene. Just kidding! They never used to do that. You are expected to know about this stuff on your own. Consider this chapter your baby care primer.

So first, let's talk candidly about diaper rash. No it isn't pretty, but there are several steps you can take to stop it. Next, it's on to belly button care. Also, we'll discuss the topic of dressing your baby as well as tips on cradle cap, sun block, dental care and more. And let's talk about your baby's private parts—you've got questions and we've got the answers, handily divided into boy and girl sections.

Q. When can I clip my newborn's nails?

Around three to four weeks of life.

The fingertip and nail are stuck together for the first few weeks. Attempts to use a nail clipper will result in drawing blood. For now, you can use a nail file and give your baby a manicure.

Helpful Hint

You can place socks on your baby's hands if he is scratching his face and you want nice pictures.

Q. When can I use diaper wipes?

Now.

Most hospital nurseries use gauze pads soaked in water for diaper cleanups. This is done to prevent potential skin irritation. The truth is that most babies have no problem with typical diaper wipes.

Helpful Hint

Some parents like to keep anti-bacterial hand sanitizer at the changing table (for mom and dad's hands). It's not a bad idea, since you need to keep your hands and your eyes on your baby.

DR B'S OPINION

"Bring your own diaper wipes to the hospital. If your baby's skin gets irritated, then you can use water and gauze pads. After your first diaper change cleaning meconium (see elimination chapter), you will understand why I recommend using diaper wipes."

Q. How many layers of clothing does my baby need to wear?

As many as you do.

Babies live at the same body temperature as we all do. They will be comfortable in the same number of clothes as you are. It is true that your baby loses heat a little more quickly than you, so keep an eye on him in cooler weather.

Reality Check

Parents often dress their babies for an arctic freeze in July. Then they wonder why their baby has a heat rash.

Old Wives Tale

My baby will catch pneumonia if he gets cold.

Your baby's body temperature will drop if he is outside in cold weather for a prolonged period of time and is not dressed for it. Pneumonia is an infectious disease. It does not infect people who are cold; pneumonia infects people who *have* a cold.

Q. How often do I clean the belly button?

Do not be afraid of it. Clean it three to four times a day until the cord falls off.

Babies cry because the rubbing alcohol you are using is cold . . . NOT because it hurts. The rubbing alcohol should be applied to the BASE of the bully button, where the gooey stuff is—exactly where you are afraid to go.

The alcohol keeps the bully button from getting stinky. A recent study showed that alcohol does not make the cord fall off any faster than leaving it alone.

TREATING DIAPER RASH: 5 TIPS & TRICKS

There are basically two kinds of diaper rashes:

Irritated skin. Flat red rash caused when poop and pee break down the skin, causing redness and irritation.

Yeast infection. Raised, pimply rash surrounds an area that looks like raw meat. (Yeast likes the diaper area because it is dark, warm, and moist.)

Curious to see exactly what these different rashes look like? Check out our web site at Baby411.com (click on Bonus Material).

For basic skin irritation, creating a barrier to protect the skin from further insults is key. Here are our tips:

1. **Use petroleum jelly (Vaseline) or zinc oxide (store brand: Balmex, Desitin) at every diaper change.**

2. **Let your baby 'air dry'.** If you are feeling brave, let your baby go bare bottomed for a while. For the less ambitious types, use a blow dryer on a cool setting and dry the diaper area after cleaning.

3. **For more severe rashes, try Dr. Smith's Diaper Ointment or Triple Paste.** These products are a little thicker and more protective. Although they are available over-the-counter, you may have to ask your pharmacist to order some for you.

4. **Use pure lanolin (Lansinoh).** Many women use this for cracked nipples caused by breastfeeding. It's very expensive to recommend as a first line of defense against diaper rash, but if you have it in the house, use it.

5. **If the rash looks like yeast, try an over-the-counter anti-fungal (e.g. Lotrimin AF)**—the package will say it's for jock itch and athlete's foot. Don't be alarmed. Apply twice daily for a week.

If none of these tricks work, check in with your doctor. Most pediatricians and family practitioners have additional tips for stopping diaper rash.

Reality Check

The umbilical cord stump falls off between one and four weeks of life. Do not immerse your baby in a bath until after the cord comes off because the cord needs to be kept dry.

RED FLAG: Belly Buttons

A foul smelling belly button with pus draining from it and surrounded by red skin indicates infection (see **OMPHALITIS**). You need to call your doctor immediately.

Q. When can I give my newborn his first bath?

After the cord falls off.

For now, you can sponge your baby down. Your baby will enjoy a real bath much more than this experience. You can sponge bathe him every few days. Just make sure the diaper area is nice and clean.

Q. How often should I bathe my baby after the cord falls off?

As often as you wish.

You can bathe your baby every day if you like. Many parents and babies enjoy the time together. On the other hand, your baby does not make body odor or play in the sandbox yet. You can bathe him as infrequently as two to three times per week. In drier climates or with babies that have skin conditions like eczema, bathing LESS often is better for baby's skin.

Q. What soap products should I use on my baby?

We like Dove soap, because it is perfume and dye free. Plus, it has a moisturizer (particularly good for babies with eczema). And it's cheap. Johnson and Johnson's hypoallergenic baby shampoo is fine.

Helpful Hint

A good rule for baby products—if it smells good or has a color, don't use it on your baby.

Q. Can I put lotion on my baby's dry skin?

Sure. Just be sure it is perfume-free and dye-free.

Most newborns have dry skin from swimming around in water (technical term: amniotic fluid) for nine months. We personally recommend hydrated petroleum jelly (Creamy Vaseline, Target brand CF-Creamy Formula petroleum jelly). When it comes to dry skin, the greasier the better.

Q. My baby has acne. Should I buy some Oxy 10?

No. Do nothing and it goes away by eight weeks of life.

Acne develops from your baby's rapidly changing body hormones. It is the worst from age four to eight weeks. Putting creams and lotions on the skin only makes it worse. Most importantly, your baby is not bothered by it.

Q. What laundry detergent do I use to clean baby's clothes? Do I really need to wash everything before I use it?

It depends on the baby.

Stick with the perfume-free and dye-free rule, especially for babies with sensitive skin. But, that does NOT necessarily mean that your baby's laundry needs to be washed separately with his own expensive detergent. The whole family's laundry can be done with a product like ALL Free and Clear or Tide Free.

For the baby with sensitive skin, pre-wash items that will be touching him. It may also be helpful to double rinse the laundry. And remember to avoid dryer sheets (they all contain perfume).

Helpful Hint

Have a spray bottle of stain remover next to baby's laundry basket. You'll probably need it for the shoulders on all of your shirts, too. For more laundry tips, check out our other book, *Baby Bargains* (see back of the book for details). Another seasoned parent tip: if you've been thinking about getting a new washing machine, now is the time. Newer, front-loading washers really do clean clothes better. Considering the time you and your washer will be spending together, it is probably worth the investment.

Q. What is the scaly stuff in my baby's hair?

For twenty points, Alex, what is cradle cap?

ECZEMA: ADVICE ON DEALING WITH DRY SKIN

Some babies develop dry, scaly patches on the skin (see **ECZEMA**). It gets worse when the skin is dry. The key to keeping it in check is using a moisturizing soap and frequent application of moisturizing cream.

For some reason our family (the Fields) has been unlucky enough to be plagued by eczema. Perhaps its thanks to the ultra-dry climate here in Colorado, where the relative humidity is often measured in single digits. Mom, Dad and both boys have had it including one child with severe, chronic eczema. Here are our tips for living with this itchy-scratchy skin condition:

1. **Baths: Try Aveeno oatmeal baths.** They're non-toxic and soothing to the skin. Also, keep the bath water warm, not too hot. Hot water dries out skin. And only give baths when you're baby is really dirty. Until baby starts crawling, he won't be that dirty.

2. **Moisturize constantly.** As a side benefit, this is a great way to bond with your baby when you massage lotions or creams into his skin frequently. A room humidifier will help introduce moisture as well.

3. **Avoid perfumes and dyes.** This includes laundry detergents, soaps and bubble baths. And don't introduce antibiotic soaps either—they can be very irritating. Babies (when they're clean!) smell so great any way, why add perfumes?

4. **Observe whether eczema shows up when you start adding new foods to baby's diet.** Eliminating the offending food will obviously help. And if it happens frequently you should consider seeing a food allergy specialist.

5. **Don't be afraid to get a referral to a dermatologist if your baby's eczema gets really bad.** Dermatologists are skin experts with access to the newest treatments.

Cradle cap (see **SEBORRHEA**) is caused by baby's hormonal changes and possibly, that pesky yeast thing again. It makes the scalp and eyebrow skin get dry, flaking patches. It can last for several months.

Because it is similar to dandruff, it can be treated the same way. Anti-dandruff shampoos (Head and Shoulders, Selsun Blue, Sebulex) work well if used two or three times a week. You can also massage vegetable oil into the areas and lift the scales up with an old toothbrush. Some doctors will use an anti-yeast product like Nizoral AD shampoo (over the counter) for resilient cases.

Eyebrows can be treated with 1% Hydrocortisone cream (over the counter) twice daily for a week.

Reality Check: Cradle cap may bother you, but it doesn't bother your baby.

Q. When can my baby start using sunblock?

Now. Sunblock can be applied to newborns.

The AAP *previously* recommended that sunblock be used only in infants over six months of age (because of the potential for skin irritation). However, the risk of skin cancer (1 in 75 over a lifetime) has outweighed concerns over potential skin irritation. Suncreen is critical because sun damage and sunburn at an early age is correlated with a higher risk of skin cancer later in life. Translation: use the suncreen on that baby. Any product with a SPF of 30 is fine; anything higher is a waste of money. Other tips: try to keep baby out of the sun from 10am to 3pm every day, apply sunscreen liberally (at least a half ounce each time) and reapply frequently (every two hours).

What sunscreen is best? Check out our other book, *Toddler Bargains* (see back of this book for details) for a discussion sunscreens and which ones we found work best. Also: *Consumer Reports* has a special report on

---

THE WHOLE FOODS SCHOOL OF MEDICINE

When our oldest son developed cradle cap, we trotted down to the local health food store to find a natural treatment. Perhaps an all-natural lotion or organic shampoo? As we perused the aisles of herbs and other natural remedies, a cheerful clerk asked if she could help. Sure, what would she suggest? We were surprised at what we heard next—the clerk suggest our baby INGEST a cocktail of herbs, spices and who-knows-what-else to treat the cradle cap. As we stood there with our mouths open, we couldn't help but notice the clerk was barely old enough to vote, yet appeared confident in dispensing quasi-medical advice about how we should treat this situation. We left the store without any "medicine" and just used an anti-dandruff shampoo at home that ended up working fine.

Now, we don't relate this story to pick on health food stores or their well-meaning workers. We actually love our local Whole Foods and shop there often. When we wander from the fruits and vegetables section into the supplements isle, however, sometimes we feel like we've entered the Twilight Zone. All of the sudden, there are wild claims of miracle health cures, often without a shred of scientific proof. All that is fine for adults of course—if you think you can cure some personal malady by ingesting an herb only found growing on the underside of an iceberg floating off Peru, we say go for it. But when it comes to your *baby's* health, we urge caution. As we said in the introduction to this book, show us the science. Before diving into "natural" or "herbal" remedies for your baby, consult your doctor and reputable web sites to confirm they won't do more harm than good.

suncreen on their web site (www.consumerreports.com) that includes product tests, ratings and more.

The key to preventing sunburn is to RE-APPLY the sunblock frequently—don't buy the combo sunblock and bug repellent (we'll explain why next).

Q. When should I apply insect repellent on my baby?

There is no consensus on the answer to this question.

Mosquitoes and ticks are known carriers of illness. The most notable diseases in the United States spread by these bugs are West Nile Virus (mosquitoes) and Lyme Disease (deer ticks). The safest option to avoid mosquitoes is to stay inside at dawn and at dusk, when they are out in greatest numbers. It's also a good idea to wear light colored clothing, long sleeves, and long pants when your baby is outside.

As far as insect repellents go, the most effective products contain DEET. Other chemicals used as repellents are not nearly as effective (citronella, eucalyptus, soybean oil, IR 3535). A recent study showed that products containing 23% DEET will repel mosquitoes for five *hours*. By comparison, Avon's Skin So Soft (citronella based) repels mosquitoes for a mere 9.6 *minutes*.[1]

The only problem with DEET is that it can be absorbed into the body via the skin and cause dizziness—therefore, you should wash the DEET repellent off once returning indoors. Here are some safety tips for using DEET on your baby:[2]

1. **Don't use DEET repellents on infants under two months of age.** It's fine AFTER two months of age.
2. **Young children should not apply repellent themselves—** that's mom and dad's job.
3. **Don't apply repellent under clothing or to wounds. It goes on exposed skin—**yes, that means ALL exposed skin areas, not just the arms or legs.
4. **Don't put DEET near children's mouths or eyes—**and avoid getting it on their hands. While the American Academy of Pediatrics says products up to 30% DEET are safe for kids, it might be safer to stay in the 5% to 10% level.
5. **What about natural repellents?** Alternatives to DEET made of eucalyptus or plant-based oils like soybeans can be as effective as low-concentration DEET products. Translation: they do offer SOME protection, but only for limited periods of time. However, other "natural" insect repellents have not been proven to be effective at all. Our advice: stick to DEET repellents.
6. **DEET comes in several forms—**the liquids, sprays and lotions are effective. The DEET wristbands don't work.
7. **When you come back inside, WASH the repellent off your skin.**
8. **DEET products with a concentration of 30% are as safe as those with 10%.** 30% DEET lasts for five hours, 10% just two hours.
9. **How much DEET should you use?** That depends on how long you plan to be outdoors—10% is fine for less than two hours, etc.
10. **DEET should only be applied once a day.** Therefore, it is NOT recommended to use a combo sunblock repellant, as sunblock needs to be reapplied frequently.

The Boy Parts

Q. When can I stop using gauze around my newborn's circumcision?

This question usually comes up at the two-week well baby check. The nurses at the hospital will show you how to apply a gauze dressing and Vaseline. The skin starts to heal around three or four days after a circumcision procedure is done. It starts to look gross with a yellowish scab. You will think it looks infected, but it's not. When it looks like that, it no longer needs gauze to protect it.

Helpful Hint

A parent remarked to me, "You need to tell me the endpoint for certain things. Otherwise I'll think I'm just supposed to keep doing it." If you are still putting gauze on your six month old, you have gone above and beyond the call of duty! Bottom Line: If you don't know when to stop, ask your doctor. It will save you a lot of time and labor.

Q. How do I care for my son's circumcised penis in the long term?

Make sure you always see a definite separation between the head and the shaft of the penis.

When you change your baby's diaper, gently pull down at the base of the penis and clean the area where the head meets the shaft. This area collects dead skin (this is called smegma; memo to Seattle-area musicians, this would be a great band name). If the smegma remains there, it can cause the head and shaft to adhere together (see **PENILE ADHESION**; second memo to Seattle bands—this is NOT a good name).

Q. How do I care for my son's uncircumcised penis?

Here are four rules:

1. *Do NOT forcefully pull the foreskin back to clean the penis.*
2. *Dead skin (smegma) collects under the foreskin and will come out on its own.*
3. *Once the foreskin pulls back on its own (usually by age five years), clean under the foreskin one or two times per week with water. Always push the foreskin back down after pulling it up to clean it.*
4. *Teenagers need to clean under the foreskin daily.*

The foreskin is attached to the shaft of the penis with tight tissue called adhesions. Most of the time, these adhesions loosen up by the age of five. Some boys, however, may have adhesions into their teen years and this is still okay (but check it out with your doctor).

Rarely, the foreskin remains tight and hard to pull back (see **PHIMOSIS**). The foreskin can also get pulled back and unable to be manually brought back down (see **PARAPHIMOSIS**).

BOTTOM LINE
If your son has a red, swollen penis, or an abnormal stream of urine, call your doctor.

The Girl Parts

Q. How do I clean my daughter's private parts?

Front to back, and in every crease. Dads—time to pay attention.

Poop has bugs in it (bacteria). Pee (urine) does not. If the poop ends up in the opening to the bladder (urethra), the bacteria will climb in and grow there (see **BLADDER INFECTION/UTI**). This is a bad thing.

Look at your daughter's private parts. Gently separate the lips (labia). You will see two holes. The top hole is the urethra; the bottom hole is the vagina. These areas, including the lips, need to be poop-free zones. Wipe from the top of the genitals, down to the anus. Never go backwards and use several wipes if you need to.

 BOTTOM LINE
Don't ever hesitate to change your daughter's poopy diaper, even if it isn't your turn. Delay can lead to a bladder infection.

Mouth Care

Q. Why is my baby's mouth coated in white? Is that milk?

It is either milk or thrush (a yeast infection in the mouth).

When babies are toothless, their mouths don't have many bacteria (germs) living there. Teeth provide a home for bacteria (that's what plaque is). Remember the yeast diaper rash? Yeast likes dark, warm, wet places that don't have other germs around. A newborn's mouth is a perfect locale.

How do you tell the difference between milk and thrush? Milk wipes off and is only on the tongue. Thrush collects on the gums and inner cheeks and can't be wiped off.

Thrush requires a prescription anti-fungal mouthwash to be treated. Call your doctor.

 Helpful Hint
If your baby gets thrush, you need to sterilize any products that go in baby's mouth (rubber nipples, pacifiers), as yeast will continue to grow on these items. Breastfeeding moms frequently develop a yeast infection on their nipples when their baby has thrush. We'll discuss this more in the Dr. B's opinion box on the next page.

Q. When do baby's teeth come in?

Around six to 12 months old. There are some kids whose teeth come in earlier or later, though. Universally, the first tooth to erupt is a bottom, middle one. The rest come in randomly.

DR B'S OPINION:
TREATING MOM'S YEAST INFECTION

Let's talk about yeast infections for breast-feeding moms. As a doctor, I feel comfortable treating mom with a prescription anti-fungal cream for her breasts. But, as you might guess, most pediatricians do NOT feel comfortable prescribing any medicine for mom that has to be taken orally. Remember, your pediatrician is trained to treat kids. From a medical care standpoint, it's best to call *your* doctor for help. Note: obviously, this is one plus to a family practitioner who can treat both mom and baby at the same time.

Reality Check
Drool is not a reliable indicator of teething. All four-month-olds are drooling and usually toothless. Why? The salivary glands are getting revved up at this age to start digesting solid foods.

Q. How can I tell if my baby is teething?

Babies have a lower coping threshold and trouble settling down. The pain of throbbing gums can usually be forgotten when a baby is busy playing.

First-year molars come in somewhere between 12 to 18 months old, even if the more central teeth are not in yet. Don't be fooled when your baby starts pulling on his ears—it's most likely not an ear infection. Look in his mouth. It's often the jaw pain from the molars that causes the ear pulling. It will save you a trip to the doctor.

Helpful Hint
Try acetaminophen (Tylenol) at bedtime for teething pain. It is a very effective pain medicine and lasts longer than topical gels (Numzit, Oragel). For daytime, try frozen mini-bagels or a cold teething ring to gnaw on.

Q. When do I start cleaning baby's teeth?

When he has teeth!

Start regular tooth care when your baby's first tooth comes out. Use a wet washcloth to wipe the teeth, twice daily. You need to clean your baby's teeth AFTER the last feeding of the night. Otherwise, you will promote tooth decay (cavities). You can start using fluoride toothpaste when your baby can spit it out (around age three years).

DR B'S OPINION

"I do not recommend alternative medicine teething products. Some of these include belladonna (a chemical toxic to the nervous system) and caffeine (it's hard to sleep after an espresso shot) as ingredients."

HYGIENE

NEW PARENT 411: BABY TOOTHPASTE

Let's talk baby toothpaste. Fluoride-free "kid's" toothpaste is okay to use for infants, but the sweet taste encourages your baby to suck on the toothbrush as soon as you get it in his mouth. Bottom line: special baby toothpaste is not really necessary—it's expensive and it's hard to maneuver the toothbrush with the baby sucking.

Q. When is the first trip to the dentist?

It depends.

For most children, the first trip to the dentist is at an age that they will be cooperative enough to sit there (between ages two and three years). For children who are at higher risk of tooth decay, the American Academy of Pediatrics and American Dental Association recommend that first trip happen at a year of age. Kids that fall into the high risk category include:

◆ Kids whose mothers have cavities
◆ Kids with special medical needs
◆ Kids with teeth who sleep with a formula bottle or breastfeed throughout the night
◆ Kids with plaque buildup on their teeth.

FYI: Tooth decay is contagious. Plaque is bacteria that can be passed from person to person. So it is NOT recommended that parents share food utensils or clean dirty pacifiers by using their saliva (that's kind of gross if you think about it, anyway!).[3]

Q. My baby has a snotty nose. What can I do about it?

All newborns have nasal congestion for four to six weeks after birth. It's not a cold.

Some congested babies are extraordinarily loud. They may snort, snore, cough, and sneeze. It is all normal. If the congestion interferes with feedings or sleep, use saline nose drops to clear the mucus.

Saline is just salt water (1/2 tsp salt to 8oz water). You can make it or buy it. It is impossible to overdose and can be used any time your baby has thick mucus or congestion. Shoot several drops in each nostril before feedings. *You don't need to suck it out with a bulb syringe.*

The saline will either make your baby sneeze or loosen the mucus enough for the baby to swallow it.

BOTTOM LINE

Leave the bulb syringe at the hospital!
Too many parents irritate their baby's nostrils to the point of nosebleeds with the bulb syringe. I had a family push air into the nose instead of evacuating the syringe first. The baby was shocked and held its breath. The parents were shocked and called 911.

Notes

Chapter 5

Nutrition & Growth

"A baby is an inestimable blessing and bother."
~ Mark Twain

What's in this Chapter

- ◆ **What growth charts mean**
- ◆ **How infants grow (height, head size, weight)**
- ◆ **Teeth**
- ◆ **Calories & nutrition for the first year**
- ◆ **Feeding schedules, or lack thereof**
- ◆ **Vitamin supplements**
- ◆ **Overeating, obesity, and the Body Mass Index**
- ◆ **Calcium, fiber, and iron**
- ◆ **Once your child turns one**

Welcome to the world of food. This section of *Baby 411* is dedicated to growth and nutrition—first, we'll look at the general questions you might have about your baby's growth, like what those ominous-looking growth charts really mean. We'll also discuss HOW your baby will grow (height, head size, weight), as well as the needed calorie and nutrition for the first year. Should you put your baby on a feeding schedule? We'll hit that hot-button issue here, as well as discussing vitamin supplements, obesity and your baby's needs for calcium, fiber and iron.

The next two chapters (six and seven) will get into the nuts and bolts of nutrition, as we discuss liquids (breast milk, formula, juice) and solids (baby and table foods). But first things first—let's dive into Baby Nutrition 101.

Infant Growth

Q. At my baby's well checks, my doctor charts her growth on a chart. What's this for?

Growth charts help your doctor follow the trends of your child's growth.

Your baby's height, weight, and head size are checked every well child visit. (Weight is usually checked at sick visits too—to assess the severity of an illness (e.g. dehydration) and in case medication needs to be prescribed). The percentiles on the charts compare your child to other children the same age and gender in America. (For example, a boy in the 75th percentile for height is taller than 75% of boys his age.) See Appendix F for growth charts (birth to 36 months) for boys and girls.

The key issue: is your baby's growth consistent? In other words, if your child is at the 50th percentile for height at three months, he should roughly be at the 50th percentile at six months. What if your child's height and weight percentiles are significantly different? We'll address the issue with a discussion of the Body Mass Index later in this chapter. Also later: what if you child's head size is growing too fast or too slow? We'll cover that too.

Q. How much weight can I expect my baby to gain in his first year?

Here are some general guidelines. Babies double their birth weight by four to five months of age. They triple their birth weight by one year, and quadruple their birth weight by age 2. After age 2, kids gain about four pounds a year until they hit puberty.

For example: A seven-pound newborn should weigh about 14 pounds at five months and 21 pounds at one year.[1]

Q. How tall will my baby grow in his first year?

Your baby will grow ten inches in his first year, and another four inches by age two. After that, he'll grow three inches a year from ages three to five, then two inches a year until he hits his growth spurt at puberty (rule of thumb is 10-4-3-3-2 inches per year).[3] For example: A 20-inch tall newborn should be about 30 inches tall at one year.

Q. Can you predict how tall my baby will be?

For boys: Add five inches to Mom's height and average that number with Dad's height.

For girls: Subtract five inches from Dad's height and average that number with Mom's height.

This number is your baby's growth potential. Of course, some people exceed their potentials and some people never reach their potentials.

The first fairly accurate height predictor is the measurement taken at age two years. Kids have established their growth curves by then. A good rule of thumb is that kids are half of their adult height at age two.

PREEMIES & CATCH-UP GROWTH

Babies born prematurely experience a phenomenon called **CATCH-UP GROWTH.** Most preemies catch up to their peers by the age of two. Your baby's measurements can be plotted on the term baby growth chart both by *chronological age* (determined by birth date) and by *corrected age* (determined by due date).

The head catches up the fastest, followed by weight, then height.[2]

Q. Why do you measure my baby's head size?

Because your baby's brain is also growing at a tremendous rate. Most of this growth occurs in the first two years of life. We want to make sure this is happening, and that the skull is providing enough room for this to happen (see **CRANIOSYNOSTOSIS**).

Some babies have huge heads (see **MACROCEPHALY**) and some babies have tiny heads (see **MICROCEPHALY**). Most of the time, this is thanks to their gene pool. The apple doesn't fall far from the tree. A baby's head size percentile may be completely different than his height or weight percentiles—and that's okay.

The average newborn head size is 35 cm. It grows 12 cm in the first year, and then only 10 cm more for an entire lifetime![4]

Q. When does the soft spot (fontanelle) close?

Anywhere between nine to 18 months. The fontanelle gives the brain the growing room it needs.

Pediatricians rely on that soft spot to provide clues for fluid status (dehydration), infection (meningitis), and problems inside the skull (brain tumors, hydrocephalus).

Q. When will my baby's teeth come in?

Anytime between five and 12 months.

Teeth may erupt as early as two months, but that is a rare event. And all you should expect is one tooth by a year of age.

As a rule, the first teeth to erupt are the bottom middle teeth (medial incisors). After that, it's anyone's guess. There is no order to further eruptions. Frequently, a baby's one-year molars will come in before the middle or eye teeth (incisors/canines).

By the way, once the teeth arrive, you need to clean them! See Chapter 4, "Hygiene" for teeth cleaning tips.

Infant Calorie and Nutrition Needs

Q. How quickly will my newborn grow on a day-to-day basis?

Faster than you want them to.

After you look at the following stats, you will never buy newborn clothes as baby gifts again. You can also understand why babies need to eat all the time. It takes a lot of caloric energy to grow that much.

On a day-to-day basis, here is what you can expect:

◆ *Birth to four days old:* A weight LOSS of 5-10%. As we discussed earlier, babies are born with extra baggage for the trip out into the world.

◆ *Four days to three months:* A weight GAIN of about 2/3 to one ounce a day (1/2 lb a week). Note: newborns should be back to birth weight by their second week doctor visit.

♦ *Three months to six months:* A weight gain of about 1/2 to 2/3 ounce a day (1/2 lb every 2 weeks).

♦ *Six months to 12 months:* A weight gain of about 1/4 to 1/2 ounce a day (3/4 to 1 lb per month).

Q. How many calories does my baby need to eat?

It depends on her age.

The calculations are listed on the next page, but please don't get too wound up about these numbers. Do NOT do calorie counts on your baby. As you can see, your baby's calorie needs will increase as she grows.

Real mom tip: baby's appetite can vary from day to day. This advice also applies to older children. Focus on what your child eats over the space of a week, not every meal. Obsessing over every ounce of milk/formula or spoonful of rice cereal isn't healthy for you or your baby.

That said, here's how many calories a baby typically needs to eat per day (given your baby's weight in kilograms): For babies birth to six months they should consume 110-115 calories per kg in 24 hours. Babies six to 12 months need 100-105 calories per kg in 24 hours. Don't know your baby's weight in kilos? To convert pounds to kilograms, divide the weight in pounds by 2.2. For example, a baby weighing seven pounds would weigh 3.2 kilograms.

Now that we have all the formulas, let's figure out how many calories a seven-pound newborn will need each day to grow normally. Your little bundle of joy needs 368 calories per day (3.2 x 115). Breast milk and formula have 20 calories per ounce. So divide 368 by 20 calories per ounce and you'll find that your baby needs to consume about 19 ounces a day. But, once again, obsessing over every ounce will only give you an overwhelming need for Zantac.

A word on preemies: premature babies have higher calorie needs to achieve catch-up growth. Some babies go home from the Neonatal Intensive Care Unit (NICU) with a higher calorie diet requirement. This is achieved with either a higher-calorie formula or a special human-milk fortifier that is added to expressed breast milk.

COMMON CONVERSIONS

For the mathematically challenged (that is, us writers) and for those who have forgotten the metric system, here are the common conversions you'll need to digest this chapter:

cc (cubic centimeter) or ml (milliliter) are ways of measuring fluid volumes.
1cc = 1ml.
5cc or 5ml = 1 teaspoon
15cc or 15 ml = 1 Tablespoon
3 teaspoons = 1 Tablespoon
There are 30cc per ounce, or 2 Tablespoons per ounce (oz)
There are 16 ounces (oz) in 1 pound (lb)
There are 2.2 pounds in 1 kilogram (kg).

There will be a quiz on this next Tuesday.

Q. Can you show me how a baby's calorie needs change for the first year of life?

Okay, here is an example, but remember this is a ballpark figure:[5]

Age	Weight (lbs)	Weight (kg)	Calories (per day)	Range (cals/day)	Breast milk or formula per day
Newborn	7 lbs	3.2 kg	368	350-700	19 oz
1 month	8 lbs 4 oz	3.75 kg	432	"	22 oz
2 months	10 lbs 2 oz	4.6 kg	530	"	26 oz
3 months	12 lbs	5.5 kg	630	500-850	31 oz
4 months	13 lbs 14 oz	6.3 kg	720	"	36 oz
6 months	16 lbs 8 oz	7.5 kg	787	600-1000	40 oz
9 months	19 lbs 8 oz	8.9 kg	930	700-1200	liquid + solid food
1 year	21 lbs	9.5 kg	1000	"	liquid + solid food

BOTTOM LINE

Do NOT calculate your baby's dietary needs at every moment. You will drive yourself, your spouse (and your doctor) nuts. This is especially challenging to do if you are breastfeeding and can't see the volume. It's just helpful information to help you gauge things.

The Big Picture: Nutrition For The First Year

The details will become clearer to you as you read through the next couple of chapters, but here is the big picture:

1. **Babies need either formula or breast milk exclusively for the first six months of life.**
2. **From four to six months of age, solids can be introduced as dessert but not as nutrition.** In other words, AFTER you nurse or bottle-feed your baby, then you can offer a taste or two of solid food. Families with a high risk of food allergies should hold off on solid foods until six months of age. (for details see solid nutrition chapter)
3. **From six to nine months of age, a baby eats more solid foods,** so he cuts back on liquid nutrition volumes.
4. **From nine to twelve months of age, a baby usually eats three solid meals a day** and takes 20 to 30 oz of breast milk or formula.
5. **After a year of age, formula is replaced by whole milk,** with a goal of 16 oz or dairy serving equivalent a day. Solid food intake becomes three solid meals and one to two snacks per day. Families may choose to continue breast feeding after one year of age, but kids need additional sources of nutrition.

So let's sum this up in chart form on the next page:

NUTRITION & GROWTH

? ?

AGE	LIQUIDS	SOLIDS
0-4 months	breast milk or formula only	none
4-6 months	breast milk or formula, about 40 oz/day	as dessert after liquids
6-9 months	yes, but cutting back	solids becoming more important
9-12 months	breast milk or formula, 20-30 oz/day	3 solid meals a day
12 months +	switch to cows milk, 16 oz per day	3 solid meals plus 1-2 snacks

See later in this chapter for information on calcium and dairy requirements at one year of age. For a more detailed chart of liquids and solids, see Chapter 7, "Solid Foods."

Reality Check

Babies have "off" days and growth spurts. So, your baby may not be as predictable as you would like when it comes to meals. Occasionally, he will be less interested in feedings. And sometimes, he will seem like he hasn't eaten in days.

Feeding Schedules

Q. I've heard about putting my newborn on a feeding schedule. How do I do it?

You don't. Your baby does it for you.

The phrase "newborn feeding schedule" is an oxymoron. Newborns are learning how life works outside the womb. Before birth, they were on a 24/7 feeding schedule. Now, your newborn will have to rely on her innate sense of being hungry when her body needs energy. However, she will not have a neat and tidy schedule.

Newborns need to eat about eight to 12 times in a 24-hour day. This may be every 1 1/2 hours for a few cycles, then four hours later, then two hours, etc. Somehow, in 24 hours, they do it. This is called "ad lib" or feeding on demand. Ideally, parents (and their doctors) would like their baby to have "'cluster feeding'" of every 1 1/2 hours during the day and a nice four hour stretch at night. But, short of divine intervention, there is little that can be done to *make* this happen.

For parents of preemies: Premature babies *really* need those feedings frequently. Their smaller tummies, and need for catch-up growth often require feedings every two to three hours until they are at least four months old. (That is, four months from the original due date, not the actual birth—their so-called corrected age).

BOTTOM LINE

Although newborns can't be put on a schedule, by four months of age, your baby WILL BE capable of regular feeding and sleeping patterns. Some lucky moms and dads will have a baby that falls into a predictable feeding/sleeping pattern by two months of age.

DR B'S OPINION:
BABYWISE OR BABY FOOLISH?

As a new parent, you'll probably hear about a book called *On Becoming Babywise*. Released in 1995, this best-selling guide instructs parents to rigidly schedule their newborn's feedings (called "parent directed feeding"). The result? Babies were showing up in their doctor's offices malnourished—and falling off of their growth charts. The American Academy of Pediatrics was so concerned they issued a media alert about the teachings of this book. The AAP advised parents that "newborns should be nursed whenever they show signs of hunger, such as increased alertness or activity, mouthing, or rooting….Newborns should be nursed approximately eight to 12 times every 24 hours until satiety."[6]

Here's the take-home message: Lower your expectations. Yes, your baby IS in charge of your house right now. That'll change in about 18 years. Or 26.

nutrition

Q. My six-week-old seemed to have somewhat of a feeding schedule . . . but now seems insatiable. Is my milk drying up?

No. Babies often have growth spurts at three weeks and six weeks of age. They will have feeding frenzies during those periods of time. As your baby's demands increase, so will your milk supply. (For details, check out Chapter 6, "Liquid Nutrition").

Old Wives Tale
Adding rice cereal to formula or expressed breast milk will make your baby sleep through the night.

The truth: Only if your baby has heartburn. Let's think about this in a scientific way. Formula has 20 calories per ounce. If your baby is taking a six oz bottle, he gets 120 calories. A teaspoon of rice cereal flakes has about five calories. It's not providing any calories to fill them up. But it is heavier. If your baby has acid reflux, he will be happier but he still won't sleep through the night!

Special Concerns

Q. My 6 month old has dropped his weight percentiles from 75% to 25% since his four-month visit. What happened?

He's begun to eat solid food. Solid foods contain *significantly* fewer calories than formula or breast milk. When babies are given solid foods *before* their milk, it reduces the amount of formula or breast milk they drink. Don't get carried away with feeding your baby solid foods until he can take one or two jars (two to four oz. of solids) at a sitting. What many parents don't realize is that your baby will tell you when he or she wants more. If your little one is finished, you'll know it. And until she's asking for more, don't push the solid food. See more on solid foods in Chapter 7.

Q. My nine month old seems to be dropping on his growth percentiles. Is he malnourished?

Probably not.

Babies these days are born much bigger than they used to be (good for them, bad for Mom's pelvis)—thanks to good prenatal care. But not all babies turn out to be sumo wrestlers. Their genetic makeup (i.e. Mom and Dad) determines their ultimate size. Big babies that have more average sized parents start to plateau, showing their truer growth curves as they approach a year of age.

Your doctor will check for iron deficiency anemia at this age, as this can also be a cause of poor growth (a drop in growth percentiles). If your baby is dropping off the growth charts, your doctor should perform a thorough evaluation to see what's wrong.

Q. My baby has dropped off the growth charts for his weight. What is wrong with him?

No, your baby hasn't joined Weight Watchers behind your back. The official term for this problem is **FAILURE TO THRIVE.**

Babies whose weight percentiles started off fine, then plateau or fall below the third percentile need to be evaluated. The causes are various and include: poor feeding routines, incorrect formula preparation, gastroesophageal reflux, malabsorption of food from intestinal problems, kidney disease, metabolic disease, hypothyroidism, and anemia.

An extensive medical evaluation is usually performed, unless a cause is found easily. If no cause is identified, a higher calorie diet is initiated and baby's weight is checked frequently.

Vitamin Supplements

Q. Does my baby need a Vitamin D supplement?

It depends.

Breast milk is perfect nutrition with one caveat. Occasionally, there is not enough Vitamin D in breast milk for your baby's growth. Mother Nature planned on children producing Vitamin D in their skin after sun exposure. She did not plan on the creation of sunblock that blocks UVB rays—an essential component of Vitamin D synthesis. Vitamin D deficiency causes **RICKETS**, a bone malformation (see glossary).[7] Because it is impossible to determine the amount of sunlight every baby needs to make enough Vitamin D (skin color and sunblock complicate the equation), the American Academy of Pediatrics issued new guidelines for Vitamin D supplements in April, 2003.

Vitamin D supplements of 200 IU per day are recommended by two months of age for:

1.   Babies who are exclusively breast-fed.
2.   Babies who are breastfed and receive less than 500 ml (17 oz) of supplemental formula daily.
3.   Babies who are formula fed but eat less than 500ml (17oz) of formula daily (preemies).

DR B'S OPINION:
SUPPLEMENTS

I recommend Tri-Vi-Sol (a three vitamin solution that includes Vitamin A, D, and C). Use one dropper-full for the baby, once a day. Tri-Vi-Sol is available over the counter or from web sites like DrugStore.com. I also suggest that Mom stay on her prenatal vitamins. This isn't for the baby— it's for Mom's health.

nutrition

4. Children who have little sunlight exposure and drink less than 500ml (17 oz) of Vitamin D fortified milk daily.

Q. Does my baby need an Iron or vitamin supplement?

There are a few kids who will need this.

Iron is needed to carry oxygen (on your red blood cells) to your body. Babies are born with a large iron bank, thanks to Mom. As withdrawals are made from the bank, the supply needs to be replenished via baby's nutritional intake. By six to nine months, the original stores are gone and baby is on his own. So, it becomes important for baby to get iron in the diet. Formula fed babies get the right amount in their iron-fortified formula. Breast fed babies, after six months of age, need an additional source of iron. The easiest way to get it is in iron-fortified cereal (all baby cereals contain iron). That's why we recommend starting solid food by six months of age (see Chapter 7, "Solid Nutrition" for details).

Iron deficiency causes **ANEMIA** (see glossary). Anemia causes fatigue, poor weight gain, and poor intellectual functioning. We routinely check for iron deficiency anemia at either the nine-month or one-year well check. If your baby is anemic, we'll recommend an iron supplement.

Babies who eat a relatively "balanced" diet do not need multivitamins. So, we don't routinely recommend iron or multivitamins for all babies.

BOTTOM LINE: If you are formula feeding your baby, DO NOT BUY A LOW IRON FORMULA. Your baby needs the iron to grow. (see Chapter 6, "Liquid Nutrition," for more details)

Helpful Hint

If your doctor prescribes an iron supplement for your baby, do not give it with a dairy product (e.g. breast milk, formula, whole milk). The calcium and iron compete for absorption in the digestive tract and will decrease the amount of iron that the body gets.

PREEMIES & IRON SUPPLEMENTS

Premature babies go home from the hospital on iron supplements because their rapid rate of growth requires it. Depending on your doctor's recommendation, your baby may continue on iron supplements through the first year of life. Also: most preemies head home with a multivitamin recommendation as well.

Q. I've heard about fluoride supplements. Does my baby need this?

Fluoride is known to prevent tooth decay. Your baby is probably getting fluoride from tap water (from mixing formula or cereal with tap water). But you should check to be sure your community adds this to tap water—call your local water department or public works agency to confirm this.

As we mentioned earlier, your baby's teeth will start to erupt from five to 12 months of age. If your community does NOT add fluoride to the water supply or you have a house that is on well water, your pediatrician can prescribe a fluoride supplement for your baby starting at six months of age.

Remember, if you are exclusively breastfeeding after six months of age and your child is not eating cereal mixed with tap water, your baby also qualifies for flouride supplements.

Just to recap—babies need fluoride supplements starting at *six months* of age if:

1. You use bottled water to drink and/or mix formula.
2. Your baby eats ready-to-feed formula and does not drink tap water.
3. You have well water.
4. You use tap water but your community does not add fluoride to its water supply.
5. Your baby is exclusively breastfed and does not drink tap water.

For details, see Appendix A, "Medications."

Overeating, Obesity, And The Body Mass Index

Q. I am concerned that I am overfeeding my baby. Is that possible?

It is unlikely, but it can happen in rare cases.

Let's look at this rationally. Most infants do not think, "I'm full, but that dessert looks pretty good." That is a *learned* behavior in our society. Most infants will eat until their tummies are full and stop. If they do overindulge, they usually just throw up.

But, it is a good idea to learn your child's cues. Some new parents think their baby needs to eat every time he cries. This becomes a set up for obesity.

It's a good idea to institute new "House Rules" in your kitchen as your baby approaches a year of age. See below for some astounding facts on the childhood obesity epidemic and ways to prevent it.

The Rise In Childhood Obesity

The United States is super-sized, to paraphrase an article in *U.S. News and World Report* (Aug. 19, 2002). A startling fact: the number of overweight school-aged children has *doubled* in the past 20 years. Why? Here are the reasons:

1. Lack of activity. Children spend more time watching TV (an average of three hours per day) and playing on computers than ever before.

2. **Eating Out and "take out" food.** 34% of our calories are eaten outside of the home. Restaurant food has more fat, salt, and sugar than home prepared meals.

 NEW PARENT 411: AVOIDING OBESITY

Set up the right routines while your baby is an infant and toddler. Here are our tips:

1. Keep your child physically active.
2. Make restaurant food a treat. McDonald's should be a once a month treat—not a weekly outing.
3. Offer appropriate serving sizes. Start with two tablespoons per serving. Offer seconds on fruit and vegetables.
4. Banish the "Clean Plate Club." Don't force your child to eat. Yes, there are starving children in India, but they won't be eating your leftovers.
5. Make juice a low-priority item.
6. Keep the four C's out of your pantry: cola, chips, cookies, and candy. If you have to go out of the house to get these items, they will truly be a treat.
7. Be a good role model. Your child is watching what you are eating.
8. No TV while food is being served. Watching the tube while you eat encourages that couch-potato thing. Don't watch the news during dinner—tape and watch it after the kids go to bed.

One of the realities of being a parent is that you often end up eating what your kids eat. That's how you end up at the end of baby's first year still wearing those prenatal pounds. What to do? Here's a tip: buy one kind of cookie as a special treat for your child. And make it a kind you don't personally like.

Next, buy healthy, yet good snacks: cereals like Rice Chex and Cheerios are great(see box below for more snack ideas). And if you are going to buy juice, stick with 100% juice products. An example: Vruit, a vegetable and fruit juice combination with no added sugar (see their web site at AmericanSoy.com). It comes in individual boxes, too, for easy transport. And be a good exam- ple to your kids. Don't drink soda in front of them day and night. Instead opt for milk or tea. In our house, when dad drinks tea, the kids aren't interested in it. But if soda is on the table they're constantly begging for a sip.

In the end, an outright ban on cookies, soda, chips and candy can backfire. As we said earlier, they should be occasional treats. Otherwise, you're going to have a kid who sneaks out to a neighbors' to indulge or spends his allowance on the sly to buy candy bars.

3. **Larger serving sizes.** Super-size servings have become the norm at all types of restaurants, not just fast food outlets. This trend toward giant portions has even crept onto our own kitchen tables.

4. **Too many sugar drinks.** This starts in toddlerhood. Don't let your child become a juice-a-holic. Kids graduate from juice to soft drinks. Believe it or not, the average teenage boy drinks *three* sodas a day.

FEEDBACK FROM THE REAL WORLD: AVOIDING THE 4 C's

You've seen the statistics and you're worried. You don't want your child to be one of them. We're talking about overweight and obese children. They are a statistic on the rise and if they start out overweight, most likely they'll be overweight adults.

You've also seen the incredible array of snack foods on the shelf at your local grocery store. So it's time to ask our experienced moms for tips on keeping your baby off the junk and excited about healthy snacks.

1. **It takes a family.** Julie DeCamp Palmer of Seattle, WA spoke for most of our readers when she said "It takes the whole family eating a healthy diet." So lead by example and don't stock the four C's in your home. For those of us who want a little of the forbidden items ourselves, eat them when your child is not around or when you're out and about without him.

2. **Presentation is important.** Healthy snacks can still be exciting to a child when they are presented with enthusiasm. One reader Tiffany Johnson from Vancouver, WA, who is also a daycare provider noted that "children like anything that isn't called what it is...i.e. celery sticks with cream cheese and raisins becomes much more appealing when you call it ants on a log. Cottage cheese with raw fruit or veggies is a hit when you make it into a face and call it clown food."

3. **Moderation.** Yes, an occasional cookie as a treat is just fine. In fact, S. Von Lengerke had a great story about her own childhood where the four C's were completely banned: "I believe everything in moderation is OK. I was raised in one of those families where we could never have soda or sweets, so my brother and I chose our friends based on their snacks. We were chubby kids. I think having some access to sweets, rather than "forbidding" them, makes them less of an allure to kids and the children, in turn, will have a healthy regard for snacks."

4. **Go with the flow.** "One item I think many parents forget is that kids' eating often ebbs and flows. Kids will be starving and eat more than Dad at one meal and turn up their noses at even favorite foods the next. It's not easy, but we offer a variety of healthy and favorite foods at meal- and snack-time and let the kids

Q. How can I find out if my child is overweight?

There is a calculation called the **BODY MASS INDEX (BMI)** that compares your child's height to his weight. The formula is applicable to children ages 2-20 years of age. The ranges vary for gender and age (because the BMI varies as kids grow).

decide if they are going to eat or not. We don't take it personally and trust that our children will eat when they are hungry. Not always easy, but usually very successful." –Wendy Stough

Not only did our readers have great tips on avoiding the four C's, they also offered food recommendations on what snacks work best in their households. Here are a few suggestions:

1. **Veggie Booty and Pirate Booty.** Manufactured by Robert's American Gourmet (web: robscape.com), the veggie variety of this puffed rice snack food is sprinkled with a blend of spinach, kale, cabbage, carrots and broccoli. Pirate Booty is a cheddar version of the snack and there is a fruit version as well. Readers report their kids love them.

2. Another reader recommended dehydrated vegetables from a company called **Just Tomatoes** (web: justtomatoes.com). Crunchy and salt- and fat-free they don't spoil like fresh food so they're great to pop into your diaper bag.

3. Other readers recommend organic products from **Hain** (web: hain-celestial.com), including their all-natural animal cookies.

4. **Organic yogurt from StonyField Farms** (web: stonyfield. com) comes in those easy to transport squeeze tubes. One mom recommended freezing the tubes for a popsicle treat!

5. **Fresh fruits and cooked veggies are the ultimate snacks.** And don't forget cheese–a terrific additional source of calcium.

6. What if you don't have access to organic foods or don't want to spend extra money to buy them? Stick with snacks like **pretzels** that are low fat and available in low salt varieties. **Breakfast bars** are popular snacks. **Dried fruits** are also portable, nutritious snacks. Just make sure they aren't a choking hazard.

7. When you find a great product, check to see if they have a web site. We discovered that they are full of nutritional information, fun games and even e-coupons for their products.

NUTRITION & GROWTH

? ?

Here's the formula:

$$\frac{\text{Weight in lbs.}}{(\text{height in inches}) \times (\text{height in inches})} \times 703 = \text{BMI}$$

For children, the risk for obesity is a BMI of 85-95%. An overweight child has a BMI of 95% or higher. To check your child's BMI, go to www.KeepKidsHealthy.com (click on "Useful Tools" and then the "BMI Calculator").

The BMI range for ADULTS is based on the number derived from the calculation above:

Healthy BMI   18-25
Overweight BMI   25-30
Obese BMI   Greater than 30

For more information on body mass indexes for both children and adults, check out the Centers for Disease Control's website at: www.cdc.gov/nccdphp/dnpa/growthcharts/bmi_tools.htm

Calcium, Fiber, And Iron

Q. Are there any nutrients that children eat too little of?

Calcium, fiber, and iron. Let's take a look at each:

1 **CALCIUM.** The requirements change as children grow. For ages one to three years, children need 500 milligrams per day (mg/day). Kids ages four to six need 800 mg/day. Kids ages seven to 14 need a whopping 1300 mg/day. If your child has a milk intolerance or allergy, try calcium fortified orange juice, broccoli, rhubarb, or tofu as alternative calcium sources. If you are looking for a vitamin supplement that contains calcium, get one with Vitamin D added (it helps the body absorb calcium better).

Calcium Content Of Foods

Food	Calcium content (mg)
8 oz cup of milk	250 mg
1 slice of cheese	200 mg
1 cup of ice cream	175 mg
4 oz cup of yogurt	200 mg

Note: As you can see, milk is the most efficient way of getting calcium. Other dairy products, while rich in calcium, may also include less desirable ingredients such as salt and sugar. The lesson: use other diary products in moderation, but milk is best.

2 **FIBER.** The fiber requirement for children is calculated by: *Age in years + 5 = Number of fiber grams/day.* Example: a two-year old needs seven grams of fiber day. However, there are no established guidelines for children under one year of age.

Adults need 25-30 grams of fiber per day. The average American diet doesn't come anywhere close to our daily needs. Not only does fiber make your child a regular guy or gal, it also has potential benefits to reducing heart disease. So, make it a little family project to increase everyone's fiber intake.

The best way to get a kid to eat fiber is through the bread and grains food group. Green leafy vegetables, while high in fiber, are not the most popular food items for kids. Also, many parents don't realize that the source of fiber in many fruits is the skin, which usually gets peeled off before a child gets to the fruit.

For details on fiber foods, see Chapter 8, "The Other End."

3 **IRON.** We have already chatted about this one. It's important to have a daily intake (10 mg/day) for growth and brain function.

Good Sources Of Iron

Meat, poultry, fish, bread, enriched pasta, dark green vegetables (spinach, broccoli, kale), legumes (dried beans, soybeans, lentils), eggs*, nuts/seeds*, peanuts and peanut butter**, dried fruits (raisins, etc)*, cereals (infant as well as grown up breakfast cereals are iron fortified). *Note: Eating iron in combination with Vitamin C (orange juice, etc), helps the body absorb iron.*

*Items only for kids over one year of age.
**Because of risk for lifelong and life threatening allergy, consider avoiding until at least three years of age. See discussion of peanut allergies in Chapter 7, "Solids."

Happy Birthday, You're Turning One!

Yes, your child is turning one! How exciting, no? Here is a look at the "food pyramid" for a one year old. On the next page is a table that goes into more detail.

The Food Pyramid for a One Year Old

Fats & Sweets Group
Eat less!

Milk Group

Meat Group

Vegetable Group

Fruit Group

Grain Group

Source: BabyCenter.com

The serving size is listed beside the food item.
The average calorie intake for a 1-3 year old is 1300 calories.

Breads/Grains	**4-6 servings/day**
Whole wheat bread	1/2 slice
cooked cereal, rice, pasta	1/4 cup
cold cereal	1/2 cup

Fruits/Vegetables	**4 servings/day** **(1 Vitamin A/ 1 Vitamin C)**
Vitamin C	
citrus, berries, melons,	1/4 cup
tomatoes, broccoli, potatoes,	
cauliflower	
Vitamin A	
peaches, carrots, peas,	2 Tbsp.
green beans, melons, apricots	
Other	2 Tbsp.

Milk/Dairy	**4 servings/day**
Whole milk	1/2 cup
Cheese slice	1 slice (1 oz)
Yogurt	4 oz
Ice Cream	1/2 cup

Meat/Protein	**2 servings/day**
Beef, chicken fish, pork	2 Tbsp
Egg	1 egg
Beans	1/4 cup

Fats	**3 servings/day**
Butter, mayo, ranch dressing	1 tsp

Q. My one year old is on a hunger strike. Help!

Very few one year olds have a world cause they support that passionately!

The *toddler diet* appears as your baby approaches one year old. The typical toddler eats well once every three days or eats one good meal in 24 hours. The food that is loved for one week straight will be refused the next. A good strategy is to offer three food choices in a meal. Pick one that is sure to be a hit—the others are trial offerings. If your child refuses everything, *do not make another meal for him.* Mealtime is over. Don't worry, your child will eat at the next opportunity.

All humans have both a hunger and thirst drive that compels us to fulfill our calorie and fluid needs.

Chapter 6

Liquids

"In short, breastfeeding occurs above the eyebrows as much as or more than it occurs in the mammary glands."
~ Judithe A. Thompson

For the first six months of your baby's life, you have only to make one decision about her nutrition: breast or bottle. Make that breast milk or formula. And you can guarantee that decision won't occur in a vacuum: friends, neighbors, relatives and complete strangers at the grocery store will want to weigh in on what's "best." But you are the only one who can make that decision for your baby.

This chapter will offer you the pros and cons of both breast milk and formula. We promise we won't make judgments about your choice. Yes, we all know that without question, human breast milk is the perfect nutrition for human babies. However, millions of children have been formula fed and lived to tell about it. Including the authors of this book.

And eventually, you'll be addressing the question of what other liquids to serve your child. These include water, juice and cow's milk. We'll discuss these other liquids in this chapter as well.

Breast Milk

Q. I have heard that breastfeeding is best for babies, but what are the real advantages?

There are advantages for both baby and mom. Let's take a look at each:

Breast-Feeding Advantages for Baby:
Mother's milk:

1. **Has the ideal ingredients for a human body.** Manufactured products (that is, formula) are approximations of the real thing.
2. **Carries the mother's antibodies to protect baby from various infections.**
3. **Is hypo-allergenic.** It is rare to be allergic to human milk.
4. **Contains products that stimulate brain development.** (A recent study showed that babies who were breastfed for the first nine months of life may have higher IQ's as adults than their formula fed peers.).[1]

Breast-Feeding Advantages for Mom:

1. **It may be the easiest way to lose those pregnancy pounds and still eat like you are a professional wrestler.**
2. **It is always ready to serve, at the perfect temperature.**
3. **It is free.** Formula can cost $500 or more for the first six months alone.
4. **It may reduce your risk of breast cancer.** A recent study published in the journal *Lancet* showed that for every two years spent breastfeeding, a woman's lifetime risk of breast cancer goes down by 5%. Currently, one in eight women will get breast cancer.
5. **It is a wonderful way to feel close to your baby.**
6. **It can be a form of birth control,** but don't rely on it exclusively (unless you want a toddler and a newborn in the house!)

BOTTOM LINE: Breastfeeding is worth the effort it takes to learn how to do it.

Q. How long should I breastfeed my baby?

The American Academy of Pediatrics recommends breastfeeding for the first year of life. The latest statistics show that 75% of American babies go home from the hospital breastfed. But, only 30% are still breastfed at six months of life. The numbers are even lower for babies who are breastfed until one year of age.

Why Women Stop Nursing . . . It's Not for a Lack of Milk!

There are many reasons why women choose to stop nursing. Most of the time it is *not* due to poor milk supply.

Breastfeeding is a learned process. It's not as natural as you might think. Babies know how to suck, and Mom's body knows how to make milk. But the technique of getting the baby latched on to the areola (the whole colored area—not just the nipple) requires a great deal of patience and sometimes *four* hands. Throw in a hormonal roller coaster after delivery and you'll understand why many women give up. Learning how to breast-feed is analogous to learning how to drive with a manual transmission.

Mothers who survive the technique test get to move on to the engorgement torture chamber. This is what happens when the milk actually comes in. Your breasts will be more impressive than your neighbor's boob job. Your husband will want to take pictures. *You* will wish that it is a bad dream and hope that your old breasts will be back when you wake up. This too shall pass. If you make it to the two-week mark, you are on cruise control. That should be your goal. You may need a great deal of moral support to get to two weeks, however.

And speaking of support... the newly crowned grandmothers arrive on the scene in the first few weeks of your baby's life. Since most of them fed their babies formula, they feel helpless. They will watch you struggle with breastfeeding and throw in little zingers like, "It's so much easier to formula feed—I never had this trouble." Put Grandma to work cooking dinner for you, changing diapers, and soothing your baby. She is an expert in those categories. And this will give you the freedom to concentrate on breastfeeding your baby.

A poignant comment from one mom we interviewed: "If everyone would just leave the baby and I alone, we could figure it out!" Truer words were never spoken. However, if you are at wit's end, utilize your pediatrician and a lactation consultant. Lactation consultants (LC's) are medical personnel trained to handle breastfeeding challenges. I have only one warning. Get a recommendation for a lactation consultant from your obstetrician or pediatrician. Lactation consultants who have a relationship with your doctor are likely to be "team players." This is helpful when everyone is working towards the same goal—your success! There are some militant lactation consultants who, we think, convey the wrong message about breastfeeding. These consultants consider "artificial milk" (their term for formula) to be Satan's brew. Mothers who encounter these well meaning people come in my office crying and feeling guilty if breastfeeding is unsuccessful.

The final problem is going back to work. Working moms, in general, have trouble finding time to pump. To completely keep up with your baby's demands, you need to pump every three hours (nearly impossible, right?). That's why stay-at-home moms are more successful with breastfeeding. It's hard to do it all, ladies.

Breast milk truly is the ideal food for your baby. We suggest that all mothers breastfeed. The decision to stop breastfeeding is rarely due to poor milk supply. If it doesn't work out for you, we're glad that you at least made the attempt.

Denise's Opinion: Sometimes, the criticism you get about your decision to breast-feed comes from unlikely sources. Sample: grandparents. This generation seldom breast-fed their babies—it just wasn't fashionable. And the idea of baring your breast in front of them (especially grandfathers) makes them squeamish to say the least. Here are some suggestions for how to deal with their objections.

1. **When in your own home, you have a right to nurse in your living room.** It's your house, your rules. But your dad will probably appreciate it if you either cover yourself with a shawl or warn him before you whip out your boob.

2. **At their house, be discreet.** Try nursing in a bedroom if you know it makes them uncomfortable.

3. **When they ask you why you're still nursing your baby at ten months,** calmly inform them that the American Academy of Pediatrics recommends that babies breast feed until a year of age.

4. **When they ask, "Why can't we just give baby a bottle so**

DR B'S OPINION:
GRANDPARENTS & BREASTFEEDING

There are some things about babies that will never change. But there are many things we have learned in the past 20 or 30 years that are different than what our parents were taught (like using car seats, for instance). Learn grandparents' trade secrets for soothing your crying baby because they have been there and done that. Learn the 411 on current pediatric trends in this book.

we can participate in feedings," promise that they can when your baby's nursing is well established and you can pump a bottle or two.

Getting Started Breastfeeding

First, some definitions to help you understand breastfeeding lingo:

1. **Colostrum.** The first milk that your breasts produce. Some women start making (and leaking) it before the baby is even born. It is a high protein drink, filled with mom's antibodies that provide an immunity boost to the newborn. It has fewer calories than mature milk because of a lower fat content.
2. **Mature Milk.** The milk that arrives on the third or fourth day after birth. It is about 50% fat.
3. **Foremilk.** The milk that comes out in the first several minutes of feeding. In general, it contains slightly less fat. Babies who 'snack' end up getting mostly foremilk, leading to more frequent feedings (and possibly, fussy moods).
4. **Hindmilk.** The milk that comes out in the later part of a feeding. It is slightly higher in fat than foremilk. Babies who drain a whole breast in a feeding tend to be more satisfied, for good reason.
5. **Engorgement.** When mature milk is produced initially, mom's breasts may feel full, tender, and hard.
6. **Plugged ducts.** An area of the breast has obstructed milk flow, creating a hard, tender lumpy area. These areas are at risk of getting infected (mastitis—ouch). See tips below for more info.

And, some info on breastfeeding gear…

◆   **Breast shells.** Plastic devices that pull out inverted nipples.
◆   **Nipple shields.** Plastic devices that protect sore or cracked nipples. Unfortunately, they limit the amount of milk that flows to the baby's mouth.
◆   **Lanolin.** A thick emollient that helps heal cracked nipples. Brand names: Lansinoh, Pur-lan. Available at breastfeeding boutiques, and even Wal-Mart.

THE FACTS OF LIFE—A.K.A. SCIENCE OF BREASTFEEDING

Keep in mind these four tips on the "science" of nursing your baby:

1 **BREAST MILK PRODUCTION IS A SUPPLY AND DEMAND PHENOMENON.** You should have no trouble making enough milk if the demand is there. Nursing at least eight times in 24 hours promotes a good supply.

2 **COLOSTRUM, THE FIRST MILK, IS ALL YOUR BABY NEEDS FOR THE FIRST FEW DAYS OF LIFE.** Mature milk, the high fat stuff, arrives when your baby needs it—around the fourth day of life.

3 **ALL BABIES ARE EXHAUSTED BY THE BIRTH PROCESS** and are not very interested in eating for the first 48 hours. They latch on, get cozy…and fall asleep after five minutes. This behavior will change (at almost the same moment you leave the hospital!)

4 **BABIES ARE BORN WITH 10% EXTRA BAGGAGE TO CARRY THEM THROUGH THE FIRST FEW DAYS OF LIFE.** They will lose 5-10% of their birth weight—expect that. Do not think you are failing at breastfeeding because your baby is losing weight.

Q. What do I need to know about my baby's first few days of breastfeeding?

Let's break this down, day by day…

First Day of Life (0-24 hours old):

1. Nurse your baby for the first time within an hour or so of his birth. He will be awake, alert, and interested.
2. At two hours of life, he will be exhausted and hard to arouse for several (three to four) hours. Don't get too worked up about trying to nurse right now. Take a nap yourself.
3. Frequency goal: six to eight feedings in the first 24 hours of life.
4. Your baby will probably fall asleep at the breast after a few minutes of nursing. An acceptable feeding session for today is five to ten minutes per breast.

Second Day of Life (24-48 hours old):

1. Today's goal is working on your technique. It may take a second set of hands to position the baby while you hold your breast. You will fly solo eventually. See tips to survive the first two weeks later in this chapter.
2. Frequency goal: eight feedings in 24 hours. Do not let your baby sleep more than four hours at a stretch or you will have trouble meeting this goal.
3. Length of feedings goal: five to ten minutes per breast.
4. If your nipples are cracked and bleeding, you need help with your technique.

Third Day of Life (48-72 hours old):

1. Your baby is suddenly awake and sometimes, insatiable. As long as your baby has lost less than 10% of his birth weight (and has

no other risk factors-see below), keep your chin up and resist the temptation to supplement with formula. Your baby's demand is precisely what your body needs to create the supply of milk.

2. Make sure your technique is okay and you are comfortable when your baby latches on.
3. Frequency goal: eight feedings in 24 hours (it should be an easy goal to reach today!)
4. Length of feedings goal: at least ten minutes per breast.
5. You may feel that your baby is on your breast non-stop. If that is the case, take a break if you have nursed for more than 45 minutes. Let someone else have a chance to soothe your baby. (Letting baby suck on someone's finger may be helpful.)

Fourth Day of Life (72-96 hours old):

1. Hello milk! There is usually little question of whether or not your milk has arrived. How will you know? Your breasts will be much larger, heavier, and tender. You should feel full before you nurse, and soft after you nurse. You should also see milk when you burp your baby (and sometimes when you shower). Your baby's poop will also tell you the milkman has arrived. See Chapter 8 "The Other End" for more.
2. If your breasts are rock hard and your areola (the darker colored ring around your nipple) are flattened against them, you are officially engorged. This lasts for a day or two. See troubleshooting tips below.
3. Frequency goal: eight feedings in 24 hours. Do not let your baby sleep for more than a four hour stretch.
4. Length of feedings goal: at least ten to 15 minutes per breast. Once your milk supply is well established (around four weeks of life), some women prefer to nurse with one breast per feeding. For now, use both at each feeding as it stimulates your milk production.
5. You should be on your way now. Your baby should be gaining about an ounce a day.

Looking ahead…

The Two Week Mark: If your full term baby is at or above birth weight at his check up, you have my blessing to let your baby sleep as long as he wants at night.

The One Month Mark

Your baby should be more efficient at feeding sessions. You may prefer to nurse on one breast only and alternate at each feeding. Some babies prefer this because they are more likely to get to the richer hindmilk and are more satisfied. Your body makes enough milk for one complete feeding in each breast. You can start expressing (pumping) breast milk now that your supply is well established. See more about pumping later in this chapter.

Helpful Hint

When you are told that babies feed every two to three hours, time is measured from the BEGINNING of one feeding until the

NEW PARENT 411: ANXIETY AT CHECK OUT

You will go home from the hospital with a shrinking baby and no 'mature' milk in your breasts. Understandably, this often creates great anxiety for new parents. Your baby will do just fine with colostrum as long as your breast milk comes in around the fourth day. The circumstances that interfere with this perfect plan are:

1. Jaundice (elevated bilirubin).
2. Prematurity or small gestational age (small for dates).
3. Loss of more than 10% of birth weight.
4. Delay in milk's arrival.

Some doctors schedule follow-up appointments for babies at the fourth or fifth day of life to make sure things are heading in the right direction.

It's a good idea to keep a breastfeeding diary (see our handy two week survival guide earlier in Chapter 3) that tracks both feeding and elimination for the first two weeks. If the milk is going in, it will come out the other end. If you are still uncertain of how things are going, schedule an appointment!

beginning of the next. If the feeding session itself lasts 45 minutes or an hour, that may leave less than an hour before it's time to nurse again.

Your goal is to nurse at least EIGHT TIMES a day. This may be every two to three hours or it may be a series of cluster feedings every 90 minutes, followed by a four-hour stretch. As long as the number of feedings add up to eight in a 24-hour period, it is fine.

Old Wives Tale
"My doctor told me I didn't have enough milk."

The truth: Doctors in the 1960's thought breast milk was supposed to come in immediately after birth—and hence when it didn't appear in day one or two, panic bells went off. We now know that it is Nature's Way (to quote Steve Irwin, Crocodile Hunter) to have colostrum first and milk later. This is one of the reasons why our mothers did not breastfeed us.

BOTTOM LINE: Be prepared for the 72 hour Colostrum Zone. Your mature milk will arrive soon enough.

RED FLAGS
Check in with your baby's doctor if:

1. You don't have a dramatic change in your breasts by the fifth day of life.
2. You don't hear your baby swallowing when he is at the breast.
3. Your baby's poops have not changed from black tar (meconium) to a yellowish color by the fourth day.
4. Your baby does not have at least five wet diapers on the fourth day.
5. Your baby is sleepy and hard to arouse for feedings.
6. Your baby is nursing non-stop.

Top 10 Survival Tips for The First Two Weeks

And now, from the home office here in Austin, TX:

1. Make sure your baby is latched on to your areola and not just the tip of your nipple.
2. If it hurts for more than a few seconds, take your baby off your breast and reposition him. Do not be a martyr.
3. If the position you are using is not working, try another one. See below for more comments on positions.
4. Have a spouse or willing volunteer get the baby's open mouth to your breast while you hold your breast. Have this person pull down your baby's chin gently with their finger.
5. Ask for a nipple shield (a plastic covering with a hole) if your nipples are too tender or cracked to nurse comfortably. This is a controversial option because the volume of fluid coming to baby is reduced. But it may make the difference for some women if used for a day or two. If you choose this option, have a lactation consultant follow up with you.
6. One word: LANOLIN. Various brands (such as Lansinoh) of this ointment are sold to provide comfort to healing nipples. It's also great for baby's bad diaper rashes.
7. Use both breasts during each feeding to stimulate milk production. Once your milk supply is established at four weeks, it is fine to nurse on one breast per feeding. One exception: Veteran moms may have plenty of milk to accomplish this sooner.
8. Sleep when your baby sleeps. Your baby should not sleep more than a four-hour stretch in the first two weeks.
9. Don't be afraid to ask for help.
10. Don't give up. The first two weeks can be rough, but then it will all be worth it!

Breastfeeding positions

◆ **Cradle hold:** Baby's head rests on Mom's forearm with his belly next to Mom's.

◆ **Football hold:** Baby's head rests on Mom's hand with his body coming underneath Mom's armpit. (Good for after a C-section, large breasted moms, preemies, and twins.)

◆ **Side-lying:** Baby and Mom lie sideways and face each other. (Popular at night feedings)

◆ **Dancer hold** (not pictured): Baby lies in a sling, freeing up Mom's hands to hold her breast and position Baby.[2] (Good for babies with a weak suck or poor seal).

Helpful Hint

To take your baby off of your nipple without causing excruciat-
ing pain, place one of your fingers into the corner of his mouth
and break the suction seal. Pulling down on his chin also works.

Infant Feeding Behaviors

Newborns can be divided into five types of feeding styles. Identifying
what type your baby is may help you understand how to help him feed
better. The types listed below were characterized by a study done in the
1950's, but are still relevant today:

1. **The Barracuda.** This little guy attacks the breast and gets down
    to business. Mom's nipples sometimes pay the price for this style.
    Be prepared.
2. **The Excited Ineffective.** Yes, this is the baby who is so excited
    to eat that he loses his latch. Calming, then reattempting to latch
    helps until baby figures out the routine.
3. **The Procrastinator.** The baby who waits until the milk is in to
    bother with eating. There is no rush. Let him be.
4. **The Gourmet.** She must mouth the nipple, have a taste test, then
    begin the meal. Again, there is no need to rush. Let her do her thing.
5. **The Rester** (similar to a cow who grazes). He takes his own sweet
    time. He eats for a few minutes, rests, then continues. Don't rush
    him. He will eventually finish the meal and eat well if left alone.[3]

Trouble Shooting: The Top Eight Breastfeeding Challenges

When breastfeeding goes wrong, these are the usual suspects:

1. **Poor position.** There are several positions that keep you and
    your baby comfortable. If one is not working, try another one.
    See list above.
2. **Poor latch.** You should hear your baby swallowing/gulping.
    Clicking is NOT a sound you should hear. Get your baby to open
    wide, with curled lips. Make sure his nose and chin are next to
    your breast. Don't let go of your breast until your baby is secure-
    ly latched on. Poor latch leads to problem #6 (sore nipples).
3. **Nipple problem.** Large areola (the pigmented part of the
    breast) and inverted nipples pose a challenge. The football hold
    may help get baby latched on to large areola. Stimulating invert-
    ed nipples to stand out prior to nursing may help. Breast shells
    (see page 92) also help inverted nipples.
4. **Mouth problem.** Babies with tongue thrusting and tongue tie
    can have poor technique. See more about tongue tie below.
    Babies who thrust their tongues forward while nursing can be
    taught how to suck correctly (with a lot of patience and profes-
    sional help).
5. **Poor milk supply.** Remember, milk supply is based on demand.
    If your baby is not stimulating you enough, use a breast pump to
    help rev up the supply. Pump for a few minutes after each feed-
    ing session.

6. **Sore nipples**. See box on the next page for tips.
7. **Engorgement.** See below for tips.
8. **Plugged ducts.** Equate this to a clogged pipe. The milk backs up and causes a hard, lumpy, tender area. Massage these areas while you nurse. Use a heating pad. Nurse or pump frequently (at least every three hours). Beware of any redness on the skin or fever. Plugged ducts are the precursor for a breast infection called mastitis (see page 106 for more info).

Helpful Hint

Sometimes a baby has a poor sucking technique because he has a slight tongue tie (**ANKYLOGLOSSIA**). This leads to cracked, painful nipples in Mom and poor intake because baby has trouble compressing the nipple. If you think this may be a problem, let your pediatrician know about it. The thin piece of tissue causing the problem can be easily clipped.

Engorgement

Q. **My breasts look like I have had implants and my baby can't get latched on. I make Anna Nicole Smith look like Kate Moss. Help!**

Welcome to engorgement. Don't worry, this is only a two or three day experience at most.

When your body first starts making milk, it sometimes gets carried away. This also happens if your baby takes less volume or suddenly starts sleeping through the night. Here are some ways to feel better:

1. **Pump or manually express for a few minutes before getting baby latched on.** Your nipple will stand more upright, be soft, and compressible.
2. **Pump or manually express only to soften the nipple.** Pump off after feedings only if your baby is unsuccessful in nursing. Otherwise it can create an even greater supply of milk.
3. **Wear a bra 24 hours a day for support.** No underwires, ladies.
4. **Take a hot shower to encourage let down.**
5. **CABBAGE LEAVES.** Yes, they really can help. Try this: wear chilled cabbage leaves as a nursing pad in your bra. Leave them on for up to 45 minutes, three times daily.
6. **Put a bag of frozen vegetables** on your breasts for ten to 20 minutes after nursing if your breasts are hard and not leaking.
7. **Encourage your baby to nurse at least ten minutes on each breast.** This is the time women usually get desperate and wake their babies up to relieve their own discomfort.
8. **Take some acetaminophen (Tylenol).** Yes, it's safe to use while breastfeeding.[4]

Breastfeeding References

Yes, you can buy another book. Here are some of our favorites:
A great one for parents is *The Nursing Mother's Companion* by

SORE NIPPLES: 7 TIPS FOR RELEIF

Experienced breast-feeding moms share these tips:

1. Good hygiene is key. Let nipples air dry and change nursing pads frequently. Cotton bras let more air through.
2. Make sure you have a good latch and position. That's what probably got you where you are right now. You don't want to continue to injure your nipples.
3. Lanolin. Using a protective cream will help the healing process. Apply *after* feedings.
4. Acetaminophen (Tylenol) is fine to use.
5. Nipple shields. As we have already discussed, these are controversial because they inhibit the flow of milk. Use for a limited time only—until the thought of nursing doesn't make you want to cry anymore.
6. Shorter feeding sessions are more tolerable.
7. If you need to use a pump and express your milk temporarily, use a hospital grade pump. (For details on pumps, see below).[5]

Kathleen Huggins, R.N. It will hold your hand and give you 25 different ways to relieve engorgement.

Breastfeeding: A Guide for the Medical Profession by Ruth Lawrence, M.D. is the book most doctors rely on for advice on this topic.

Reality Check
Pacifiers and breastfeeding

Babies are soothed by sucking. In the first two months of life, this may be the only thing that reliably settles your baby. Letting a breastfed baby use a pacifier is a controversial issue amongst lactation professionals. Some argue that pacifiers create confusion for babies who suck pacifiers differently than the breast. Others report that babies can use a pacifier for 'non-nutritive' sucking and nurse just fine.

In our opinion, breastfeeding and pacifiers are not mutually exclusive. But, it is wise to wait on introducing a pacifier until your baby is a confident breastfeeder (around one week old). A reasonable alternative to the pacifier is a parent's finger. The other obvious alternative is to offer your breast for comfort nursing. This may or may not be for you.

BOTTOM LINE

 If you opt to use a pacifier, we suggest getting it out of your baby's life by three or four months of age when he no longer needs to be soothed by sucking. For more information, see Chapter 11, "Discipline."

Expressing Milk

Q. Why do some women express their breast milk (that is, pump)?

Many mothers pump to survive engorgement. You can pump off the excess milk to get more comfortable and baby can have an easier time getting latched on. For working moms, it's essential to pump to maintain breast milk supply. For stay-at-home moms, it allows you to escape your house for a little while.

Q. How do I pump and store my milk?

Here's is what you need to know:

◆ Wash your hands.
◆ Clean all breast pump apparatus thoroughly.
◆ Use sterilized opaque plastic bottles (polypropylene) or polyethylene disposable bags for collection of milk. See below for a discussion of disposable bottle bags.
◆ Expressed milk can be refrigerated and used within two to five days.
◆ Expressed milk can be frozen for up to three months in the back a standard freezer (top part of refrigerator). Avoid storing breast milk on the bottom of a freezer, as that area may warm up during a defrost cycle.
◆ Expressed milk can be frozen for up to 12 months in a deep-freezer.
◆ Remember to put a collection date on the bottles or bags! Use the oldest milk first.
◆ Yes, you can combine expressed milk from different pumping sessions together in one container. Just keep it going for a full day, then divide the milk up into individual servings.
◆ Start with four oz servings of milk to freeze. Store six to eight oz servings when your baby is three months old. Leave room in the container. Fluids expand when frozen.
◆ Newly expressed breast milk can sit out at room temperature for up to eight hours. But it's wise to refrigerate it as soon as possible.[6]

Reality Check

Plastic disposable bottle bags are very convenient for storage. You can pour the milk directly into them, put on a twist tie, and freeze. For use, immerse the bag in a bowl of warm water to thaw it out.

Here is the downside: many of those great antibodies in Mom's milk stick to the bags and don't get to baby's mouth. Most lactation professionals prefer the hard polypropylene bottles (frosted plastic) for breast milk storage.[7]

Another reality check: Breast milk can be different colors (white, yellow, blue, brown, black) and that's okay. Once it is frozen, it can smell kind of like soap. It's not spoiled—use it.

Q. How do I serve my expressed breast milk?

Warmed and gently shaken. Some tips:

1. Thaw frozen milk in the refrigerator overnight.
2. Warm it up by placing the bottle into warm water.
3. Do not microwave it! It zaps the Vitamin C out and may lead to hot spots that can burn baby's mouth.
4. The milk will separate into water and fat. Mix the bottle up before serving.
5. Once the milk has been thawed, it will last in the refrigerator for up to 24 hours.
6. Thawed milk is good for one hour at room temperature.
7. An unfinished breast milk bottle is good for up to four hours at room temperature. Just don't reheat it or cool it.

Reality Check

Very few insurance companies will cover the cost of a breast pump or a private lactation consultation, despite the obvious medical advantages for both.

THE LOW DOWN ON BREAST PUMPS

You can rent a hospital grade pump, purchase an electric pump, or purchase a manual pump.

A smart move: rent a pump when you go home from the hospital. Renting lets you figure out whether you need a pump long term, without making a serious financial commitment. Most hospitals offer rentals or at least provide a list of medical supply companies in the area that rent pumps.

Moms who are returning to work and plan to pump, can rent for an extended period of time, or can later buy their own. We like the hospital grade dual pump. You can control the speed and pressure, which less expensive models don't allow. For working moms, efficiency is key. You can pump both breasts simultaneously in 15 minutes with a high-grade pump. A Medela brand "Lactina" will cost $30-75 per month to rent. It pumps 50 cycles per minute (baby sucks about 60 times/minute) at a comfortable pressure.

You can purchase a hospital grade equivalent product (Medela brand 'Pump In Style') for about $275. It has the same double pump as a hospital grade pump. If you are looking at less expensive models, remember to look at the cycle speed and pressure.

You might get a manual pump as a shower gift. This is convenient for emergencies or travel. The mechanism is similar to operating a bike pump. Your arm may get tired out long before your breasts have emptied.

FYI: For an in-depth discussion on buying a breast pump (including brand name reviews) as well as the best milk storage options, check out our other book *Baby Bargains* (see back of this book for details).

Q. When can I introduce a bottle?

Ideally, at four weeks of age.

Introduce one bottle a day of expressed (pumped) breast milk at four weeks of age. Why?

DR B'S OPINION

◆ Dad gets involved.

◆ Mom can go out to get her hair cut (remember you are nursing every 2-3 hours).

◆ Baby learns that food comes in different packages.

A common mistake is waiting until the end of maternity leave or when you want a date with your spouse to try a bottle. Once a baby is in the breast-only mode, he is less flexible about change.

Q. My baby is refusing to take a bottle. Help!

"It is very healthy for your marriage to leave your baby at home with a loving family member or friend! I frequently prescribe this form of mental health therapy to my families. Dinner or a movie (you won't have time for both) is much cheaper than marital counseling."

Babies are smarter than you give them credit for. They can see and smell Mom if she is anywhere in sight. Get out of the house and let someone else feed your baby the bottle.

Babies have thirst and hunger drives. No matter how stubborn your baby is, he will eventually accept a bottle of your breast milk if he is not given an option.

This is not cruel or unusual punishment.

Considerations for Mom

Q. I've heard I need to restrict my diet while I am breast-feeding. Is this true?

Not really.

Human milk is remarkably uniform despite differences in women's diets. It is always a good idea to eat healthfully for both you and your baby, though. There are actually very few restrictions. Here are the recommendations, according to the Institute of Medicine:

1. Avoid diets that promise rapid weight loss.
2. Eat a wide variety of foods including breads/grains, fruits, vegetables, milk and dairy, meats or meat alternatives daily.
3. At least three servings of milk products daily.
4. Specifically eat Vitamin A rich foods- carrots, spinach, greens, sweet potatoes, cantaloupe.
5. Drink water when you are thirsty.
6. Caffeine-containing products (cola, coffee) are suggested in moderation (two servings or less per day). The caffeine enters the breast milk.

DIETARY RESTRICTIONS FOR CERTAIN CIRCUMSTANCES

When there is a strong family history of food allergies, your doctor may recommend that Mom stay away from peanut-containing products, eggs, wheat, or dairy. Two and a half percent of all newborns have a hypersensitivity to cow's milk. Occasionally, babies with a milk allergy can have problems if their breastfeeding moms have milk products in their diet (see "I Give Up" story below). For more information on food allergies, see Chapter 7, "Solid Nutrition."[10]

7. Avoid eating shark, swordfish, king mackerel, and tilefish because they may contain high levels of methyl mercury which can interfere with neurological development.[8]

8. It's okay to eat 12 ounces or less of shellfish, canned fish, small ocean fish, or farm raised fish/per week.[9]

Feedback from the Real World: "I Give Up"

One of our readers sent us a note, in desperation, regarding her baby's problems. The mom had been exclusively breastfeeding her baby. She wrote, "it breaks my heart to hear her scream all the time... to have your child be so obviously unhappy and/or in pain all the time is the worst feeling in the world...I think it's time for me to give up (breastfeeding) because nothing else I've tried seems to work." A milk protein allergy was ultimately diagnosed.

Our response: You are not alone. Babies who suffer from this problem leave both baby and parents in misery. But do not fear—your child will not be like this forever. Some babies outgrow this problem by six months of age, and over 80% outgrow it by age five. Babies who are breastfed and have a milk protein allergy can still have problems because mom's milk/dairy intake can end up in the breast milk. If you want to continue breastfeeding, you need to avoid ALL products containing milk or dairy. There are often hidden dairy sources, so it's not only the obvious dairy products you need to avoid. Check out the web site FoodAllergy.org for more information.

FYI: Babies with classic milk protein allergies have blood streaked poop/diarrhea.

Old Wives Tale
You need to drink excessive amounts of water when you are nursing.

The Truth: Your body will increase its thirst drive to accommodate for your fluid needs. You don't need to go overboard.

FYI: Your daily caloric needs will be higher if you are breastfeeding. The average recommended daily allowance for non-pregnant women is 2100 calories. With breastfeeding, the recommendation is 2700 calories.[11]

DR B'S OPINION

"Babies will get what they need from breast milk, at the expense of Mom's body. I recommend continuing your prenatal vitamins if you are nursing."

breastfeeding

Old Wives Tale
You need to avoid gassy foods like beans because it will make the baby gassy.

The truth: You may want to avoid gassy foods because other people might not want to be around you. Your baby is unaffected by this food choice.

Q. Is there any truth that some foods in my diet will make my baby fussy?

Yes, but there is no reason to restrict your diet unless you identify a problem. Foods that *might* cause a problem: cabbage, turnips, broccoli, rhubarb, apricots, prunes, melons, and peaches.[12]

Q. Can I drink any alcoholic beverages while I am nursing?

Yes, in limited amounts.

Alcohol enters the bloodstream and the breast milk anywhere from 30-90 minutes after ingestion. The levels in the milk drop quickly. Each individual's metabolism is slightly different. So, a good rule of thumb is to avoid nursing for at least two hours after drinking.

I'd suggest you limit your intake to one alcoholic beverage, sporadically, if you are nursing.

DR B'S OPINION

"The only dietary restrictions I recommend are for caffeine and alcohol. I had the personal experience of drinking one Coke while nursing my son and had a baby who would not go to sleep for several hours. We were both miserable!"

Old Wives Tale
Drinking alcohol improves your milk supply.

The truth: Drinking alcohol may help relax an overstressed mother, but it does not improve breast milk volumes or let-down reflexes.

Q. Are there any medications I need to avoid while I am nursing?

Yes, lots of them.

The short answer to this question is, always inform your doctor that you are breastfeeding. That way, a medication choice for you can be made safely. You can always call your child's doctor, or your pharmacist to double check.

See Appendix A, "Medications" for more information.

Q. I love exercising. Any problems with that while I am breastfeeding?

If you exercise vigorously then nurse, your milk may have a sour taste that your baby may not like. Exercise produces lactic acid in your body,

DR B'S OPINION:
MEDICATIONS AND BREASTFEEDING

Mothers frequently call me about medications they are taking and if they are okay to use while breastfeeding. Although I sound smart knowing all the answers on the phone, I find the answers in a book called *Medications and Mother's Milk* by Thomas Hale, Ph.D. If you are planning on nursing for the long haul, or have a chronic medical condition, it might be worth having this gem on your book-shelf at home. (Find it at www.iBreastfeeding.com or 800-378-1317.)

which goes into your breast milk. It's not harmful, it just tastes funny. There have also been anecdotal reports of infant fussiness up to six hours after Mom's exercise/nursing session. Here are some suggestions:

♦ Pump or express for a minute or two before nursing.
♦ If your baby gives you a strange look, use some stored breast milk for that feeding!

Q. I am going back to work after my maternity leave. How am I going to make this breastfeeding thing work?

Setting aside time, having a progressive workplace, and being committed. Yes, Moms, you can try to do it all. And, some women are able to go back to work AND provide breast milk to feed their babies. It may take some trial and error to figure out what works for you, but here are some ideas.

1. Leave for work a little early and pump BEFORE you start working.
2. Invest in a high-powered, double pump. You can successfully pump in 15 minutes with one of these models.
3. Let your boss/co-workers know of your intentions. You may be surprised at how understanding people are.
4. Think about where you will be able to pump and how often.
5. Think about where you will *store* your expressed milk until you get home. It can sit in a cooler with ice packs if you don't have access to a refrigerator.
6. Start stockpiling expressed milk BEFORE maternity leave is over.
7. Be prepared for being exhausted the first few weeks. It does get better.
8. If you don't have enough breast milk for the whole time you are away, supplementing with formula is okay. Your baby will benefit from any milk you can provide.

Q. I have a fever, can I still breast feed?

Absolutely!

Your body is producing antibodies to whatever infection your body is fighting. Those antibodies are going directly to your baby. If you have a cold or upper respiratory infection, not breathing on your baby would be helpful!

Contact your doctor (obstetrician, preferably) if you have a fever short-ly after the birth of your baby. You could have a bladder infection, womb infection, or mastitis.

Q. So, what is mastitis?

A breast infection due to raw nipples and germs from your baby's mouth. Pediatricians try to stay out of Mom's health issues, but we are frequently asked to make this diagnosis.

New mothers often have trouble with their baby's latch initially, leading to raw and cracked nipples. This lets baby's mouth germs enter Mom's breast. Symptoms include fever, chills (like you have the flu), pain/swelling/redness of the breast. Women are usually afflicted with this one to four weeks after delivery.

Treatment requires antibiotics (you need to call your OB for this) and continued elimination of breast milk from the breasts. Yes, this means you either need to continue nursing or pumping through this unpleasant experience. Your baby will not be harmed—it's *his* germs that did this to you!

What causes mastitis?

1. Cracked nipples (mostly from poor latch technique)
2. Plugged milk ducts (from incomplete emptying at a feeding, tight clothes)
3. Missed feedings (lack of nursing or pumping for several hours)
4. Stress and exhaustion
5. Rapid weaning (lack of nursing)

If you notice that you have a tender, painful area on your breast—do something about it ASAP. Massage the area while you nurse or pump to unclog the duct. Apply a warm compress to the area. Nurse or pump every two to three hours. And get some sleep![13]

Q. My nipples are burning every time I nurse. Why?

This is likely to be a yeast infection.

Again, pediatricians try to stay out of Mom's medical care, but parents often ask their opinion. Yeast infections also come from your little one's mouth. Babies (who are toothless) have some bacteria in their mouths, but not nearly as much as we do (because plaque goes along with teeth). Yeast likes dark, warm, moist, low bacteria places. So, newborns often get yeast or **THRUSH** infections in their mouths. It looks like curdled milk that can't be wiped off the gums, cheek lining, and roof of their mouth.

If your breasts burn and you experience shooting pains every time your baby nurses, check your baby's mouth, and check with both your obstetrician and pediatrician. A family practitioner should be able to handle both of these problems.

Your baby can get an antifungal mouthwash and you can get an antifungal cream or oral medication.

Special situations

Q. I am adopting a baby. I have heard that I can take a medicine to stimulate my milk supply. Is this true?

Yes. There is a medication called metoclopramide (the brand name is Reglan) that helps some women produce milk. This is also used for women who have trouble producing enough milk for their babies. While there are natural remedies to stimulate milk production, there is no scientific data on how effective these are.

Q. I am unable to breast-feed, but I want my baby to be breast-fed. Is there some place I can buy breast milk?

Yes. There are a few programs across the country called Mother's Milk Banks that sell breast milk. The donors are rigorously screened prior to acceptance of the milk. Check with your area hospital's lactation services or the La Leche League to see if there is a program near you.

On the flip side, if you have more milk than your freezer can handle, consider making a donation!

Q. I have twins and want to breast feed. How do I make it work?

You will have enough milk. The question is, will you have enough time?

The key is getting both babies fed at the same time. Otherwise, it will be a challenge to get any sleep. Start this routine from day one and you will have more success.

When it comes to multiples, you will do a little more scheduling and a little less feeding 'on demand'. If you are able to get some hired or volunteered help around the house, things may be less chaotic for you.

The football hold and/or the cradle hold work well for simultaneous feeding sessions. It's probably wise not to have one breast exclusively designated for one baby. That way, they will accept either breast in the long run.

Q. I have a baby who was born prematurely. Anything special I need to know about breastfeeding?

Yes—it's even more important to breast-feed these little ones.
Here are some special considerations:

1. Many premature babies get tired easily while nursing. If you no longer hear your baby swallowing, take him off the breast and burp him. Then return to feeding.
2. Many premature babies have poor technique (sucking, latching). Get professional help (from a lactation consultant) if you are having trouble.
3. You may be supplementing with formula or expressed breast milk for a while. Don't give up.
4. Weigh your baby once or twice weekly to make sure he is gaining, ideally, an ounce a day. Eventually you can stop doing this— check with your doctor.
5. The football hold works well for little preemies. That way you have better control of positioning and latch.
6. Give baby skin to skin time. This stimulates your milk production (and promotes bonding!)

Weaning

Q. When should I wean my baby off of breast milk?

When one or both of you is ready.

The American Academy of Pediatrics recommends breastfeeding for at least a year, with the addition of "complementary" solid food by six months. Hopefully, both you and your baby will enjoy nursing for at least that long. Some nursing teams (mother and baby) opt to continue even after one year.

So, the right time to wean is when one or both of you thinks it is time to stop. That time may be when your baby refuses the breast, when you decide you want your body to yourself, or when your three-year-old is able to ask for your breast by name. It is really a personal decision.

Reality Check

Americans tend to nurse their babies for less time than many other cultures. In some cultures, women nurse one child until the next one arrives. These same women have lower rates of breast cancer. Food for thought.

Q. I am planning to wean my baby. How do I do it?

Slowly and methodically.

If you stop breastfeeding abruptly, your body will be unhappy with you. Milk ducts get clogged (and infected). With that said, here is a typical strategy:

1. Create a timetable for the projected target date of nursing completion.
2. Eliminate one nursing session every three or four days, two to three weeks before your target date. The length of time for the entire weaning process depends on how many times a day you are currently nursing.
3. If you are weaning prior to one year of age, replace that feeding with either previously expressed breast milk or formula.
4. Eliminate the first morning and last evening feeding at the end of the weaning process.
5. Once you have completely stopped nursing, you may continue to leak milk for a week or two.
6. Wear an old bra (non-nursing), even though it is a little binding.
7. If your breasts feel so full that they are going to explode, pump or manually express just enough milk to get comfortable.

Q. I want to continue breastfeeding, but my nine-month old seem to be weaning himself. Is that okay?

Yes, but you may gently encourage him to continue. Babies go on strike (from formula or bottles, too) for various reasons.

◆ Some babies get distracted during feeding sessions when they realize the world is pretty interesting. Nurse in a boring, dark, quiet place.

- Some babies don't want to suck if they are teething. Try using acetaminophen to relieve teething discomfort.
- Ear infections and nasal congestion can also discourage a baby from nursing. Check in with your doctor.

If none of the advice above helps, transition to formula in a bottle or a cup (depending on your baby's age and skills). Transition to whole milk if your baby is over a year of age.[14]

Q. If I stop breastfeeding before my baby is one year old, what do I offer him instead?

Commercial-brand formula is the acceptable substitute for breast milk in the first year of life.

Note: whole milk, soymilk, goat's milk, and rice milk are NOT substitutes for breast milk in the first year of life.

The Big Picture: Breastfeeding for the First Year

Okay, let's sum up this breast-feeding section with an overview of nursing for your baby's first year:

Birth to 2 weeks: (18-24 ounces/day)

Breast fed newborns tend to eat every two or three hours. That adds up to eight to 12 times in a 24-hour day. They may cluster feed as frequently as every 1 1/2 hours (that's from the beginning of one feeding to the beginning of the next). If you are expressing breast milk and feeding via a bottle, your baby will probably take two or three ounces at a feeding.

Babies who try to nurse more frequently than every 90 minutes are nursing for comfort—BEWARE OF BEING THE HUMAN PACIFIER. Babies have no other way of consoling themselves. They can't just pull it together and settle down. Sucking is extremely soothing. So, if it has been less than 90 minutes since the beginning of the last feeding, try using your finger to let him suck. Your breasts will thank you. Note: If your baby is truly nursing non-stop, go get your baby weighed. Make sure you have enough milk supply.

On the flip side, your baby may take a four-hour stretch before feeding again. In the first two weeks of life, do not let your baby go more than four hours without feeding. Why?

- Breast milk is a supply and demand phenomenon. To get your supply established, the demand must be there.
- Your breasts will feel like they are going to explode. If that four-hour stretch is during daylight hours, you are in for a long night of cluster feedings.

2 weeks to 2 months: (20-32 ounces/day)

Once your baby is two weeks old, you can relax a bit. Your milk supply will be better established and your baby will have regained his birth weight. If he sleeps through the night, let him! You may need to pump to get comfortable during the night, but don't wake a sleeping baby. By the way, this is unlikely to happen. If it does, don't tell your friends about it. They will hate you.

This feeding "pattern" goes on for at least the first two months of life. While this seems a bit erratic, it is normal for a newborn is to be irregular with her feeding (and sleep patterns).

2 to 4 months: (30-40 ounces/day)

Your baby will start to have some regularity! He will have more predictable wakeful periods and sleep periods. Hopefully, you will be down to one or two night feedings. If you are returning to work and pumping, plan on four ounces per feeding at two months of age and up to eight ounces per feeding at four months. *Babies usually max out at 40 oz per day at four months of age.*

4 to 6 months: (36-40 ounces/day)

You can look forward to five or six breast feedings a day. You should be able to get an evening stretch of six hours without nursing. Six hours is considered "sleeping through the night", although this is probably not your definition.

You may be introducing solid food at this point (see the next chapter on solid nutrition). Solid food is dessert. Your baby needs the same volume of breast milk for a while.

6 to 9 months: (28-36 ounces/day)

Your baby will nurse four or five times per day. You should be done with night feedings. If you are not, do some problem solving with your doctor. You may enjoy those cuddly moments nursing in the middle of the night, but these are not a necessity. Your baby is comforted and used to feeding at night. Frequently, so is Mommy. If both of you are enjoying this situation, keep doing it.

If one of you (Mom) is not enjoying it and wants more sleep, read Chapter 9, "Sleep."

THE HISTORY OF BABY FORMULA

1700's: 'Wet nurses' were paid to breast feed infants who could not be fed by their mother.

1800's: Milk from other animals was used as a substitute.

1700's   **1800's**

1838: The ingredients of animal milk and human milk were analyzed. We learned that cow's milk had a higher protein and lower sugar content which could cause problems for infants trying to digest it. This led to the first chemical "formula" that was added to cow's milk.

1870's: Nestle made the first infant formula that only required water to be added. It was very expensive and therefore quite unpopular.

The inventions of evaporated milk (1883), pasteurization (1890), and the refrigerator (1910) allowed parents to make infant formula in the comfort of their own home.

9 to 12 months: (20-30 ounces/day)

Babies are well into solid foods and start to wean—that is, their volume and frequency of nursing decline. Your baby may nurse three or four times per day.

By one year of age, babies wean to 16 to 24 oz per day. At this point, you deserve a gold medal of honor. If you and baby are ready, you can stop breastfeeding.

We recommend switching to whole milk with Vitamin D added at one year of age. The goal is two cups of milk per day (or dairy serving equivalents). Remember, breast milk is low in Vitamin D and iron. So, if you want to go beyond a year of nursing, find other nutritional sources for these nutrients.

Formula

Q. Is it okay to feed formula to my newborn?

Yes.

Although it is wonderful to breastfeed, it is also acceptable to feed your baby infant formula for the first year of life. But consider these points:

1. **It's expensive.** Expect to pay $500 for the first six months (and up to $800 during the first year) if your baby tolerates the least expensive cow's milk based product (hypoallergenic formula costs $1000).

2. **Prep time.** It isn't a pretty sight—your baby screaming at you at 2am while you frantically mix a bottle of formula. Of course, your efficiency at preparing formula will improve over time, but the prep time is still a significant factor.

3. **Intolerance.** Human milk is made for human babies—it makes sense that it is more easily tolerated. It's more likely your baby will have an intolerance to formula. But, most babies do just fine.

1940-1960: Parents made infant formula out of evaporated milk, water, and corn syrup or sugar. The elaborate process of making formula daily provides much of the basis for the Old Wives Tales you hear about formula today.

1900's ——————————————————→ **PRESENT DAY**

1960's: Commercial formulas become popular due to a reduction in cost and ease of preparation. Breastfeeding rates drop sharply.

1970's: Only 25% of newborns left the hospital breastfeeding. As a result, the parents of this generation are the most formula fed babies in recorded history.

1980's and 90's: New scientific studies that point out the benefits of breastfeeding over formula spur a renaissance in nursing.

2003: 75% of babies go home from the hospital breastfeeding, but only 30% are breastfed beyond six months of life.[15]

Q. I have chosen to feed my baby formula. What formula do you recommend?

The cheapest cow's milk based formula with iron you can find. Get a warehouse club membership now, if you don't have one already. In general, the cheapest formula are the generic or store brands sold at discount stores like Wal-Mart and Target. Buy in bulk to get the maximum savings.

Here is an overview of these products. Dr. Lewis First, a well-respected pediatrician, deserves credit for the explanations below. He classifies formula into three categories: Coke, Diet Coke, and Caffeine Free Diet Coke. We'll also provide you the brand names for each type in the following list:

DR B'S OPINION

"Yes, I was formula fed and managed to make it to Harvard Medical School. Your child can lead a perfectly normal life if he is formula fed. Although we encourage you to breastfeed your baby for obvious benefits, your baby will be fine if he is formula fed."

◆ **Coke =** Cow's Milk Based Formula with iron. This is the formula tolerated by most babies and recommended first by most doctors.

Name brands include: Enfamil Lipil (DHA)*, Enfamil with iron, Similac Advance (DHA),* Similac with iron, Carnation Good Start. There are also generic or store brand cow's milk formula found at Wal-Mart, Target, and your grocery store.

* *We'll discuss DHA (and the similar fatty acid ARA) later in this chapter.*

◆ **Diet Coke =** Soy Protein Formula with iron. Some doctors recommend soy protein formula for babies who seem intolerant to cow's milk formula. (Note: this intolerance is NOT an allergy to milk protein, which is addressed with the formula type discussed next). "Intolerance" is a vague term for extremely gassy babies, or those who throw up more formula than they keep down. About 25% of American babies are fed soy formula. Soy formula is also an option for parents looking for a vegetarian-based alternative to cow's milk-based formula.

Name brands include: Prosobee (by Enfamil), Isomil (by Similac), Carnation Alsoy. As you might guess, there are also generic/store brand soy formulas sold at Target and Wal-Mart as well.

◆ **Caffeine Free Diet Coke =** Protein Hydrosylate Formula with iron. The Dom Perignon of formulas, these are for babies with a **MILK PROTEIN ALLERGY**, not merely an intolerance to regular milk-based formula. Common brand names for this type of formula include Enfamil's Nutramigen and Similac's Alimentum. Babies who are allergic to cow's milk protein have diarrhea with blood and/or mucus in their poop. Occasionally, babies with milk protein allergy also have a soy protein allergy. Some babies need this formula for the entire first year—but, based on a family history of food allergies and the severity of the baby's reaction to milk protein, your doctor may attempt a trial of soy formula before one year.

Name brands include: Nutramigen (by Enfamil), Alimentum (by Similac).

DIFFERENCES BETWEEN BREAST MILK & FORMULA

To understand the differences, you need a brief chemistry lesson here. Milk contains fat, protein, and sugar. Use the following table as a reference:

	Human Milk	Cow's Milk formula	Soy Formula	Protein Hydrosylate
Calories	20 cals/oz	20 cals/oz	20 cals/oz	20 cals/oz
Protein % **of calories**	5%	10% Nonfat milk, whey	10% soy protein	10% casein hydrosylate
Fat % **of calories**	54%	50% Vegetable oil	50% Vegetable oil	50% Vegetable oil
Carbohydrate **% of calories**	41% Lactose	40% Lactose	40% Corn syrup/ Sucrose	40% Corn syrup/ Sucrose
Live cells **Antibodies**	Yes	No	No	No
DHA, ARA	Yes	Some brands do	Some brands do	No

Special notes:
1. Human milk has lactose sugar.
2. Soy formulas replace cow protein with soy protein and are lactose free.
3. Protein Hydrosylate formulas are the most hypoallergenic because the protein is pre-digested.
4. All formulas in the table contain the recommended daily iron requirement for babies. Avoid low-iron versions of formula unless specifically directed by your doctor.
5. Note that 50% of the calorie intake comes from fat.
6. The major formula companies are adding very long chain polyunsaturated fatty acid derivatives of Omega-3 and Omega-6 (DHA and ARA). These are present in breast milk and some studies suggest they promote vision/brain development. (For more on this topic see DHA below).

Helpful Hint

Do not switch formulas without the blessing of your pediatrician or family practitioner. Most babies who are gassy and fussy will be gassy and fussy for the first three months of life no matter what they are eating. (For details, see Chapter 11).

BOTTOM LINE

All marketed formulas are tested extensively and required by law (Infant Formula Act 1986) to contain minimum levels of 29 different nutrients.

WHAT ARE DHA AND ARA? LIPIDS?

DHA stands for Docosahexaenoic Acid. ARA stands for Arachidonic Acid. DHA and ARA are also called "lipids." Walk into your grocery store and you'll see lots of formula cans hyping their added lipids. So, what is this stuff? Lipids (DHA/ARA) are polyunsaturated fats that occur naturally in breast milk. They are also found in fish oils, egg yolks, and algae/fungal oil.

There has been a fair amount of research done on these fatty acids because they are present in nerve tissue and the eyes. Some studies show improved vision and scoring on infant developmental testing when babies have DHA and ARA in their diets. Other studies, however, show absolutely no statistical differences with these nutrients. There is currently no strong data to support the addition of these fats to infant formula, other than it makes the formula more similar to the contents of breast milk. The bottom line: the jury is still out on DHA and ARA.

The DHA/ARA added formulas cost 15-30% more than standard formula. But there is one way to save if you want to go with a DAH/ARA-added formula: generic and store brands of formula sold at discount stores are now adding this ingredient as well.[16]

Soy Formula

Considering soy formula? The American Academy of Pediatricians (AAP) recommends soy formula for the following reasons:

- ◆ Full term babies who are not breastfeeding and whose parents want a vegetarian alternative to cow's milk-based formula. Soy formula is considered a safe alternative.
- ◆ Full term babies with galactosemia or hereditary lactase deficiency.
- ◆ Full term babies with documented (diagnosed) transient lactase deficiency.
- ◆ Babies with documented (diagnosed) IgE-mediated allergy to cow's milk.

The AAP does NOT recommend soy formula for:

- ◆ Preterm infants with birth weights less than 1800g (4 lbs).
- ◆ Prevention of colic or allergy.
- ◆ Infants with cow's milk protein-induced enterocolitis/enteropathy (i.e. food allergy causing blood in stool)[17]

Q. My doctor recommended an expensive name-brand formula with DHA. When I asked for a suggestion for a cheaper store brand, he said that option is inferior. Do doctors get kickbacks from formula companies for recommending name brands?

It's not likely. While there have been news stories about doctors caught taking kickbacks from pharmaceutical companies for recommending certain-name brand prescription drugs, we've never seen any evidence of that with pediatricians and formula.

Of course, doctors receive boatloads of free samples from formula companies. And it's fair to say that some may recommend a name brand formula based on their familiarity with that company (thanks to those samples).

As we stated earlier, we don't think there is any significant difference between store-brand and name-brand formula. Yes, we realize that some formula companies market their formulas as being "easier to digest" than competitors, but we think that's just hype.

What about DHA/ARA? Again, the jury is out on this subject. As we discussed earlier in this chapter, some researchers think the additives *may* enhance a baby's brain and visual development. BUT, there is no definitive scientific proof on this. Yes, the FDA says DHA and ARA are safe . . . but unproven. While most pediatricians are taking a wait-and-see approach on this subject, some parents are willing to spend the extra 15% to get formula with these ingredients. (Generic, store-brand formulas also have DHA/ARA versions as well—that should help with the price differential).

While it is fair for a doctor to have a preference for one formula brand or another, berating you for asking for a less-expensive option is not appropriate.

Q. So which is better, cow's milk formula or soy formula?

The consensus here: cow's milk. Why? Cow's milk-based formula is a better source of protein than soy, according to research studies. But neither are without controversy . . .

Q. I heard that cow's milk formula causes diabetes?

A recent article in the *Wall Street Journal* pointed out "some researchers suspect cow's milk formula may increase the risk of type 1 diabetes in certain children, although the science behind this theory is far from conclusive." Again, the science is NOT there to draw any conclusions on this.

Soy formula also is somewhat controversial.

DR B'S OPINION

"If you think Coke and Pepsi have an intense rivalry, check out the competition between formula companies. Despite the hype and personal preferences, the products are basically equivalent in each category."

Some researchers think soy formula may interfere with reproductive or immune functions when given in high doses to infants. Why? Soy formula contains phytoestrogens, which is a plant version of estrogen. While this chemical has shown to lower the risk of certain cancers in adults, it is unclear what effect it is has infants. Again, however, there is NO proof that soy formula is harmful to babies.

We don't mention these controversies to scare you, but you should be aware of them as you might hear discussion of this online and among parents. Just because a researcher has a *theory* about a particular product, it should NOT inspire panic in parents. [18]

As always, we'll track these controversies and put the latest updates on these issues on our web site at Baby411.com (sign up for our free newsletter for breaking news items).

Reality Check
I've heard that soy formula causes Attention Deficit Disorder (ADD). Is this true?

No. This fear stems from a study that purported to show a link between one ingredient in soy formula (manganese) and neurological disorders like ADD. But let's take a closer look at that study. Researchers fed baby rats extremely high doses of manganese—some 38 times greater than the level found in formulas. Surprise! These toxic doses caused developmental problems in the rats. The bottom line: Soy formula has been around for over 40 years and is considered acceptable by both the AAP and the Food and Drug Administration. If you give toxic doses of anything to rats (or people), bad things happen to them![19]

Q. I have seen other formulas on the shelf at the grocery store. What are they used for?

These would be classified as the "gourmet formulas." Most are made for babies with particular problems. A few are made as optional products, which are not based on a medical necessity. See the following section for more on gourmet formulas.

The Gourmet Formulas

1. Lactose Free Formula
Lactose intolerance occurs in older children and adults. Babies are rarely born with this problem. Lactose intolerance can occur temporarily after an infant has a stomach virus. Some stomach viruses break down the human enzyme "lactase" which digests the lactose sugar, creating a temporary intolerance. This can go on for one to six *weeks* after the virus.

When babies are allergic to formula, it is usually the milk *protein* that is the problem, as it is the most allergenic part of the food. It is rare for a baby to have a problem with the milk sugar (lactose). Human milk has lactose in it and it is perfect nutrition.

2. Isomil DF
This delicacy is made for babies who are experiencing a stomach virus. Not only has the lactose sugar and cow's milk protein been removed, but 6 grams of fiber is added per liter of formula. You're thinking, why give fiber to a child with the runs? Believe it or not, fiber actually bulks up watery stools. This formula can be used for the duration of a stomach bug to cut down on the water loss that occurs with intestinal infections.

3. Low Iron Formula
In our opinion (and we're not the only ones), low iron formulas should be taken off the market. Iron is the key ingredient to red blood cells. Iron carries oxygen to your whole body. Formula companies sell this as an alternative product, but put a disclaimer on the package that babies need iron supplementation if they are eating this stuff. Huh? Some doctors recommend this formula for breast-fed babies who take an occasional supplemental bottle. In reality, the parents who are using this product are those who believe their baby is constipated from iron-rich formula—and hence using the low-iron stuff will solve that problem.

The American Academy of Pediatrics sees no role for the use of low-iron formulas in infant feeding and recommends that all formulas fed to infants be fortified with iron (more than 6.7mg/100kcal–this is present in standard formulas with iron).[20]

Old Wives Tale
Iron is constipating.

The truth: If your baby is constipated, he needs more fiber in his diet, not less iron. If you doubled your size in four or five months, you'd need that much iron, too.

4. Enfamil AR

All babies spit up a little. But babies who suffer from heartburn (a.k.a. gastoesophageal reflux), look like the Exorcist. Thickening the formula can help keep it from coming back up. So pediatricians often recommend parents add a teaspoon of rice cereal to each bottle to make the formula heavier. After trying this at home, however, I can tell you that the formula gets clumpy and it requires minor surgery on the rubber nipple to get it out of the bottle. No fun.

Enfamil AR solves this problem by adding rice starch to their regular cow's milk formula. This is much easier to use (especially in concentrated form), reducing your frustration. You will still need to use bottle nipples with a larger hole to get the formula to flow, however.

It is an old wives' tale that adding rice cereal will make your baby sleep through the night. But those old wives would be correct if they are speaking about babies with reflux.

5. Carnation Follow-up and other "toddler" formulas

According to Carnation, their Follow-Up formula is designed for babies from four to 12 months of age. This product contains more calcium (120mg per 5oz) than its competitors' standard infant formula (78mg per 5oz). The manufacturer's theory: babies over four months have a higher calcium requirement than those under four months of age.

Other formula companies have tried to jump on this bandwagon as well, but this time with "toddler formulas" designed for one to three year olds. The formulas, with added vitamins, are pitched to parents as an allegedly better substitute for cow's milk.

Is any of this necessary? We say no. Follow-up (for four to 12 month olds) and toddler formulas (for one to three year olds) are generally a waste of money. The calcium content of standard infant formulas is appropriate for birth to 12 months of age. After one year of age, a baby can drink

---

FORMULA FOR PREEMIES

There are higher calorie formulas made especially for babies who are born before 34 weeks gestation or less than four pounds. These formulas have more calories, more protein, more calcium, and more phosphorous than standard formulas. Some babies will switch to standard formula, but the premature formulas can be used for a whole year if necessary for growth.[22]

---

whole milk—at a savings of 80% compared to the cost of toddler formula! The American Academy of Pediatrics Committee on Nutrition concurs. They do not recommend using toddler follow-up formulas for healthy children who have low risk of nutritional deficiency.[21]

Q. Do you have a preference of powder, concentrate, or ready to feed?

Pick the cheapest—powder.

Why? Babies who start on the more expensive concentrate or ready-to-feed formulas develop a preference for it, as it is a little thicker than powder based formula. So, if you start on the expensive stuff and try to switch to cheaper powder, you may find some resistance on part of your child (to put it mildly).

Sure, ready-to-feed formula is convenient for travel, but, again, is very expensive. Concentrate has to be refrigerated once you open the can and is wasted if you are taking a bottle on the go (and you don't use it).

Powder is portable. Just add water to the powder if you need an "emergency" feeding. Powder also needs no refrigeration until it's mixed with water.

FYI: the nutrients are the same for all types of formula!

Old Wives Tale
The ready to feed formula is easier to digest.
The Truth: The ready to feed is convenient, a little thicker, and a lot more expensive. All products are digested exactly the same way.

Helpful Hint
If you choose ready-to-feed formula, you will need to consider a fluoride supplement for your baby after six months of age if you are not giving him any water (since no water is added to prepare the formula)

Q. Do I need to sterilize the bottles, boil water, or use bottled water to mix the formula?

No, no, and no.

You don't need to sterilize the bottles after the first time you take them out of the package. You can clean them with warm water or put them in the dishwasher. Your baby isn't sterile once he leaves the hospital nursery and is exposed to real world germs on a daily basis.

You don't need to boil the water you use to mix formula because the American water supply is clean. Formula companies have instructions to boil the water on the package because their products are distributed worldwide. Note: If you have well water, you need to get your water tested before your baby arrives to make sure it isn't contaminated.

If tap water is fine for you to drink, it's fine for your baby, too. In fact, your tap water likely has fluoride added to it (check with your local water department). Fluoride prevents tooth decay. If you are a bottled water family, then you need to get a fluoride supplement for your baby once he is six months old.

Sterilizing bottles and boiling water are all based on the kitchen chemistry our mothers and grandmothers performed to prepare formula in the olden days.

Helpful Hint

Look at the mixing instructions on the formula can. Powder requires one scoop per two ounces of water. Liquid concentrate is one ounce of formula per one ounce of water. Ready-to-feed is ready to go (DON'T ADD water). This may seem obvious to you. But if you screw up, your baby gets either half of the calories he needs or rocket fuel.

My mother-in-law (who is a very bright woman) mistakenly bought ready-to-feed formula for her third baby (my future husband) and added water because she thought she had purchased concentrate. Her astute pediatrician identified the problem at the baby's two-week well check when he wasn't gaining weight. Sure, this baby ended up nearly six feet tall as an adult, but we figure he could have topped Shaq's height if this mistake was caught earlier.

Q. Which bottles/nipples do you recommend?

There are so many products out there. You'll end up trying a few out to discover your baby's preference. Some have advantages that may be appealing to you: disposable bottle bags, curved bottles, air free mechanisms (Dr. Brown's bottles—no relationship to the author of this book). The nipple manufacturers all claim to be the most like Mom's nipples—Playtex and Avent are the most popular in this category.

Lactation consultants seem to like the Avent nipples best. They believe there is less nipple confusion when they are used. Lactation consultants also recommend holding the bottle in a more horizontal position so babies have to work a bit harder to get the milk. Why? Bottles are usually much easier to feed from so babies get "lazy."

Note: There are newborn nipples (low flow), older baby nipples (higher flow), and cross cut nipples (highest flow). You can switch to the older baby nipples at four months. The cross cut nipples are better for babies with reflux who drink thickened formula.

For an in-depth discussion of bottles (including brand reviews and money-saving tips), check out our other book, *Baby Bargains*. See the back of this book for details.

Reality Check

Feeder bottles (solid food dispensers) are unnecessary. Your baby needs to learn how to eat, *not drink* his solid food. (See the next chapter for more).

The Big Picture: Formula Feeding for the First Year

Birth to 2 weeks: (18-24 oz)

Newborns tend to eat two to three ounces every three to four hours. For the first two weeks, wake your baby if it has been more than four hours since the last feeding. Once baby has regained birth weight, he can sleep as much as he wants (good luck)!

2 weeks to 2 months: (20-32 oz)

You will see a gradual increase in volumes at feedings. By two months, babies usually take around four ounces per feeding, about every three hours.

2 to 4 months: (30-40 oz)

Your baby will eat six to eight ounces per feeding, and *max out at about 40 oz per day at about four months of age.*

When the volumes go up, the number of daily feedings go down. So, a baby who chugs 8oz at a feed can eat five times a day and sleep through the night. Parents often ask if they can space out the frequency of daytime feedings. NO! Use common sense here—if your baby eats every two to three hours during the day, you will all be sleeping at night.

Babies who take smaller volumes at each feeding will need to eat more often. These tend to be babies who suffer from heartburn. (**GASTROE-SOPHAGEAL REFLUX**). We'll have more on this in Chapter 8, "The Other End."

4 to 6 months: (40 oz)

Babies continue to take 40 oz per day of formula. You will be introducing solid foods at some point. Solid food is only dessert and is a poor source of calories (see Chapter 7, Solid Nutrition). *There should be no reduction in the volume of formula.*

6 to 9 months: (28-36 oz)

Your baby will start to wean—decreasing volumes of formula as his intake of calories from solid food increases.

9 to 12 months: (20-30 oz)

Your baby will decrease drinking formula to a minimum of 24 oz per day. At one year of age, your baby will usually drink three 8 oz bottles. This will then be replaced by whole milk that is Vitamin D fortified. *The goal is 16 oz a day (which is two cups a day) of milk.* The equivalent of dairy products is also fine.

It's time to kick the bottle habit at a year. Don't get stuck here. You don't have a baby anymore. You have a toddler. If you want a baby in your house, go have another one. Yes, your child will be quite capable of drinking via a cup, sippy cup, or cup with a straw. He will not go thirsty.

Other Liquids

Q. Does my baby need any water?

Not until six months of age.

The reason: your baby is already getting water. It's naturally mixed in breast milk and artificially mixed in to prepare formula. Your baby gets plenty of water. After six months of age, go for it.

Note: Babies who are exclusively breast fed or fed ready-to-feed formula AFTER six months of age will need a source of fluoride if they don't drink any water. These babies can either eat cereals mixed with tap water, have juice that has been diluted with tap water, or get a fluoride supplement with a doctor's prescription.

Q. When can I give my baby juice?

What's the rush?

Pediatricians, as a general rule, are not very enthusiastic about juice. Sorry, juice producers of America. Here are the reasons:

1. Juice provides little nutrition. Vitamin C has to be added to many juices to give them any nutritive value. Otherwise, juice is just a form of liquid sugar.

2. Juice is filling, which decreases a child's appetite for more nutritious foods.

3. Drinking juice throughout the day (especially in a bottle) causes sugar buildup on the teeth. This, in turn, creates *high dental bills.*

4. A sugar-loaded diet causes diarrhea.

> **DR B'S OPINION**
>
> *"I recommend starting juice after six months of age. Offer no more than eight ounces per day. Diluting it half and half with water is even better. I also suggest introducing juice in a cup not a bottle."*

BOTTOM LINE: Children with poor weight gain, chronic diarrhea, or rotten teeth often are juice-a-holics.

Helpful hint

Kudos to the V-8 company. They have created a V-8 Splash drink that contains carrot juice (an excellent source of Vitamin A). It comes packaged in a kid sized juice box and tastes like fruit juice. Tropicana Healthy Kids Orange Juice also contains Vitamin A, C, E, and has calcium added. Another great product: Vruit (web: americansoy.com). A blend of both fruit and vegetable juices, they are 100% juice.

Q. When can my baby drink from a cup?

Any time after six months of age.

Your long-term goal is to have your baby drinking from a cup at his first birthday. Babies usually get the hang of it between six and 12 months.

Reality Check

Once your baby has teeth, you need to wipe them or brush them after the last feeding (before bedtime). Your baby shouldn't be falling asleep while he is eating by the time he has teeth anyway. (See Chapter 9 "Sleep" for details.)

DR B'S OPINION: SIPPY CUPS

A popular item among parents is the no-spill sippy cup. I have never been a fan of these because the sucking mechanism to get the fluid out is similar to a bottle. Dentists dislike sippy cups because the flow of liquid heads straight to the back of the top front teeth. In short, sippy cups can promote tooth decay.

I'd prefer to have your baby drinking from a straw if he hasn't quite mastered the art of drinking from a cup.

Q. When and how do I switch to cow's milk?

At one year of age, cold turkey.

Your baby still needs a high fat diet because his brain development is on overdrive. The American Academy of Pediatrics recommends whole milk until *two years of age*.

After the second birthday, your child should drink what the rest of the family is drinking. This should be *skim milk*, everyone. The fat will clog your baby's arteries just like it clogs ours.

Q. What do you think of alternative dairy products compared to cow's milk?

Only soy milk has the same amount of calories as whole milk, but less of those calories come from fat (and 12 to 24 month olds still need the fat). The preferred dairy beverage of choice is whole cow's milk. Here is a comparison:

8 OUNCE SERVING	WHOLE MILK (3.5% FAT)	SKIM MILK (0.1% FAT)	SOY MILK	RICE MILK
Calories	150 calories	80	150	130
Calories from FAT	70	0	35	20
Total fat	8 grams	0	4	2
Sodium	115 mg	125	140	90
Carbohydrate	11 grams	12	22	28
Cholesterol	35 mg	0	0	0
Protein	8 grams	9	7	1
Vitamin A	yes	yes	no	yes
Vitamin C	yes	yes	no	no
Vitamin D	yes	yes	no	yes
Calcium	50%	50%	<10%	50%
Other nutrients			iron	B12

Q. What do you think of organic milk?

It's expensive.

Some families prefer to buy organic, pesticide free products. Others don't. There is no public health group that recommends the use of organic milk over store brand cow's milk. It's your call.

Q. Is it okay to use formula after a year of age?

It is not the appropriate diet for a child over age one. For babies who are failing to thrive, your doctor might recommend a dietary supplement (such as Pediasure, Carnation Instant Breakfast). Using formula for convenience when you are out and about isn't harmful, but is unnecessary. Using formula for nutrition is a waste of money.

Chapter 7

Solids

*"Raising kids is part joy
and part guerilla warfare."
~ Ed Asner*

WHAT'S IN THIS CHAPTER

- ◆ **HOW TO TELL IF YOUR BABY IS READY TO EAT SOLID FOOD**
- ◆ **WHAT IS RICE CEREAL?**
- ◆ **STAGE 1 OR FIRST FOODS**
- ◆ **MAKING YOUR OWN FOOD**
- ◆ **FOOD ALLERGY**
- ◆ **FOOD INTOLERANCE**
- ◆ **THE BIG PICTURE— HOW MUCH TO OFFER AND WHEN**
- ◆ **FOOD LABELING**

This is the chapter you have been waiting for! After months of feeding your baby a liquid diet, you're looking forward to those photos with peas all over your baby's cute little face. And friends and relatives can get into the act of feeding baby too.

You are allowed to read this chapter at any time, but don't put it into action until your baby is at the legal eating age— four months old (or older).

After reading through the general nutrition and liquid nutrition sections already, you know that solid food is the equivalent of *dessert* at four months of age. Solid food becomes a *nutritional supplement* to breast milk or formula at six months of age. It's not until your baby is taking larger amounts of solid foods (seven to nine months of age), that it starts to replace some of the nutrients that liquid nutrition offers.

Before we get going, let's define some baby food lingo:

- ◆ **Stage 1 Food.** The first solid food given to babies. Pureed. Most easily digested, least allergenic. Examples: rice cereal, fruits, vegetable, except for berries and citrus
- ◆ **Stage 2 Food.** More complex to digest, more allergenic solid food. Chunkier texture. Examples: oatmeal cereal, barley cereal, mixed cereal, meats, pastas, dairy, papaya, mango, guava).

◆ **Stage 3 Food.** Most complex solid food. Very chunky. Comparable to table food.

◆ **Finger foods.** Food your baby can feed to himself. Good for independence, fine motor skills. Examples: teething/biter biscuits, small pieces of fruit/vegetables, crackers, pasta wheels, Cheerios, ground meat, canned chicken.

◆ **Table food.** What you eat.

Babies progress through the solid food experience based on three factors:

1. Food allergies. Start with the least allergenic foods first.

2. Oral motor skills. Babies cannot start to eat solid food until they know how to swallow it.

3. Texture complexity. Start with pureed foods, move up to chunks, then pieces. Babies cannot move up to pieces of food until they know how to gum it or chew it before swallowing. Some babies develop preferences for certain textures (or lack of texture).

Q. My mother wants to feed my two-month-old solid foods. I've heard this is a bad idea. Help!

Your mother will tell you that she fed you rice cereal at two months of age and you did fine. Here is your ammunition to keep the baby spoon out of Grandma's hands:

1 STARTING SOLID FOODS WILL **NOT** MAKE YOUR BABY SLEEP THROUGH THE NIGHT. Most babies start sleeping through the night by four months of age. It is not because their tummies are full of rice cereal, but because they are developmentally able to by that age.

2 INTRODUCING SOLID FOODS AT AN EARLY AGE (BEFORE BABIES CAN DIGEST THEM) MAY RESULT IN FOOD ALLERGIES.

3 SOLID FOOD IS SPA CUISINE. As you already know, breast milk and formula are the only items that should be on the menu for babies birth to at least four months. These products contain 50% fat and thus, are loaded with calories (20 calories per oz). Next time you go to the grocery store, do some research in the baby food aisle. Rice cereal has 60 calories per 1/4 cup (when 2 1/2 oz of formula has been mixed with the flakes). A jar (2 1/2 oz) of 'Stage 1' carrots has 25 calories. Your baby would need to eat almost 3/4 cup of cereal or six whole jars of carrots to replace one bottle or breastfeeding session. You'll be lucky if your baby eats two tablespoons of cereal or 1/2 jar (1 oz) of carrots in a feeding session.

4 TELL GRANDMA THAT YOUR DOCTOR TOLD YOU NOT TO START SOLIDS UNTIL AT LEAST FOUR MONTHS OF AGE. Use your doctor as an excuse any time. We don't mind.

Q. My baby is four months old now. How can I tell if he is ready to eat solid foods?

PREEMIES & SOLID FOOD

Because eating solid food requires a certain level of oral motor skill, many premature babies are not ready to eat solid food until their corrected age (based on due date) is at least four months old. Also, preemies tend to need lots of extra calories for catch up growth. Liquid nutrition is a much better source for calories than solid food.

Try it out and see what happens.

From an allergy standpoint, he should be able to tolerate 'Stage 1' foods (see below). It's more a matter of knowing what to do with a bit of food on the tongue (**ORAL MOTOR SKILLS**). Some babies are ready at four months; some aren't ready until six months. Your baby will tell you if he is ready. Try putting a spoonful of rice cereal on his tongue. If he swallows it, he's ready. If he spits it back out at you, put the box away and try again next week. *There is no hurry to start solids.*

BOTTOM LINE: There is a great deal of variability amongst babies (and their doctors) about when they are ready to eat solid food. Solid food before six months of age is really just for fun, anyway.

Q. What is rice cereal?

You will find it in the baby food aisle in a box.

Rice cereal is often the first food a baby eats. You buy it in a box as dry flakes. Mix it with either expressed breast milk or formula (otherwise it tastes like cardboard). Be sure you read the packaging. *Some rice cereal already has formula added.* This can be a problem for a baby with a cow's milk allergy. Make sure the cereal is pretty watery—not the thick texture you would eat. Make about two tablespoons worth. You can always make more.

Offer it as a snack *after* baby has had breast milk or formula. If you try to feed him solid food when he is hungry, you won't be able to shovel it in fast enough. By four months of age, your baby could probably win a chugging contest with the speed he guzzles down 160 calories (eight ounces of liquid).

Try one feeding a day of rice cereal for four days before embarking upon other foods. Cereal should be offered daily because it is a great source of iron. Once your baby is at least six months old, you can experiment with tastier cereals (oatmeal, barley, and other grains).

Q. What other foods should I offer to my four-month-old baby?

Rice cereal and Stage 1 foods are fine for four to six-month olds. Stage 1 foods include carrots, sweet potatoes, mashed potatoes, squash, green beans, peas, bananas, peaches, pears, plums, prunes, and applesauce. All of these foods are pureed.

Q. How often do I introduce a new food?

After your baby has mastered rice cereal, forge ahead and introduce one new Stage 1 food every three to four days. You are introducing foods slowly because you are looking to see if your baby has any food allergies (see a discussion on this topic later in this chapter).

Q. How often do I feed my baby solid foods?

Start with one feeding a day and work up to three feedings a day.

Always feed your baby his breast milk or formula first. Then offer solid food as a between meal snack. Remember, until your baby eats several jars of food, he's drinking his calories. When your baby is only eating rice cereal, one feeding a day is fine. When he has a repertoire of foods, you can feed him three times a day.

Old Wives Tale

Introducing fruits before vegetables will give your baby a sweet tooth.

The truth: Your baby will either like vegetables or not. The order of introduction has nothing to do with it. When your baby is a toddler, he won't eat *anything*.

Q. My five-month old started solids and now his skin is turning yellow—HELP!

You are what you eat!

Babies are often introduced to a series of yellow vegetables (carrots, squash, sweet potatoes). All of these vegetables are rich in Vitamin A (carotene). This vitamin has a pigment that can collect harmlessly on the skin producing a condition called **CAROTINEMIA**. The difference between this condition and jaundice (high bilirubin level) is that jaundiced babies have a yellowing in the whites of their eyes. Sweet potato lovers don't have that. See Baby411.com (click on "Bonus Material") for a great picture.

Q. Can I make my own baby food?

Absolutely. There is nothing special about prepared baby foods, other than being prepared. After six months of age, it's actually preferable to offer food from your table. That way, your baby will get used to your cooking!

DR B'S OPINION:
BABY FOOD COOKBOOKS

I bought a baby food cookbook for my husband, our chef, when our first child was born. (Being in the kitchen actually makes me nervous!) The recipes amused him. The recipe for carrots was: 1. Steam carrots. 2. Puree. 3. Serve.

My advice—don't bother buying a baby food cookbook. Just use a food processor or blender and puree your home cooking. You can pour the food into ice cube trays (perfect serving size) and freeze them. It's easy to thaw out and serve.

Q. What do you think of organic baby food?

It's a lifestyle choice.

As stated before, some parents think this is important. Others don't. There is no consensus in pediatric medicine that recommends organic foods over other prepared baby foods. If you are interested in organic foods, it's much cheaper to prepare your own baby food from organic fruits and vegetables.

All processed Stage 1 foods (Gerber, etc.) are preservative and additive free. The Stage 2 and 3 foods do add other ingredients, so you may want to check the packaging.

Q. How do I know if my baby has a food allergy?

Look for an impressive rash, profuse vomiting, or horrible diarrhea.

Allergic reactions are not subtle. If your baby has a few dots of a rash or a diaper rash, it's not because of the food you just introduced.

Allergic responses occur within minutes or at most four hours after an exposure. A chemical in the body called **HISTAMINE** is released in massive quantities with an allergic reaction. Histamine can cause a tingling or itchy mouth, mouth or lip swelling, shortness of breath, and dramatic diarrhea. You may also see hives (raised borders of red plaques or mosquito bite looking with a circle around it). See our web site at Baby411.com (click on "Bonus Material") for a picture.

The extreme scenario is called an **ANAPHYLACTIC REACTION.** This is when loss of consciousness and airway swelling occurs—obviously, this is life threatening and you need to call 911. This is very unlikely to ever happen, particularly with a Stage 1 food— they are extremely well tolerated.

Infants who are more at risk for food allergies are those with parents who are very allergic. These babies' risk of having a food allergy may be as high as 20%. Compare that to the general population, which has about a 2% risk of food allergies. Children who have asthma have a higher risk of having a more serious allergic reaction if they have a food allergy.

BEHIND THE SCENES: WHAT IS "ORGANIC"?

The USDA has recently regulated the labeling of all of these "natural" products so that people know how natural a product really is. Organic products are meats, poultry, eggs, and dairy products made from animals that did not receive antibiotics or growth hormones or fruits and vegetables grown without pesticides or petroleum based fertilizers. Organic farms are certified by a government inspector. Here are the rules:

◆ *100% Organic* must have a USDA seal on it.
◆ *Organic* is made of 95-100% organic ingredients.
◆ *Made with Organic Ingredients* is made of at least 70% organic ingredients.

Q. What is a food intolerance?

This term refers to an adverse reaction to a food or food product, not an allergic response.

Allergic reactions produce histamine. Food intolerances do not. If a baby has a food intolerance, he might have stomach cramps or bloating. You'll probably avoid that food in the future, but he'll never have a life-threatening (anaphylactic) reaction if he is exposed to it.

(Example: An adult with a lactose intolerance gets diarrhea when he drinks milk, but doesn't get hives).

Q. What foods are more likely to cause food allergies?

Here is the Top 10 List, from the home office in Buda, Texas:

1. *PEANUTS/Peanut Butter.* We'll discuss this in detail next.
2. Egg whites. (the *white* part—egg protein is the problem)
3. Shellfish (crab, lobster, shrimp, scallops, oysters)
4. Fish.
5. Tree nuts (walnuts, cashews, etc).
   These will be referred to as the "Top Five"
6. Wheat
7. Cow's Milk
8. Soy
9. Citrus fruits, berries
10. Cocoa

Food Allergies Stats

◆ 2.5% of newborns have a cow's milk allergy. 80% outgrow it by age five.
◆ 1.5% of children are allergic to eggs.
◆ 0.5% of children are allergic to peanuts, but of those with the allergy, only 20% will outgrow it.
◆ Most food allergies occur in the first three years of life (6% of all children).
◆ Only 2% of adults have a food allergy, and of those, 50% are allergic to either peanuts or tree nuts.[1]

Q. Can my baby have a milk protein allergy if I am breastfeeding?

Yes. Food proteins are passed into mom's breast milk, and cow's milk protein is no exception.

Babies with a milk protein allergy may have blood streaked poops, diarrhea, and poor growth. The problem may be seen in the first few weeks of life with a baby fed cow's milk based formula. In breastfed babies, it may not be a problem for a few months.

Q. So when can I feed my child a peanut butter and jelly sandwich?

Okay, let's talk peanuts and peanut butter.

Here's the scary fact about peanut allergy: it is life threatening. That's right, kids with a peanut allergy can die from ingesting less than one peanut. Another scary fact: only 20% of kids who have peanut allergy will outgrow it!

Here is the party line from the American Academy of Pediatrics on peanuts: for families with NO history of food allergies, the AAP suggests your baby can eat peanuts or peanut butter after one year of age. For "high risk" families (that is, those with a history of food allergies), the AAP says you should avoid the top allergy foods (including peanuts) until age three. And mothers of those families should avoid these foods while nursing.

However, you may find some variability of opinions amongst pediatricians and allergists. After having personal experience with this one, we'd suggest ALL children avoid peanuts and peanut butter until after age THREE—or longer if possible. Since peanut allergies are life-long and so dangerous, it doesn't pay to roll the dice on this one. And studies show that when you introduce peanuts LATER in life (like after age three), there is a much lower chance of developing this allergy.

What about avoiding TRACE amounts of peanuts? You probably don't have to worry. Some products have warnings that they MAY contain trace amounts of peanuts because they are processed on machines that also process products made with peanuts. Bottom line: While you should stay away from peanuts and peanut butter until age three, eating food that MIGHT contain a trace of peanuts is kosher after a year of age.

HIDDEN SOURCES FOR DANGEROUS FOODS.

So, you know to avoid peanuts for your child until they are three years of age (or even better, five years of age). And obviously, that means no peanut butter or peanut M&M's. But are you aware of how peanuts and other potential food allergy dangers are hidden in other products? Candy and cookies (as well as fresh baked goods) are a flashpoint—undeclared soy, wheat, nuts and eggs are common in baked goods. Even if you try to read the label, you can miss mention of a product when it is in tiny six point type. Finally, consider the stealth uses of dangerous foods—did you know that some Chinese restaurants seal their egg roll wrappers with peanut butter? Ethnic food restaurants can be a landmine of potential problems, especially when servers may not even know the ingredients of food on the menu.

Now, we're not trying to make you overly paranoid here. But as a parent, you have to be vigilant—especially when your baby gets older and goes over to friends' or relatives' homes. If in doubt ask to speak to the manager or chef and don't forget to warn all your friends and relatives every time you drop your child off. In fact, it may be a good idea to get a MedicAlert bracelet for your child when he gets older. It reminds him of his allergy as well as the adults he's with for the day.

For more information, check out the web. Food Allergy Network's website (FoodAllergy.org) has a brochure you can download called "Preventing or Delaying the Onset of Food Allergies in Infants." It also provides an FAQ, alerts and school resources.

Feedback from the Real World: Ben's Story

Want to hear something really scary? How about the story of Ben, my son, and how we discovered his life threatening peanut allergy. When Ben was one year of age, we decided we could add peanut butter into his life. Being a confessed peanut nut (I've searched the Southern U.S. for the best peanut butter pie–haven't found it yet but I'm still looking), we thought this would be a tasty addition to his diet. Besides, most parenting books say you can add peanut butter at age one and we had no history of severe food allergies in our families.

Shazam! He immediately swelled up like a tomato. This was our first experience with an allergic reaction. Hives hit him like a ton of bricks. We practically threw him in the car and raced down the mountain (yes, we did live in the mountains at the time) to the doctor's office. There we were informed that he was allergic to peanuts. After treating the hives, the doctor mentioned that this would probably be for life and the next time could be life-threatening anaphylaxis (after eating one peanut he could stop breathing and die). We next visited with an allergist who confirmed the diagnosis with a "peanut challenge" test.

So what now? Well, we see the allergist once a year. And we have to carry an epinephrine injectible pen with us everywhere we go. In fact, there is an Epi-Pen at school, at Nanna's, at our house and in my purse. We had to teach Ben to read labels on food, never share at school and never, ever take food samples without first checking with us (Sam's Club is a nightmare sometimes!). It's no wonder a recent study showed that kids with peanut allergy suffer from more stress than kids with diabetes.

The good news: scientists are developing a vaccine (TNX-901) that may someday save my son and other peanut allergic kids from an accidental ingestion. But until then we're amazingly careful about everything that goes in his mouth. My wish, however is that no other parent have to deal with this scary allergy. That's why my recommendation, as discussed above, is to avoid nuts altogether until your child is at least three years old. And longer if you can. It's worth waiting a bit for that PBJ experience.

Helpful Hints

1. If your baby does have a food allergy, get educated about hidden sources of the problem food.

2. Know how to read an ingredient label. Products containing milk include: casein, sodium caseinate, whey, or lactoglobulin.

3. Be a detective. Deli slicers are often contaminated with milk because both cheese and lunchmeat are sliced on the same machine. Many candies without peanuts are processed in the same location as those with peanuts.

FOOD ALLERGIES AND ECZEMA

Food allergies are one of the key precipitating factors for eczema. 37% of kids with severe eczema have a food allergy. The eczema improves when the food offender is eliminated from the diet. The vast majority of food offenders are the Top 8 foods on the list earlier.[2]

Q. What is the best way to avoid food allergies?

Good question. Introduce more highly allergenic foods later.

There is a lot of research to prove that early exposure to these risky foods lead to more food allergies—some that can last a lifetime.

Since human milk is made for human babies, it is the least likely to be problematic for a baby. Babies can have food allergies to both cows' milk protein and soymilk protein.

Recently, there has been some research done on nursing mothers eliminating highly allergenic foods from their diets to prevent "sensitizing" their infants. The science is: the breakdown products of these foods end up in breast milk. So far, the jury is still out. For families with a *significant* history of food allergies, it may be a good idea for breastfeeding moms to avoid peanuts and tree nuts in their diet.[3] If there is no family history of food allergies but allergy symptoms are discovered in the baby, removal of milk, eggs, fish, peanuts, and tree nuts are suggested.

Q. Okay, so when can I try these high allergy foods with my baby?

For *low risk* babies, the Top 5 list (peanuts, egg whites, shellfish, fish, treenuts) can be introduced after the first birthday—preferably after three years. If you can wait on peanuts later than three years, even better. For *high risk* babies (family history of food allergies, asthma), wait on the Top 5 until three years old.

BOTTOM LINE

For high-risk allergy families, the AAP recommends:
1. Breastfeeding to reduce the incidence of food allergies.
2. Breastfeeding mothers avoid peanuts and tree nuts while nursing.
3. Introduction of solid food after six months of age.
4. Introduction of peanuts, tree nuts, and seafood after three years of age.
5. Introduction of eggs at two years of age.
6. Introduction of milk and soy products at one year of age.[4]

Q. What is a good reference if my baby does develop a food allergy?

Check out the Food Allergy Network at www.foodallergy.org. Or call, (800) 929-4040.

How Food Allergies are Tested

There are four basic ways to test for a food allergy, but be aware that nothing is perfect science:

1 **ELIMINATION DIET.** Eliminate the food from the diet for three to six weeks; see if there is an improvement in symptoms (i.e. eczema, diarrhea, etc).

2 **SKIN TESTING.** Skin prick tests detect a true allergic response (see IgE below) to a food. If skin testing shows an allergic response, RAST testing can be done for confirmation.

3 **CAP-RAST** TEST. Blood test detects an elevation of the body's IgE antibodies (an allergic response chemical). RAST testing is useful because it can identify some food allergies. However, not all food allergies cause an elevation of IgE levels. The newer CAP-RAST tests have been shown to be 95% predictive in food allergies for milk, eggs, peanuts, and fish.

4 **FOOD CHALLENGE.** When a person is known to be allergic to a certain food, periodic (annual) RAST testing may show a decrease in allergy response levels. A person can try a certain food again in a controlled medical setting to see if he is still allergic to a particular food. (This does not mean at your kitchen table).[5]

Can you outgrow a food allergy?

Most kids outgrow food allergies to milk, eggs, soy, and wheat by the time they are five years old. Over 50% of kids will outgrow their food allergies by the age of one. The foods that tend to be lifelong problems are peanuts, tree nuts, fish, and shellfish.[6]

Q. Are there any other foods my baby shouldn't eat?

Yes. Here are three:

◆ *Honey*: Wait on honey until your child is one year old. Honey contains *clostridium botulinum* spores that can cause botulism in an infant. (Infant's digestive systems are relatively sterile compared to ours and can't kill the spores).

◆ *Choking Hazards:* Raw carrots, celery, popcorn, potato chips, nuts, hard candy, hard meat, fruits with seeds, raisins, hotdogs, and grapes (unless cut lengthwise). Wait on these foods until your child is really good at chewing (two to three years).

◆ *Artificial sweeteners:* There is no official party line on this one, but there is no reason to offer these products to babies.

Q. My baby is six months old now. What can he eat?

Start at Stage 1 foods. Then advance to Stage 2-3 Foods and start feeding him off of your plate.

At this point, you may have tried rice cereal, fruits, and vegetables. If your child is doing well, expand his diet. Keep in mind, it's also okay if you are just getting started with solids.

Now is the time to start good eating habits, and give your baby a feeling that mealtime is enjoyable. (That means, don't worry about making a mess.) Solid foods should still be a supplement and not replacement of calories. Your baby will tell you he is done by turning his head, spitting out his food, and/or throwing it on the floor.

As far as food allergies, your baby should be ready to tolerate most foods now. Stage 2 and 3 foods are fine from an allergy standpoint. However, your baby may not like the textures. They are chunkier than the Stage 1 pureed foods. These foods contain complex grains (wheat, barley, oats), dairy, and meats. Remember: Avoid egg whites, peanuts/peanut containing products, fish/shellfish, and nuts (the top five). Everything else is fair game.

So, if the food on your plate looks good to your baby, let him try it. This includes a variety of safe ethnic foods. You will know he is ready because he will be watching every spoonful that goes into your mouth. Don't worry about herbs and spices you use in seasoning. Your baby needs to get used to your methods of food preparation.

Some fun food ideas include: oatmeal or mixed cereal, whole milk yogurt, cottage cheese, cream cheese, wheat crackers, and cooked egg yolk (the yellow part).

Helpful Hint

Remember to offer cereal daily. Babies older than six months old need to have a source of iron in their diets. Check the previous chapter for a list of foods that are good sources of iron.

Q. My baby is nine months old. What can he eat now?

Almost anything (except the Top 5). This includes 'finger foods'.

Your baby is ready to feed himself when he uses his index finger and thumb to grasp things, otherwise known as the *pincer grasp.* Finger foods include: Cheerios, pieces of banana, pieces of pears or peaches, small pieces of cheese, whole wheat toast, soft meats (my personal favorite is the chicken in a can—it's next to the canned tuna fish at the store), graham crackers, and teething biscuits. And you thought solids were messy before...do not make a big deal out of it—just clean it up. Kids sense frustration and will have mealtime anxiety if you make it an issue. Your child can be toothless and enjoy solid and finger foods. They can gum just about anything.

As far as amounts, your baby should be taking enough solid food at a sitting to cut back on the volume of liquid nutrition. He'll take one to two jars of Stage 2 foods or two servings (three oz) of table food. (See the "Big Picture" table at the end of this chapter.

Helpful Hint

Now is a good time to take that CPR class you have been meaning to take. It's unlikely you will ever need to utilize your skills, but it s always good to be prepared.

CELIAC DISEASE: A RARE CAUSE OF CHRONIC DIARRHEA

As babies start to eat cereal grains (wheat, barley, and oats), a rare disorder can become apparent—celiac disease. Other names for this disorder are celiac sprue or gluten sensitive enteropathy. There is a particular protein called "gluten" found in all of these grains. People with Celiac Disease form an immune response to the protein gluten that causing injury to the intestinal lining. The result: chronic diarrhea, failure to thrive, vomiting, and bloating to name a few symptoms. This is a genetic disorder; so more than one family member may have this problem.

If you have a family member with this disorder, or notice a change in your baby after introducing these foods, check in with your baby's doctor.

Q. My nine month old refuses any food that has a texture to it. Help!

This is called **TEXTURE AVERSION.**

Some babies prefer smooth, pureed foods well into their second year of life. If he is otherwise developing normally, I'd consider your baby a little eccentric, but normal.

Babies with texture aversions, adverse reactions to sensory stimulation, and developmental delays may be worth talking to your doctor about (see **PERVASIVE DEVELOPMENTAL DISORDER, SENSORY INTEGRATION DISORDER**).

Q. What are the food expectations for a one-year old?

To join the family at the dinner table, and eat what the family is eating.

The goal is for your child to graduate to table foods (what you eat) at one year of age. He should eat three meals and two snacks per day. He should drink whole milk (16 oz or dairy serving equivalent), juice (less 8 oz per day), and water out of a cup. Say goodbye to bottles.

Q. Is it okay for my one year old to eat fish?

Yes. The few restrictions are: shark, swordfish, king mackerel, and tilefish. These fish contain high levels of mercury, so the Food and Drug Administration has recommended that these be avoided for young children. It is also recommended to contact your local health department about any warnings on fish caught in area lakes. Canned tuna is okay in small amounts (less than 12 ounces/week).

The Big Picture For Liquid And Solid Nutrition

Age	Liquid Nutrition	Solid Nutrition	Solid serving size
4-6 months	32-40 oz **5-6 meals**	Maybe cereal* Maybe fruit/vegetable* **1-2 feedings/day**	2-4 Tbsp (1-2 oz) 1-2 items at each meal **0-8 oz/day** Pureed foods.
6-9 months	24-32 oz **4-5 meals**	Cereal Fruit/vegetable Meat Grains Dairy (limited amt) **3 feedings/day**	2-4 Tbsp (1-2 oz) Two or three items at each meal, or a whole Stage 2 jar. **8-14 oz/day** More textures.
9-12 months	20-30 oz **3-4 meals**	All of the above Table foods **3 meals/day**	3-4 Tbsp (2 oz) Three items at each meal, or a Stage 3 jar. **10-15 oz/day** Bite size pieces.

*Solid nutrition from 4-6 months is completely optional.

Key Points To Remember

◆ Prepared baby food jars: Stage 1= 2oz serving. Stage 2 = 4 oz serving. Stage 3 = 5-6 oz serving.

◆ Remember that breast milk and formula have 20 calories per ounce. A 2.5 oz jar of Stage 1 carrots has 25 calories.

◆ Do not reduce the amount of liquid nutrition until your baby eats enough solid food to replace the calories. This gradual taper begins somewhere between six and nine months. This is when a solid meal is at least a four to six ounce serving.

◆ Every baby is different!

Notes

Chapter 8

The Other End

"Gil, why are you standing there?"
"I'm waiting for her head to spin around."
~ Parenthood

This chapter addresses a subject taboo at most dinner tables. We are going to have a candid discussion about poop (as well as gas, burps, pee and spit up, too). Why spend a whole chapter on poop? Let's be honest—you'll have LOTS of questions about this subject. And you'll be looking at lots of it too! The average baby goes through 2300 diaper changes in the first year alone.

Parents have concerns because baby poop does not look like theirs. If it does, your baby has a problem. And as you might imagine, changing at least eight diapers a day also results in a pre-occupation with diaper contents.

Before we go too far, it's a good idea to go over the terminology we'll be using in this chapter:

◆ **Stool.** Your digested food garbage that is eliminated through your anus. Stool also has bacteria germs in it (these germs help us digest our food). Just so we're on the same page—it's also known as poo, poop, feces, caca, Number 2, bowel movement... for this book, we will use the term **POOP**.

◆ **Urine.** The garbage that your kidneys clean out of your bloodstream that is eliminated through your urethra (the hole in the penis or the hole above the vagina). Urine is sterile (germ

free). Otherwise known as pee, pee-pee, wee-wee, wet diapers...for this book, we will use the term **PEE**.

◆ **Gas.** The air inside the intestines that is a by-product of the food
transit through it. When babies eat 24 hours a day, their intestines
move 24 hours a day, *and* make a whole lot of gas. The gas slows
down when the intestinal transit slows down, around six weeks.

◆ **Burps.** The air that gets swallowed comes back out of the esophagus. Because babies exclusively suck and swallow their nutrition for
the first four months of life, burping feels good after a big meal.
Some babies suck very aggressively and ingest a large air bubble.
When this air bubble comes up, often so does the whole meal.

◆ **Hiccups.** This is caused by a muscle spasm of the diaphragm (the
muscle that divides the chest and abdomen). All babies have
some hiccups, a few have a lot of hiccups. This sometimes is a sign
of sensory overload (i.e. over stimulation). There is nothing wrong
with your baby. You may just want to soothe him.

Newborn Poop

Q. What should my newborn's poop look like?

Black tar.

In the first 24 hours of life, your baby should pass a poop called **MECO-
NIUM**. This has the color and texture of black tar. It looks like this because
the baby has swallowed some blood while inside the womb. The black tar
contains some digested blood. (Good to remember if you ever see poop
that looks like this again from your baby or a family member).

As your baby starts to eat breast milk or formula, the poop will change
color and texture. This happens on about the fourth day of life. (Remember,
they don't eat much the first few days.)

Q. My newborn is breastfed. What should his poop look like?

Grey Poupon (or crab mustard, as my Baltimore friends would say).

Breast milk poop is very watery. In fact, many parents worry that their
baby is having diarrhea if they have never changed a breast-fed baby's
diaper before. It's watery because the breast milk is so easily digested, it
goes right through the intestines and leaves very little solid garbage to be
pooped out.

Parents often wonder how they will know when their baby is having
diarrhea. The answer is the *frequency* of poop increases. Breastfed babies
often poop with every feeding for the first six weeks of life. Some babies
will poop less frequently than that, sometimes only once every few days.
Do not worry unless the consistency of the poop looks like yours.

The color is often yellow. But, ***any shade of yellow, green or brown is
okay.*** Florescent green is okay too.

DR B'S OPINION: GREEN POOP AND FOREMILK?

Some mothers hear that green poop is a sign that their baby is only getting the foremilk and not the richer hindmilk. (For a discussion of foremilk and hindmilk, see Chapter 6, "Liquids"). I think the way to tell if a baby is getting hindmilk is to look at the feeding patterns and growth charts, not the poop color. Babies who get foremilk only tend to be snackers who eat frequently (they don't fill up as well). They also gain less weight if they miss out on the fatty hindmilk.

Q. My newborn is formula fed. What should his poop look like?

Strained peas.

Formula poops tend to be greener than breast milk poop. But, as we mentioned, any shade of yellow, green or brown is okay.

Formula poops are also thicker and pastier than breast milk poop. It takes longer to digest formula in the intestines, so more water is absorbed before the "final product" comes out.

Q. How often do formula fed babies poop?

Formula fed babies poop less often because the "transit time" through the intestines is longer. These babies may poop three or four times per day or once every couple of days. The frequency slows down even more at six weeks of life.

RED FLAGS: Worrisome Poop

If you see/note any of these, call your doctor immediately:

1. Your baby doesn't poop in the first 24 hours of life (see **MECONIUM PLUG OR ILEUS**).
2. Your baby's poops look bloody, tarry, or mixed with mucus (see **BLOOD IN STOOL**)
3. Your baby's poop looks like yours. (see **CONSTIPATION**)
4. Your baby has a stomachache and poop that looks like grape jelly (see **INTUSSUSCEPTION**)
5. Your baby's frequency of poop doubles or triples (see **DIARRHEA/GASTROENTERITIS**)

Q. My baby grunts and his face turns red when he poops. Is this normal?

Yes.

Try lying down and pooping some time. See what your face looks like. This does NOT mean your child is constipated. There is actually a term for this phenomenon—The Grunting Baby Syndrome.

Q. My three-week-old usually poops with every feeding. Now, he hasn't gone in 24 hours. Is he constipated?

No.

Please read this carefully. Constipation is diagnosed by the FIRMNESS of the poop, NOT THE FREQUENCY (or infrequency) of pooping. *Concerned parents often think their baby is constipated when they are not.* Newborns to six week olds usually poop several times a day. Occasionally, though, they may take a day off. That's when you call the doctor in a state of panic. The answer is, "Be prepared for the Mother Load." Some babies may poop once or twice a week. That's fine, as long as it is soft when it comes out.

Your baby is constipated when the poop looks like logs, rock balls, marbles, or deer pellets. See below for tricks of the trade for relieving constipation.

Old Wives Tale
The iron in formula causes constipation. My mother-in-law told me to switch to a low iron formula.

The truth: There isn't enough iron in formula to make a baby constipated. And without the iron, your baby won't grow. Don't switch formula. Try some of the tricks below and read the formula section in the Chapter 6, "Liquids."

Trade Secrets For Relieving Constipation

1 **RECTAL THERMOMETER TRICK.** If your baby is straining and not having any success, insert a rectal thermometer in his anus for about a minute. Trust me—this is the most dispensed phone advice by any pediatrician's office. You can read the exact details on how to insert a rectal thermometer in Chapter 15, "First Aid." This usually provides the inspiration your baby needs to get moving. (And no, they don't mind having it done like you would!)

2 **PRUNE JUICE COCKTAIL.** If your baby is regularly irregular, he may need some extra fiber to move things along. Try one teaspoon of prune juice per feeding (mixed in formula or given separately to breast fed babies) until you get the desired consistency of poop. You can adjust the volume to what your baby needs (that is, anywhere from one to five teaspoons a day). Prune juice has both fiber and sorbitol (sugar) that pull water into the poop to make it softer.

Hint: Buy store brand prune juice—not the stuff in the baby food section. Baby prune juice is mixed with apple juice and is very expensive by comparison.

3 **KARO COCKTAIL.** Some pediatricians recommend using karo syrup instead of prune juice to pull water into the stool. I don't use it because there are some anecdotal reports of botulism spores in karo syrup (similar to the concerns we discussed about honey in the feeding chapter).

4 **WASH IT OUT.** Sometimes, babies need drink a little water to soften up the poop. I wouldn't offer more than an ounce or two, though, to an infant under six months of age.

5 THE GLYCERINE BULLET. For immediate relief, use a glycerine suppository to get dramatic results. These suppositories can be purchased without a prescription at the grocery store or pharmacy. Frequently, the label will read 'infant' suppository. The suppository looks like a bullet made of soap. Insert it directly into the anus. It dissolves as you push it in. Be prepared for the fireworks.

If these tricks don't work, call your doctor. Pediatricians always have a few more tricks like this up their sleeves!

Q. My six-week old breastfed baby used to poop at every feeding. Now she only goes once a day. Should I be worried?

No. This is normal and you should be thankful.

Babies are born with intestines that work 24/7. They work that way to keep the nutritional juices flowing. By six weeks of age, things start to slow down. This is called slower intestinal transit time. Mature breast milk is also mostly digested, so there is very little garbage to eliminate.

As long as the poop is soft, your baby is fine. So be grateful you have fewer diaper changes!

Solid Food Equals Solid Poop: Older Babies

Q. My four month old started rice cereal and now she is constipated. Help!

Rice cereal has this effect on some babies. Offer only one feeding a day of rice cereal and introduce higher fiber foods sooner rather than later. Pureed prunes are a Stage 1 food and add both fiber and taste to rice cereal. See below for more fun fiber foods.

Q. How much fiber does my child need to eat?

The equation is Age in Years + 5 = Total daily fiber requirement (in grams)

This equation doesn't apply for babies under a year of age. Breast milk contains no dietary fiber, so there are no requirements for babies from birth to six months. From six to twelve months, fiber is introduced in the diet via solid foods. The daily needs vary by individual and there are actually no established guidelines. But studies have shown that children who are constipated eat significantly less fiber than their "regular" peers.[1]

Reality Check

You, Mom and Dad, need 25 to 30 grams of fiber per day no matter how old you are. Most Americans do not eat enough fiber. The way to get your child to eat fiber is for you to have it in the house and eat it yourself. If you don't realize this yet, your baby is watching every move you make!

Q. Which foods are high in fiber and more importantly, which ones will my child eat?

This is my favorite fiber food list. Some foods will be off limits under a year of age and are designated with an asterisk (*)—these are choking hazards. Kids usually find the bread/grain category the most appealing. Take careful note of serving sizes. The sizes listed below are sometimes more than even a one year old will eat. We've noted in bold print the highest fiber foods (or the ones that pack the biggest fiber punch).

PRODUCT	SERVING SIZE	FIBER GRAMS/SERVING
Bread/Grains		
Whole wheat Bread	1 slice	2 grams
White Bread	1 slice	0
Pepperidge Farm HeartyWheat Crackers	3 crackers	1 gram
El Galindo Wheat Tortillas	**1 tortilla**	**9 grams**
Hodgson Mill Whole-wheat pasta	2 oz.	6 grams
Brown Rice	1/4 cup	0.9 grams
Cereal		
Baby Rice	1/4 cup	0
Baby Oatmeal	1/4 cup	1 gram
Baby Mixed	1/4 cup	0
Cheerios	1/2 cup	1.5 grams
Quaker Oat Bran	1/2 cup	2.4 grams
Quaker Oatmeal Squares	1/2 cup	2.5 grams
Kellogg's Nutragrain bars	1 bar	1 gram
Wheat germ	**1 Tbsp**	**1 gram**

(I like wheat germ because you can sneak it into food and your child might not even notice)

Fruit (raw)

Note: The peel is often the part of the fruit that contains the fiber. Since most kids hate the peels, the fiber ends up in the garbage disposal and not in your child.

Apple (with peel)	1/2 medium	1.8 grams
Apricots	1/4 cup	0.8 grams
Banana	1 whole	2.7 grams
Blackberries	1/4 cup	1.8 grams
Dried Cranberries*	1/4 cup	1.5 grams
Grapefruit	1/4	1 gram
Grapes	1/2 cup	0.5 grams
Orange	1/2	1.5 grams
Pear (with peel)	1/2	2.1 grams
Prunes	**1/4 cup**	**3.5 grams**
Raisins*	1/4 cup	2 grams
Raspberries	1/4 cup	2 grams
Strawberries	1/4 cup	0.8 grams
Watermelon	1/2 slice	0.5 gram

PRODUCT	SERVING SIZE	FIBER GRAMS/SERVING
Vegetables (Usually unpopular with children, however.)		
Broccoli	1/4 cup	1.4 grams
Corn	1/4 cup	1 grams
Green beans	1/4 cup	0.7 grams
Green peas	1/4 cup	2.2 grams
Lima beans	1/4 cup	3 grams
Pinto beans	1/4 cup	3.7 grams
Refried Beans	**1/4 cup**	**3 grams**
Squash (baked)	1/4 cup	2 grams

Q. Now that my nine month old eats a large amount of solid food, what should his poop look like?

Soft and solid.

The more your baby eats like you do, the more his poop will look like yours. It should always be easy for your baby to pass. It has a cow patty appearance when your baby sits on it after he poops.

By the way, some foods don't get completely digested as they pass through the intestines. It's normal to recognize last night's corn, carrots, etc. in your child's poop.

RED FLAGS: Worrisome Poops For Older Babies

1. **Streaks of blood.** If the streak is on a hard, firm poop, it's probably due to a tear in the anus as the poop was passed. Worth checking out, though.
2. **Streaks of blood/mucus.** More concerning for infection, particularly if poop is loose/diarrhea. Be prepared for a homework assignment (providing your doctor with a fresh poop specimen). This can also be a sign of a food allergy.
3. **Clay (white) colored poop.** Also known as **ACHOLIC STOOL.** This can occur in conjunction with a stomach virus. But, worth checking out with the doctor
4. **Looks like meconium again.** Black, tarry poop can be a sign of bleeding in the upper part of the intestinal tract (because the blood has had time to get digested). This may indicate irritation and inflammation in the intestines. Your doctor will do a test to check for blood in the poop.
5. **Grape Jelly poop.** The doctor term for this is actually "currant jelly stool". This is a medical emergency. It is a sign of **INTUSSUS-CEPTION** where the intestines have kinked.
6. **Bulky, REALLY stinky, greasy, floating poops.** This may indicate difficulty with absorption (see **MALABSORPTION**).

Helpful Hint
Pepto Bismol makes poop look black like meconium. Pepto Bismol is *not* currently recommended for infants. Just thought you'd be interested for your own sake.

Q. My baby just had a BLUE poop. Help!

Your baby is not an alien. It's either natural or artificial food coloring.

To the best of my knowledge, blue poop is never a sign of illness. Blue colored kid juices and kid yogurts (Hi-C) are often the culprits.

Beets cause a dramatic red hue in both poop and pee.

Q. I am interested in toilet training my baby. Is it too early to think about this now?

Yes. Your baby will be in diapers for a long time.

Being toilet trained is a developmental milestone, just like learning to talk and walk. Milestones can be encouraged, but the child has to achieve it on his own. Your child needs to be able to sense the urge to pee and poop (not just after he has gone). His only incentive to be toilet trained is the desire to be clean (regardless of how many toys you buy him). If he runs around in a poopie diaper and could care less, he is miles away from this milestone.

Girls usually train around 2 1/2 years of age. Boys train around 3 or 3 1/2 years. There is no need to purchase a potty seat any time soon. All it will do is collect dust in your bathroom. For more information on this subject, look on our web page (www.Baby411.com) for details about our other new book, *Toddler 411.*

Spit Up, Regurgitation, And Vomit

Q. My newborn spits up all the time. Should I be worried?

No. Most babies spit up after meals. They are born with a loose muscle between the esophagus (swallowing tube) and the stomach. This muscle, called the gastroesophageal sphincter, will tighten up by about six months of age. Until then, liquids travel down into the stomach. Then some will return into the esophagus and mouth. By definition, most babies have **GASTROESOPHAGEAL REFLUX (OR ACID REFLUX, GER)**. They spit up effortlessly and with small volumes.

RED FLAGS: When to worry about acid reflux

1. If your baby spits up large volumes consistently, he won't gain weight (see **GER TREATMENT**).
2. If your baby cries or arches after feeding, with or without spitting up. The stomach acid is irritating his esophagus. (See **GER TREATMENT**).
3. If your baby has Exorcist-style, projectile vomiting after every meal, call your doctor immediately. (see **PYLORIC STENOSIS**).

Q. My baby is four-months old now and is spitting up more than he did when he was younger. Should I be worried?

No.

It takes six months for the sphincter muscle to tighten up. As your baby takes larger volumes of breast milk/formula, larger volumes will come up. Hence, it gives the appearance that your baby's reflux is getting worse instead of better.

Q. Okay, my baby is nine-months old and still spitting up. Should I be worried?

No. You're just at the end of the bell curve. Most babies will have graduated from spitting up by six months, but there are a few stragglers.

Q. How can I tell if my baby is suffering from acid/gastroesophageal reflux?

Everyone is usually miserable from this. Your doctor can help you make the diagnosis on this one.

This is usually the problem behind fussy, "colicky" infants. Most parents are convinced that their infant either has horrible gas pains, a milk allergy, or colic. They also think that they are inadequate as parents because their baby is always fussy and they haven't figured out how to make them feel better. Some adventurous parents will unsuccessfully try Mylicon (an over-the-counter medicine which makes big gas bubbles into little gas bubbles) drops, switching formulas, or eliminating dairy from breastfeeding Mom's diet before scheduling an appointment with their doctor.

How do we make the diagnosis? We look at the time the fussiness occurs, and what seems to make it worse. *The first rule: babies with reflux don't always spit up–(spitters are really easy to diagnose).* Some babies experience heartburn when the stomach acid comes up into the esophagus with the milk. If it doesn't make it all the way up to the mouth, you won't see it. Babies with heartburn often cry during and shortly after feedings. They can also cry when lying down (for example, on the changing table) because this lets the acid to come up. They may try to arch their backs or thrust their heads back to alleviate the pain. This happens around the clock, making a very unhappy baby.

Colic is ruled out by the frequency of the behaviors. Babies with colic are also unhappy. However, they are only unhappy for three hours a day (say, around 5pm to 8pm). Colic starts at three weeks of age and lasts until three months of age. If your baby has been fussy since two weeks of age and is always fussy, it's probably not colic and most likely acid reflux. (See the next chapter on sleep for more about colic).

Milk allergy or intolerance is ruled out by exploring some details about baby's poop. A true milk allergy causes mucus and/or blood in loose poop. If you have a fussy baby with normal poop, the food is not the problem. A therapeutic trial of changing formula or Mom's dairy elimination will not improve a reflux baby's symptoms.

THE BOTTOM LINE

Most babies outgrow their symptoms of acid reflux when the esophagus muscle tightens up. For many babies, this is around six months of age. A few babies will continue to have problems up to their first birthdays.

TRICKS OF THE TRADE TO TREAT ACID REFLUX

If your baby is uncomfortable from the heartburn associated with acid reflux, or is not gaining weight, there are many options to reduce the severity of the symptoms. Start by using the following tricks at home. If that doesn't work, consider a medication (which will require a prescription).

1. Keep your baby upright for 20 minutes after feedings. This lets the food travel out of the stomach into the small intestine before moving baby around.

2. Offer smaller volumes of feedings more frequently. Babies often figure this out themselves. They have more discomfort with large meals, so they learn to become snackers. It's not great for parents' schedules, but is more comfortable for baby.

3. For infants under three months of age: let your baby sleep in his car seat. Keeping the head upright 30 degrees keeps food going downwards instead of upwards. For infants over three months of age, you can prop up the crib mattress with a purchased wedge or pillow UNDER the mattress. It's not terribly effective, though, because many babies roll all over their crib.

4. For formula fed or expressed breast milk babies: Add one teaspoon of rice cereal to each bottle (or use Enfamil AR—see Chapter 6, "Liquids" chapter). Thicker milk is heavier and stays down better. You will see the same effect with solid food.

5. Medications. Babies use the same antacids as adults. Many products are over the counter for adults, but are by prescription-only for kids. Some products are not approved by the FDA for use in children, but are routinely used by both pediatric gastroenterologists and pediatricians. The options are listed below. (For details, see Appendix A on mediciations.)

- Zantac (Ranitidine)
- Prilosec (Omeprazole)
- Prevacid (Lansoprazole)
- Reglan (Metoclopramide)
- Tagamet (Cimetidine)

If you reach the point that your baby needs medication, he likely has a pretty irritated esophagus lining from constant stomach acid burns. The medication prevents further insults, but it takes at least a week for the irritation to heal. So, don't expect a miraculous change in your baby's behavior after just one dose of medicine. Give the medicine for a week, then see if it is working.

Parents are often leery of giving medication on a daily basis to their babies. Understandable. However, these medications are safe to use daily, as a general rule. Once your baby outgrows the problem (about six months old), the medicine is no longer needed.

Reality Check

Your baby does not have acid reflux because your Great Uncle Harry has acid reflux. Nor will your baby develop a hiatal hernia because of acid reflux. The acid reflux that adults suffer from has the same symptoms, but for different reasons. Your baby has acid reflux because he is a baby.

Q. Occasionally, my baby will throw up his whole feeding. Should I worry?

No.

When babies eat aggressively, they suck in a lot of air. When that big air bubble comes back up with burping, often the whole feeding does too. Unlike adults, babies often throw up and then want to eat again.

The only time to worry is when the whole feeding gets thrown up at *every* feeding. This is a red flag for pyloric stenosis. This is a medical emergency caused by a narrowing of the muscle between the stomach and small intestine. It usually occurs at six to eight weeks of age because the muscle seems to narrow over time.

 ### RED FLAGS: Vomiting

1. Vomiting Bile. Bile is a fluorescent green/yellow color that can indicate a blockage in the intestines. It is especially worrisome if associated with stomachache or a bloated looking tummy, or fever. Call your doctor ASAP.

2. **Vomiting blood or "coffee grounds."** In newborns, blood in baby's spit up is often from Mommy's cracked and bleeding nipples. Beyond that time, blood in vomit warrants a call to the doctor. Blood that has been partially digested by the stomach looks like coffee grounds when it is thrown up. Both of these symptoms can be caused by bleeding in the esophagus or stomach.

3. **Vomiting repeatedly over six hours**. Excessive vomiting can be caused by stomach viruses (see **GASTROENTERITIS**), food poisoning (see **BACTERIAL ENTERITIS**), or an intestinal blockage (see **ACUTE ABDOMEN**). Most of the time, it's a stomach virus. It's time to check in with your doctor after six hours because your baby can get dehydrated.

4. **Vomiting associated with fever and irritability.** This is how meningitis presents in a baby. Babies have a unique "window" to the brain with their soft spot (fontanelle) on their heads. A full, bulging soft spot occurs with meningitis. Call your doctor immediately.

5. **Morning vomiting.** Babies don't get morning sickness. It's incredibly rare, but vomiting exclusively in the morning is a symptom of increased pressure in the skull. This can be caused by abnormal fluid collections or a mass (i.e. **HYDROCEPHALUS**, **BRAIN TUMOR**). Both of these abnormalities cause a full, bulging soft spot (fontanelle). This definitely needs to be checked out.

Q. What should I feed/let my baby drink while he is vomiting?

Nothing.

When your baby is actively vomiting, give him nothing to eat or drink unless you want to see it come right back out.

Wait until it has been at least an hour since the last vomit to test the waters. Start with Pedialyte, which is basically Gatorade made specifically for babies. Give one teaspoon every five minutes. Don't let your baby chug as much as he wants. He will be very thirsty. If he takes a full bottle worth on an unsettled stomach, it's destined to be thrown up. He'll get about two ounces an hour for the first couple of hours. If the Pedialyte test fails (more vomiting occurs), call your doctor.

Once the Pedialyte stays down, resume formula or breast milk.

Q. What are the signs of dehydration?

Lethargy, dry skin and lips, sucken soft spot (fontanelle), and decreased urination (less than three wet diapers in 24 hours—or no wet diaper in eight hours).

Another measure is weight loss, which is checked in the doctor's office. If your child is vomiting and/or having diarrhea, *start tallying how many wet diapers your baby is having*. Your doctor will ask you that question when you call or come in for an appointment. For more info, check out Chapter 15, "First Aid."

Urine

Q. My newborn urinated only once in his first day of life. Is this normal?

Yes.

All you can expect is one wet diaper on baby's first day. We just want to know that the pipes are working. Your baby might pee twice on his second day of life. The wet diapers will start to accumulate once your baby is drinking more. By day four of life, you should get at least four wet diapers. This should reassure you that your baby is getting something to drink when you are breastfeeding.

Q. These diapers are so absorbent, how can I tell if my baby has urinated?

Put a tissue in the diaper and you can see the pee.

In the first week of life, keep track of wet diapers. This information is also useful if your baby is vomiting and has diarrhea.

Another hint: diapers with pee in them feel heavier than dry ones.

Q. My newborn looks like he has blood in his pee. What is it?

Take a closer look. Does it look like brick dust? Is it powdery and on the *surface* of the diaper (whereas the pee is soaked in)

If the answer is yes to these questions, it's not blood. These are **URIC ACID CRYSTALS**. When newborns are a little dehydrated (in the initial 10% weight loss mode), the pee is more concentrated and less watery. This causes one of the ingredients of pee, uric acid, to separate out. That's what you are seeing. Uric acid crystals are nothing to worry about. For a picture of this, see Baby411.com.

Q. My newborn looks like she has blood in her diaper. What is it?

This is the equivalent of a menstrual period. It's not in the pee.

Baby girls' bodies respond to their mother's hormones. There is frequently some bleeding and vaginal discharge in the first few weeks of life. This is normal.

Q. I've heard that baby girls are prone to bladder infections. How can I prevent them?

Good hygiene.

A brief anatomy lesson here. Girls have a very short tube (urethra) that attaches the bladder to the outside. The urethral opening sits just above the vagina. Just below the vagina is the anus. Remember that poop has bacteria in it and urine is sterile. If the poop ends up in the nooks and crannies surrounding the urethra, the bacteria (usually E.coli) can climb into the urethra and grow in the bladder causing a bladder infection. Girls in diapers are particularly prone to infections. The best ways to prevent infection are:

◆ *Change a baby girl's poop diaper ASAP.*
◆ *Wipe "front to back".* Dads—this means start cleaning your daughter at the urethra and wipe downwards to the anus. Never go the other direction! Gently separate the labia and be sure to clean well in there.

Boys rarely get bladder infections because the urethral tube is much longer from the bladder to the opening (the urethra tube is inside the penis and the opening is at the tip). It's much harder for those bugs to travel that far.

Q. How do you diagnose a bladder infection in a baby?

Foul smelling urine, cloudy urine, and particularly, *fever in a baby with no obvious symptoms* (i.e. no runny nose, cough, or diarrhea).

This is one of the top reasons why we want to hear from you if your baby under three months of age has a fever. *Untreated* bladder infections can quickly lead to kidney infections (and even meningitis) in infants under six months of age.

If your baby is in diapers, and has a fever with no obvious symptoms, your doctor will need a urine sample to look for infection.

Q. Are some babies more prone to bladder infections than others?

Yes. There is an uncommon abnormality of the urinary system that causes urine to flow backwards into the kidneys called **VESICOURETERAL REFLUX (VUR)**.

Any pre-pubertal child who has a bladder infection needs to be tested for this abnormality. There is also a hereditary factor. Siblings of affected children may get screened as well. Three to five percent of all girls and 1% of boys will get a bladder infection before puberty. Also, 40% of these children have vesicoureteral reflux. Take home message: It's worthwhile to be tested for VUR.[2]

Reality Check

There is a 60% chance of a child having vesicoureteral reflux if a parent has the disorder. There is a 30% chance of having VUR if a brother or sister has the disorder.[3]

Burping

Q. Do you have any tips on burping my baby? I spend 20 minutes trying to burp him and nothing happens.

It's either going to happen or it won't. It's not your technique or patience that does the trick.

Burps are the result of swallowed air during feedings. Once your baby is an efficient eater (by four months old), he's also likely to be an efficient burper.

For the first few months of life, stop in mid-feed to burp your baby. There are basically three techniques.

1. Baby is upright on your shoulder, and you rub upwards on her back.
2. Baby is sitting in your lap, upright, and you rub upwards on her back.
3. Baby is lying face down on your lap, and you rub upwards on her back.

If it has been more than ten minutes, the burp ain't happening on your watch. Unfortunately, your baby may sleep for 20 minutes, then wake himself up when he burps. Welcome to parenthood. Just do what you can.

DR B'S OPINION

"Notice that the burping technique involves rubbing. I watched my brother burp his twins once and considered reporting him to child protective services. Patting and hitting aren't really necessary!"

Hiccups

Parents ask a lot of questions about hiccups. Here is what you need to know:
1. Hiccups don't hurt.
2. Hiccups are not a sign of an underlying disorder.
3. Don't worry about hiccups—doctors don't.

Gas

A nice way to exit this chapter.

Q. My baby has more gas than me. Should I be worried?

No.

Your baby has more gas because he sucks in a lot of air and because his intestines are on high alert 24 hours a day.

Most of the time, babies don't really care that they have gas. And don't be embarrassed, it's the only time in your child's life when people will think it's cute when he toots.

Q. What can I do about my baby's gas? Are Mylicon drops okay to use?

Not much, and sure, it won't hurt.

Gas is one of the biggest obsessions of newborn parents. Some parents believe it is the root of all evil... the reason that the baby is unhappy... the reason why nobody is sleeping. The truth is—IT'S NOT THE GAS. But, if you feel compelled to do *something* (which is a common feeling of all parents), it's okay to try those Mylicon drops. (See below for gas tips.)

The good news; the gassy phase will pass by age two or three months.

Q. I'm breastfeeding. Will eliminating high fiber foods from my diet fix my baby's gas problem?

No, but it will give you, Mom, a constipation problem.

This is rarely the cause of baby's gas. You can try an elimination diet, but it's usually not the problem.

Q. My baby is colicky. Is it because of gas?

No. Gas gets a bad wrap.

See the the next chapter (sleep) for information on colic. Eliminating gas won't solve your colic problem.

NEW PARENT 411: HELPING YOUR BABY PASS GAS

Here are three tips from seasoned parents:

1. Infant massage. This is a comforting way to help your baby relax. Pressing gently on baby's belly sometimes gets the gas out.

2. Warm bath. This also works by relaxing your baby.

3. Mylicon (simethicone) drops. This over the counter medication is safe for babies, including newborns. It makes big gas bubbles into little gas bubbles. Some parents swear by it, others see absolutely no difference in their baby's demeanor.

Notes

Baby 411

Sleep, Development & Discipline

Chapter 9

Sleeping Like a Baby

"Whoever coined the phrase, 'sleeps like a baby' never slept with one!"
~ Anonymous

Who needs sleep?
well you're never gonna
get it

Who needs sleep?
tell me what's that for

Who needs sleep?
be happy with what
you're getting
There's a guy who's been
awake since
the Second World War
                    —Barenaked Ladies

New (and veteran) parents struggle with their baby's sleep habits—it's a fact of life. Everyone warned you about it, but you weren't buying it. At first, the excitement of being a parent gives you the momentum to make it through the first few weeks of sleep deprivation. Then, the novelty begins to wear off. You are exhausted and desperate for a good night's sleep. You'll ask friends and relatives for tricks that worked for their babies. It's no wonder that books on infant sleep are a booming section at your local bookstore.

If you are reading this chapter before your baby is born, good for you. You will be prepared for what lies ahead. If you are already in the desperate category— don't worry—we can help you, too.

Before we give you all of our sage advice on this subject, it is *essential* that you understand the science of sleep.

Knowing the basics will help you appreciate the advice and avoid the common mistakes parents make.

The Science Of Sleep

Q. Do newborns have the same sleep patterns that adults do?

NO. That's why you cannot expect them to sleep like we do. Here are four important concepts you need to understand:

1 **TYPES OF SLEEP.** There are two basic types of sleep: REM and Non-REM. REM is stands for **R**apid **E**ye **M**ovement. Here are the differences between the two.

	NON-REM SLEEP	REM SLEEP
Muscle movements	relaxed	active (stretches, sucks, vocalizes)
Brain activity	relaxed	active (dreams)
Occurrence	1st part of night, PM nap	2nd part of night, AM nap

Newborns spend 50-80% of their sleep in REM sleep while adults spend only 25% of their sleep in REM. The result: babies are very active when they are asleep. In fact, all that kicking you felt in the womb was not just your baby's wakeful time. A fair amount of that activity occurred while your baby was in REM (active) sleep. And that pattern continues even now. Your baby will be noisy and moving around, but he is not awake.

BOTTOM LINE: Your baby's sleep activity and noises do not mean you need to feed or help him.

2 **SLEEP CYCLES.** Humans go through a series of sleep cycles throughout an evening's rest. Adults tend to bunch all the Non-REM cycles first, and then go through REM cycles. Babies do more flip-flopping of Non-REM and REM cycles. Each sleep cycle has a beginning and an end, where a person goes from light sleep to deep to light again, before entering the next cycle. Humans recheck their environments and body comfort at that time. At the end of each sleep cycle, a partial wakening occurs. Babies may whimper or briefly cry out during this time.

BOTTOM LINE: Leave your baby alone when he has a partial wakening. He will enter into his next sleep cycle if you leave him alone. If you intervene, you will wake him up. As the saying goes, let sleeping babies lie.

3 **LENGTH OF CYCLES.** The average adult sleep cycle lasts 90 minutes. The average newborn sleep cycle lasts 60 minutes.

BOTTOM LINE: Your baby has shorter sleep cycles than you. It can take several months until he has mature sleep patterns like an older child.

4 **CIRCADIAN RHYTHM.** The human body has a biological clock that registers 24.5 to 25 hours in a day. This is called a circadian rhythm. It is affected by both light exposure and a body chemical called melatonin. Babies follow their mother's circadian rhythm in the womb probably because of melatonin levels. Once outside the womb, they have exposure to light and must form their own circadian rhythm.

BOTTOM LINE: It takes several weeks for a baby to get their circadian rhythm sorted out. If you lived in the dark for nine months, you'd probably be a little confused too.

Newborn Sleep Issues

Q. Okay, now I understand why my newborn has erratic sleep patterns. But, how can I get my baby to sleep at night instead of during the day?

This is called Day-Night Reversal. It usually takes three or four weeks to resolve.

The best way to help your baby through this is to stimulate him during the day and keep things low key at night. Talk to your baby during daylight hours and encourage any wakeful periods he has. At night, do your feeding routine with little interaction. Only turn the lights on if you have a poopy diaper to clean. If your baby decides he wants to have a slumber party, he can party on his own. You don't have to entertain him.

These nocturnal habits usually resolve by three to four weeks of age. See "Sleep Tips" below in this chapter for more advice on the first couple weeks of life.

Q. How much should a newborn sleep?

About 16 to 18 hours total a day.

But here's the cruel part: most newborns will not sleep more than four hours at a stretch. They need to eat frequently and their little bodies know it.

Check out the table in the setting up good habits section later in this chapter to get an idea of how sleep changes through the first year of life.

BOTTOM LINE: Most newborns have six or seven stretches of sleep every 24 hours. Feedings occur in between these stretches.

Helpful Hints
Three Sleep Tips for the First Two Weeks of life
◆ *Wake your baby up if he has slept longer than 3 1/2 hours during the day.* When your baby has day-night reversals, he may have his one long stretch of sleep in the middle of the day. Discourage this! Otherwise, you will be in for a long night of cluster feedings.

◆ *Do not let your baby sleep more than five hours straight during the night.* He needs nutrition to grow. He also needs to stimulate your milk supply to come in if you are breastfeeding.

◆ *Your job is to sleep when baby sleeps.* Become nocturnal. Don't even think about doing laundry when your baby crashes in the afternoon. Go to bed!

Q. When can I expect to sleep through the night?

Now that you are an expert in "sleep-ology," you can appreciate the following fact: it takes (on average) *17 weeks of life* for an infant to develop mature sleep patterns. Yep, that's about four months. Think about that for a moment.

The definition of "sleeping through the night" is six hours of uninterrupted sleep. That will feel like a great night's sleep by the time you get there![1]

FYI: As the parent of a six YEAR old who often wakes up (and wakes us up) during the night to go to the bathroom, the concept of "sleeping through the night" is only a fuzzy and abstract concept that exists for childless couples.

Old Wives Tale
Giving your baby rice cereal helps him sleep through the night earlier.

The truth: Food has nothing to do with it.

Q. My friend says that their baby slept through the night at four weeks of age! That's not fair! How can this be?

Odds are, your friends are lying—or will soon be proved wrong when their baby reverts back to a normal sleep pattern (that is, waking up during the night). Sure, lightning sometimes strikes and a one month old will sleep through the night . . . for one night.

DR B'S OPINION

"If your full term, healthy baby is still not sleeping six hours straight by six months of age, it's not your baby's fault. It's probably yours. Read the section later entitled, Undoing Bad Habits."

Or even a month. But then, as we'll discuss later, she may relapse into waking up during the nighttime.

Another explanation for these wild claims: dads. When we hear about a baby that miraculously slept through the night from birth, this claim usually comes from the proud new dad. Of course, the baby wasn't sleeping but daddy was—mom still had to get up several times a night!

By the way, some babies *will* sleep up to 12 hours a night as early as two months of age, but it's not the norm. If your baby is a terrific sleeper, don't mention brag about it—you'll jinx yourself for the next baby!

Q. How do I get my newborn to fall asleep? He seems to have trouble relaxing.

It would be nice to have the baby who awakens to feed and then goes right back to sleep. More likely, you have the baby who eats and then fusses until you help him return to the Land of Nod.

After you and your baby get to know each other better, you will figure

New Parent 411:
Top 5 Tips for Getting a Newborn to Sleep

1. **Suck to soothe.** If you are so inclined, your breast may become the human pacifier. If this approach is not for you, use your finger or a pacifier in your baby's mouth to encourage sucking. This is fine for the first two months of life (more on pacifiers in later in this chapter).
2. **Move around.** Rocking, swaying, and bouncing (you will have the veteran-parent-hop down quickly) are effective.
3. **Sing, in or out of tune.**
4. **Snug as a bug.** Swaddling (see page 162), sleeping in a bassinet, or even sleeping in a car seat may do the trick.
5. **Go for a car ride.**

out what helps him settle down.

Newborns are born with immature nervous systems. That means, they don't have the ability to pull it together, relax, and fall asleep. The most reliable way babies know how to settle down is to suck. See the box above for our Newborn Sleep Tips.

Q. How long should my newborn sleep in a bassinet?

Two or three months max.

You are not setting up any permanent habits the first two months of life. Babies become aware of their surroundings around three to four months of age. That's when you need to set up a permanent routine.

For now, newborns prefer to be snug. They like to sleep in bassinets or even their infant car seat (both are fine) until they decide they want to stretch out. I recommend transitioning over to the crib by three months of age. Another factor: some playpens with a bassinet insert have weight limits that are usually exceeded by two or three months of age.

Old Wives Tale
Too much holding and rocking will spoil your baby.
The truth: You cannot spoil a newborn. Remember, babies don't have the ability to settle on their own. Do what it takes to get your baby to sleep. *However, you need to grow as your baby does. Your six-month-old will be quite capable of settling down on his own.*

Sleep Safety Tips

Q. I've heard about sudden infant death syndrome (SIDS). What is the official recommendation about infant sleep position?

The "Back to Sleep" Campaign is promoted by the American Academy of Pediatrics and various other health organizations. The official recommendation is that babies sleep on their backs from birth to six months of age to reduce the risk of SIDS.

Our own parents put us on our bellies to sleep. Any grandparent will tell you that babies sleep better on their tummies. They are right. However, numerous studies have proven that this sleep position significantly increases the risk of sudden infant death. It seems to be caused by the infant smothering himself—a pocket of carbon dioxide forms around the baby's face when she is face down in a mattress or soft bedding. Babies don't have the neck muscles to move their heads and, sadly, that's how some SIDS deaths occur.

Before the Back to Sleep Campaign began in 1992, 5000 babies died per year in the U.S. from SIDS. Today, that number is down by over 40%. Let's take a look at a graph that shows how the SIDS rate plummeted as parents stopped putting baby to sleep on their stomach:

US SIDS rate versus the % of babies sleeping on their stomach

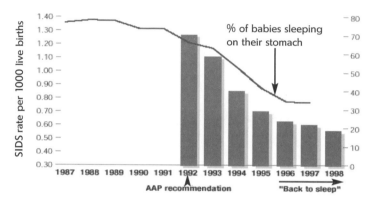

Source: Contemporary Pediatrics, Vol 17, No. 9

Q. If I put my baby on his back to sleep, I worry that he could throw up and choke. Or get more stuffy noses. Is that right?

Actually, a recent study came to the OPPOSITE conclusion! Yes, that is a common fear about putting baby on his back to sleep. But a study of 3,733 infants in a respected pediatric journal found that "babies who slept on their backs did not spit up and were less likely to develop fever or stuffy nose than babies who slept on their bellies," according to a summary of the study that appeared in USA Today. Not only does putting baby to sleep on their back reduce the risk of SIDS, but it appears to reduce other problems like spitting up and stuffy noses![2]

Q. Are there any other known risk factors for SIDS?

Yes. Here are the top six:

ROOM TEMPERATURE. The cooler the room, the better. SIDS occurs more frequently in the winter months when babies are bundled and the heat is on. Believe it or not, the recommended "safe" room temperature to reduce SIDS risk is 68 degrees.

? ?

SLEEP

2 **SOFT BEDDING.** All those beautiful bedding sets need to stay out of the crib. The heavy quilts, pillows, and blankets cause the ambient temperature of the crib go up. Babies can also smother themselves in the bedding.

3 **SMOKING.** Babies whose parents smoke have a higher risk of SIDS. So, if you can't do it for yourself, stop smoking for the most important thing in your world.

4 **ETHNICITY.** Native Americans and African Americans have a much higher risk of SIDS than other babies. It's unclear exactly why this is, but overlapping factors (such as higher smoking rates among some minority groups) may play a role.

5 **FAMILY HISTORY.** There may be a higher incidence of SIDS when a previous family member has had it.

6 **HAND-ME-DOWN MATTRESSES.** A 2002 study published in the British Medical Journal pointed to a possible link between SIDS and second-hand mattresses. Researchers found babies that died of SIDS were three times more likely to have slept on a used mattress. Exactly how this is related is not clear—perhaps toxic bacteria from milk, urine or saliva grows in the mattress and contributes to the SIDS death of the subsequent child who uses the mattress. As a result, we recommend using a NEW mattress for each child.[3]

Helpful Hints
◆ *What should you do with that baby quilt you got as a gift?* Use it as a wall hanging. Or buy a special quilt rack for your baby's nursery. You can always use it on the floor as baby gets older. Put a few toys out and encourage some supervised tummy time. Another alternative: some crib bedding makers are substituting lighter-weight blankets for thick quilts in their sets.

◆ *Don't borrow a crib older than a 1990 model.* The safety standards changed in 1989. The width between crib slats in older cribs was more than 2 1/2 inches apart, creating an entrapment hazard.

Q. What bedding items are acceptable to place in the crib?

A fitted sheet and a light receiving blanket. Of course, you don't even have to use a blanket—baby can just sleep in a sleeper or be swaddled. Or consider a new alternative: the sleep sack (pictured here is the SleepSack from HALO Innovations, web: www.halosleep.com). These "wearable blankets" provide warmth but cut the SIDS the risk, as babies can't crawl under them or become entrapped. Again, the key goal here is to not over-heat your baby—putting your child in a sleep sack and cranking up the thermostat is a no-no.

What about crib bumpers? Suffice it to say, these are a controversial item. We have a long discussion of the pros and cons of bumpers in our other book, *Baby Bargains*. To sum up, we believe crib bumpers are purely optional. One important point: if you decide to use them, remove the bumpers after your baby can pull herself up to a standing position (usually around eight to nine months). Why? Babies who can stand can use those bumpers to escape from the crib!

Pictured here is the Consumer Product Safety Commission's suggestion for how baby should sleep in their crib. Note there are no bumpers or other soft bedding in the crib. The thin blanket is tucked in the mattress at one of the crib to keep it from moving around.

Q. Is it okay to swaddle a baby in his crib?

Yes.

Newborns like to be snug for the first couple months of life. Think about it. They are used to being in a confined space. Your friendly nurses from the hospital probably taught you the "burrito wrap" technique of swaddling your baby. If not, see the box below.

Swaddling works well for the first six weeks of life, until baby wants to stretch out.

Q. Okay, I put my baby on his back to sleep. What do I do if he rolls over?

Let him sleep!

Your baby probably won't figure out how to roll over until he is at least four months old. Once he starts doing it, you can't stop him. The next morning, you will find him in a completely different position than the way you left him!

If it makes you feel any better, once babies can physically clear their nose and mouth by turning their heads, the risk of SIDS is lower.

Q. I'm concerned my baby might choke if he sleeps on his back. Should I be?

HOW TO SWADDLE A BABY—AKA BABY BURRITO WRAP

And now, the six steps to swaddling your baby:

1. Take a square receiving blanket and turn it diamond shaped on a flat surface.
2. Take the top corner and fold it towards the center of the blanket. You now have a horizontal line at the top.
3. Place your baby on the blanket with his neck at the level on the horizontal line.
4. Bring the bottom corner up to the baby's belly button.
5. Bring one side corner over the baby and fold over the other side of the belly.
6. Bring the other side corner over the baby and fold over on the other side.

Voila!

No.

Babies have a gag reflex that protects their airway when they vomit (all humans do). There is no increased choking risk.

As a side note, babies with gastroesophageal reflux do better with their heads elevated 30 degrees (the angle of a car seat). They experience less heartburn that way. (That's the way I sleep, too, after overindulging on Tex-Mex food). These babies sleep better with a wedge under their mattress or may sleep in their car seats for the first several weeks of life.

Q. Can I cheat, and let my baby sleep on his side?

That's a bad idea.

The research on SIDS was done on the back sleep position, not on the side. There is no data at this time to support side sleeping.

Q. Can I buy one of those breathing motion detectors and let my baby sleep on his stomach?

Again, a bad idea.

This won't prevent SIDS. It leads to more parent anxiety and disrupted sleep when the alarm goes off accidentally. The motion detectors you buy at the store are not the same as "apnea monitors" that some premature infants use after they are sent home from the hospital.

Q. My baby has a flat head and a bald spot on the back of her head from this sleep position. Is this permanent?

No.

As your baby starts to roll over, the head shape will round out. All babies lose their hair around four months, and then grow new hair in.

You can help with the head shape issue by giving your three to four month old some tummy time when he is playing. This promotes neck and back muscle strength. It also helps them learn how to roll over. (It's easier to roll from stomach to back than the reverse).

Q. Is there any greater or lesser risk of SIDS with a family bed?

No.

There has been a great deal of speculation, but no data, regarding this issue. To date, there is no risk OR benefit in relationship to SIDS and a baby co-sleeping in his parents' bed. One caveat: *Maternal obesity, tobacco, and alcohol use are other factors that DO correlate in an increase* in suffocation and SIDS.

Bottom Line

Here are the Top Ten take-home messages on sleep safety:

1. Put your baby to bed on his back.
2. Keep soft bedding out of the crib.
3. Keep the room temperature cool (68 degrees).
4. Don't over bundle your baby with too many bedclothes. Swaddling in one light blanket is okay.

SLEEP

? ?

5. No smoking.
6. Use a crib made after 1990.
7. Buy a new, firm crib mattress.
8. Make sure the mattress fits into the crib snugly, without gaps.
9. Take bumper pads out of the crib by six months old.
10. Lower the mattress height to the lowest level *before* your baby starts to pull on the railings to stand up.

Deciding On The Family's Sleep Routine: a.k.a. The Family Bed vs. Solitary Sleep Debate

This debate is worthy of an introduction before we get to the details. Where your baby sleeps is completely your decision. There is no right or wrong answer—the right answer is what works for *all* of you. There are advantages and disadvantages, whichever choice you make. We'll give you the information to make an educated decision about what is best for you.

Here are the options:

♦ **The Family Bed (Co-sleeping):** Parents and children sleep together in the same bed.
♦ **Solitary Sleep:** Each child sleeps separately in his own bed.
♦ **The Desperation Move:** Parents prefer that their baby sleep in his own bed, but end up having him in their bed out of sheer exhaustion and frustration with their inability to get their baby to sleep in his crib. (See undoing bad habits section later in this chapter.)

Q. What are the advantages of a family bed?

The main advantage is convenience.

For a breastfed newborn, it's very easy to eat at night. As soon as he stirs, his mother is there for him. This is also convenient for Mom, who might fall asleep shortly after (or during!) those middle-of-the-night feeds. Recent data suggest that co-sleeping babies nurse more frequently and take larger volumes of breastmilk at night than their solitary sleeping peers.[4]

Family bed advocates claim there are other advantages to co-sleeping. These include: better parent-infant attachment, sense of security, sense of trust, and protection from SIDS. But there is no statistical data or scientific proof to back up these claims.

Many parents choose this option simply because it feels good to snuggle up with their baby.

Just a bit of trivia: in the United States, 12.8% of infants sleep in a family bed regularly. The percentages are higher in ethnic and lower-income groups.[5]

Q. What are the disadvantages of the family bed?

Potential for SIDS and smothering risk.
The American Academy of Pediatrics pol-

DR B'S OPINION

"Having a well-adjusted and happy child has nothing to do with where he sleeps!"

icy position warns against the family bed, cautioning families to AVOID co-sleeping if a parent is obese, uses alcohol, or smokes tobacco.

Solitary sleep advocates argue that co-sleeping families get poor sleep and prolong the time that a baby starts sleeping through the night. They also feel that co-sleeping interferes with a baby's ability to become an independent being.

One way to address this issue is to use a hybrid method of co-sleeping—putting the baby in a co-sleeper (pictured). This port-a-crib attaches to the adult bed, allowing a parent to easily reach the child for feedings or comforting. But the baby really is in its own space instead of sleeping in the bed.

 Bottom Line
An eighteen-year study on parent-child bed sharing:
A landmark study came out recently that evaluated children who slept in a family bed as infants and young children and compared them to their solitary sleeping peers. These children were studied from birth through age 18 years. *The data showed that co-sleeping had no statistically significant benefits or problems.*[6]

Q. What are the advantages of solitary sleep?

Better and potentially safer, sleep.

As stated above, breastfed babies who co-sleep are up more often at night to feed. For certain populations (obese/smoking/drinking parents), the crib is a safer place for baby to sleep.

Q. What are the disadvantages of solitary sleep?

Consistency is required.

A baby who is used to sleeping alone in his own bed may have more sleep disruptions when families travel or sleep away from their home. It also requires taking a portable crib on trips or making arrangements to borrow one at your destination.

 DR B'S OPINION:
THE FAMILY BED

One of my colleagues used to say, "The family bed is a wonderful form of birth-control." Be honest with yourself. Many women lack the energy and interest in sexual relations after the baby is born. Don't use the baby in your bed as an out. It's important that BOTH parents want baby in bed with them. *The reality of the family bed is that Dad often ends up on the couch to get some sleep.*

Also, remember the discussion about babies having mostly REM sleep? Babies are noisy and mobile a good portion of the night. If you are a light sleeper, the family bed may not be for you. And let's be honest—even if you are a heavy sleeper, having an infant cry/fuss/feed every two hours is enough to wake the dead.

Babies who sleep alone need a consistent sleep ritual and often a transitional object (the proverbial security blanket) to wind down.

Q. With all of these night feedings, my baby ends up falling asleep on me. I don't want a family bed—will this be a problem in the future?

For the first two months, do anything that buys you some sleep.

Babies are very malleable for the first two to three months of life. You are not setting yourself up for having a five-year-old in bed with you.

Your goal should be to have a consistent sleep routine by four months of age.

Setting Up Good Habits (two months and up)

Let's take a look at the sleep requirements of a child from birth to 2 years of age:

INSIDER SECRETS: TOP 10 COMMANDMENTS FOR

1 **TEACH YOUR BABY TO FALL ASLEEP ON HIS OWN.** Remember those sleep cycles? The cycle consists of light to heavy to light arousal before entering the next cycle. At the end of each cycle, humans re-check their environment and change body position (move a pillow or blanket, roll over). By three to four months of age, your infant will be aware of his world. If he falls asleep on a parent's shoulder and gets moved to a crib, or falls asleep when he is drinking or sucking a pacifier, that is what he will be expecting when he arouses at the end of his sleep cycle. Translation: be careful of sleep "crutches" like the pacifier. Put your child in a crib or bassinet when he is sleepy . . . but before he falls asleep. If the child always falls asleep on your shoulder, he will expect to see that shoulder at the end of every sleep cycle.

2 **BE CONSISTENT.** Kids do best with routines. Predictable is comfortable. You will learn that rapid transitions and unexpected activities promote anxiety and outbursts in your child. (see temperament chapter for details) Have a routine for both nap and bedtime and stick with it by the age of four months.

3 **YOUR CHILD SHOULD ALWAYS SLEEP IN THE SAME PLACE FOR NAPS AND NIGHTTIME.** That's not the car seat or the infant swing anymore. Reality check: yes, every now and again your child may fall asleep in a car seat, especially after a long trip on the weekend for example. That's OK on an occasional basis. But when you are at home, keep the sleep place the same.

4 **NAP TIME AND BEDTIME SHOULD BE APPROXIMATELY THE SAME TIME EVERY DAY.** That goes for vacations, visits to relatives, etc.

Sleep requirements, birth to 2 years (in hours)

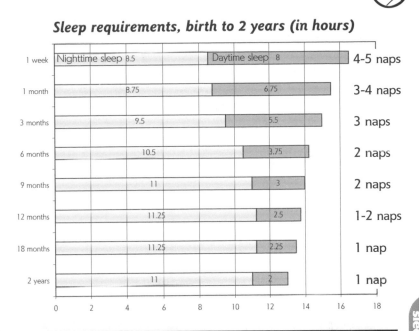

1 week	Nighttime sleep 8.5 / Daytime sleep 8	4-5 naps
1 month	8.75 / 6.75	3-4 naps
3 months	9.5 / 5.5	3 naps
6 months	10.5 / 3.75	2 naps
9 months	11 / 3	2 naps
12 months	11.25 / 2.5	1-2 naps
18 months	11.25 / 2.25	1 nap
2 years	11 / 2	1 nap

0   2   4   6   8   10   12   14   16   18

ESTABLISHING A SLEEP ROUTINE (2 TO 4 MONTH OLDS)

5 **ALWAYS FOLLOW YOUR SLEEP RITUAL.** Bath, feeding, (teeth brushing), story-time, songs, prayers...you might do the Cliff's Notes version of a book or song if it has been a long day, but still do it.

6 **START YOUR SLEEP RITUAL BEFORE YOUR CHILD IS TIRED.** Don't wait for the yawns and eye-rubbing to begin the routine.

7 **EARLY TO BED, LATE TO RISE.** Sounds like it wouldn't work this way, but it does. Babies actually sleep better when they go to sleep early. An "overtired" baby does not sleep longer —so, you are not buying time to sleep in by putting your baby down later in the evening. Trust me on this one.

8 **GET RID OF THE PACIFIER BY FOUR MONTHS OF AGE.** Your baby is very aware of his world. If he falls asleep with a pacifier in his mouth, he will cry when it falls out. At 3am. And 5am.

9 **BABIES NEED REFRESHER COURSES ON SLEEP ETIQUETTE AFTER TRAVEL, ILLNESS, OR TEETHING.** When consistency is broken, it takes a few days to get back on track. If you don't remind your baby of what to do, he will remain on a disrupted sleep schedule.

10 **DON'T TREAT YOUR FOUR MONTH OLD LIKE A NEWBORN.** Your baby will take advantage of your naiveté. Four month olds are capable of falling asleep on their own if given the opportunity to do so.

? ?

DR B'S OPINION:
FOUR MONTH OLDS AND SLEEP

Your four-month old baby is aware of his surroundings. If he falls asleep in your arms and you sneak him into bed, he will awaken at the end of his sleep cycle (every 90 minutes) looking for comfort. If your child is awake when you leave the room, he will fall asleep alone and content. You'll hear him on your baby monitor discussing his day with inanimate objects. Your baby is growing up—it's time to accept that change and adapt to it.

Behind the Scenes
Is there a correlation between parents' behavior and infant's sleep?

A recent Canadian study showed that many infant sleep disorders were based on parents' excessive intervention in comforting them to sleep. These parent behaviors with their five month olds included:

1. Putting a baby in bed *after* he was asleep.
2. Remaining in the room *until* the baby was asleep.
3. Taking the baby out of his bed to comfort him.
4. Parent feelings of inadequacy.

A significant percentage of these babies continued to have sleep problems well into their third year of life.

BOTTOM LINE: Don't just wait for your baby to outgrow his sleep issues—it may be a long time waiting. And, the issues may belong to the parent and not the baby.[7]

Q. How do sleep patterns and needs change as my baby grows?

Here's what you can anticipate:

◆ *Birth to two months.* Newborns sleep 16-18 hours a day. They have day-night reversals, and rarely sleep for more than a four-hour stretch at a time.

◆ *Two to four months.* On average, babies sleep 15-16 hours a day. They are usually taking three naps per day. If you are lucky, your baby may sleep for a six-hour stretch.. It is still too early to train your baby to sleep. But, here are three tips to get a few extra minutes of precious sleep:

1. Walk, don't run, to your baby's bedside when she starts to cry. She might just roll over and go back to sleep without your intervention.
2. Try soothing your baby without offering food at a night wakening.
3. Encourage feedings every two to three hours during the day. The more your baby eats in the daylight, the less he will eat in the moonlight.

Continued on page 170

SLEEP

? ?

THE TOP TEN MISTAKES PARENTS MAKE WITH INFANT SLEEP ROUTINES

1. Sneaking baby into bed. Your baby falls asleep in your arms, and then you sneak him into his crib. Compare this to the following scenario.[8] You fall asleep on the couch in front of the TV. Your spouse picks you up and carries you into your bed. When you wake up in your own bed, you are disoriented and alarmed. Your baby feels the same way—and hence, wakes up and wants your arms back!

2. Falling asleep while eating. Your baby falls asleep when he is drinking (breast or bottle). When he stirs, he is in a different place and not eating anymore.

3. Falling asleep with a pacifier. Here is the comparison:[9] You fall asleep with your head on your pillow. In the middle of the night, your spouse steals your pillow. When you wake up, you are confused and probably annoyed.

4. The Trained Night Feeder. Your baby gets used to eating a snack or a meal in the middle of the night, so he continues to be hungry at that time. Equate this to working the nightshift and having your lunch break at 3 am. Yes, your body will work up an appetite if you are used to it. Stop eating at 3am, and your body will no longer be hungry. Parents frequently continue these feedings well beyond six months of life because they don't know any better and their babies continue to demand it.

5. Inconsistent schedules. Babies are creatures of habit. Adjust your schedule as much as possible around your baby's. Don't change your baby's bedtime because you got home late from work and missed spending time with him. Pushing back your baby's bedtime for selfish reasons is always a recipe for disaster. Tomorrow is another day.

6. Missed naps. The better your baby sleeps during the day, the better he will sleep at night. Being overtired actually creates sleep disturbances. So, don't run errands when it is your baby's naptime.

7. Late to bed equals EARLY to rise. This is really true, even though you would think the opposite. As we've said, overtired babies sleep poorly.

8. Interventions at partial wakenings. Just because your baby stirs at night, does not mean he needs your help. We all stir at the end of each sleep cycle (every 90 minutes). If you go in "to help," you will wake your baby up. If these partial wakenings are waking you up, turn off the baby monitor. If your baby really needs you, you will hear him.

9. Bringing baby into bed when you don't want him there. Babies get used to routines. If you consistently bring your baby into your own bed when he cries, this is what he will expect. He will continue to cry until he gets what he wants. If the expectation is not there, the behavior won't exist.. Make a plan between BOTH parents and STICK WITH IT.

10. Not letting your baby learn how to self-soothe. The ability to soothe one's self is a learned skill. This skill can be mastered by six months of age, if your baby is given the opportunity. Yes, both thumb sucking and comfort objects (see below) are acceptable. Those Old Wives are correct about "spoiling" if you coddle your *older* baby.

◆ *Four to six months.* The average four to six month old sleeps a total of 14-15 hours a day, with two naps included. Your baby should be sleeping AT LEAST six hours at night. Some babies will sleep up to 12 hours at night. Yes, everyone in the house should be getting sleep by now. . .but if this is not happening, you need help. Do not be convinced that your baby NEEDS to be up at night. In fact, everyone will be happier if your child is sleeping at night. Sometimes parents aid and abet their baby's bad sleep behaviors. We'll discuss the reasons why babies this age continue to wake at night in the next section of this chapter.

◆ *Six to 12 months.* On average, these babies sleep 13 to 14 hours per day, with two naps included. Most babies sleep ten to 12 hours straight at night. Yes, your prayers were answered! If your baby is still waking up for night feedings or comfort, you need help. See "Undoing Bad Habits" below.

Undoing Bad Habits (Four to 12 months and Beyond): Solving the Sleep Problems That Parents Create

If you have a baby who is still not sleeping at least six hours a night, or you are bringing your child to bed with you out of desperation (and not choice), this section is for you. Admitting you have a problem is the first step!

Q. My baby started sleeping through the night at three-months old. She is five-months old now and waking up in the middle of the night again. Help!

Babies who are early to start sleeping through the night (less than three months old) frequently start up again when they become aware of their surroundings.

These are babies who never needed the sleep rituals before. They just fell asleep eating and were placed into bed. Now, they are alert little beings and need to learn how to fall asleep on their own.

When your former perfect baby starts having night wakenings, it will be at the end of a sleep cycle (a multiple of 90 minutes after bedtime). That's when you know the sleep routine you have created has backfired on you. Start using a sleep ritual that lets your baby fall asleep on his own.

DR B'S OPINION:
BEEN THERE, DONE THAT

I am a parent of young children. I have walked in your shoes. I know that irrational thoughts seem rational at 3 am. It SEEMS EASIER to just bring your baby in bed with you or nurse them to sleep. But it is not the right answer anymore.

Once you are on the other side (sleeping through the night), you'll say, "What was I thinking?" I am happier with myself and my relationship with my children when we have all slept at night.

Q. My baby uses a pacifier to fall asleep. When should we stop offering it?

By four months of age.

In the first two or three months of life, babies have very few ways to soothe themselves. Parents usually figure out within the first few days of bringing their baby home that a pacifier buys everyone some sleep. This approach is fine for the first few months.

BUT, do not use a pacifier beyond four months of life. Trust me. This is the time when you need to set up the routines you plan to keep. Remember the pacifier/pillow analogy? If the pacifier falls out in the middle of the night, your baby will be looking for it.

You don't want to have a baby who is capable of sleeping through the night waking *because* the pacifier is out. If the pacifier isn't there to begin with, he won't be looking for it. See Chapter 11, "Discipline and Temperment" for more details.

Helpful Hints

◆ Don't place dozens of pacifiers in your baby's crib so he can find one on his own.

◆ Don't go in every 90 minutes to put a pacifier back into your baby's mouth.

◆ Don't buy a glow-in-the-dark pacifier so your baby can find it at night. I promise that your four-month-old can fall asleep without the pacifier.

◆ Don't get stuck treating your four-month-old like a newborn!

Q. My baby can only fall asleep nursing/taking a bottle. When will he outgrow this?

When you stop allowing it.

Again, for the first two months of life, anything goes. After two months, you have eight weeks to get your baby to fall asleep without drinking. If your four-month-old falls asleep eating, wake him up just enough so he knows he is getting into bed and you are leaving the room.

Q. Are comfort objects okay to use?

Yes.

Comfort objects are also called transitional objects because they function to help babies' transition away from their parents.

Use a little blanket or small stuffed animal that can go to bed with your baby starting at four to six months old.

Q. My nine month old still has a middle of the night feeding. Is there something wrong with him?

He is a trained night feeder. There is nothing wrong with him. You've just allowed him to get part of his nutritional needs met during the night beyond when he needs them. Healthy, full term babies are all capable of fasting for ten to 12 hours at night by six months of age.

Stop the night feeding and he will stop being hungry. That's easy to say, right? Offer water at 3am and see what happens. It's likely to be rejected the first night. And yes, your child will protest. The second night, offer water again. The protesting will be less lengthy. By the third night, your baby won't bother to wake up.

Reality Check

It's likely that your nine-month old has at least one tooth. Therefore, offering milk at night without brushing his teeth afterwards may be a set up for cavities (milk has sugar in it). Be honest—you aren't getting out the toothbrush at 3am after your child has crashed on your shoulder. The answer: STOP THE NIGHT FEEDING.

Q. What sets off disrupted sleep patterns?

Travel, teething, and illness. Any change in routine will disrupt a child's perfect sleep pattern.

Q. How do I get my baby back on track after a disrupted sleep schedule starts?

A quick refresher course in nighttime etiquette is helpful.

Your baby will have a protest rally in his crib. But you need to let him cry. If you choose an alternative method of soothing, that will be the method your child adapts to. See below for a discussion of the Ferber method.

Q. There are so many books written about infant sleep. What do you think about them?

If you are looking for more information, there are a few books that are worth reading.

Here are our opinions of the leading sleep authors and their books. First, the table on the next page sums up the background and theory of each guru. Then below we offer a more detailed description of each.

SOLVE YOUR CHILD'S SLEEP PROBLEMS, FERBER.

Theory: "What parents view as abnormal wakenings in the night are actually normal. What they do to treat the 'abnormal' wakenings—namely going in to help their child go back to sleep—is actually causing the disturbance."

For the first four months of life, parents need to create positive sleep associations, routines, and rituals. If your baby is not sleeping through the night (six hours of uninterrupted sleep) by five or six months of age, it is time to train or untrain (break bad habits) your baby to stop the night wakenings.

Note: Babies under four months of age are not neurologically mature enough to settle and console themselves. This method is not intended for that age group.

The Sleep Guru Table

AUTHOR/BOOK	BACKGROUND	THEORY	GRADE
Ferber Solve Your Child's Sleep Problems	M.D.-Director of Sleep Lab, Boston Children's Hospital, Harvard	Ferber Method. Intervals of intervention extinguish night wakenings	A+
Weissbluth Healthy Sleep Habits, Happy Child	M.D.-Director of Sleep Disorders Program Children's Memorial Hospital, Chicago	Sleep deprivation. creates a vicious cycle. Break cycle cold turkey.	A-
Hogg Secrets of the Baby Whisperer	Nurse	E.A.S.Y. Eat, Activity, Sleep, Your Time	B
Pantley The No Cry Sleep Solution	Mother of 4	Pantley Method. Comfort baby until he is almost asleep.	C
Sears The Baby Book	Pediatrician	Attachment Parenting. Babies belong in contact with parents 24/7—asleep and awake.	C-
Ezzo/Bucknam On Becoming Babywise	A pastor and his friend, an obstetrician turned pediatrician	Parent Directed Feeding. Don't let the baby dictate when it is time to eat.	F

Ferber Method, in a nutshell:

1. Do not let your baby fall asleep feeding, rocking, or being stroked by you.
2. Provide the identical sleep ritual (books, songs, cuddling) at nap and bedtime.
3. Have your baby sleep in the same place for naps and bedtime.
4. Avoid crutches. (i.e. pacifiers)
5. Put your baby down relaxed, but not asleep.
6. If your baby protests, make brief appearance at increasing intervals (add five minutes *each* time) to reassure your baby that you have not abandoned him. This is NOT intended to console your baby. In fact, he will yell louder. Eventually your baby falls asleep on his own.

Pros: This method works! And it works quickly—in three or four nights.

Dr. Ferber is truly one of the world's experts on sleep disorders in children. His book thoroughly explains the science of sleep at a level that parents can understand. He explains his method clearly with good detail and examples.

This book also addresses the gamut of all childhood sleep disorders, not just infant sleep problems. It is an excellent reference for night terrors, bedwetting, sleep walking, etc.

Cons: Yes, your child will cry. Yes, the first night will be ugly. The second night is less ugly. The third night is manageable. The fourth night, your baby has a smile on his face and so do you. Your baby will be fine. Parents are always guilt-ridden when they hear their baby crying. More on this later.

As in every method, there are occasional setbacks. Illness, teething, and travel create sleep disturbances. Kids need an occasional refresher course (shorter than the initial training) to remind them what they are supposed to do at night.

Grade: A+

2 HEALTHY SLEEP HABITS, HAPPY CHILD, WEISSBLUTH.

Theory: Good sleep is critical to good behavior and functioning. Overtired children have a lower frustration tolerance (short fuses), more behavior problems, and more difficulty falling asleep. Parents perpetuate their child's poor sleep habits unintentionally with their actions. These mistakes are thoroughly explained.

Weissbluth Method, in a nutshell:

1. Set an earlier bedtime to get baby down BEFORE he is overtired. This may limit the evening playtime after a working parent comes home, but makes for a happier child.
2. Naptime should be preserved at all costs.
3. Let your baby learn the process of falling asleep by letting him do it on his own.
4. If your baby is already in a vicious cycle of being overtired, end this cycle abruptly by letting him 'protest cry' until he falls asleep on his own (after four months of age). This is called Plan A, and it takes one night to accomplish.
5. Plan B is a more gradual approach offered for parents who can't handle Plan A.

Pros: This method works quickly—in one or two nights. Dr. Weissbluth provides an understandable, in-depth discussion of sleep physiology. His philosophy makes a lot of sense.

The author provides true stories that will hit home with many of the parents that read this book. There is even a chapter written by a psychiatrist that is very insightful about parenting styles and how these styles impact a child's sleep routine.

Cons: Can be one very long night of crying (both on the part of the baby and the parent). Many parents don't have the stamina to let their child cry for more than 15 minutes, even if it is in their child's best interest. (see why parents can't let their child cry later in this chapter).

The author spends 200+ pages explaining sleep and he does it beautifully. But it takes a while to get to the brief action plan.

Grade: A-

3 SECRETS OF THE BABY WHISPERER, HOGG.

Theory: Parents should control bedtime.

Baby Whisperer Method, in a nutshell:

1. Identify your baby's tiredness cues.
2. Put baby to bed before he is overtired.
3. Put baby down when he is relaxed, but not asleep.
4. Give the baby a "dream-feed" before parents go to bed. (Baby is asleep and parents feed him).

Pros: Ms. Hogg has a charming way of explaining sleep behaviors and parent mistakes. Her whole plan is to teach parents how to find their baby's window of opportunity to fall asleep.

The author supports the appropriate foundations for good sleep without pretending to be a sleep authority.

Cons: If you miss the "window of opportunity," you are screwed. Ms. Hogg then sticks parents with the unpleasant alternative—several hours of patting and soothing until baby is finally relaxed enough to fall asleep.

I also disagree with the "dream-feed" concept. This presumably fills the baby's tummy up to avoid middle of the night feedings. I am bothered by this approach for two reasons: first, don't encourage a child to eat when he isn't hungry. This leads to obesity. Second problem: cavities. Many parents continue night feedings long after their baby has teeth (six months of age). Unless you plan on brushing your child's teeth after that dream feed, you will be paying for your dentist's kids to go to college.

Grade: B

4 THE NO CRY SLEEP SOLUTION, PANTLEY

Theory: Babies develop associations with sleep that become a crutch (co-sleeping, feeding to fall asleep). Pantley says breaking these bad habits by letting the baby cry is insensitive and cruel. The focus is on establishing good routines and earlier bedtimes before missing the window of opportunity.

Method: Author provides 20 ideas that promote good sleep associations and routines. She tested her method on 60 families with infants.

Pros: Some families just can't listen to their baby crying. This book provides some ideas for establishing sleep rituals.

We agree with many of the author's comments on establishing sleep routines, although none of them are unique to her book. She does a nice job of addressing how to transition a co-sleeping child to his own bed.

She suggests that parents compile data on their own child and then make a personal plan for addressing their child's sleep disturbances.

Cons: Author admits that following her approach may take up to *eight weeks* to be successful. Perhaps a prescription for Prozac could be included for the parents when they buy her book. Most sleep-deprived parents are at the end of their rope at week ONE! We'd venture to say that any baby (with or without her method) sleeps better after two months of living and growing.

Ms. Pantley focuses on families who choose "attachment parenting" and the family bed. Her answer to reducing night feedings is to pretend to be asleep—not very realistic. This is not a book written by an expert.

Grade: C

5 THE BABY BOOK, SEARS.

Theory: Babies need positive sleep associations. To Dr. Sears, this means your baby should be skin to skin with you during sleep. Dr. Sears once said in a Child magazine interview (1998), "Why would a parent want to put her child in a box with bars in a dark room all by herself?"

Method: The family bed fosters attachment parenting. There is no reason to force your baby to sleep through the night or discontinue night feedings.

Pros: Many cultures use the family bed.

Cons: Co-sleeping is perfectly acceptable for families who choose it. However, we find that usually only one parent is in favor of the family bed (the mother). Dad agrees to the family bed because his wife is exhausted from the frequency of having to get up for breastfeeding sessions. Eventually, Dad moves out to the couch or the spare bedroom to get some sleep.

The family bed is not for all families. Dr. Sears' approach makes families feel guilty if they choose not to sleep with their child. That's hard for us to support.

Grade: C-

6 ON BECOMING BABYWISE, EZZO AND BUCKNAM

Theory: Parents create a high need baby by having a "child-centered universe" approach to family life. The authors promote a family-centered lifestyle whereby the baby must adapt to the needs of the family. It is up to the parent to schedule feedings, wake time, and naptime.

Babywise Method, in a nutshell:
1. From birth to eight weeks of age, feed the baby every three hours during the day. At night, let the baby sleep.
2. If the baby awakens before the scheduled "first morning feeding," wait to see if he will fall back asleep without feeding.
3. If the baby must eat, readjust the feeding schedule for the day—but try not to make a habit of it.

Pros: According to the authors, 98% of their babies are sleeping through the night at eight weeks of age. Yet, the authors offer no scientific proof that their method really works. Yes, this book has become a best seller . . . no doubt because it lulls parents into thinking that by "taking control" of the situation, everything will be all right. Sure, babies do love consistent routines, but this book goes overboard with the rigid feeding schedule.

Cons: When this book came out, there was an outcry from pediatricians. When parents followed this method to the letter, babies became dehydrated and did not gain appropriate weight (called failure to thrive).

This book is so contrary to mainstream pediatric practice that the American Academy of Pediatrics issued an alert regarding their concerns with this book.

Memo to the authors of the *Babywise* book: If parenthood is such a chore, don't become one. Having a newborn in the house is exhausting. Newborns need to eat frequently (yes, sometimes even MORE than every three hours) because their body metabolism functions that way. If you dou-

DR B'S OPINION:
WHICH SLEEP METHOD IS BEST?

By far, my patients' families have had the most success with Dr. Ferber's technique, known as "Ferberizing."

In my opinion, this is the most rational way of setting up good sleep habits. Unfortunately, some parents read a negative review of the book or hear how the Ferber technique failed one parent . . . and therefore, believe it can't work for them. Some exhausted parents come to me and say "I just can't let my child cry" or "I tried it and it doesn't work." In some cases, these parents have never read the Ferber book . . . or have not followed the technique correctly. So, we'll try to de-mystify Ferber in the box on the next page.

bled your weight in four months and your brain size in a year, you would eat all the time, too! Messing with Mother Nature by forcing your child into rigid feeding schedules is not only foolish, it's dangerous.

Grade: F

Q. If the Ferber technique is so successful, why doesn't it work for every parent?

The key word here is *parent*.

Most parents are unsuccessful because they do not follow the technique correctly or are not committed enough to endure the three-night experience.

Here is my pep talk to give you the incentive to persevere.

1. What you are doing currently is not working.
2. Nothing is medically wrong with your child.
3. Nothing will happen to your child if he cries.
4. Your child will not hate you or feel you have abandoned him. Your baby will be HAPPY to see you the next morning and you'll be happier to see him.
5. Your infant is currently in charge of your house! It's time to change that.

Now, we realize number five sounds a bit like the *Becoming Babywise* book we discussed earlier. But let's separate the subjects—the Ezzo's mantra is a rigid *feeding* schedule intended to eliminate night feedings and wakings with *newborns*. We think that's dangerous. And the *Babywise* authors insist parents start the rigid routine immediately. Dr. Ferber does not suggest using his method until your child is five or six months old and is actually capable of self-soothing at night and no longer requires night feedings for nutritional needs.

Feedback from the Real World
One parent wrote of her nine month old twins:
"You'll be interested to know that they slept through after the second night. I guess they were as ready as I was."

SLEEP

? ?

This comes from a parent of a nine month old I care for:

"You told me she was just manipulating me with waking up for bottles and rocking. When I said, "I'm not letting her cry. I can't listen to her cry all night. I have to get up in the morning to go to work." You said, "I wouldn't give this advice if I hadn't tried it." I left your office and went straight to the bookstore for Dr. Ferber's book. I read it and started that night. By the third night, my daughter was sleeping through the night. **The technique**

THE FERBER TECHNIQUE, DE-MYSTIFIED

1. Be consistent with your sleep routine at nap and at bedtime.
2. No falling asleep rocking, eating, or sucking a pacifier.
3. Comfort object/Lovie is allowed after four months of age.
4. Get your child relaxed, put him in his crib, and say goodnight.
5. Your child will start complaining.
6. Wait five minutes before returning to the nursery.
7. When you enter the nursery, make your response short and sweet (no more than 60 seconds). Tell your child you love him and say goodnight. Do NOT pick him up, rock him, or feed him. Leave the room. This lets your child know you have not abandoned him.
8. Your baby cries louder. (No surprise here)
9. Wait ten minutes before returning.
10. Repeat step 7.
11. Your baby sounds possessed.
12. Wait 15 minutes before returning.
13. Repeat step 7.
14. Wait 20 minutes before returning...

This process lets your baby know that you haven't abandoned him, and requires *him* to do the work to fall asleep (yes, he is quite capable). The first night will be very difficult to tolerate. You may reach the "Wait 30 minutes" mark (which will be almost two hours of intervention) before your baby falls asleep. **Don't back down.** That will only convince your baby that if he cries long enough he will get what he wants. When your baby wakes up the next morning, he will be happy to see you.

The second night is much easier. The night's events will last half as long as the first night.

The third night may last only ten minutes.

By the fourth night, your baby will have adjusted to his new sleep schedule.

Some final thoughts:

1. This technique only works when your baby is old enough to have the neurologic maturity to settle on his own (five or six months old).
2. I always recommend doing this over a weekend. Otherwise, you will be cursing Dr. Ferber and me the next day at work.
3. You can't give in or give up once you start.
4. Buy Dr. Ferber's book. It's worth every penny.

was not 'just shut the door and let them cry' as others had told me. The philosophy, statistics, and true cases were so convincing. And, the exact method was so different than what I had heard from other parents. Thank you for not blowing me off as a hypochondriac and giving me the tools I needed. Thanks again for putting up with one more mother!"

Q. I know I am being a wimp, but I don't think I can listen to my baby cry.

Think to yourself, "There is nothing wrong with my child."

Yes, your baby is mad that he is not getting his way. You will see a lot of this behavior in the years to come (a preview of the toddler and teenage years)! Remember when you were 16 and your parents didn't let you borrow the car? Did you still love them? Your child will still love you, even when you set limits on their behaviors (including sleep).

For the long three nights ahead of you, I prescribe:

1. Planning your next vacation.
2. Renting some videos.
3. Making love with earplugs—a novel idea, I know.

You get the idea. Find something else to do other than lie there in your bed listening to the drama going on in the nursery. Be strong. You can do it.

Sweet dreams.

Nap Schedules

Q. How much should my baby be napping?

Here's the timeline:

- ◆ *Birth to two months:* three to four naps per day (mostly waking up to eat and going back to sleep)
- ◆ *Two to four months:* Three naps per day
- ◆ *Four to 12 months:* Two naps per day

Babies usually cut back to one afternoon nap a day shortly after their one-year birthdays. Some will keep that nap until kindergarten. Most (like my own kids) give it up by three years old.

FIVE REASONS PARENTS CAN'T LISTEN TO THEIR BABY CRY

1. You feel like you are helpless and not 'doing anything' for your baby (not true).
2. You are a working parent and feel guilty (don't).
3. You think you will cause your baby to have long-term emotional scars (you won't).
4. You think you are an inadequate parent if you can't get your baby to settle down (you aren't).
5. You think something must be wrong with your baby (probably not).

---

sleep

Q. When will my baby be on a nap schedule?

By four months, maybe earlier. Follow your baby's lead.

At two months of age, you will have more predictability in your lives. Your goal, at this point is to start having a schedule by four months of age. You follow your baby's plan and work around it.

Naptime can begin within 30-45 minutes of your daily goal. But try as much as you can to be consistent. Overtired babies are not exactly the life of the party. Things happen and delays sometimes are unavoidable. Just be prepared. . . but you will pay for it!

Remember, from birth to two months, anything goes. If your baby falls asleep in the car, that's fine. This is a popular parent trick. But by four months, avoid it.

Put your baby down awake and follow your same sleep routine as at bedtime. View naptime as your baby's downtime. If he chooses to talk for 30 minutes instead of sleep, so be it.

By six months, you should have the nap thing down. If you don't, it's time to Ferberize. The only difference with the Ferber nap technique is that if your intervention goes on for more than an hour, that is the end of naptime. That may equate to a baby who is not actually sleeping during naptime for a period of three days.

Q. How long are naps supposed to be?

Thirty minutes to three hours.

It depends on the child. By four months of age, your baby should have two or three naps per day. One is likely to be a catnap in the morning. The afternoon nap may be a three-hour marathon.

By a year of age (12-21 months), the morning nap is lost, and your baby will take a 90-minute hour to three-hour afternoon siesta.

Q. My baby never naps at daycare and comes home cranky. Help!

Some babies just don't do well with group naptime. They prefer solitude.

See if your daycare center is willing to put your baby in a private area to take his naps. If this is not a possibility, you may need to rethink your childcare options.

Q. I have an older child that is in school. My baby's naptime falls right at the time I pick him up from school. He either misses his nap or falls asleep in the car, only to be awakened when we get home.

Naps are an important part of your baby's schedule. Enough that it is worth looking into carpool options. Perhaps you could drive in the morning and a friend could pick your child up from school. Don't sacrifice that nap if you can help it.

Beyond The First Year

Q. How long will my baby sleep in his crib before graduating to a big bed?

As long as he still likes it.

That can be as old as three years of age. I don't recommend toddler beds or convertible beds. When your child starts trying to climb out of his crib, take the mattress out and put it on the floor. Put up a safety gate in front of his doorway. That way, he'll have free reign of his room, but not the whole house.

Q. We have a one year old and are expecting again. Should I take the older baby out of the crib when the new one arrives?

No.

A bassinet will buy you a couple of months with the newborn. Then, see if the older child still likes his crib. If the answer if yes, borrow or buy a crib for the younger baby until the older one graduates. (see information above about purchasing a new mattress)

Otherwise, you are asking to have a toddler roaming free around your house at night.

Q. Can we use a small travel pillow in the crib?

After a year of age, it's okay.

Special Situations

Q. I have twins. Is it okay to let them share a crib?

Yes. Until they start waking each other up.

For the first two months, both babies will sleep snugly and not get in each other's way. After two months, it's probably wise to give them the space they need to move around—that means two cribs. It's fine to have them share a room.

Q. Do you have any recommendations for how to get both babies to sleep through the night?

The answer is the same as for single babies. Set up the right routines and rituals.

The only difference is with feeding times. See Chapter 6, "Liquid Nutrition" for how to coordinate night feedings with multiples.

Q. I have a baby who was born prematurely. Will it take longer for him to sleep through the night?

Yes. It may be as long as 17 weeks beyond your baby's *due date*, not their birth date.

Premature babies are neurologically immature. They also need more calories for "catch up growth." Night feedings will be necessary for a longer period of time than full term babies need.

Chapter 10

Development

"I have found the best way to give advice to your children is to find out what they want and then advise them to do it."
~ Harry S Truman

Okay, you've heard the conversations on the playground: "Janey was walking at only ten months." "Well, my little Henry was saying his first words at four months. " You know—competition starts early. Now if you're pregnant as you read this you're probably wondering when they *should* start walking and talking. And if you have a child already, you may be one of those quiet moms who doesn't join in the above boasting conversation. You may be wondering if your beautiful baby is behind. That's what this chapter is here to tell you.

When can your child roll over, when should he, and when is he developmentally delayed? And what is important to worry about and bring up to your doctor during well check visits? This chapter provides the key to understanding how your child's brain works. Knowing what to expect will help you know how to respond to your child's needs as he is growing. This is required reading *before* you get to the next chapter, "Discipline and Temperament." We'll refer back to this stuff, so don't jump ahead.

Your first lesson: DO NOT COMPARE YOUR BABY TO OTHER CHILDREN. We know, you just can't help it. You watch other kids in playgroups, at the park, and in your own family and then look at your baby. Don't do it. Every child reaches her developmental milestones at her own pace. Yes, there is a certain timeline to reach these milestones, but there is a broad range of "normal."

Q. What does development mean?

The way a child evolves in muscle skills (large and small muscles), language skills, social and personality skills, and intelligence. This is different from the term "growth" which refers to physical body changes. We'll define some key terms on this topic next.

◆ **Gross Motor Development**. This refers to using large muscle groups to function (i.e. arms, legs, torso). *Milestones:* rolling, sitting, crawling, climbing, walking, running, throwing, and kicking a ball. *FYI: Gross motor development is mastered in a "Head, shoulders, knees, and toes" direction. Remember these milestones by the numbers 3-6-9-12:*

  ◆ Three-month-olds have achieved *head* control. (no more head bobs)
  ◆ Six-month-olds have *shoulder* and trunk support. (rolling over, sitting up)
  ◆ Nine-month-olds have *knee* control and can stand up holding on, and walk with support.
  ◆ 12-month-olds have control of their feet and *toes*, standing alone and taking steps.

◆ **Fine Motor Development**. This skill involves using small muscle groups to function (i.e. fingers). *Milestones:* batting with hands, grabbing, picking up objects, feeding oneself, holding food utensils, holding writing utensils, coloring, and writing.

◆ **Oral Motor Development.** The ability to use mouth and tongue muscles. *Milestones include:* swallowing, chewing, and talking. Newborns only have the ability to suck, swallow, and cry.

◆ **Language Development.** This refers to the ability to communicate with others. The pre-requisites for language development are oral motor development and the ability to hear and process language (see receptive language skills below). *Milestones:* cooing, babbling, stringing sounds together, imitating noises, and using words purposefully. There are two sub areas of language development:

  ◆ *Receptive language skills.* The "input" that babies get in the form of words is understood long before they start talking. Babies can follow directions (if they are in the mood) before they say any words.
  ◆ *Expressive language skills.* This is language "output". When people refer to a child having language delays, it is usually an expressive language delay (i.e. they aren't talking yet). If there is a concern for an expressive language delay, your doctor should always check to be sure there is not a receptive language delay, too (a hearing problem, or an **AUDITORY PROCESSING DISORDER**).

◆ **Social-Emotional Development.** This is how a child adapts to his world. *Milestones:* smiles responsively, knows parents, asks to be held, laughs, imitates, plays peek-a-boo, anxiety towards strangers, anxiety from being separated from loved ones, seeks independence.

Social skills are a learned process. And, parents are the most important role models for a child. Children interact in social situations quite differently at different ages.

◆ **Cognitive (Intellectual Development)**. This refers to how a child figures out his world. Babies are like a big sponge. They absorb vast quantities of information on a daily basis and learn how to decipher it all. And you thought your learning curve was steep with this new parent experience. Imagine what your baby's brain is going through!

Milestones: follows people and objects in field of vision, expresses needs, explores toys, prefers routines, knows how to get people's attention, understands cause-and-effect (that is, banging this toy makes noise), object permanence (things still exist even if not in view), remembers frequent visitors, limited problem solving skills

Q. How do I know that my baby is developing normally?

You come to visit the pediatrician or family doctor for well baby checks.

Many parents think that well baby checks are "just for shots." They're not. At every well baby check, your doctor will ask a series of questions to be sure your baby is developing all five types of skills at an appropriate pace. Don't expect these questions to be asked at sick visits because these are "problem-focused" appointments.

If a delay in any of the developmental areas is detected, it may be followed for a period of time to see if your baby "catches up" or a referral may be made to a specialist in that particular field.

This is an extremely important part of both the parent and doctor's job description. If you have concerns about your child's development, don't be shy about it. There is never a downside to getting your concerns checked out.

Q. I've heard the term "developmental milestones." What does it mean?

These are individual skills that your baby progressively masters as he matures.

The series of questions your pediatrician asks are based on expected milestones at specific ages. Some babies will show off and demonstrate their new tricks in the office. In most cases, however, doctors rely on your descriptions for the rest. Remember, there is a *range* of time for when milestones are achieved.

Q. Can I have a milestone checklist so I can follow along?

Yes, as a matter of fact, the Denver Developmental Checklist can be downloaded from our web site at Baby411.com. Click on Bonus Material to find it.

Remember, no obsessing over this list and do not tape it to your baby's crib and check the boxes when he passes each milestone. This is by no means a perfect test, but it is a helpful guide for doctors to screen for developmental delays.

As you will see, many of the checklist items for the first year of life are for motor skills. Language and social skills come later. Cognitive skills are incorporated into both language and "personal-social" skills.

There is a very low criterion to "pass" a test so that children with normal skills are not falsely considered delayed. In light of this, if a child does "fail" a test on the Denver Checklist, it is quite likely he has a developmental delay in a certain area. In such a case, the doctor will investigate this further either in her office or via referral to a developmental specialist.

To score this test, draw a vertical line down the page at your child's age. The white bar indicates the milestone we are looking for. The gray bar shows the end of the normal spectrum (where at least 90% of the kids tested will pass). If you look at any particular age, there are some milestones your child should definitely have achieved and some that are okay if he hasn't achieved yet.

Q. What is the significance if my child fails in his milestones?

Maybe something, maybe nothing.

This is a non-committal answer, but it is the truth. Some children will have an isolated delay in one particular developmental area (that is, just motor skills, just expressive language skills, etc.). With a little help and encouragement, these kids catch up to their peers and you might never notice a problem later on. For others, it may always be an issue. For instance, a child with gross motor delays may grow up to be a non-athletic kid. A child with expressive language delays may turn out to have a learning disability. Both of these children might also be a varsity football player or the valedictorian. It just might take a little more work for that kid to succeed in those areas.

The children we are most concerned about are those with delays across the board, termed "global developmental delays." These children are more at risk to never catch up to their peers. When children continue to have global delays by the age of three years old, they are ultimately diagnosed with mental retardation. There is a range from mild to severely affected children. Doctors evaluate these children for genetic and metabolic (they way the body breaks down certain chemicals) defects when they are diagnosed.

Q. I've heard a lot about autism in the news. What is it, and when do I worry?

AUTISM is another diagnosis doctors make based on developmental delays. Autism is a term used for children with severe language delays and inappropriate social interaction skills. There is a range of disorders under the heading of "Autism Spectrum Disorder." These include the diagnoses of **PERVASIVE DEVELOPMENTAL DISORDER** and **ASPERGER'S SYNDROME.** Children with autism are usually diagnosed by 18-21 months of age when language delays are obvious. However, other clues to the diagnosis appear long before that time. These children do not have social smiles and avoid eye contact with their parents. Cuddling does not soothe them. In fact, their behavior worsens with touching. These kids do not regard and take interest in toys. Bright lights and noises often bother them. Because of their repulsion of sensory stimuli, they turn inwards and perform repetitive self-soothing behaviors (rocking, head banging, spinning).

BOTTOM LINE: *Children with autism have autism long before their first birthdays, even though their "official" diagnosis occurs in their second year of life.* This is one of the arguments that proves the measles

(MMR) vaccine given at one year of age does not *cause* autism (see Chapter 12, "Immunization/Vaccines" for details).

Q. My baby bangs his head frequently. Does he have autism?

No.

Many babies have behaviors that they perform repeatedly. The repetition is soothing for them. Unless your baby has multiple symptoms (unsocial, poor language, etc.), your baby is not autistic. By the way, babies have the same self-preservation instincts that we do, so they really won't hurt themselves by head banging.

Q. If my child has a developmental delay, where can I get help?

Want to use a FREE service that makes house calls?

There is a government program called *Early Childhood Intervention*. (It's not exactly free because your taxes have paid for it.) Every town has an agency. Look yours up in the phonebook. Your child's development will be screened over the phone. If he qualifies as having a delay, a specially trained physical therapist (large muscles), occupational therapist (small muscles), or speech therapist (language, mouth skills) will show up at your doorstep and do a formal assessment. If help is needed, a regular therapy schedule will be set up.

The other option is to get a referral from your pediatrician to a private specialist in your area. Easter Seals also has a national program that provides services based on ability to pay. You can contact them at www.easter-seals.org or at (800)-221-6827.

Denise's opinion: We've all been at the park and noticed a child who seems to be "hyper" or "slow" or "aggressive" or non-communicative. But no matter how tempting it is, keep your opinions to yourself. Besides, behavior problems on the playground probably have more to do with kids who are tired or hungry than with some kind of serious brain dysfunction.

As the parent of a learning disabled child, I can tell you that no outsider would have known he was anything but normal until he got closer to school age. And kids who *seem* to have delays and problems often sort them out and have no issues by the time they reach kindergarten.

But if you notice your child doesn't seem to be keeping up with other kids his age physically or socially, be sure to bring it up to your doctor at the next well visit. If you don't say anything, your doctor may not notice subtle signs in a ten or 15-minute visit.

Feedback from the Real World
Special babies, Extraordinary Parents: Meredith's Story
"When we first learned of Meredith's diagnosis (developmental delays) our first worry was that there would be nobody to take care of her in the future when we were gone. We now realize that dwelling on that is giving up any hope for the present. When Meredith was finally able to throw a ball, we celebrated all the years in therapy that got her to that moment. When she was able to catch the ball, we marveled that it happened the very next day."—Sarah Barnes and Jim Hemphill, parents of Meredith Hemphill, age 6 (diagnosis: agenesis of the corpus callosum).

WHERE TO GET HELP

◆ *Head Start and Early Head Start programs:*
   www.ehsnrc.org
◆ *Parent training:* www.patnc.org
◆ *Early Intervention for children birth to three years:*
   www.nectas.unc.edu

Q. My baby was born prematurely. Does the same developmental checklist apply to him?

Yes, but not at first.

Babies born more than five weeks early have some catching up to do from both a growth and development standpoint. Your baby's chronological age will be corrected by their gestational age (age in months at time of delivery). So, the expectations will be lower initially. Babies will catch up with their peers developmentally by one year of age.

Now that we've talked about general developmental milestones and delays, we want to explain a bit about intellectual development and social/emotional development. We'll explore theories from two prominent doctors with their thoughts on the stages your child will go through throughout his life.

How Your Baby Learns

Ever wonder how your baby learns all the amazing things she does? How does she go from being a little lump at birth to a smiling, talking, walking dreamboat by her first birthday? Dr. Jean Piaget, the father of the major accepted theory for cognitive (intellectual) development, believes that a child's brain processes and understands information in different ways at different ages. As a parent, it's helpful to know what "stage" of brain development your child is at, because *your child's reasoning will be different than yours*. And if you are educated about those differences, hopefully, you'll be less perplexed and frustrated by them.

So here is the big picture, stage by stage:

Sensory-Motor: Age birth to two years

Babies learn by hearing, feeling, tasting, smelling, moving, and manipulating (that is, using their Five Senses). Babies are "**EGOCENTRIC**". In their minds, the world revolves around them. They continue to think this way until about age six or seven years old (although you might think that some adults haven't outgrown this stage yet!).

◆ *Birth to one month:* A newborn comes equipped with immature reflexes (sucking, rooting, grasping). He will learn how to use and coordinate them. Newborns have no concept of "self."

◆ *One to four months:* Babies realize that they have body parts, and can control them. If you see your baby staring at his hand, it's because he has discovered it.

◆ *Four to eight months:* Babies are more interested in the world. They realize their actions can make other people do things. They start to manipulate objects and explore with their mouths. But, people and things don't exist unless they are within a baby's visual field. They do well with routines and predictable events with their limited memory banks.

◆ *Eight to 12 months:* Babies grasp the concept of *object permanence*. A baby realizes that a person still exists even when he leaves a room. The same goes for toys, food, etc. A baby this age has a limited repertoire of techniques to explore a new situation. They use their *memory* of what 'worked' in the past to approach something unfamiliar.

◆ *12 to 18 months:* Toddlers have more sophisticated approaches to problem solving (although it won't feel that way to their parents). They experiment systematically. Toddlers go through a "trial and error" method of attack. Things are explored more with hands than with mouths. They CAN follow directions. (It's a matter of whether or not they CHOOSE to).

◆ *18 to 24 months:* As these kids approach two years of age, they can do "trial and error" in their minds, and figure out the solution to a problem (i.e. simple puzzles). They will figure out language, and start to pretend.

Pre-Operational: Age two to seven years

Kids have the concept of "symbols" representing things (i.e. language, pretend play). Their level of reasoning is based on *their* viewpoint. They are not capable of taking someone else's perspective. They have primitive logical thinking. For example, a full juice cup will look like it has more in it than a half-full water glass.

Concrete Operational: Age seven to eleven years

Kids this age can think logically, order and classify items, compare, and sequence information. But, everything is black and white—there is no *gray* zone.

Formal Operational: Age 12 to Adulthood

This is the age of abstract reasoning— when a child can "think outside of the box." A teenager can take a hypothetical situation and reason it out.[1]

Your Baby's Social and Emotional Growth

As one of the most influential psychologists of the 20th century, Erik Erikson continues to influence our view of social and emotional development today. His theory suggests that personality development rests on how a person deals with a series of stages in his life. A person's sense of identity depends on the outcome of eight crises or conflicts. If a person does not successfully resolve a particular conflict, the unresolved issue persists in later life.

People can also regress to prior stages during times of stress (that is, a four-year-old returns to the Terrible Two's when a baby sister is born).

Again, the big picture....

Trust vs. Mistrust: Birth to 18 months

Infants learn to trust their parents. They learn that their needs are met. Babies who do not get appropriate care have a sense of distrust and apprehension around others.

Autonomy vs. Doubt: 18 months to three years

Children are seeking independence and are trying to gain confidence in their abilities. This happens while parents are trying to set limits on inappropriate behaviors. (This meeting of the minds is also known as the Terrible Two's). Children need a certain autonomy to rely on their own skill, or else they will begin to doubt themselves.

Initiative vs. Guilt: Three to six years

Children thrive on decision-making and accomplishments. If parents do not support these experiences, the child feels guilty for trying to be independent.

Industry vs. Inferiority: Six to 12 years

Children gain confidence in their skills and want to learn. With failure or lack of support, children feel inferior to others.

Identity vs. Role Confusion: 12 to 18 years

Simply put, teens either figure out who they are and what they want (sense of self) or they are confused and reliant on their peers.[2]

Now you know the theories behind how babies develop. So you're probably wondering how to put them to work. This is the section for you. Here we're going to discuss how to foster appropriate development for each age and stage. Keep in mind the idea is not to "train" your child to be the next Beethoven, Mary Cassat or Bill Gates.

Birth to Two Months of Age

Q. So what is a general idea of how my baby will develop in the first two months?

Here is a thumbnail sketch.

You may think that your newborn spends his whole life eating and sleeping, but he is actually learning a great deal. Babies are born with an immature nervous system (brain, spinal cord, nerves). So, most of what you see develop is not dramatic in the first two months of life. Instead, development is happening with a baby's neurological system. *Milestones include:*

◆ *Newborn reflexes.* Babies suck and turn their head instinctively when you rub their cheeks. They will also grasp anything placed in the hands. If you gently drop their heads back, they will flail their arms out and open their eyes. These reflexes should go away by six months of age.

◆ *Motor skills.* Babies are born with poor head and neck stability. Over the first two months of life, they gain better head control. They should move both arms and legs equally well. A dominant side or hand preference is NOT normal.

◆ *Vision.* Newborns have 20/400 vision. They are not blind. But, they can only see clearly about eight to 10 inches in front of them. Putting your face right up to theirs is very entertaining for them. Babies like contrasts (hence, all of the black and white toys at trendy baby stores). By the time your baby is two months old, he will be able to see one to two feet in front of him. He should also be able to fix his eyes on an object and follow it side to side.

◆ *Hearing.* Newborns are born with normal hearing. They startle to loud noises. Babies recognize their parents' voices. They have heard you inside the womb.

◆ *Social.* Newborns are interested in your face. By two months of age, if you smile at your baby, he will smile back (called a social smile). Under six weeks of age, any smiling is a mere coincidence, or gas.

◆ *Language.* Initially, babies cry to express all of their needs. As they approach 2 months, babies will start to "coo" (ooo and ah noises). They may even start to laugh and squeal.

Q. What kind of developmental stimulation should I provide my birth to two-month-old?

Give them lots of time with you. Here is a break-down:

1. Sensory-motor:
   ◆ Give your baby interesting things to follow with her eyes (your face, colorful toy).
   ◆ Listen to music; play with rattles, music boxes.
   ◆ Let your baby touch different objects (your face, your hair, the dog).
   ◆ Give your baby short (five minutes) bursts of time on her tummy to work on shoulder and stomach muscles.

2. Language:
   ◆ Start a *reading ritual.* Set aside reading time EVERY day until your child packs up and goes to college. There is a great deal of research that proves infants who are read to at early ages have stronger language and cognitive skills than their peers.
   ◆ Infants respond best to rhymes and good illustrations. See the end of this chapter for a list of good books for kids age birth to one-year-old.

3. Social:

◆ Spend time talking and smiling at your baby.

Q. My newborn does not have good head control yet. Is it okay to use an infant baby carrier (Snugli/Baby Bjorn)?

Yes. Holding your baby in your arms 24/7 gets old quickly. These carriers provide enough head support and allow you to use two hands to get something done.

Q. My two-month-old's eyes cross frequently. Should I worry?

No. A baby's eye muscles are weak initially and frequently are not in sync with each other.

Doctors start testing for lazy eye muscles (see **AMBLYOPIA**) from six to nine months of age. If you notice that one eye turns in, turns out, or only one eye has a "red eye" effect in photographs, let us know. Note: a two month old can follow your face as you move it in front of him. A three month old can follow it for a full 180 degrees.

Old Wives Tale
Letting an infant bear weight on his legs will make him bowlegged.

The truth: Babies like to bear weight on their feet with your support. It's fun—and it won't make them bowlegged.

Two to Four Months of Age

Q. What milestones should I expect my two to four month old to achieve?

◆ *Gross Motor.* Your baby should have good head control by three months of age. If you lift his body from a lying position, his head should come up at the same time and not lag behind. He may or may not roll over. By four months old, he should bear weight on his legs if you stand him up. Most babies can lift their heads up when lying on their stomachs.

NEW PARENT 411: READING PROGRAMS

The Reach Out and Read program encourages 15-20 minutes a day of reading to young children. Books are given free of charge to underprivileged children via doctors' waiting rooms. First Lady Laura Bush also has a national program called Ready to Read, Ready to Learn, which promotes reading time in preschools.

The benefits of reading to children at an early age are clear.

◆ *Fine Motor.* Your baby will start to realize that his hands are useful. At first he will bat at objects, then start to grab successfully around four months. (This is when moms usually stop wearing hoop earrings and pull their hair back). Your baby should also be able to bring his hands together.

◆ *Language.* Babies are really experimenting with their voices at this age. They will move on from cooing to laughing and squealing. They may start to "blow raspberries" (spray saliva). This is particularly fun at mealtime. They also experiment with the volume of their voice.

◆ *Vision.* Your baby's vision improves to about 20/40 by four months of age. So, he will be able to see you across the room.

◆ *Social/Personality.* Your baby will try to imitate social contact with you. Smiling, tickling, and laughing are very entertaining for your baby.

Q. What developmental stimulation can I provide for my two to four month old?

◆ *Motor.* Give your baby more tummy time (five to ten minutes) several times a day. He will let you know when it's time to turn over. Activity gyms are fun because they can start to bat and grab at the objects.

◆ *Language/Social.* Keep that reading ritual going. When you are out and about, talk to your baby. He is your companion, so treat him like one. Tell him where you are going and what you are doing. You may feel silly telling him what you are putting in your grocery cart, but all those vocabulary words will be recorded in his growing brain.

Four to Six Months of Age

Q. What developmental milestones will I see with my four to six month old?

◆ *Gross Motor.* Your baby will sit up with your assistance, then "tripod sit" with his hands supporting him between his legs. Eventually, he will sit up without support.

◆ *Fine Motor.* Your baby has mastered grabbing. He will start to use his fingers more than just his hands. He will "rake" objects to get them into the palm of his hand by six months. He will also start to transfer objects from one hand to the other by six months old.

◆ *Oral Motor.* Your baby will figure out how to maneuver his tongue to swallow solid food by six months of age (see Chapter 7 "Solids"). This is one reason why it is not recommended to offer solid food before this age.

- *Language.* Your baby will start making the first recognizable sounds of language. Consonant sounds usually progress from B's to D's to M's. This means, you'll first hear "ba-ba" then "da-da" then "ma-ma". The "Ba-Ba" occurs around six months of age. Your baby should also turn to you when you are talking to him by six months.

- *Social/Cognitive.* Your baby is very aware of his surroundings. He knows his family and friends. He knows his room and his crib. Four month olds already thrive on the routine and the expected. But even at six months of age, your baby will not have the concept of "object permanence". So, if you leave the room or a toy leaves his sight, it no longer exists.

Q. My six-month-old is sitting up but he never rolled over. Should I be worried?

No. Welcome to the anti-SIDS generation.

It is easier to roll from tummy to back, than from back to tummy. Babies of our generation spend significantly less time on their tummies because of the "Back to Sleep" campaign to prevent Sudden Infant Death Syndrome. As a result, babies these days often master rolling over about the same time as sitting up (or skip rolling over entirely). Rolling over used to be a four-month milestone. Sitting up is a six-month milestone.

Q. What can I do to foster my four to six month old's development?

- *Gross Motor.* Because babies of this age group aren't quite sitting alone yet, the stationary Exersaucer toys are great. They give babies a sense of independence, and free up their hands to play. However, we don't recommend using them for more than ten or 15 minutes at a time. Some studies have shown that babies who can't see their feet and legs because of the trays on these toys can have delays in walking. Also, be sure to give babies lots of floor time to work on rolling and balancing.

- *Fine Motor.* Give your baby large plastic or plush toys to grab, manipulate, and mouth. Yes, mouth is used as a verb here. Everything your baby examines will go into his mouth to test out. Toys that make noise are fun. The plush caterpillars that have different sounding objects in each segment are popular.

- *Language.* You know the drill by now. Read to your child on a daily basis. Use board books and those designed for tub time (that is, they're waterproof)—these give your child a tactile experience as well.

- *Social/Personality.* Babies are keenly aware of facial expressions. Get a cheap plastic mirror for hours of fun—your baby will sit there and stare at himself.

RED FLAG: Avoid Walkers

The American Academy of Pediatrics strongly discourages the use of walkers. Babies drive these things without taking a driver's ed course. Walkers allow babies to get places that their knees or feet would never take them. This sometimes means falling down a flight of stairs.

New walkers now have some safety devices built in meant to keep them from falling down stairs. Because of the new safety requirements, there has been a marked decline in the number of injuries caused by walkers. However, the Consumer Product Safety Commission reports that there were still 6200 injuries from walkers that required a hospital visit in 2001.

Pediatricians see numerous head injuries every year as a result of walkers. Even if a child doesn't fall down the stairs, she can still run into low tables and chairs and knock items off tables (like hot drinks and glass vases, for example). And older, used walkers without the new safety devices are definitely death traps.

Six to Nine Months of Age

Q. What are your expectations for a six to nine month old?

♦ *Gross Motor.* The main milestone over these three months is loco-motion. Your baby will figure out how to get to where he wants to go. That may be achieved by rolling, crawling, or "cruising" (walking while holding onto furniture). Some babies skip crawling. Because of this, if you look at the Denver Developmental Checklist, you'll notice that crawling isn't listed. Meanwhile, your baby should also be able to get from lying down to sitting, and from sitting to standing up (holding on to something).

♦ *Fine Motor.* Your baby will refine his reaching and grabbing skills. The crude "raking" will change to a "pincer grasp" (picking things up between index finger and thumb). Things like lint and dirt on the floor will suddenly become very interesting. This correlates with the ability to self-feed (see finger foods in Chapter 7, "Solids").

♦ *Oral Motor.* Your baby should be able to maneuver his tongue and chew food with teeth (or gums).

♦ *Language.* Your baby should be progressing into the D's and M's. We expect a nine month old to say "Dada" and "Mama", but don't expect them to know the meaning of those words until about 14 months. Everything you are saying is recorded in your little one's big brain. His receptive language is quite good (that is, he understands what you are saying). *Your nine month old understands the word, "No". Whether he chooses to response to it is another story.*

◆ *Cognitive/Social.* Ah, the light has turned on. Somewhere between six and nine months, your baby will have achieved *"object permanence"*. This is a MAJOR concept. He realizes that people and things still exist, even if he can't see them anymore. So, if you leave the room, he will look for you. This, understandably, creates some anxiety (see "separation anxiety" in the next chapter).

◆ *More social issues.* Another concept that arises is *stranger anxiety.* Not only will your baby want to know your every move, but he won't want to hang out with anyone but you. Don't get too frustrated. When your baby is so independent that he wants nothing to do with you, you will look back fondly at these days. Your baby also is picking up social cues. He will smile to engage others. He might wave bye-bye by nine months of age. He also is starting to figure out how to express his needs nonverbally. Finally, your baby will start testing the limits of his world. At nine months old, your real parenting job begins. You need to set limits on your baby's behaviors STARTING NOW (see Chapter 11, "Discipline").

◆ *Vision.* Your baby's vision is 20/20 by six months of age.

Old Wives Tale
A baby who skips crawling and walks first won't be able to do higher math.
The truth: Where did this one come from? I crawled before I walked and still couldn't figure out calculus—so there. It has no bearing on intelligence.

Q. What developmental stimulation can I provide for my six to nine month old?

◆ *Gross Motor.* Provide a SAFE environment for your baby to move around in (see safety section below). Your house is now his playground.

◆ *Fine Motor.* Provide SAFE toys for your baby to feel, touch, maneuver, and taste. Babies explore with their hands first, then their mouths. If you are buying toys, pick ones that make sounds or lights when manipulated. Before you rush to Toys'R'Us, look around your kitchen. Old measuring cups, Tupperware, seasoning bottles (sealed shut), pots, pans, and wooden spatulas are often a hit with this age group. If you actually venture to a restaurant, those individually wrapped crackers are a real crowd pleaser until your meal arrives.

◆ *Language.* Do you have a bookstore frequent buyer's card yet? Get one. Use your local library as your baby gets older, but for now buy some cardboard books (called board books) of your own. Your baby's library will double as his teething toys.

◆ *Even More Language.* When you speak to your baby, use single words and short phrases. Otherwise, you will sound like the teacher in the Peanuts cartoon to him. Your baby will start to show you what he wants. Instead of saying, "Oh, do you want the rubber ducky?" say, "Duck?" That will teach him the vocabulary word he is looking for. The same language rules apply for discipline. Instead of saying, "Oh, no, Honey, don't bite Mommy's shoulder!" say, "No biting." (Yes, there is more coming on this in the next chapter).

◆ *Social/Personality.* Your baby is a social being and is very responsive to family members. Your baby will imitate the way you respond to situations. He follows your lead. Be a good role model. Since your baby now has object permanence, playing peek-a-boo is fun. It's also fun to hide toys under a blanket and let your baby look for them. How easy it is to amuse a child this age!

Nine to Twelve Months of Age

Q. What are the developmental milestones for a nine to 12 month old?

◆ *Gross Motor.* Your baby should definitely have his sea legs. He should be able to stand holding on to someone's hand or a piece of furniture. He probably will be able to pull up to stand and get back down to a sitting position. One day, you'll go into the nursery some morning and be shocked to find your baby standing up in his crib grinning at you. Your baby may or may not be taking his first steps at his birthday party. It's still within developmental limits to be walking by 15 months old.

◆ *Fine Motor.* Your baby should be good at picking up small items. He will also start banging objects together. Babies this age get really good at pointing.

◆ *Oral Motor.* Your baby should learn how to drink liquids from a cup. Ideally, she will be able to drink from a real cup, but most parents seem to prefer the no-spill sippy variety. Drinking from a straw is also something that works well for a child this age. By one year of age, your baby should graduate from a bottle to a cup (see Chapter 6, Liquids for details).

◆ *Social/Personality.* As your baby approaches his birthday, he will be very good at expressing his needs non-verbally. There is a universal "point and grunt" that babies around the world know how to do. As his expressive language improves, there will be less frustration due to communication barriers.

◆ *Anxiety.* Separation anxiety peaks at nine to 12 months, then again at 15 to18 months. Remember, that anxiety stems from the fear that you are leaving permanently. Ease these fears by kissing your baby goodbye and telling him when you will be back. Keep it short and sweet, and make your exit.

◆ **Language.** From nine to 12 months, your baby may start to say "Mama" and "Dada" and mean it. He may also say a word or two (but it's more likely to happen if you have a girl). Regardless of sex, your baby will speak with great confidence in some foreign language. If you listen to him (via monitor) in his crib at night, you should hear a whole monologue going on. This singsong intonation of speech is called "jabbering". Even though there aren't any vocabulary words, you know your baby has been listening to you.

Babies start to imitate their parents' activities. You may catch him pretending to dust and sweep. You may have a cleaning buddy!

Your baby will make it clear that she wants to be in charge and independent (in simple terms, it's her way or the highway). *It is important to begin discipline and limit setting.*

Your child will have conflicting moods. He may happily leave you behind, but then call for your help. Your availability as a consultant teaches your child to turn to adults for problem solving. Your child's sense of self (ego) is developing. Praising your child for small accomplishments gives him confidence.

Q. My one-year-old son isn't talking yet. All of the girls in his playgroup are yakking up a storm. Should I be worried?

Girls are talkers. Boys are walkers.

There is no question that girls learn language skills more quickly than boys. And once we start talking, you can't shut us up! Boys tend to reach motor milestones more quickly than girls—hence the roughhousing and athletic skills that you see later on. It's very interesting to watch. Clearly, parents have some hand in the way children develop along gender lines, but a lot of it is pre-determined.

Q. We speak two languages in our house. Will our child learn both?

Yes. She will have excellent receptive language skills in both languages (that is, she'll understand both) long before she speaks either language.

Q. What can I do to foster my baby's development from nine to 12 months?

◆ **Gross Motor.** Offer a wide-open space for your child to roam. Start playing with a ball. Toys that can be pushed are fun for babies who are walking (lawn mower, grocery cart, baby buggy).

◆ **Fine Motor.** Play patty-a-cake. Offer toys that your baby can bang together. It's also fun to get "cause and effect" toys (your baby pushes a button that causes a toy to move or make a noise; Jack-in-the-Box). Now is the time to buy "the classics". These toys are called stacking cups (plastic cups of various sizes) and shape sorters (cylinder with plastic shapes and matching holes in the top). Toys that can be filled and dumped are also entertaining.

- **Social**. Let your child participate in activities of daily living. While you are cooking dinner, let your baby "cook" his own meal on the floor with old pots and pans. While you are cleaning up, give him a towel, too. Start reviewing body parts with your child as a part of his vocabulary. You can also begin giving jobs to your baby. He should be able to follow one-step directions (such as "Bring me the ball.")

- **Language**. Books, books, and more books. Picture books with a single picture and word on each page encourage vocabulary words. Remember to converse with your child as your companion. Continue to identify items in single words and short phrases. Singing songs helps with language skills, and helps pass the time in traffic. Your baby doesn't mind if you can't carry a tune.

If you're looking for a great resource on the best toys to buy for your child, check out the *Oppenheimer Toy Portfolio* (web: toyportfolio.com). The book and accompanying web site rate and review toys, books, videos, software and music for kids. You can find age appropriate toys that are geared toward stimulating your child's development.

Don't forget friends' toys. When you take your child to another kid's house for a play date, they get exposed to a whole other set of toys. Some parents even get together and toy swap so their kids get different toys but don't have to spend oodles of money on them. Not to mention the social interactions baby will experience in a new environment.

Q. When should I buy shoes for my baby?

When he is a good walker.

There is no medical reason to wear shoes. Most babies use their toes to grasp the floor when they are trying to walk. For this reason, we encourage your baby to travel the house in bare feet. If you are out in public, by all means, put shoes on your child. You don't need to buy expensive shoes. But, it is a good idea to get your child's foot measured when you buy that first pair of shoes to ensure proper fit.

NEW PARENT 411: CAR SEATS & HEAD CONTROL

Babies need to be at least 20 pounds AND one year of age to be forward facing in the car seat. Their neck support is not good enough to sustain the impact of a collision in a forward facing position until these criterion are met. Even if your baby is at least 20 pounds AND one year of age, you can still keep them rear-facing in a seat (as long as you aren't near the limit)—in fact, safety advocates recommend keeping baby rear-facing as long as possible. Most convertible seats go to 30 pounds rear-facing today—that's quite a while beyond the first birthday for most children.

Helpful Hints

◆ *Take a CPR course* and have any caregivers who are taking care of your child take one, also. The biggest potential problem for a child after nine months is choking. Kids this age do not get the famous Heimlich maneuver— they get back blows to force out the foreign object. You'll want to find out how to perform this if you don't know already.

◆ *Have Ipecac syrup* (medicine that induces vomiting) in your medicine cabinet. Have Poison Control's phone number by your kitchen phone. The national number is: 1-800-222-1222. You can find your local Poison Control number from the American Association of Poison Control Centers' web site at aapcc.org. Always call poison control first if your child has ingested something. If they instruct you to give Ipecac, then proceed. Not all toxic chemicals should be removed by vomiting because they can burn the esophagus and mouth when coming back up.

Q. Where can I get information about toy safety? I have heard about baby product recalls.

Check out the U.S Consumer Product Safety Commission Hotline on the web at cpsc.gov or toll free at 1-800-638-2772.

Q. When can my baby start watching TV?

The American Academy of Pediatrics would say two years of age, for no more than 30 minutes a day. Most doctors, in general, do not find much benefit in television in providing developmental stimulation for children of any age. Here are the arguments against TV:

1 **TV IS A LOW ENERGY ACTIVITY.** If the TV is on, your child is sitting down (unless you are doing an aerobics video). Americans have an obesity problem, partially due to a sedentary lifestyle. The average school age child watches an astounding three hours a day. Amazing, eh?

2 **IT'S A PASSIVE WAY TO LEARN INFORMATION.** Children learn much better when they are actively participating in the learning activity. Yes, Sesame Street might help your child learn his letters— but your time working with him will be more effective. Yes, kids' TV has become more interactive in recent years (witness Dora the Explorer, Blues Clues and even Sesame Street). But that still doesn't take the place of active learning.

3 **MANY PROGRAMS ARE INAPPROPRIATE FOR CHILDREN.** For instance, the evening news can be very graphic and disturbing. Even children's programs can be problematic. Have you watched a cartoon lately? The average cartoon has 20 violent scenes per hour. The violence that occurs does have an impact. Studies have shown a direct influence on children's behaviors after watching cartoons.

4 **TV PROVIDES A DISTORTED VIEW OF THE WORLD.** As your child gets older (teen years), he or she will view TV as a mirror of the real world. Do you want your child to think the world of sitcoms is reality? Think about the amount of sexuality on many of these shows.

New Parent 411: Top 14 Safety Tips

Now is the time to make your home child-safe. Put 'this one on the Honey-Do List.

Children start to explore their world as a natural part of their development. Make their world safer so they can accomplish their goals. Here are the Top Safety Tips:

1. *Safety gates need to be at the top and bottom of the stairs.* The best and safest option is to permanently install gates (instead of using pressure gates).
2. *Electrical outlets need to have plastic safety covers.*
3. *Get down on the floor* and look at the world through your child's eyes. Electrical cords and telephone cords need to be moved behind furniture.
4. *Toxic cleaning products in lower cabinets need to be moved.*
5. *Cabinet locks on cabinets* with knives, glass containers, and china.
6. *Coffee tables and fireplace hearths with corners need safety bumpers.*
7. *Anchor bookshelves to the wall.*
8. *Get toilet lid locks so your baby cannot fall in.*
9. *Set your water temperature under 120 degrees.*
10. *Get cord shorteners or wall brackets to avoid dangling drapery cords.*
11. *Remove any toys hanging over the crib by the time your baby is five months old.*
12. *Keep medicine out of reach.* Be especially watchful of grandparents who come to visit. They are more likely to a) be taking a medication and b) be leaving it out on a bathroom counter.
13. *If you drop something, pick it up.* Otherwise, your baby will do it for you and stick it into his mouth.
14. *If you are a gun owner (remember I live in Texas, y'all), lock 'em up.* Guns should *never* be accessible to children.

For more safety advice and which safety products are best, check out our other book *Baby Bargains* (see back of this book for details). We have a 25+ page chapter on this subject alone.

So, here are some suggestions:

◆ *After your child turns two or order, limit the amount of time your child watches TV a day.* Thirty minutes to one hour is a reasonable goal

◆ *Know what your child is watching.* Any PBS show is usually a good bet. Cartoon Network shows require a parent preview. Yes, that means sitting down and watching "Jimmy Neutron" *without* your child to see if that show is appropriate.

◆ *Watch TV WITH your child.* Talk about what you are seeing. Stress to your child the "make believe" part. As your child gets older, explain the advertisements.

◆ *Have a family TV.* One in five American children have a television in their bedrooms. That means there is no supervision of what kids are watching. *You* need to be the V-chip—don't put a TV in your kid's room.

◆ *There is no good reason for a baby under one year of age to be watching TV,* even if the video is "designed" to boost your baby's intelligence. It hooks them on TV. Yes, that means Baby Einstein videos too. They won't make your child into Einstein, Mozart or anyone else.

◆ *Don't watch TV at meal times*—that means kids' shows or the news. This sets up the couch potato syndrome.

Q. What do you think of "Mommy and Me" and other community programs for babies?

These are a mixed bag. For the most part, Mommy gets more out of these programs than babies less than one year of age. Look for programs that focus on singing, story time, and finger plays. The more motor oriented programs (Gymboree, Little Gym) are more appropriate for toddlers (over one year in age). One tip: watch a class or two before you sign up so you aren't wasting your time.

Q. What books do you recommend if I want to learn more about child development?

Touchpoints by Dr. T. Berry Brazelton. He has a beautiful style to approaching development, developmental stimulation, and the challenges within these topics. Brazelton has a "cup is half full" way of viewing your child's struggles with growth and independence.

DR B'S OPINION:
BABY SIGN LANGUAGE

Yes, baby sign language is very trendy . . . and something fun to do with your baby.

Notice, we did not say that it promotes language development. Babies around the world figure out how to express their needs without words. Remember, "point and grunt" is universal. For babies with severe expressive language delays, it may be helpful to teach some signs to minimize their frustration in communicating with others. But that's a rare case.

What I have seen in my practice is babies who have learned the signs for "more" and 'drink'. Their sign language vocabulary is certainly not extensive. But, the time spent working one on one with your baby doing any activity is invaluable, so we won't discount the merits of this popular parent trend.

NEW PARENT 411: FINDING THE BEST TOYS

The best place to find great toys are to look in your own home. Old bowls, wooden spoons, measuring cups, and Tupperware can entertain a child more than you think.

But, if you are in the market for toys, it is worth doing a little research. *The Oppenheimer Toy Portfolio* is a great resource (it's both a book and web site). Visit their website at www.toyportfolio.com.

Q. Can you give me some ideas for age appropriate toys for babies?

Here are some guidelines:

Infants birth to six months:
Look for: bright primary color, clear lines, features, human faces
Fine Motor (Manipulatives): soft blocks, rattles, squeeze toys, keys on a ring, activity gyms.
Other sensory activities: Tape recordings of you singing or reading a story, music boxes, mobiles, mirrors, hand held puppets

Infants six to 12 months:
Look for: things safe to go in the mouth, things to stack, pour, dump, things to push, turn, or press, things to open and shut
Gross Motor Play (large muscles): Push toys, Low climbing platform
Fine Motor: soft blocks, easy puzzles, squeeze-squeaky toys, pop-up boxes containers to empty and fill, nesting cups, water toys
Other sensory: music boxes songs, tapes, tapes of you

This list is derived from The Consumer Products Safety Commission guide called *Which Toys for Which Child: A Consumer's Guide for Selecting Suitable Toys, Ages Birth Through Five.* Check out their website at cpsc.gov for your own copy.

Recommended books for kids birth to age one

Margaret Wise Brown: *Good Night Moon, Runaway Bunny, The Big Red Barn*
Eric Carle: *The Grouchy Ladybug, The Very Busy Spider, The Very Hungry Caterpillar*
Eric Hill: *Where's Spot?*
Golden Books: *Pat The Bunny, The Pokey Little Puppy*
Nancy White Carlstrom: *Jesse Bears' Yum Yum Crumble*

Notes

Chapter 11

Discipline & Temperament

"Any child can tell you that the sole purpose of a middle name is so he can tell when he's in trouble." - ~ Dennis Fakes

WHAT'S IN THIS CHAPTER

- ◆ FIGURING OUT YOUR BABY'S TEMPERAMENT
- ◆ THE HIGH MAINTENANCE BABY
- ◆ TIPS FOR SOOTHING THE SAVAGE BEAST
- ◆ PACIFIERS
- ◆ COLIC
- ◆ INFANT MASSAGE
- ◆ TIPS ON PLANTING THE SEEDS OF DISCIPLINE
- ◆ SEPARATION ANXIETY
- ◆ MASTURBATION
- ◆ THUMB SUCKING
- ◆ BITING AND BEING BITTEN

Every parent will go through it. You can see it coming. Your son snuck out last night to hang with his buddies after you explicitly told him he couldn't. So he's grounded. You took the car keys. He has to bum a ride to school or, worse, take the bus. Maybe you remember when you did exactly that or something like it.

Okay, so you don't have to worry about this scenario yet, but you do need to set up the foundation for what seems like a lifetime of discipline. And now that you know all about child development, you can take all that knowledge and apply it to guiding your child's behaviors today and into the future.

But before we get to discipline, we'll need to discuss temperament. Call it the "getting to know the real you" section of the book. Once you figure out your little angel's temperament, you can tailor your discipline issues to fit him like a glove. Or at least that's the theory.

Believe it or not, your baby's doctor may be a good resource to help you sort through these issues. If she doesn't have all of the answers, she can point you in the right direction to get the answers.

Temperament and discipline issues are the toughest part of your job description. Here is a general list of what you will be facing this first year:

AGE	ISSUE
0-3 months	Learning your baby's temperament
	Colic
3-4 months	Night feeding/ sleep issues
9 months	Separation anxiety
	Stranger anxiety
	Night wakenings
	Limit setting
12 months	Aggressive behaviors (biting, hitting)

Adapted from the Harriet Lane Handbook, 2002

Temperament: Getting to know YOUR baby

Every baby is different. We know that's not news to you. No matter how much advice you get, or how many books you read, no one can tell you what YOUR child's emotional needs will be. You will realize when you have a crying baby on your hands that you'd better figure out your child ASAP . . .or check into the nearest mental health facility.

Q. What are the typical temperaments of babies?

Landmark research done in the 1970's described the three main types of temperaments. Every child doesn't fit into only one category all the time, but here are the groups:

1 **EASY CHILD.** Surprisingly, 40% of kids fit in this category. These babies have regular eating, sleeping, and elimination habits. They are usually happy and easy going. They are interested in exploring new things and don't mind change.

2 **DIFFICULT CHILD.** Only 10% of kids fit in this category—although if it happens to you, it is a 100%! These babies have more irregular eating, sleeping, and elimination schedules. They have trouble with change, transitions, and new experiences. These babies are intense.

3 **SLOW TO WARM UP CHILD.** About 15% of kids fit here. These kids are also difficult because it takes them a while to adjust to change in environment or care provider. They hide in their shells when they encounter a new situation.

4 **THE REST.** Thirty-five percent of kids don't fit into any of the above categories and have "mixed" temperaments.[1]

BOTTOM LINE

Figuring out what type of baby you have will help you to *anticipate* how your child will react to certain situations. Plus, you'll have a better idea on how to make his world (and yours) a better place.

For example, a difficult baby needs extra time getting into his car seat without a fight. Plan extra time in your schedule for coaxing if you have some place you need to be.

Real world parent story: It always amazes us to watch our child-less friends decide to go somewhere (like a restaurant). They just pick up their keys, lock the door and poof! they're gone. For parents of children, it is a 20 (or 30 or 40) minute odyssey that first involves finding shoes/socks, coats, toys, books, etc. Then someone has to have a diaper change. It then takes more time to buckle in the car seat, only to discover a child has forgotten their toy and then the process repeats. As a parent, outings require the pre-planning that usually goes into staging a small-scale military invasion—remembering to bring that diaper bag (honey, do we have any wipes?), wallet, purse, keys . . . as well as your sanity. Then add in a "difficult" baby and you may as well just stay home.

Q. What is your view of infant temperament?

There are high-maintenance babies and low-maintenance babies. If you are blessed with a high maintenance baby, recruit family and friends to help out.

High-maintenance babies require more physical and emotional strength from their parents. These babies get walked around, rocked, and soothed more than their low maintenance friends. Parents of these babies are exhausted and frequently at wits end. They have irrational thoughts about giving their baby up for adoption. Don't worry—you are not alone.

Low-maintenance babies need little intervention, and therefore need little discussion here.

Q. Do infant temperaments have any prediction on future personality?

Yes.

Elements of a child's temperament will persist through a lifetime. However, all humans adapt to their environment and change to succeed in the face of life's challenges. In English: the way you respond to your child has a *tremendous* impact on your child's personality. It's that heredity vs. environment thing—both have an influence on behavior.

Q. I have an extremely active baby. Can you tell if he has Attention Deficit Disorder (ADD)?

No.

Attention Deficit Disorder is a diagnosis based on the shortened attention span of a child compared to peers his age. All babies under one year of age have fleeting abilities to pay attention to anything for very long. It's virtually impossible to make a diagnosis of ADD in a child less than three years of age.

Will your very active baby ultimately have ADD? Only time will tell. As we discussed in the previous chapter, armchair quarterbacks (namely, other parents at your local park) may be quick to offer a diagnosis for your child on this subject. Don't listen to them!

Q. Why is my baby crying?

Because he can't talk. The average baby cries one to four hours a day.

If you had no other way of communicating you'd be crying, too. Babies are trying to tell you something when they cry. It's your job to play detective and figure out what it is. Yes, there are certain types of cries (I'm hungry, tired, in pain), and that will give you some clues. The truth is, when you spend 24 hours a day with your crying baby, you will get each other figured out—we have no doubt about it. Welcome to Hell Week—you are about to be initiated as a parent.

Read the box below for a reasonable cry management approach:

Reality Check
A recent study done at a clinic for babies with colic showed that two-thirds of the babies referred actually had gastroesophageal reflux (i.e. heartburn).[2]

BOTTOM LINE
The mistake most parents make is that they give their newborn more credit than they deserve. Newborns have simple needs. Your baby is not nearly as sophisticated as the baby in *Look Who's*

NEW PARENT 411: THE 3 RULES OF CRY MANAGEMENT

Rule #1: DON'T PANIC—the most important advice!

Rule #2: Go through your baby's To Do List. Is your baby crying because she:
- ◆ Needs to eat?
- ◆ Needs a diaper change?
- ◆ Is overtired and having trouble falling asleep?
- ◆ Is a high-maintenance baby and doesn't know what he wants?

Rule #3: Rule out medical causes if crying persists over two hours straight. A good rule of thumb is that medical reasons for crying are generally not fixed by holding and rocking your baby. For example, your baby may be saying:
- ◆ I'm having heartburn. (This is probably the most common medical reason—see **GASTROESOPHAGEAL REFLUX**).
- ◆ I have colic. I do this every night. (See later in the chapter for more discussion on colic.)
- ◆ I have a fever. (If your baby is under *three* months old, call your doctor ASAP.)
- ◆ I have gas, constipation, or milk intolerance (Memo to new parents: usually this is NOT the cause, but every parent is convinced that this is the problem).
- ◆ I have a really serious medical problem (also rare, but that's why you should call your doctor).

Talking. They don't cry because you are a bad parent, because they are lonely, or because you have gone back to work and they are mad at you.

Most of the time, your baby just can't pull it together to fall asleep and needs some soothing. Depending on your baby's temperament, that may mean a little—or a lot—of soothing.

Old Wives Tale

Picking your newborn up every time he cries will spoil him.
The truth: Your newborn does not have a neurological maturity to relax and settle down on his own. You need to do the work to comfort him—*given his age.* From birth to two months, you do whatever it takes. There is no such thing as spoiling a newborn. As babies reach four to six months of age, they are quite capable of self-soothing. Wait to see if your baby can settle on her own before intervening.

Top Ten Tricks for Soothing a New Baby (under four months of age)

1 **LET YOUR BABY SUCK ON YOUR FINGER.** Sucking is incredibly soothing for newborns. Pacifiers are okay, too. (More on this below).

2 **DO THE BABY BURRITO WRAP.** Swaddle your baby in a receiving blanket. They are used to being snug in the womb, without limbs flailing around. See Chapter 9, "Sleep" for details on how to do this.

3 **ROCKING.** Either sitting in that expensive rocking chair you bought, or walking around and gently swaying baby back and forth in your arms. (Much as YOU would like to be sitting in that chair, babies often prefer you to walk around.) Singing or humming is also helpful.

4 **GO FOR A WALK IN THE STROLLER.** A change of scenery often helps baby and parent.

5 **GO FOR A CAR RIDE.** When parents call me about prolonged (over two hours straight) crying, I tell them to go for a car ride. If a few trips around the block don't make the crying stop, I'll tell them to keep on driving to the nearest emergency room.

6 **USE A VIBRATING INFANT SEAT OR INFANT SWING.**

7 **TAKE A TRIP TO THE LAUNDRY ROOM.** Put your baby in his car seat and place on top of the dryer. Turn on the dryer. Vibration is particularly helpful for colicky babies. Don't leave your child unattended, however.

8 **GIVE YOUR BABY A BATH.**

9 **TRY SOME INFANT MASSAGE.** (see below for more info)

10 **PUT YOUR BABY IN BED AND LEAVE HIM ALONE.** If you have tried everything and now you are crying, too, it's time to let your baby cry it out. They are truly exhausted at this point and will fall asleep on their own.

DISCIPLINE

? ?

Q. What is the party line about pacifiers?

Pacifiers are okay to use for babies *under four months of age*. Let's look at this in a developmental way.

◆ Newborns are neurologically immature.

◆ Newborns are soothed by sucking.

◆ If babies don't find their own thumb, or suck on your finger, they will use Mom's breast as a pacifier. *Remember, it's Mom's choice whether or not to accept this role.*

Here is why should you *stop* using a pacifier after four months of age:

1. Babies over four months of age have many other ways to console themselves.
2. Pacifiers become a crutch for naptime/bedtime, car rides, etc. If the pacifier falls out during these times, you will have a crying baby. If the pacifier isn't there to begin with, you won't have a problem.
3. Prolonged pacifier use creates a high arch in the mouth and protruding upper teeth. It's easy for doctors to tell which toddler is a pacifier addict. Their mouth shapes are a dead giveaway.
4. Pacifiers encourage perpetuation of the "oral exploration" phase of child-hood. As children approach their first birthdays, they stop exploring everything with their mouths and start using their hands. If they continue their oral fixation using a pacifier all the time, they continue to mouth everything well into their second year of life. If your child is in daycare, you are asking for illness when shared toys are going into your child's mouth.

DR B'S OPINION

"Nothing drives me nuts more than to see a three-year-old walking around the mall with a pacifier in his mouth. In fact, my husband gets great joy in pointing these kids out to me to see my reaction."

BOTTOM LINE: The longer the pacifier remains in your baby's world, the harder it will be to kick the habit. A four-month old will forget about that old pacifier within a day or two and move on.

Reality Check

Anti-pacifier lobbyists argue that pacifiers interfere with breast-feeding and create nipple confusion. We disagree. Babies learn very quickly that Mom's breast gives them milk, and your finger or a pacifier doesn't. If they are truly hungry, they will reject the pacifier and wail for Mom.

Q. What is colic?

If I had the answer (and the solution) I'd be rich.

This problem is known as the Rule of Threes. A three-week-old baby with colic cries for about three hours straight daily until he is three months old. This occurs in about 15% of babies. The crying usually occurs in the early evening time, just when dad is coming home from work and you are attempting to eat dinner.

The problem seems to be related to immaturity of the gastrointestinal system. Through the years, pediatricians have tried medications to reduce gas, relax the intestine muscles, or cause sedation. None of these medications help. Vibration can be somewhat helpful. Time is really the best medicine. All babies outgrow colic with time.

BOTTOM LINE: The difference between a baby with colic and one with heartburn (gastroesophageal reflux) is that colicky babies act this way for specific periods during the day. Babies with heartburn do it all day long.

Q. I heard that white noise can help soothe babies who have colic. But then I heard about a study that said white noise can damage a baby's hearing? What's up with that?

Yes, it seems conflicting to us too. Here's the scoop: a recent study published in the journal *Science* showed that rat pups exposed to white noise (such as radio static or an air conditioner's hum—no words or varying sounds involved) led to developmental delays in the hearing center of the brain.[3] Extrapolate that to humans and some scientists think that those white noise machines are a bad idea. The other side of the debate: researchers point out that white noise is similar to what babies hear when they're sloshing about in the womb—and that noise runs 24 hours a day! So at least for the first few weeks, listening to white noise can help an infant cope with all the silence outside the womb.

Our opinion: white noise is NOT a bad thing, especially in moderation. If white noise is helpful for a baby who has real colic, by all means use it. But don't expose your baby to white noise constantly—and turn it off once your baby falls asleep. Wean him off the sound once the colic goes away (at about three months of age).

Q. What can I do about colic?

The eternal parent question. We are always compelled to do *something* to make our babies feel better. In this case, the answer is that YOU need the help, not your baby.

You think I'm kidding, but I'm not. Your baby is screaming, but he will be fine. You need an escape before you go over the edge. Moms are already sleep-deprived and hormonal. Throw in an inconsolable baby—*daily*—for eight to ten weeks and you'd be justified in asking for the jumbo size gallon of Prozac at this point.

Here is what you should do:

1.   Recruit loving friends and family to come over from 5 to 8pm a night or two a week. You leave.
2.   If #1 isn't an option, put your baby in his crib and step outside for a few moments.
3.   Put your baby in a sling or carrier and run the vacuum cleaner. You probably haven't had a chance to clean the house in a while anyway. We're not being cruel, just realistic here.

4. Seek professional help for yourself if you can't take it anymore—this is not a sign of weakness or poor parenting skills.

5. For those parents who are really desperate, and will spend any amount of money to stop the crying. There is a product called "Sleep Tight" which attaches to the baby's crib to simulate the vibration and noise of a car going 55mph. For a mere $140, it can be yours. Check out www.colic.com or call 1-800-NO COLIC. Another idea: those vibrating bouncer seats ($30 to $40) have been the savior of more than one parent of a colicky baby.

Tips and tricks for dealing with colic could fill an entire book—and, in fact, one doctor has already written an excellent book on this. Dr. Harvey Karp, a pediatrician in Santa Monica, CA, has developed a terrific method for soothing colicky babies. His *Happiest Baby on the Block* book (Bantam, $13.95) focuses on five steps to mimic the baby's experience in the uterus: swaddling, side/stomach position, shhh sounds, swinging and sucking. We highly recommend Karp's book.

Reality Checks

◆ *A common parent thought is, " I can't listen to my baby cry."* That is exactly the way nature intended it to be. All animals have a certain noise that is disturbing to their elders and that prompts them to take action. As a doctor, I listen to children cry all day long in my office and completely tune it out. When I get home and my own children cry, it drives me nuts. Parents (including me!) need to learn to take their own emotions out of the picture. View crying as a form of self-expression and it won't raise your blood pressure. Remember this rule: Most of the time, YOUR CHILD IS FINE.

◆ *Parents at the end of their rope need to walk away from their baby. NEVER SHAKE a baby.* Babies who are colicky or high maintenance have a significantly higher risk of being abused. A baby's brain is very fragile. If he is shaken, the motion can lead to blindness, brain damage, or death.

Q. What do you think about infant massage?

Everyone benefits from a massage.

The power of touch has known therapeutic value. Not only are babies soothed, but parents are too. Learning infant massage teaches parents how to feel more comfortable holding and handling their babies.

Infant massage classes are a popular trend. Check with your local hospital or parenting magazine for information in your area.

DR B'S OPINION

"Spouse massages are also very important. Often our energies get focused on the baby and our spouses get treated like chopped liver."

Q. When should I encourage my baby to have a favorite toy?

The official term is *transitional object.* Six months of age is the perfect time to introduce it.

Remember that *object permanence* concept? Babies start to realize that parents still exist when they leave their viewing field between six and 12 months of age. The transitional object or toy is the friend that travels with your child when you aren't there. They are making an emotional "transition" to seeking an alternative source of comfort. The object may be a doll, blanket, or even a piece of parent's clothing.

Your child will likely have his comfort object for a while. He will give it up before going to his first slumber party (age seven to eight years is normal).

Helpful Hint

Try to pick a transitional object you don't mind carrying around everywhere. One of my patients clung to his mother's satin nightie. Another important point: buy EXTRA objects. Once your child has a favorite "lovie" (such as a stuffed animal or blanket), be sure to buy extra identical ones. Odds are, the lovie will get lost or destroyed—and that isn't a pretty scene. Having back-ups is important for everyone's sanity. Also: be careful when you attempt to wash a lovie—a much-loved stuffed animal can easily fall apart in a washing machine. Hand washing or using the delicate cycle (and not drying) is important.

If you've ever seen those kids who seem to have their parents wrapped around their little finger (think Veruca Salt from *Charlie and the Chocolate Factory*), you know you want to avoid that fate. But how can you prevent that future behavior in your cute little baby? Even though you now know how your baby's brain works, you still may not have all the right answers in every discipline situation. Why? Because your child is really smart and has figured YOU out. So let's move on to setting up a good discipline foundation that can hopefully take you through the tougher times to come.

Planting The Seeds Of Discipline

Q. At what age should I start to discipline my baby?

By nine months of age.

Planting the seeds of discipline is CRITICAL. From birth to eight months, your parenting job is easy. It is physically exhausting but doesn't require too many mental strategies to succeed. At about nine months old, you will start playing chess with your child and will continue to play for a lifetime. Here are the rules of the game:

Discipline is the process of teaching your child to be an independent being. Your job is to give your child a **SUPER-EGO**. This is a Freudian term that refers to a person's internal control that limits inappropriate behavior from occurring (that is, self-control). In other words, your discipline implants a device in your child's hard drive that he will carry with him wherever he goes. That way, your child will do the right thing even when you aren't around.

Let's review your child's development. A nine to 12 month old is exploring, not purposefully destroying, his environment (your house). He uses his memory of what has worked before to approach the unfamiliar, so everything ultimately ends up in his mouth (and hence, a safety hazard). He has figured out how to get other people to repeat behaviors (if you scream when he bites you, he will bite you again). He is egocentric—the world revolves around him (how could a phone call be more important than him?) He wants independence, but doesn't quite have the motor skills to accomplish his goals (refusing to let you feed him). He has developed a sense of trust with his parents and caretakers. He doesn't want anyone to leave him, even to go to the bathroom (separation anxiety). Are we having fun yet?

When the baby I just described is *your* baby, it's time to get to work.

BOTTOM LINE

Consistency is the key to making a discipline plan work. If there is an adult who ignores a behavior that other adults reprimand, the behavior will continue to occur. Grandparents are usually the worst in this department— and kids know it! It's like having a substitute teacher.

Q. What should be included in our House Rules?

Anything dangerous or potentially painful to the child or others.

These are behaviors that are *never* acceptable. These include pulling on cords, touching the stove, putting fingers in electrical outlets, turning on bathtub water, biting, hitting the dog and so on. Look around your house and add to your list.

Q. What is a discipline management plan?

How adult caretakers will respond to inappropriate behaviors.

Everyone has his or her own style. Most parents will think back to their own parents' approach and remember what worked. You and your spouse need to come up with a uniform strategy that both of you feel comfortable enforcing.

Q. Do you think it's okay to spank my child?

No.

We never recommend using physical force to punish a child. Your child learns from you. If you are violent when you are angry, your child will be that way, too. We know that your first reaction when your child hits you is to hit back—DON'T. You're older than your child remember?

BOTTOM LINE: The goal of discipline is to *teach*. If you want a well-behaved child, you need to be well behaved as their role model.

NEW PARENT 411: PLANTING THE SEEDS OF DISCIPLINE

1. Make your house kid safe, so you don't have to say "No" to everything your child touches.
2. Make up a set of "House Rules" that all caretakers enforce.
3. Make up a discipline management plan with consequences— again, that all caretakers enforce.
4. Know that your nine-month old understands the word, "no", but wants to be sure you really mean it. Yep, this is called *testing limits*.

11 TIPS FOR DEVELOPING A DISCIPLINE STYLE

1 **AVOID AS MANY CONFLICTS AS POSSIBLE.** Make your house kid safe. Don't push your child past his threshold. For example: running too many errands, missing naptime, waiting forever at a restaurant. For eating out, we have a ten-minute rule—if the wait is over ten minutes, it's time to go elsewhere. Obviously, eating early is a good way to avoid lengthy waits for a table.

2 **ANTICIPATE CONFLICTS.** If you see your child heading towards the stereo, move him elsewhere or offer him a toy. Obviously, parents develop a sixth sense for this—soon, you'll be able to scan a room and predict the future (that is, zeroing in on your baby's next conflict).

3 **ANTICIPATE ATTENTION-SEEKING BEHAVIOR.** Be prepared for trouble when your attention is turned elsewhere. If your child gets into trouble when you are cooking dinner, let him "cook" on the kitchen floor.

4 **PICK YOUR BATTLES.** Saying "No" twenty times a day loses its effectiveness. Believe it or not, I had a parent tell me her child thought his name was "No." Categorize behaviors into major errors, minor ones, and those too insignificant to bother with. Minor infractions are negotiable with an older child.

5 **ACT IMMEDIATELY.** Discipline when the behavior occurs, not after the fact. Otherwise, your child won't remember what he is getting in trouble for. Never say: "Just wait till your father/mother gets home!"

6 **MAKE YOUR COMMENTS SHORT AND SWEET.** Speak in short sentences such as "No hitting." This is much more effective than, "Johnny, you know it's not nice to hit the dog." Believe us, you lost Johnny right after "you know."

7 **FOCUS ON THE BEHAVIOR, NOT THE CHILD.** Be sure to state that a particular behavior is bad. NEVER tell your child that HE is bad.

8 **REMIND YOUR CHILD THAT YOU LOVE HER OR HIM.** Always end your intervention with a positive comment. It reinforces the reason that you are teaching her how to behave.

9 **USE AGE-APPROPRIATE AND TEMPERAMENT-APPROPRIATE DISCIPLINE TECHNIQUES.** You need to adapt to your baby and find a discipline style that works well with your individual child. What works at nine months might not work when your child is two. He's had time to figure out your strategy!

10 **DON'T YELL.** It's not the volume of your voice, but the tone that gets your point across. Remember *The Godfather?* He never needed to yell. Some of the most effective discipline we've ever seen has been whispered.

11 **CATCH YOUR CHILD "BEING GOOD."** Praise for good behavior is so important and helps encourage more of it. Think of it as fertilizer for her conscience.

Q. At what age does the Terrible Two's start? My one year old is already acting terrible.

The Terrible Two's is a misnomer. It actually starts when your child declares independence from you.

We usually see this behavior start around 18 months and last until age three, but some kids are ahead of their time.

My advice is to have a glass of wine at dinner for the next two years. Just kidding—sort of. My other advice is to give your child the opportunity to feel like he is in control of his world. You are really in charge, but he doesn't need to be reminded of that 24 hours a day. When there is an opportunity for *him* to choose something, let him (picking out a snack, a toy to play with, etc.). Also, don't bother to discipline for minor infractions. It's not worth it and limits the amount of conflicts that arise.

Q. What is a temper tantrum and how should I respond to it?

A physical release of anger. You need to let it happen.

Tantrums are frequently seen in toddlers, but some kids like to start early. When your child is at the end of his rope, he may have an emotional breakdown. This involves kicking, screaming, crying, and flailing

8 TRIED & TRUE DISCIPLINE TECHNIQUES

Here are some tips to keep the peace in your house and foster your child's self-control.

1. Ignore. If it's not a major infraction, ignore the behavior. If your child doesn't get a rise out of you, she will stop doing it.

2. Redirect. Move your child to a different activity. Children repeat the same inappropriate behavior to see if they can get away with it. It often takes numerous times and consistent redirection of the same misbehavior until you can eliminate it. Don't give up.

3. Use Humor. It works beautifully with power struggles. Instead of digging in to the trenches and holding your ground on the situation, change to an upbeat approach. Your child will do the same.

4. Time Out. Yes, it really does work. The premise is that your child is removed from his play and must sit out for a period of time. Your child gets one minute for every year of age. Kids under age two rarely sit in isolation for the time requirement. Little ones can sit facing away from you on your lap. You do not talk to them or interact. Time out is reserved for particularly inappropriate behaviors and it should be used every time the behavior occurs.

around on the floor.

Your job is to give him a safe place to have it out. Do not respond to your child while he is in the midst of this performance. When he is done, you can scoop him up and discuss things.

Just for fun, as parents, we also like to rank our children's temper tantrums much in the way scientists score hurricanes. There are Category 1 and 2 fits, which like minor hurricanes involve a minimal amount of damage. Then there are the serious tantrums—up to and including the big ones we like to call Category 5.

Once we took our two year old to a train show, something he absolutely loved. Until it was time to go. They were closing it down and turning out the lights (we had been there for an hour or more). Suddenly, our son launched into the most amazing Category 5 tantrum—a one-hour scream-fest. You just had to marvel at the intensity of it all. Of course, at the time, we wanted to give back our parent license and go into the Federal Parent Witness Protection Program.

Reality Check

A word of caution: If you give in to a situation when your child has a tantrum, you have just taught him that a tantrum is an effective way to get what he wants. Be strong!

5. Positive Reinforcement. Catch your child being good. Tell your child how proud you are when they are behaving well. This will pay off.

6. Avoid Negative Reinforcement. Any attention (good or bad) that you pay a child is attention. So behaviors that cause a reaction from you (even a negative reaction) are likely to be repeated by your child. This concept is called negative reinforcement of a behavior. Think before you react.

7. Give Choices/Teach Consequences. As your child gets older, he (who is seeking independence) will appreciate being given choices. Instead of getting into a power struggle, let him pick the consequence of his actions. Example: If your child insists on picking out his pajamas (which might take a long time), then he will opt not to read books that night. One real world parent tip: LIMIT the number of choices any baby is offered. Too much choice can be overwhelming.

8. Loss Of Privileges. As your child gets older, he will appreciate that certain activities are special. You can reinforce consequences of actions by withholding special activities for misbehavior. The most important activity in your child's world is special time with a parent (not TV time, dessert, etc). Use this to your advantage.

Bottom Line: Whatever discipline style you use. BE CONSISTENT. If your child knows he can get his way if he persists, he will.

Q. What sets off a temper tantrum?

Anything and nothing.

Look at your child's world through your child's eyes. He has poor language skills and can't tell his parents everything he needs and wants. He hasn't mastered all his motor skills to accomplish certain tasks. He isn't sure where his activity boundaries are and is told "no" numerous times a day. Add in an egocentric perspective that Mom and Dad can read his mind (if he thinks it, everyone knows what he is thinking). Finish with the unattainable goal of complete independence.

Being tired, bored, and hungry are also contributors to ugly behavior.

So, when you pick out the wrong pajamas at bedtime and your child explodes, don't think it's just the P.J.'s.

Special Situations: Tips & Tricks

Q. How do I deal with separation anxiety? Can I just sneak out of sight?

Before, you could leave the room and your baby might not have cared. Now, if you leave the room, he wants to know where you're going. This is about the time you will keep your bathroom door open so your baby doesn't panic every time you answer nature calls. (That bathroom door often remains open for the next several years. I have to remind myself when we have company to close mine. But I digress). It is CRITICAL that you tell your baby where you are going. You will think it is better to "sneak out" of the house when you leave, so your baby doesn't cry. But, you are NOT helping your baby with his anxiety—you only make it worse. He doesn't know if you are leaving for a minute or for a lifetime. If your baby is prepared for your departure, he will protest for a few minutes and then move on.

Q. My child freaks out with strangers. How do I make him more comfortable?

Be patient. All babies, but especially the slow-to-warm-up ones, are afraid of strangers. They need some time to check out these people and make sure they are okay. And "strangers" to a baby might include a grandparent who lives out of town.

To help the situation, let your baby watch this person before handing him over. Then, stay in your child's view for a while after the hand off.

It's probably a good idea to have consistent caregivers while your child is in his stranger anxiety mode (nine to 15 months).

Q. My baby is playing with his genitals. How do I make him stop?

He is normal and you don't need to stop him.

The official term is **MASTURBATION**. It is amazing how quickly babies find these body parts, and yes, it does feel good to touch them. P.S. Erections are also normal.

For now, there is little you can do to limit this behavior. As your child gets older (18 months) you can start explaining to him that it's okay to touch down there, but only when he is at home/in his room. This is a good segue into a discussion that no one else touches or looks down there except for Mom, Dad, and Doctor.

Masturbation is in the same category of self-soothing behaviors as thumb sucking. You won't be able to eliminate these behaviors, but you can limit where and when they are occurring.

Reality Check

Boys aren't the only ones exploring their pleasure zones. I had a female patient who would ride the high chairs at restaurants. Needless to say, her parents didn't take her out to eat much.

Q. My nine-month old enjoys having food fights in our kitchen. Help.

A budding John Belushi. Children start to play with their food when they are no longer eating it. When the food starts to fly, mealtime is over. Your child will quickly learn that he is excused from the dinner table when more food ends up on the floor than in his mouth.

Q. My nine-month old awakens every three hours at night and screams. Am I being manipulated?

Yes. Go back to the chapter on sleep and read it again! Do not pass go, do not collect $200.

Q. My child is one year old and we can't break the bottle habit. Help!

Treat your toddler as a child, and he won't act like a baby. Bottles tend to perpetuate the oral phase of development. Get rid of the bottle before it really becomes a test of wills. Teach your child to drink from a cup or with a straw, so there is no need for a bottle in his life.

Q. My one year old sucks his thumb. How can I stop it?

You can't. The thumb goes everywhere your child does. This is another self-soothing activity. As your child gets to be around 18 months, you can reason with him about where it is appropriate to thumb suck (in his bedroom) and where it is not (out in public). This will limit the behavior to certain times when your child needs to have some down time.

I've never seen a thumb sucker beyond age seven.

Q. My child holds his breath when he gets angry. What do I do?

Nothing. At worst, he will faint. It is human nature not to inflict harm on oneself. If your child holds his breath long enough, he will lose consciousness and start breathing spontaneously. This sounds really cruel, but a *breath holding spell* is potent ammunition for a little kid to get his way. If you want to win the battle, you can't give in.

Note: If your child has numerous breath-holding spells, check in with your doctor. Occasionally, this can be related to iron deficiency anemia.

Q. My child is biting me. What do I do?

Don't bite back. And whatever you do, don't scream.

When babies are teething, they often start to gnaw on whatever is available. This may be a parent's shoulder or Mom's nipple (OUCH!). It's not malicious. But, if you respond dramatically, it will encourage your baby to bite again.

Your response: Take your baby off your body and place him on the floor. Calmly and sternly say, "No biting." Do not pay any attention to your baby for one minute. Your baby yearns for your attention so this is a good punishment. Lick your wounds later, out of sight from your baby.

It may take 20-30 times before your baby gets the message, but he will.

Q. My child is biting/being bitten at daycare. What do I do?

Talk to the daycare director and do an observation in the classroom.

There is a biter or hitter in every room. A good childcare program will be constantly watching the children and be able to prevent Hannibal Lecter, Jr. from successfully drawing blood from another child.

Reality Check

My son's kindergarten teacher had a wonderful motto. "If I'm doing my job, I don't have to discipline these kids." The point is, children who have the opportunity to bite or hit are those that aren't being watched closely enough by an adult caregiver. The problem is not the child's but the caregiver's.

Finally, here's when you know you're getting through to your kids: My 4-year-old was watching a football game on TV with my husband. One of the teams called time out. My daughter astutely asked, "Daddy, why is the team in Time Out?"

THE QUIET ZONE—WHEN YOU ARE REALLY IN TROUBLE!

When our oldest son became a toddler, we had our share of discipline problems. In hindsight we think he was a pretty well behaved guy. But we learned one important tip we wanted to pass along to all you first time parents: if your rambunctious child is unusually quiet, check it out quick.

You see, Ben normally exhausted us and once, when we were sitting in the living room resting from a particularly long day, we began to notice how quiet the house was. Hmmm, should we investigate? Boy it was hard to give up the couch, but eventually we pried ourselves loose and meandered to the kitchen. There we were presented with the sight of our son Ben covered head to foot (no exaggeration) with flour. We immediately turned around and walked back to the living room to laugh our heads off. And of course we took lots of pictures. But then we all had a sit-down to explain exactly why Ben *wouldn't* be doing that again.

So even to this day, if the house seems too quiet, we are quick to check things out. And while most of the time all is okay, you never know when your oldest child will be using every inch of tape to turn his little brother into a mummy.

SECTION 4

Baby 411

Sickness & How To Avoid It!

Chapter 12

Vaccinations

*"No man is an island,
entire of itself; every man is
a piece of the continent, a
part of the main..."*
~ John Donne (1572-1631)

It's time to jump right into the deep end of one of the most controversial subjects you'll find in parent circles—vaccines. Nothing seems to stir the blood these days more than a good ol' fashion debate on vaccinating your child.

Before we get to our take on this debate, let's go back in time a bit. Well, more than a bit. How about three million years? While watching the Discovery Channel show *Walking with Caveman* with our kids, a thought occurred to us—why did we survive while other early humans didn't?

Hundreds of thousands of years of human evolution boiled down to this: survival meant more than making tools and finding food more efficiently. The "cavemen" that evolved into our ancestors had one crucial advantage—they had imagination. They could plan for the future. And it was the evolution of imagination and our ability to anticipate the future is what made the crucial difference. What resulted was a sense of responsibility . . . to ourselves and to our society.

We don't think we ever appreciated that responsibility more than on September 11, 2001. We suddenly felt closer to every person in this country, and we felt stronger about our civic duty to work together as a community.

So, what's all this pontificating have to do with vaccines? It's that responsibility issue again. Just look at a bit more recent history: in the 1890's, people would have seven or eight children in their families and only half of them would survive childhood. Just go to an old graveyard some time and look at the ages listed on the headstones. Many of the diseases that killed those children are now prevented by vaccination. It's a fact: vaccinations, single-handedly, have increased the life expectancy of our nation's children.

Again, you might say "so?" Well, the key to a vaccine's success is that *everyone* in the community gets vaccinated. Think about that for a minute. As a society, we are often taught to think just about ourselves—and to be suspicious of the Establishment. Or the Government. Yet, vaccines won't work if a large number of folks just choose to opt out of the system and their responsibility. Germs are rather simple creatures . . . they just look for a new person to infect. They don't play politics.

A Bit of History

So where did the idea of vaccinations develop? It took centuries of observation as well as trial and error. (And sometimes, error meant death.) The first real step was describing the disease, in this case, smallpox. Smallpox was a deadly disease that, historically, wiped out entire civilizations. The earliest descriptions can be found as far back as the ninth and tenth centuries among Turks. In fact, "inoculation" or the infecting of a person with the disease in hopes of introducing a mild form and then creating immunity was practiced in Asia. In the 1700's an English aristocrat, Lady Mary Wortly Montagu, was living in Constantinople and learned of the practice of inoculation (known as variolation). She had her son inoculated and subsequently, brought the practice back to England.

At about the same time, an English country doctor, Edward Jenner, made an interesting connection: farmers who had been exposed to cowpox (a common disease in cattle at the time) never seemed to get smallpox infections during epidemics. He began to study the idea that vaccinating humans with cowpox virus would make them immune to smallpox. In 1798 he published a paper on his idea and called it "vaccination." Not to say, by the way, that Dr. Jenner's idea was accepted with completely open arms. In the nineteenth century there did emerge a group opposed to vaccination led by Mary C. Hume. See, even the anti-vaccination lobby has been around a long time! Of course, in those days, you could be prosecuted for refusing to vaccinate.[1]

People were inoculated with a small amount of cowpox virus on their arm. It caused a localized infection at that site (hence, the scar that we Thirty-Somethings and above bear). And true to Dr. Jenner's hypothesis, it provided protection against smallpox disease. In 1972, the United States stopped vaccinating against smallpox because it was no longer a threat to the population. In 1977, the last case of smallpox occurred in Somalia. In 1980, the World Health Organization declared the world free of smallpox, thanks to a global effort to immunize all children.

The success of the smallpox vaccine and scientific discoveries led to the evolution of many vaccines. These new, safer vaccines are extremely effective in preventing diseases and epidemics that our grandparents and parents can still remember.

Today's Paradox—Have Vaccines Been Too Successful?

As you can see, vaccinations are one of the greatest achievements in medical history. Above all other advances in public health, vaccinations have significantly decreased infant and childhood mortality. Yet, amazingly, doctors have to convince many of today's parents that immunizing their child is extremely important, not "optional." Most parents have not spent a night in a pediatric intensive care unit with a child who has HIB meningitis, watched a child gasping for breath with whooping cough, or seen a child die with a Strep infection as a complication of chickenpox. Sadly, every pediatrician has had one of these experiences and has known that the child's illness or death could have been prevented by vaccination.

That's the bitter irony of today's vaccine "debate." As a vaccinated society, we've made diseases like whooping cough so rare that parents have no idea today how devastating it was and still can be. Hence it is easy to pontificate about real or imagined risks with vaccines when you don't see the real devastation the original disease created.

Reality Check

The concept of "public health" has been around since antiquity. Obviously, rulers had a vested interest in keeping their subjects healthy so they had a society to rule. Through the years, governments have been responsible for managing numerous programs. The most important advances in public health have been vaccination programs, water purification, and waste disposal/sanitation systems. The only way for public health to work, though, is for all members of the community to follow the same rules.

BOTTOM LINE

The decision to vaccinate your child impacts the health of other children in the community. Choosing NOT to vaccinate your child is choosing to put your child AND your community's children at risk. This is a public health issue, not just a personal one. As

---

OUTBREAK: IT COULD HAPPEN TODAY

Let's get even more serious here. European settlers who "discovered" the New World had a very effective way of finding land to settle on. They brought their germs from the Old World and infected Native Americans. Although most germ sharing was unintentional, there are historical reports of English soldiers giving smallpox infested blankets to Native Americans to purposely "remove" them from their land. Biological warfare has been around for a long time.[2]

Fast forward to the present day. One obvious real-world example: SARS (Sudden Acute Respiratory Syndrome). Here's a new virus that in a matter of weeks spread around the world and killed hundreds. Thanks to today's modern air travel system, a bug can go from a regional problem to a worldwide epidemic in a blink of an eye. SARS, like many of the diseases we vaccinate for, is a VIRUS. There is no medication to stop the spread of infection—despite our scientifically advanced world.[3]

vaccinations

a parent, you want to make the right choices for your child to protect them. We want you to ask questions. We want you to be informed. And we want you to get your child vaccinated. YOUR decision impacts OUR children.

The Top 15 Vaccine Questions

1 **WHAT ARE VACCINES?** Vaccines are materials that are given to a person to protect them from disease (that is, provide immunity). The word vaccine is derived from "vaccinia" (cowpox virus), which was used to create the first vaccine in history (smallpox).

Modern medicine has created many vaccines. Vaccines PREVENT viral and bacteria infections that used to cause serious illness and death.

2 **HOW DO VACCINES WORK?** Here is your microbiology lesson for today. Your immune system is your body's defense against foreign invaders (viruses, bacteria, parasites). Vaccines prepare your body to recognize foreigners without getting infected. A vaccine revs up your immune system to make antibodies (smart bombs with memory) for the signature of a particular germ. So, if your body sees the real germ, voila! You already know how to fight it off.

There are three types of vaccinations: inactivated, live attenuated, and inactivated bacterial toxins:

◆ *Inactivated vaccines* do not contain any living germs. An immune response forms against either a dead germ, part of the germ (recombinant DNA), or a protein or sugar marker that sits on the outer layer of the germ (its signature). Very cool. These vaccines are safe to give to immune-compromised people. The only down side is that several doses of the vaccine are needed to provide full, lifelong protection against disease. Some of these types of vaccines include: *Flu, Hepatitis A & B, HIB, Pertussis (whooping cough), Inactivated Polio, Prevnar.*

◆ *Live attenuated vaccines* are weak forms of the germs that cause infection. An immune response occurs just as if your body had the infec-

FIVE BIGGEST MISCONCEPTIONS ABOUT VACCINES

Pop online to any of the anti-vaccine web sites out there today and you'll find a plethora of misconceptions, untruths and worse about vaccines. Here are the top five we hear most often:

1. Diseases disappeared before vaccines were introduced. *No!*
2. Vaccines cause illness and death. *Reactions are very rare.*
3. Vaccine preventable diseases are rare. *No!*
4. Multiple vaccines overload the immune system. *No!*
5. There is a government conspiracy to inject cancer-causing agents into our children. *What can we say to that one?*

Source: CDC and Dr. Brown's patients

tion. So, one or two doses of vaccine gives you lifelong protection. These vaccines are not given to immune compromised people because it can make them sick. Examples include: *MMR, Oral Polio, Smallpox, Tuberculosis, Varicella (chickenpox).*

◆ *Toxoids* (inactivated bacterial toxins) are vaccines that create a defense against the toxin (poison) that a bacteria germ makes. Examples of toxoid vaccines include: *Diphtheria, Tetanus.*

BOTTOM LINE

There are two critical points for vaccination to work:
1. You need to be vaccinated.
2. Your neighbor needs to be vaccinated.

This concept is called herd immunity. And yes, you are a member of a herd. When 90-95% of "the herd" is protected, it is nearly impossible for a germ to cause an epidemic. Think of germs as rain. Vaccination is a raincoat. Even with a raincoat on, you can still get wet. You need an umbrella, too. The umbrella is 'herd immunity'. Those who don't vaccinate expect someone to share their umbrella when it rains. But society can only buy umbrellas TOGETHER. And raincoats aren't made for newborns—they need umbrellas!

3 **WHAT ARE THE DISEASES WE ARE PRO-TECTED AGAINST WITH VACCINATION?** Good question. You are probably unfamiliar with most of these diseases since we don't see them much anymore. After you see this list, thank your parents for immunizing you.

As you read through the list, note that some diseases are viruses. Antibiotics kill bacteria only. Doctors have no medications to cure the viral infections. See section on "vaccine specifics" for details on all of these diseases and the vaccines.

DR B'S OPINION

"I refuse to care for patients whose parents refuse vaccinations. I care about my patients as I do for my own children. I wouldn't be able to sleep at night if my kids weren't protected."

SEVEN TRUTHS ABOUT VACCINES

Let's contrast those misconceptions about vaccines with these truths:
1. Vaccines save lives. They have single-handedly reduced infant mortality rates.
2. Lower immunization rates mean higher disease & mortality rates.
3. Misinformation is everywhere—the web, media, and playgroups.
4. The decision NOT to vaccinate is a decision to accept the consequences of the disease.
5. The decision NOT to vaccinate is a decision to put your community at risk for epidemics.
6. Vaccines are not 100% safe.
7. Your parents have respect for vaccinations because they have seen these diseases.

Deaths drop by 99%!

Doubt the effectiveness of vaccines? Let's look at the facts. Here is a chart that compares the annual deaths by vaccine-preventable diseases in 1901 compared to 2001 in the United States.[4]

Disease	1901 Deaths	2001 Deaths	Decrease	Type of germ
Smallpox	48,164	0	100%	virus
Diphtheria	175,885	2	100%	bacteria
Tetanus	1,314	27	97.9%	bacteria
Pertussis	147,271	5,396	96.3%	bacteria
Polio	16,316	0	100%	virus
Measles	503,282	108	100%	virus
Mumps	152,209	231	99.8%	virus
Rubella	47,745	19	100%	virus
Congenital rubella	823	2	99.8%	virus
HIB	~20,000	183	99.1%	bacteria
Hepatitis B	200,000	80,000	60%	virus

4 **HOW ARE VACCINES TESTED TO MAKE SURE THEY'RE SAFE?** Vaccines are researched extensively for an average of 15 years before being approved for use.

A pharmaceutical company conducts medical research trials in a series of stages. Once safety is proven, the vaccine is tested in several thousand volunteers to make sure the vaccine actually works. These volunteers are followed for at least one year to be sure that no serious side effects occur.

Nothing in this world is 100% foolproof, including vaccine science. But the research trials that occur before licensing are very rigid. If you think there are a lot of vaccines on the market, imagine how many didn't make it through the research phase of development.

The Food and Drug Administration (FDA) governs this whole process. The FDA is the watchdog for any medication that is sold over-the-counter or by prescription. There are extremely high standards that must be met before any product is allowed for human use.

After a vaccine is approved for use, long-term follow-up studies are done to assess for side effects, adverse reactions, and potency over a lifetime.

5 **WHY IS MY CHILD GETTING MORE SHOTS THAN I DID?** Because vaccinations are one of the most important advances in modern medicine. There has been a tremendous effort to create more vaccinations because they are so effective in preventing serious infections.

Many of the vaccine preventable diseases are viruses. These viral infections cannot be treated with medicine once an infection occurs (for example, Hepatitis B).

Vaccines that protect against bacterial diseases are often serious ones, and resistant to many antibiotics (for example, Prevnar).

6 **CAN MY BABY'S LITTLE BODY HANDLE FOUR OR FIVE DIFFERENT VACCINATIONS GIVEN AT ONCE?** Yes, probably better than you!

On any given day, your baby is exposed to literally thousands of germs (it doesn't matter how spotless your house is). Exposing your child to five to eight different germs in the form of vaccines is a spit in the bucket.

Young children have better immune responses to vaccines than adults and older children. So, they will form adequate immune responses to various vaccines *simultaneously*. (This is studied extensively before a vaccine is licensed).

Also, the diseases that the vaccines protect against are the most severe in infants and young children. Your doctor wants to get those vaccinations in as quickly and as efficiently as possible.

Q. Can't you just give one big shot that has all the vaccines in it?

Medical science is working on it!

There have been a few combination vaccines licensed for use. The largest combination vaccine is called Pediarix. Pediarix includes DTaP, IPV, and Hepatitis B. The problem is that some vaccines are less effective when they are sitting together in a solution. Even if your doctor uses the Pediarix shot at the two, four, and six month visits, the HIB and Prevnar vaccines are administered separately.

Hopefully, there will be more combination vaccines in the future.

Helpful Hints
Top Five Tips to Make Shots Less Painful

1. Distraction. Blow in your child's face, or pull out a new toy.

2. A spoonful of sugar. Put a little sugar water on a nipple or pacifier. It is a known pain reliever (analgesic).

3. Acetaminophen (Tylenol). It's a great pain medicine. Be sure to check with your doctor for the correct dose for your baby's weight.

4. Numb it. There is a prescription anesthetic cream called EMLA that can be applied one hour before shots are administered. The downsides: a) Pain is not just from the needle going through the skin but also from the fluid injected into muscle. b) You may not know where to place the cream.

5. Freeze it. There is a cold 'vapocoolant'spray that can be placed on the skin just before the injections. A few doctors use it. It works slightly better than the distraction technique.[5]

7 **WHAT GROUP MAKES DECISIONS ABOUT VACCINATIONS FOR CHILDREN?**
There are four governing panels of experts in infectious diseases that make recommendations for vaccinations. These smart folks include: American Academy of Pediatrics (AAP), American Academy of Family Physicians (AAFP), Advisory Committee on Immunization Practices (ACIP), and the Centers for Disease Control (CDC). Because there are several groups involved in this effort, there is some variability in vaccination schedule recommendations.

8 **MY BABY HAS A COLD. SHOULD I HOLD OFF ON THE VACCINATIONS HE IS DUE FOR?**
No!

This is a common misconception of parents. We cannot stress how important it is to get your child vaccinated in a timely manner. Unless your baby has a fever of 102 or higher with his illness, he can get his vaccinations when he is sick.

9 **CAN I CHOOSE NOT TO VACCINATE MY CHILD?** Yes, but we wouldn't advise it. Choosing not to vaccinate is choosing to expose your child to potentially serious infection. It's also choosing to expose other children in society to serious, preventable diseases. Remember, your decision impacts the welfare of others. And if you think your child will be safe because everyone else vaccinates his or her kids, you'd be wrong (and very selfish, we might add).

You can also choose not to stop at a stop sign, but we wouldn't advise it!

Reality Check

Vaccine requirements for school entry vary by state. There is no one consistent policy. All 50 states allow vaccine exemptions for medical reasons, 48 states allow vaccine exemption for religious reasons and 16 states allow vaccine exemption for philosophical reasons.[9]

10 **I'VE HEARD THAT GETTING A DISEASE PROVIDES LIFE LONG IMMUNITY AND VACCINATIONS MIGHT NOT PROVIDE LIFELONG PROTECTION. WOULDN'T IT BE BETTER TO GET THE DISEASE? ISN'T THAT A MORE "NATURAL" WAY OF CREATING IMMUNITY?**

No.

The diseases we prevent by vaccination are not minor illnesses (this includes chicken pox). For instance, would you rather have your child get meningitis and die or get the vaccine? Getting chickenpox or any other disease the "natural way" does not create any more immunity than using a vaccine. And just think of the discomfort, pain and perhaps serious injury that come with getting any of these diseases.

REASONS NOT TO VACCINATE

There are very specific medical reasons to discontinue or hold off on certain vaccinations:

1. *An immune-compromised patient or family member.*
2. *Had disease (for example, if you've had chicken pox, you don't need the vaccine).*
3. *Encephalitis or degenerative brain disorder.*
4. *Allergy to vaccine or an additive in vaccine.*

If your baby has a food allergy to eggs or gelatin, or an allergy to antibiotics (such as Neomycin, Streptomycin, Polymyxin B), notify your doctor before any vaccinations are given. Several vaccines are grown in chick embryo cells and therefore contain a small amount of egg protein: flu vaccine (Flushield, Fluzone, Fluvirin), MMR, rabies (RabAvert), and yellow fever vaccine (YF-VAX). The MMR vaccine also includes gelatin.

Rabies, MMR, Chickenpox and Polio vaccines include several different kinds of antibiotics to prevent contamination of the vaccine itself. Check with your doctor if your child is allergic to any antibiotics.[6]

If your child has a food allergy to eggs, it is recommended that your child be observed for allergic reaction for 90 minutes after receiving the MMR vaccine at one year of age.[7] The flu vaccine is NOT advised for people with egg allergies.[8]

It is true that some vaccinations require a booster dose to keep antibody levels high. That is why we need to get a tetanus and diphtheria booster every ten years.

11 **WHAT WOULD HAPPEN IF WE STOPPED USING VACCINATIONS?** That's an easy one. The diseases would come back.

Vaccinations keep us from getting sick from these infections. But, all of the infections we protect against are alive and well in our world. As of today, the only disease we have completely eliminated is smallpox. And when it was eliminated, we stopped vaccinating for it. (However, "eliminated" may be too strong a word. Smallpox still exists in laboratories in the U.S. and Russia as well as potentially in rogue countries.)

Anyway, it's a simple fact: when immunization rates drop, epidemics occur. My home state of Texas currently ranks 42nd in the United States for children age three who have received the appropriate number of vaccinations. (Texans are usually very proud folks—we *aren't* proud of this statistic). Only 74% of Texas children are protected by immunization . . . which leaves a window of opportunity for epidemics. As a result, my hometown of Austin is in the midst of a whooping cough epidemic as of this writing.

Reality Check

◆ In 1990, low immunization rates led to a measles epidemic of 55,000 cases and over 100 preventable deaths in the U.S.

◆ In 2003, UNICEF sent a team to Iraq to vaccinate five million children against measles and polio prior to the second Gulf war. Why? Because these diseases flourish in cramped housing conditions (such as refugee camps). It is estimated that there could have been 10,000 deaths of Iraqi children from measles, a vaccine-preventable disease. [10]

12 **WHAT ARE THE TYPICAL SIDE EFFECTS OF VACCINATION?** Fever, fussiness, redness or lump at the site of the injection.

Inactivated vaccines cause an immediate immune response. The body mounts a response to the foreign invader as if it were being infected. The result, typically, is a fever within 24 hours of vaccination. Babies sometimes feel like they are coming down with a cold or flu (body aches, pains). Some babies prefer to sleep through the experience; some choose to tell you how they feel (fussiness, crying). All of these symptoms resolve within 24 hours of vaccination.

Live attenuated vaccines (MMR, Varicella) cause a delayed immune response. This occurs one to four *weeks* after the vaccination is given. Long after the doctor's visit, your child may wake up one morning and have a fever. This may be accompanied by a rash that looks like measles (pimples) or chickenpox (clear, fluid filled pimples). The rash can sometimes be dramatic. Both the fever and the rash tell you that your baby is forming an immune response to the vaccination. Babies are not contagious and aren't too bothered by the rash. You don't need to call your doctor. This reaction is expected.

Redness at the injection site is common. In particular, the fifth booster dose of the DTaP (at age five years) can cause a huge area of redness. This happens because our bodies already recognize these germs pretty well. Doctors get many phone calls on this reaction.

A firm lump may develop at the injection site if some of the fat in the arm/leg gets nicked as the needle goes into the muscle. This is called **FAT NECROSIS**. It usually goes away within six to eight weeks. It doesn't hurt.

RED FLAG

If your baby has a fever *more* than 24 hours after being vaccinated, it's not from the vaccination. You need to call your doctor. The only exceptions are the MMR and chickenpox vaccines given at one year of age.

Reality Check

It's okay to give your baby acetaminophen (Tylenol) to help reduce the fever and discomfort of vaccinations. The dose is not listed on the package of infant drops. It says to "consult a doctor." That's because doctors don't want you giving this medicine to a baby *three months or younger* with a fever without checking in first. Other than with shots, you need to call your doctor about fevers in this age group—see Chapter 15, "First Aid" chapter.

13 WHAT ARE THE WORST REACTIONS TO VACCINATION? These are called adverse reactions. This is the equivalent of an allergic reaction to a medication—and fortunately, they are all quite rare. With each generation of newer vaccinations, the risk of serious reactions is almost eliminated. Adverse reactions include:

1. Death.
2. Encephalitis.
3. Fever related seizure (convulsions).

Both the CDC and FDA keep close tabs on adverse reactions to vaccines via a Vaccine Adverse Event Reporting System (VAERS). Both doctors and patient families may submit a VAERS form if any adverse reaction occurs.

Keep in mind that medical illness reports do not prove an association of a particular illness with a particular vaccination. The job of both the CDC and FDA is to review each report that occurs and see if there is a pattern of subsequent illness after vaccination.

While we would be remiss if we didn't tell you that vaccinations have some risks associated with them, we want you to remember that the risk of adverse reaction is *significantly* lower than leaving your baby unprotected.

In 1986, recognizing that there are rare, serious reactions that occur as a result of vaccinating children, the U.S. Department of Health and Human Services created the Vaccine Injury Compensation Program. This program attempts to determine whether adverse reactions from vaccines are responsible for injuries or death and then to provide the victim with compensation. Since 1986 there have only been 1775 claimants. Considering there are four million babies born each year (or 68 million since the program started) and most have been vaccinated, the odds of an injury are staggeringly tiny.

Another statistic to mull over: 1.9 billion doses of vaccine were given in the U.S. from 1991 to 2001. Only 2,281 cases of allergic reactions were reported.[11] (Compare that statistic to one in 50 adults having a food allergy!)

We agree that an adverse reaction only has to happen to one child for it to be heartbreaking. But if we look at the big picture, we can point to the millions of children who might have experienced illness, disfigurement and death if diseases like smallpox or polio were not controlled by vaccinations.

RED FLAGS

Call the doctor if your baby does the following after a vaccination:
1. Inconsolable crying over three hours.
2. Fever over 105 degrees.
3. Seizure activity.
4. Extreme lethargy.

Q. How do I know that the CDC and FDA are on "our" side?

Ah yes, the government conspiracy theory.

For starters, no one working for the vaccine watchdogs (CDC, FDA, AAP, ACIP, or AAFP) receives any grant or research money from pharmaceutical companies. So there is no financial incentive to allow a bad vaccine to stay on the market. If there is concern about a vaccine, it will be pulled from the market immediately (see the example of the rotavirus later in this chapter).

Here is another consideration: Why would these groups want our nation's children to suffer chronic illness, pain, or even death? Think about it. It is in *nobody's* interest to increase infant morbidity and mortality rates.

14 WHO KEEPS A RECORD OF MY CHILD'S VACCINATIONS? You and your doctor. Your doctor keeps a record of vaccinations in your child's records. If your doctor retires or dies, you may find it difficult to locate your records. If another doctor buys the practice, the records are kept. And some states have an immunization registry that also keeps records of vaccinations.

But ultimately, YOU need to have a copy of these in your personal medical record file. You will need proof of vaccinations for many things. Any childcare or school program requires this information. Summer camps and athletic programs want the records too. If your child becomes a healthcare professional, joins the military, or is a food handler, he will also need this information.

Helpful Hint

It's a good idea to have a medical passport for your child. This should include an immunization record, growth chart, list of medical problems, list of surgeries, drug allergies, and name and dosage of any medications that are used regularly (such as asthma medicine).

Q. How do I know when my child needs booster shots?

Your doctor will remind you at each well child visit.

We wish pediatricians were more like dentists or veterinarians. Most do not usually send out reminder cards to let you know your child is due for shots. What most practices do is provide the schedule in an information packet at your child's *first* visit. Your doctor will tell you at each well check when to return. This system works pretty well unless you start missing well-child visits. Then your child gets behind on his vaccination series. You can try to catch your child up on shots when he is in for a sick visit if this happens.

Reality Check
Wanted: a national immunization registry.

There is no uniform system of tracking immunization status and sending reminder cards to patients' families. This is a concept currently being discussed by the American Academy of Pediatrics. It boils down to having a national immunization registry. Advocates of this plan feel it will improve our country's poor immunization rates. Those opposed to the plan think it invades personal privacy and creates a government health care tracking system. So, like most governmental decisions, it may take years to resolve.

15 **WHAT VACCINES ARE REQUIRED AND WHICH ONES ARE OPTIONAL?**
The answer varies state to state. It also varies depending on the frequency of disease in particular counties within a state. We have provided a table of the most recent requirements in the U.S. on our web site Baby411.com (click on "Bonus Material").

Note: Prevnar (Strep pneumoniae) is optional in all 50 states. The Hepatitis A vaccine is optional unless a particular county has 20 cases of Hepatitis A

Recommended Childhood & Adolescent

Vaccine / Age ▶	Birth	1 mo	2 mos	4 mos	6 mos
range of recommended ages					
Hepatitis B	HepB #1	only if mother HBsAg (-)			
		HepB #2			
Diphtheria, Tetanus, Pertussis			DTaP	DTaP	DTaP
Haemophilus influenzae **Type b**			Hib	Hib	Hib
Inactivated Polio			IPV	IPV	
Measles, Mumps, Rubella					
Varicella					
Pneumococcal			PCV	PCV	PCV
Vaccines below this line are for selected populations					
Hepatitis A					
Influenza					

This schedule indicates the recommended ages for routine administration of currently licensed child given at the recommended age should be given at any subsequent visit when indicated and feasible previously given. Additional vaccines may be licensed and recommended during the year. Licensed indicated and the vaccine's other components are not contraindicated. Providers should consult the per 100,000 population. States will mandate Hepatitis A vaccine for daycare and school entry if the disease is that prevalent in a community.

Vaccination Schedule

Below is the schedule for vaccinations. For details on these specific vaccines, see the following section. Note: there has been a worldwide effort to eliminate polio disease by immunizing all children. War torn countries are a challenge to this effort. In light of current world affairs, the vaccine will likely be continued indefinitely.

Disease And Vaccine Specifics

Let's talk specifics—here is a breakdown of the vaccines and the disease they are designed to stop. View our website at Baby411.com for a visual library of these diseases (click on "Bonus Material").

Immunization Schedule for the United States

hood vaccines, as of December 1, 2002, for children through age 18 years. Any dose not
▸ ▨▨▨ Indicates age groups that warrant special effort to administer those vaccines not
combination vaccines may be used whenever any components of the combination are
manufacturers' package inserts for detailed recommendations.

Diphtheria, Tetanus, Pertussis

◆ **Diphtheria**: This is a *bacteria* that causes a serious throat infection. It invades the tonsils, kills the tissue, and creates a thick pus lining that can block off the airway. It also produces a toxin that enters the blood and injures the heart, kidneys, and nerves. It is spread by respiratory droplets (coughs and sneezes). There is a 10% mortality rate from infection, even today. *Before the vaccine, 200,000 Americans had this disease every year—and 20,000 died per year.*

◆ **Tetanus**: This is a *bacteria* that causes wound infections. It is not contagious person to person. Tetanus bacteria produce spores that are found in the soil and dust around the world. These are resilient little germs, so we will never eliminate them. Tetanus spores can enter open wounds (especially puncture wounds, animal bites, and umbilical cord stumps) and make a toxin that attacks nerves. The affected nerves cause muscles to spasm (called "tetany"). These spasms prevent breathing and swallowing (lockjaw). There is a 30% mortality rate from infection.

◆ **Pertussis (Whooping Cough):** This *bacteria* causes irritation and inflammation of the throat. This swelling prevents mucus from being coughed up and creates a blocked airway, particularly for those with the smallest airways (infants). Pertussis infection initially looks like the common cold. Over time, infected people have coughing fits or spasms. As a person tries to get a breath in, he makes a characteristic "whoop." Infants, who have smaller airways, are unable to breathe at all. So instead of whooping, they stop breathing and their faces turn red or purple. Children often throw up during a coughing fit. In Asia, this illness is known as the "100 Day Cough". *Prior to vaccine development, there were 200,000 cases a year in the U.S. There were 10,000 deaths annually, mostly in infants.* The infection is spread by respiratory droplets.

Reality Check

There have been recent epidemics of whooping cough in the U.S., particularly in under-immunized communities. Boulder, Colorado has three times more whooping cough cases than the entire state because fewer children are protected by vaccination. Why? A large number of parents in Boulder and other similar communities believe vaccines are at best, a personal lifestyle choice (like nose piercings).

Here is a typical riff on vaccines that was published in the *Boulder Weekly* (May 15, 2003): "Some vaccinations are tied to serious side effects and come with a range of contraindications. Parents who think they must immunize their kids aren't likely to do the research necessary to find out if immunizations are right for their child."

Again, the emphasis is that vaccines are purely optional—and after a little web surfing, the educated parent may decide that vaccinations might not be "right" for their child. But what is right for the community as a whole? Sadly, states like Colorado give such parents an easy out by letting them sign an exemption, which enables them to enroll an unvaccinated child in public school.

Here's the ultimate irony: today's skeptical parents were vaccinated themselves, but now they are denying the same protection to their kids.

Which one of your child's friends or classmates isn't vaccinated? You can't tell, unfortunately.

Q. What is the DTaP vaccine? I've heard that it is safer to give than the DTP.

This is the vaccine that protects against **D**iphtheria, **T**etanus, and **P**ertussis (whooping cough).

The combination vaccine has been around since the 1940's. The older vaccine (DTP) was called a 'whole cell' vaccine because the vaccine was derived from a whole dead whooping cough germ. This vaccine was effective, but caused a significant number of high fevers and convulsions. A newer formulation is called the "acellular" vaccine or DTaP vaccine. The immune response is formed to a piece of the bacteria (its signature). This safer vaccine came out in 1991 and our babies are a lot happier with us.

The vaccination series is five doses total. The fourth and fifth booster doses are more likely to cause a fever or redness at the injection site because our bodies recognize it and have an immune response ready to go. After the fifth dose of DTaP, boosters of the Tetanus and Diphtheria components are given every ten years. The pertussis component is not given after seven years of age.

Unfortunately, the pertussis component is riskier to give to older children and adults. The immunity wears off over time and leaves adults as reservoirs of infection to expose infants who aren't fully protected yet. An adult whooping cough vaccine has been in the works for some time now but isn't out now as of this writing.

Q. Is it true that whooping cough epidemics still occur?

Yes. In fact, whooping cough is alive and well in the hometowns of both authors of this book (Austin, TX and Boulder, CO) as well as other communities. What do these towns have in common? LOW immunization rates. Texas has had over 100 cases of reported whooping cough and four deaths in 2003. That's four deaths … that were preventable.

Here are the facts:

1. Whooping cough epidemics occur about every three to four years.
2. Immunity to whooping cough wanes in teens and adults despite vaccination.
3. Many cases of whooping cough are undiagnosed and untreated in older people. Have you ever had a cough that just 'hung on' for several weeks? You may have had whooping cough and not known it.
4. Dropping immunization rates allow the disease to spread quickly through a community.
5. Infants are given their first whooping cough (pertussis) vaccination at two months of age. Yes, it is the youngest children are the most susceptible and have the highest risk of serious illness and death.

BOTTOM LINE: If you or anyone in the family has a chronic cough, get it checked out. It's important for you and your baby. And please get your baby vaccinated.

Polio

This *virus* attacks the spinal cord and brain. It has particular affinity for the nerves that control leg muscles and the diaphragm muscle (that helps you breathe). Polio infections leave people paralyzed, or needing a machine to breathe for them. Prior to our modern day ventilators, people survived the illness by living in iron lung machines. The virus spreads through the stool of infected people. This was a common summertime epidemic, and whole households would get the infection. Before the vaccine, there were 20,000 cases of paralysis per year in the U.S. Since 1979, there have been no cases of naturally occurring polio infection in the U.S. There were a few cases annually of vaccine associated polio disease when the live (oral) vaccine was used. In 1997, doctors switched to an all-inactivated (IPV; that is not-live) vaccination series. IPV does not cause polio disease.

Q. Why do we still give the Polio vaccine? I thought we got rid of polio disease.

Because the infection is an airplane flight away.

Polio infections occur in 30 countries around the world. There has been an extraordinary effort to eradicate the disease, like smallpox. While this may happen in our lifetime, polio is still a threat.

In the U.S., we give the inactivated form of the vaccine (a shot). The vaccine that was given from 1963-1996 was a live vaccine (a drink) that carried a small risk of acquiring vaccine-associated polio disease. As mentioned above, this is no longer used.

Haemophilus Influenza B (Hib)

This is a *bacteria* that causes a potentially fatal throat swelling (epiglottitis) and meningitis (infection of the brain lining). Despite the name, there is no relationship to influenza, the flu virus—yes, we realize that is confusing. HIB is spread by respiratory droplets (sneezing, coughing). Prior to vaccine development, there were 20,000 cases of HIB infection annually in the U.S. and 500 deaths. Most infections occurred in children less than five years old. Survivors of meningitis may be permanently deaf, blind, or mentally retarded. The development of the HIB vaccine is a true success story of modern-day medicine. The vaccine was licensed in 1985. By 1992, HIB infections were virtually eliminated (less than 200 cases per year).

Q. Does the HIB vaccine need to be given separately? My doctor uses something called Comvax.

The HIB vaccine can be given either individually (in three or four doses) or in a combination product. Examples of such combo vaccines include Comvax (which combines Hepatitis B and HIB) or Trihibit (which combines DTaP and HIB). Children form a good immunity with any of these products.

Measles, Mumps, Rubella

◆ **Measles:** This is a *virus* that infects the entire body. Infected people start out with cold symptoms and pink eye. It causes a dramatic head to toe rash, then spreads to other organ systems. These include the intestines (diarrhea), lungs (pneumonia), and brain (encephalitis). The highest rate of these complications is in children under age five. The virus is highly contagious and is spread through respiratory droplets. Measles was as common as chickenpox used to be. Before the measles vaccine, there were an amazing four million cases per year and 500 deaths per year in the U.S.

◆ *Mumps*: This is a *virus* that attacks the salivary glands. Mumps infect the glands located along the jaw line and causes a marked swelling. It also infects other body parts that swell up, including the testicles, ovaries, and brain. Mumps attacks the brain (meningitis) about 15% of the time. It can cause deafness and mental retardation in survivors. Like measles, mumps is spread through respiratory droplets. Before the mumps vaccine was developed, there were 200,000 cases per year. We now see fewer than 600 cases a year in the U.S.

◆ *Rubella* (German measles): This is a highly contagious *virus* that causes mild infection in children, but fatal or disabling infection in unborn fetuses. Rubella spreads through respiratory droplets and causes a runny nose, swollen glands, and a rash in children. If a pregnant woman gets rubella, the fetus can die in the womb (miscarriage) or be born with severe mental retardation, deafness, or blindness (called congenital rubella syndrome). An epidemic in 1964 (prior to the rubella vaccine) affected 20,000 babies.

The vaccines for measles, mumps and rubella are given together as the MMR vaccine.

Hepatitis B

This is a *virus* that attacks the liver. There are various types of Hepatitis. The most noteworthy are A, B, and C. Each type of virus is spread differently. Hepatitis B is spread through blood and body fluid (saliva, vaginal discharge, and semen) contact. It is extremely contagious. Yes, it is spread primarily by sexual contact and by exposure in the health-care field. However, children are most at risk of exposure to Hepatitis B during birth if their mother has the disease.

The infection causes skin to turn yellow because the liver is unable to metabolize bilirubin as it should (see earlier in this book for a discussion of bilirubin). It causes stomach upset and lack of appetite. Some people with Hepatitis B recover quickly, while others die. Others have a chronic infection that goes on for 20 years until they die. And, some people become carriers of the disease once they survive the infection.

Reality Check

There are *1 million* Hepatitis B carriers walking around the U.S. If this isn't enough to convince you to protect your child, Hepatitis B also in a known cause of liver cancer. Yes, the Hepatitis B vaccine is the first cancer vaccine. Before the vaccine became part of the childhood immunization series, 30,000 children were infected with Hepatitis B annually in the U.S.

In addition to the Hepatitis B vaccines, there is also a vaccine for Hepatitis A. FYI: there is no *cure* for either infection—that's why the vaccine is so important.

Q. I thought Hepatitis B was a sexually transmitted disease. Why does my baby need to get it?

Don't think of this disease as one that only happens to IV drug users or people with several sex partners. 30% of people who get Hepatitis B have neither of these risk factors.

Giving the vaccine as a part of the childhood immunization program ensures that your child gets immunized and has lifelong protection (yes, someday your child will become sexually active). Babies born to mothers who have Hepatitis B need to get the vaccination within 12 hours of birth to prevent infection.

Varicella (Chickenpox)

This is a *virus* more familiar to most of us. Prior to the development of the chickenpox vaccine, 3.7 million people got chickenpox every year in the U.S. So, most of you reading this book probably remember having this illness. What most of you don't know is that chickenpox also led to 10,000 hospitalizations and 100 deaths annually.

The varicella virus spreads by respiratory droplets and by the fluid found in the skin lesions. It is incredibly contagious. The virus attacks the whole body via the bloodstream. Infected people feel tired and run a fever, then break out in classic clear fluid-filled blisters that arrive in clusters. The average number of skin lesions is 350. Does it make you feel itchy just thinking about it? People are contagious for seven days, on average.

The virus itself can cause pneumonia and encephalitis. Even more problematic is that Strep bacteria have a field day with the open wounds when the blisters pop. These secondary infections can be deadly.

Reality Check

Even if a child has a minor case of chickenpox, he cannot return to childcare/school for seven days. This has an obvious economic impact for working parents.

Helpful Hint

The American Academy of Pediatrics currently recommends a single dose for children vaccinated under 13 and a two-dose series for those over age 13. Vaccinated children occasionally get *mild* cases of chickenpox when exposed to someone with the infection. The American Academy of Pediatrics and Centers for Disease Control are currently evaluating the possible need for a second booster shot for all children.[12]

DR B'S OPINION: CHICKENPOX CAN BE DEADLY

I cared for a five-year-old patient with chickenpox during my residency that came to our emergency room with a secondary Strep infection—she died two hours later. That experience has left an impact on me. When parents perceive that chickenpox is just a minor illness, I tell them that story.

Strep Pneumoniae (Prevnar Vaccine)

Although this is an *optional* vaccine, it is recommended as part of the routine immunization schedule by the American Academy of Pediatrics.

This is a *bacteria* that is in the Strep family. It is not the Strep that causes Strep throat. It's a distant cousin. This bacteria causes meningitis, pneumonia, blood infections (sepsis), sinus infections, and ear infections. The Prevnar vaccine protects against the top seven strains of Strep pneumoniae (there are 90 total) that cause serious infection.

Respiratory droplets spread the bacteria. Once the bugs get in, they head for the respiratory system (ears, sinuses, lungs) or the brain. They travel via the blood en route to these places. Infected people run a high fever when the bacteria are in the bloodstream. Fortunately, many infections are treated before meningitis occurs. Prior to the Prevnar vaccine, there were over 500,000 cases of serious Strep pneumoniae infections a year in the U.S. and 11,000 deaths. *In babies, Strep pneumoniae is the #1 cause of bacterial meningitis.* The highest risk groups for serious infection are infants and the elderly.

Reality Check

There are antibiotics to treat Strep pneumoniae, however, doctors are seeing more drug-resistant strains. It's survival of the fittest for germs—and these germs are some of the smartest around. Twenty percent of the Strep pneumoniae strains in the vaccine are resistant to Penicillin. Ten percent are resistant to three OR MORE types of antibiotics.

Q. Because the Prevnar vaccine is optional, should I wait until there is more safety data to vaccinate my baby?

There is plenty of safety data—immunize your baby now.

The Prevnar vaccine came out in February 2000. There was so much enthusiasm that there was a recent shortage of the vaccine. Over 20 million children have been immunized as of this writing and doctors feel comfortable saying that it is safe.

The stats on disease reduction are also impressive. There has been a 87% reduction in serious Strep pneumoniae disease (meningitis, blood and pneumonia infections) since the immunization program began.

Remember, Strep infection is most serious in younger babies. Choosing to wait on the vaccine is choosing to put your child at risk. And if your child is in daycare, I would not hesitate to vaccinate for this. Daycare children are at higher risk for Strep pneumoniae infection, particularly the drug-resistant strains.

Optional Vaccines

Hepatitis A

Q. What is Hepatitis A and is there a vaccine for it?

Another virus that attacks the liver. And there is a vaccine to prevent it. This *virus* is spread through infected poop, contaminated water and food. It spreads rapidly in childcare centers due to all the kids in diapers. Fortunately, children infected with Hepatitis A have a relatively minor illness. Some children don't even have symptoms. Adults, however, get very sick. There are over 150,000 cases per year in the U.S.

The Hepatitis A vaccine was approved in 1995. It is an optional vaccine for most people. During outbreaks/epidemics, it is a required vaccine for children in specific counties. The vaccine may be recommended for everyone soon.

Kids must be at least two years old to get the vaccine.

Helpful Hint

Hepatitis A vaccine is currently recommended in the following states: Alaska, Arizona, California, Idaho, Nevada, New Mexico, Oklahoma, Oregon, South Dakota, Utah, and Washington. These are states that have more than two cases *reported* per 10,000 individuals. (Hepatitis A is under diagnosed because children are often infected and symptom-free).[13]

Influenza

Q. What are the recommendations for the flu vaccine?

Here are the latest recommendations.
The flu shot is *recommended* for:
1. 50-years or older.
2. Immune-compromised (weak immune systems)
3. Chronic illness (asthma, heart disease, diabetes) in anyone six months old or older.
4. Health care workers
5. Pregnant women who will be in their second or third trimester during flu season (November-March).

The flu shot is *encouraged* for:
1. Children ages six months old to two years old.
2. Household contacts and caretakers of ANY child aged birth to two years.

These recommendations were revised because children under the age of two have a higher risk of complications from the flu.

The flu vaccine is an inactivated vaccine. You won't get the flu from it. It provides immunity after two weeks of getting the vaccine. The vaccine is effective for one year. The particular influenza virus strain that shows up every year is different, so we have to get vaccinated for the new bug in town each autumn.

Kids under nine years of age who get the flu vaccine for the first time need two doses given one month apart.

Currently, there is only one flu vaccine that is "thimerisol free" and allowed for use in infants as young as six months old. It's called Fluzone (Aventis Pasteur). The other flu vaccines contain a trace amount of thimerisol (12.5 micrograms per dose). The acceptable limit of exposure is over 15 times this dose (200mcg). See the section "Controversies" later in this chapter for more information on thimerisol.

Smallpox

Q. What is smallpox?

It is a highly contagious virus that causes fever and pus-filled lesions all over the body. There is a 30% mortality rate with the infection. Those who survive the illness are often permanently disfigured. Prior to the 18th century, epidemics used to wipe out entire civilizations. The United States has not seen a case of smallpox since 1949, thanks to a worldwide vaccination program.

Q. How does the smallpox virus spread?

There are a couple of ways:
1.   Face to face contact with an infected person.
2.   Coming in contact with infected body fluids (through bedding and clothes).
The good news: Smallpox virus is rarely spread via airborne particles.

Q. Is there any medication or cure for smallpox?

Currently, no. There is an antiviral medication (Cidifovir) being researched right now, which may have some benefit.

Q. How long is an infected person contagious with smallpox?

From the time a person develops a fever until all the lesions crust over and fall off (about three weeks).

If a smallpox outbreak occurred, infected individuals would likely be quarantined in their homes until they were no longer contagious.

Q. Can my baby get the smallpox vaccine?

No. There are safety concerns.

The smallpox vaccine supply that the United States government has is an old, "live" vaccine, which has significantly more risks associated with it than newer generation vaccines that we currently use for other diseases. People with immune deficiencies (HIV, on chemotherapy) could become very ill or die if they received this vaccine. Even people with eczema (severely dry skin) could die from the vaccine.

The first recommendation from the CDC was to vaccinate a community immediately if a case of smallpox was diagnosed. This is called "ring immunity." Because the incubation period is seven to 14 days from virus exposure to infection, a whole community could theoretically be vaccinated immediately and protected after a known outbreak.

The recommendations changed as of December 2002. Health care workers who would be first responders to an outbreak and military personnel in high-threat areas are now being vaccinated against smallpox.

BOTTOM LINE: As this book goes to press, there are no official recommendations for the general public to be vaccinated. We may be offered an optional *unlicensed* vaccine in 2003 or a licensed vaccine in 2004. *There is no recommendation for the vaccine to be offered to children under 18 years of age as of this writing. Check our web site at Baby411.com for updates on this issue.*

Q. Will the vaccine protect someone who has already been exposed to smallpox?

Yes. If a person is vaccinated within three days of exposure, the vaccine should be very effective in preventing infection. If a person is vaccinated with five days of exposure, the vaccine should protect against serious infection/death. This is the advantage of "ring immunity."

Q. What are the risks of the smallpox vaccine?

Let us first explain why there is more risk with the smallpox than with other vaccines discussed earlier in this chapter. The smallpox vaccine is made out of a *live* virus, called vaccinia (cowpox), which means it can cause cowpox infection in susceptible people (see below for a list of who should NOT get the smallpox vaccine).

Here's how that works: Dryvax (the smallpox vaccine made by Wyeth Pharmaceuticals and available now) is made when cowpox is injected into cows. Then fluid from the resulting pox wounds is used to make the vaccine. Ultimately, immunity occurs by giving the human recipient a minor infection of cowpox in the skin. A newer vaccine, being developed by Acambis Baxter Pharmaceuticals, will create cowpox virus synthetically (much to the relief of all those cows, no doubt) to avoid the risk of getting cowpox.

Here are several more risks to the smallpox vaccine (source: CDC):

◆ ALL vaccine recipients have lesions at the injection site for four to 21 days after vaccination. They can accidentally spread the infection on themselves and to others. The rash is very itchy.
◆ One out of three people feels sick enough to limit their daily activities.
◆ One out of 1000 people gets a rash beyond the injection site.
◆ One out of 1,000,000 people has a fatal reaction (widespread infection, encephalitis).

So, given those risks and problems, here is a list of who should NOT get the optional smallpox vaccine:
1. Pregnant women.
2. Breastfeeding women.
3. Weak immune systems—either by disease (HIV, autoimmune diseases) or by medications (chemotherapy, chronic steriod use).
4. Eczema (even if the disorder is no longer a problem).
5. Active skin wounds (chickenpox, impetigo, herpes, severe acne, psoriasis).
6. Current illness.
7. Allergy to vaccine ingredients (polymyxin, streptomycin, chlortetraycline, neomycin)
8. ***Anyone who lives in a household with people who fall into the above categories one to six!***

9. The Advisory Committee on Immunization Practices (ACIP) does NOT recommend non-emergency vaccination of children under 18 years of age.
10. History of heart disease.

Reality Check
If there is an outbreak of smallpox (that is, one reported case), EVERYONE needs to get vaccinated, regardless of relative risk of the vaccine.

Helpful Hints
Here's where to get more info on the smallpox vaccine:
◆ www.bt.cdc.gov/agent/smallpox/vaccination/facts.asp
◆ www.kidshealth.org/kid/health_problems/infection/smallpox
◆ www.nlm.nih.gov/medlineplus/smallpox.html
◆ CDC Hotline (888) 246-2675

Controversies

Let's face it, controversy sells newspapers and drives TV ratings. No one is interested in hearing about things that work as they should—and vaccines are a good example. As you might guess, vaccines have made the news lately. Unfortunately, rare adverse events and theoretical concerns tend to make more headlines than the remarkable success story of vaccinations. These problems are then seized on by vaccine opponents and spread online through the web like a, well, virus.

So, let's address this head on. Here are the controversies you might hear about with vaccines:

Does MMR Cause Autism?

Q. I've heard news reports that the MMR vaccine causes autism. Is this true?

No.

Parents also hear that vaccinations cause multiple sclerosis, diabetes, asthma, and SIDS. None of these diseases are caused by vaccination. This is the whole purpose behind the government safety monitoring system (VAERS, FDA, CDC)—monitoring for any adverse effects from vaccines. *No one wants to increase autism rates in our society.*

The study that created the controversy about the MMR vaccine came out of England in 1998 (the Wakefield study). Researchers there had a theory that the MMR vaccine led to intestinal inflammation, cracks in the intestine lining, and escape of proteins that attack the brain. This theory was formed based on a mere *eight patients* who had autism and stomachaches. The study did not provide any statistically significant data (eight patients is too small of a sample size), and the study had many critical flaws.[14] This flawed study concluded that the rise in autism was related to giving a combination vaccine of Measles-Mumps-Rubella (MMR). Prior to 1978, these vaccinations were given separately.

Numerous studies have been done since 1998 that have soundly refuted Dr. Wakefield's theory. A 1999 study showed that 498 autistic children had no statistical difference in the timing of diagnosis whether they were vaccinated or not.[15] In 2001, another study looked at autism rates in the state of California. *Researchers found that although the rates of autism had climbed from 1980-1994, the percentage of children who got the MMR vaccine was the same!*[16]

DR B'S OPINION: BAD SCIENCE

Linking autism to vaccines is bad science. Consider what else has changed since 1978 besides the way these vaccines are given to children. Pollution rates have risen, processed meats are more popular, and almost everyone owns a cell phone. To say that any of these factors has caused an increase in autism rates would be ridiculous—these are called "confounding variables."

Having a child who is autistic is challenging and frustrating as a parent. I truly empathize with these families. Families desperately want an explanation for why their child is autistic. The Wakefield study provided an answer. Unfortunately, it is not the correct answer. But concerned groups of autistic families continue to believe this study.

Q. Okay, so what causes autism?

The million-dollar question.

There has been a huge increase in the rates of California children being diagnosed as autistic (a rise of 273% from 1987 to1998). There are 13 states in the U.S. who have seen a similar rise in autism rates. Studies from Denmark also show a disconcerting increase in autistic children in the past decade.

Part of the increase in autism may be the fact that we as a society are getting better in diagnosing it.

Experts believe that autism is caused by a genetic defect. Studying twins is an obvious way to detect genetic disorders. For example, research shows if one identical twin has autism, 60% of the time, so will the other twin. To date, the exact gene has not been identified.

One interesting study that was released as we went to press on this book tied autism to abnormal head growth in infants under a year of age. While this is not a cause of autism, it is hoped this discovery may lead to better diagnosis and early treatment of autism. Follow our website at Baby411.com for new information on this topic.

Reality Check

The combination Measles–Mumps–Rubella (MMR) vaccine was introduced in 1975. That is 15 years *before* the dramatic rise in autism rates. Therefore, it is the belief of a majority in the medical community that they are unrelated.

Q. If the MMR vaccine doesn't cause autism, why is the diagnosis made around the same time as the vaccination?

DR B'S OPINION:
MMR & AUTISM

I follow the developmental milestones of all my patients carefully. I have concerns for autism and mental retardation long before a patient turns a year of age. But I keep these concerns to myself because many of these worrisome children ultimately catch up developmentally. It is only when I am sure of the diagnosis do I sit down with my families to discuss these lifelong developmental disorders.

I have never had a developmentally normal patient come in for his one year well check, get his MMR vaccine, and come back at his 15-month checkup as an autistic child. The 15-month-old who is autistic is a child I was worried about long before the one-year well check.

In another study I read, doctors noticed the same results. Developmental specialists viewed footage of children's first birthday parties (who had not received the MMR vaccine yet). The specialists accurately identified the children who were later diagnosed as being autistic.

One of the criteria used to make a diagnosis of autism is a language delay. Because children do not have significant expressive language under a year of age, doctors have to wait until 15 to 18 months to confirm a language delay and make the diagnosis. That's about the same time as the MMR vaccination, which leads some parents to wonder about autism and vaccination.

Q. Why don't we just give the MMR vaccine separately?

A reasonable question.

Separating these vaccines is impractical because it imposes three more needles for the first dose due at a year of age, and the booster dose before kindergarten. Doctors already have enough trouble getting all of the vaccinations done on time. Often your baby is already receiving four or five shots at one visit. Parents really don't enjoy watching their baby become a human pin cushion, either.

Because there is no medical reason to separate these vaccines, they are routinely given in one combination shot.

Q. If I want to give my child the measles, mumps, and rubella vaccinations separately, can I?

Yes, but it is extraordinarily difficult to get the individual doses of the vaccines. The rubella vaccine is readily available, but the measles and mumps are not. My practice has checked into this for a few families (I usually have one family a year who asks). There is a one-year waiting list to get those separate vaccines. Because these vaccines are used so infrequently, there is little manufactured in the U.S. You will also have to foot the bill for the individual vaccines. Insurance companies won't cover them because it is not the AAP's recommendation.

For families who have their hearts set on separating these vaccines, we'd suggest a trip to France. France does separate vaccinations and it's a fun place to visit.

Rotavirus

Q. I've heard about a vaccine that was taken off the market. What was the problem with it? It makes me nervous about other new vaccines.

The vaccine protected against a stomach virus called Rotavirus.

Rotavirus comes to visit every winter. Doctors always know rotavirus has arrived in a community. The littlest patients come into the office with so much watery diarrhea that parents can't keep up with diaper changes. The vomiting part is pretty miserable, too. Because there is so much water lost in the poops, infants are at high risk of becoming dehydrated. As a doctor, I usually admit one or two babies to the hospital every winter to get IV fluids. Multiply this number by 50,000 pediatricians in the U.S. That's right, this infection alone causes 50,000 hospitalizations of infants every winter. There are also about 30 deaths per year from Rotavirus. You can see why the medical community is anxious to have a vaccine for this disease.

The Rotavirus vaccine was approved in August 1998 after a study was done on 10,000 individuals. It looked like a safe vaccine. The vaccine was then given to 1.5 million children over a period of nine months. During this time, there were 15 reports of bowel obstruction (intussusception) that occurred within a week of being vaccinated. There were no deaths. The CDC immediately pulled the vaccine off the market and initiated an investigation.

Although this was certainly a setback for new vaccinations, it proves that the adverse events reporting system works (VAERS). Modifications have been made to the license process as a result of the Rotavirus vaccine. This was the first vaccine recall in over 20 years.

There may be a new Rotavirus vaccine someday. Studies are currently in the works.

The Thimerisol (Mercury) Controversy

Q. Is there anything else in the vaccine injection fluid? I've heard a lot about Thimerisol (mercury). Has the thimerisol been removed from vaccines?

Yes and yes.

There are preservatives and stabilizers in the vaccine suspensions so that the vaccinations remain potent and uncontaminated. A popular preservative *used* to be a chemical called thimerisol, which contained trace amounts of *ethylmercury*. Thimerisol was used beginning in the 1940's in vaccines. *It was removed from all required childhood vaccines in 1999.*

A quick chemistry lesson: Certain compounds have completely different properties even though they may be related. For instance, take the alcohol family. *Methanol* is anti-freeze; *ethanol* is a Bud Light. Keep this in mind when we discuss mercury. We are all exposed to small amounts of mercury. The type of mercury that has raised health concerns is called *methylmercury*. High concentrations of methylmercury can be found in tuna, swordfish and shark from contaminated waters. The information known about mercury poisoning comes from unfortunate communities that have experienced it. There is a large amount of data from the Faroe Islands, near Iceland. The people there would eat whale blubber contaminated with toxic levels of methylmercury and polychlorinated biphenyls (PCBs). Children, especially those exposed as fetuses during their mother's pregnancy, seemed to have lower scores on memory, attention, and language tests than their unexposed peers. (They were *not* diagnosed with autism or Attention Deficit Disorder, however.) [17]

Chronic exposure to liquid mercury causes Mad Hatter's Disease, named for hat makers who used liquid mercury in the hat-making process and went crazy. The disease consists of psychiatric problems, insomnia, poor memory, sweating, tremors, and red palms. Chronic mercury poisoning also impairs kidney function.

Because of the increased number of vaccinations that children get, the potential cumulative exposure to mercury became a concern in 1999.

There are three federal groups that set standards for acceptable daily mercury exposure (Environmental Protection Agency, Food and Drug Administration, Agency for Toxic Substances and Disease Registry). When the exposure was calculated, the cumulative dose was higher than acceptable levels set by the EPA only (the other groups' standards were higher). The Food and Drug Administration mandated the removal of thimerisol at that time for concerns extrapolated from data on Methylmercury.

Vaccine manufacturers have switched to using other preservatives now. The other chemicals that can be found include antibiotics (neomycin), monosodium glutamate (yes, the famous Chinese food additive), and traces of aluminum salts.

BOTTOM LINE: Thimerisol will remain in the news, the legislature, and in the courts. But it does not remain in any of the required vaccines that YOUR child will get.

Q. Does thimerisol cause autism?

No. How do we know? Three reasons:

1. Thimerisol has been removed from vaccines since 1999, but the rates of autism are still skyrocketing.
2. Mad Hatter's Disease and Autism are very different disorders.
3. Children who are autistic do not have any skin or kidney problems, which occur in mercury poisoning.

FYI: Most flu vaccines still contain trace amounts of thimerisol.

Vaccine Shortage

Q. I've heard there is a vaccine shortage. Is this true, and why did this happen?

Yes, our country has had shortages in many of the childhood vaccinations. Most vaccines are available now, though.

Now that you have read about removing thimerisol, VAERS, and the Rotavirus vaccine,

DR B'S OPINION

"Families with autistic children used to claim that the MMR vaccine caused the condition. Once that was refuted, they moved on to Thimerisol. I suspect these families will continue to look for some 'external cause' for their child's disorder. Unfortunately, interest and financial resources for autism research are being wasted on this controversy."

would you want to be a vaccine manufacturer? There used to be 15 pharmaceutical companies that made vaccinations. Now there are only four. When the others left the market, the remaining companies were forced to increase production for the needs of our entire country.

The biggest problem was the tetanus booster. We had such a shortage that state health departments kept emergency doses under lock and key. That shortage is over now.

Prevnar vaccine also experienced a shortage. This optional meningitis vaccine has been so popular since it came out in 2000, the company had trouble keeping up with the demand (1.4 million doses per month.) The shortage is now over.

Helpful hints
Where to get more information

Our advice: don't type in "vaccinations" in a Google search.. You will end up with inaccurate information from concerned groups who do a great job of creating parental anxiety. The following sites will provide *accurate* information:

- ◆ *CDC's National Immunization Program*
  www.cdc.gov/nip   (800) 232-2522
- ◆ *American Academy of Pediatrics*
  www.aap.org   (800) 433-9016
- ◆ *Immunization Action Coalition*
  www.immunize.org
- ◆ *Vaccine Education Center, Children's Hospital of Philadelphia*
  www.vaccine.chop.edu

There are also two excellent reference books written for parents:

Vaccinating Your Child: Questions and Answers for the Concerned Parent. Humiston, S., Atlanta: Peachtree, 2000.

What Every Parent Should Know About Vaccinations. Offit, P., New York: MacMillan, 1998.

Feedback from the Real World
Ryan's Story

Frankie Milley, a founder of Meningitis Angels (web: meningitis-angels.org), offered up this heartbreaking story about vaccines:

On June 22, 1998, a vaccine preventable disease called Meningococcal meningitis took the life of my only child, my son, Ryan. Thousands of children will develop meningitis each year and many will die. But death isn't the only outcome: children who survive are often left with limb amputations, organ damage, and the list goes on.

The two types of meningitis that are most common are meningococcal and pneumococcal (Strep pneumoniae). There are vaccines for both.

This vaccine preventable disease took away my identity, my right to ever be the parent at a wedding, to hold a grandchild, and to have the comfort of a child in my old age. We must work together in the United States to protect our children from epidemics which other parts of the world see everyday.

Because epidemics are a plane ride away. And vaccinations save lives.

Chapter 13

Common Infections

"A family is a unit composed not only of children but of men, women, an occasional animal, and the common cold."
~ Ogden Nash (1902-1971)

What's in this Chapter

- ◆ **What are Viruses?**
- ◆ **What are Bacteria?**
- ◆ **Antibiotic Resistance.**
- ◆ **What you always wanted to know about the Common Cold.**
- ◆ **When your child can return to childcare or play-group.**
- ◆ **Special feature— Ear infections.**

This chapter answers that age-old parent question: "So, when can my child go back to child care/play-group?" Yes, it's time to take a look at the germs that like to invade us. Infectious diseases are a large part of pediatrics. Adults have their share of infections, but the numbers pale in comparison to kids (a.k.a. human culture dishes). FYI: diseases that are not caused by infections are covered in the next chapter, "Common Diseases."

Common infections are usually caused by one of two issues—viruses and bacteria. We'll cover both in this chapter.

Most infections that your child will get are viruses. These are infections that go away on their own, without medication. One of the advantages of being a pediatrician is that in the case of viruses we do nothing, and our patients usually get better! Many parents don't understand what viruses are and feel compelled to DO SOMETHING. It often takes more time to explain to a parent that their child will get better without a prescription, than it takes to diagnose the ailment.

You will be an honorary microbiologist after reading this chapter. It will prepare you for the numerous infections coming your way. We'll go over viruses and bacteria since those are the biggies. Fungi, mites, lice, and parasites are discussed in "Things that make you itch just thinking about them." in Appendix D. That same appendix has a more complete review of specific infections we'll talk about here.

Viruses

Q. What is a virus?

These are tiny germs that need our body cells (called the "host") to survive and prosper. They contain genetic coding, DNA or RNA, material that are the building blocks to make more viruses.

Most viruses enter our bodies, reproduce for a few days, then leave to infect someone else. Examples include the cold virus and hand/foot/mouth diseases (see the table at the end of this section for a complete run-down of viruses with their common and scientific names). A few viruses like to stick around, lie dormant, and then reactivate to torture us again, such as herpes and chickenpox. Rarely, a virus kills their host—one example is HIV.

Here's some cocktail party trivia for you: according to the International Committee on Taxonomy of Viruses (7th report, 2000), there are more than 1550 virus species, divided into 56 families. Within each family, there are sometimes thousands of relatives for each virus. These identified viruses are just a small portion of what is actually out in the world.

Q. Where do viruses live when they aren't infecting someone?

Viruses can be airborne or live on surfaces for a period of hours to days. Germs live on surfaces called **FOMITES**. Fomites include door handles, grocery carts, gas pumps, changing tables, shared toys, etc.

BOTTOM LINE: Your mother was right—WASH YOUR HANDS!

Q. Is anti-bacterial soap a good defense against disease?

We have mixed feelings about this kind of soap. A Columbia School of Nursing study, funded by the National Institutes of Health, found that anti bacterial soap, when used for normal daily washing did not destroy more bacteria than regular soap. "We found antimicrobial or antibacterial soaps provide no added value over plain soap, " noted Elaine Larson, associate dean of research at the School of Nursing.

The Center for Disease Control, on the other hand, recently recommended anti-bacterial soaps for patient care settings such as hospitals and doctors' offices. They said that it reduces the number of infections transmit-

NEW PARENT 411: WHY EVERYONE IN THE HOUSE GETS SICK WHEN A CHILD HAS A VIRAL ILLNESS

Everyone gets sick because of what families do in their own homes. We hug, kiss, share drinks, touch door handles, touch hand towels, etc. We also wash our hands less in our homes than when we are out in public.

BOTTOM LINE: Think twice before you decide to finish what is left over on your child's plate. Is that half-eaten chicken nugget really worth it?

ted by health care providers. They even went so far as to recommend it for surgeons prior to surgery, replacing the age-old tradition of "scrubbing."

Finally, what about the possibility that anti-bacterial soaps are "too much of a good thing?" Some health care professionals fear that the use of anti-microbial and anti-bacterial soaps may help create new breeds of bacteria that are harder to kill.

Ultimately, the decision is up to you. You may decide to keep some anti-bacterial soap for when you are out and about or at the diaper changing table. But in most other circumstances regular soap will do just fine.

Denise's opinion: On a personal note, we have found that in the Fields' household, anti-bacterial soap aggravates our chronic dry skin (we live in a very arid climate) and eczema. We stick to regular Dove soap and wash frequently. Also those alcohol based hand sanitizers like Purell are very painful if you have cracks from eczema. We avoid them as well.

Q. Do we pass viral infections back and forth in our household?

No. Once everyone is infected, everyone is immune to that particular germ.

Q. Why is my child always getting sick?

Because he is being exposed to infectious germs he has no immunity to.

There are literally millions of germs out there. Every time your child gets an infection, he creates antibodies to a specific bug. But until your child has a large immune memory in his body's "hard drive," he will get almost every illness that comes down the pike. Most infections are spread through respiratory droplets (snot and cough secretions), saliva, and poop. Babies don't have good manners. They cough and sneeze on each other. They also explore toys in their mouths, leaving the germs behind for someone else.

Reality Check

Babies begin to get sick when they start venturing out in the world. Here are some astounding statistics:

◆ The average number of viral infections per year for kids under age five is EIGHT. Yes, you read that right.
◆ Each illness lasts seven to ten days.
◆ Most infections occur between October and April.
◆ That's 80 days of illness packed into six months of the year.

BOTTOM LINE: That's right, expect an infection every other week in the winter. And that's just the AVERAGE. If you win the sick kid lotto, you could be in for more. Astounding, eh?

Q. Why is my second child sicker than my first?

Because your older child is bringing home infections to share.

Firstborns often live in a bubble for their first year of life (unless they are in childcare). Second babies don't have that luxury. They get carted around to big brother or sister's activities. And big bro/sis share whatever infections they have acquired with the little ones.

So, it is natural for a second child to get more illnesses earlier in life than the first.

Q. Why do we only see the flu virus in the wintertime?

Viruses prefer certain times of year to attack.

When a virus arrives in a community, it spreads in an epidemic fashion for a period of weeks, then disappears. Doctors know what virus has arrived because every patient has the same illness for a few weeks. Yep, it's a fact of life—viruses are always coming to town, it's just a matter of when they arrive every year. Here are the seasonal patterns of viral epidemics:

Summer: Coxsackievirus (hand/foot/mouth), Enteroviruses (stomach, skin, respiratory, eye)
Fall: Parainfluenza (croup), Rhinovirus (common cold)
Winter: Influenza (the flu), Rotavirus (stomach flu), RSV (bronchiolitis)
Spring: Parainfluenza again, Varicella (chicken pox)

What causes these seasonal patterns? There are various factors that influence the annual epidemics of these viruses. Scientists have been studying this for years. It seems to be a combination of atmospheric conditions and host (that's us) behaviors that lead to the perfect conditions for a virus to attack. Interestingly, viruses can be found infecting people in their "off-season," but not at epidemic levels.[1]

Q. How do viruses cause infection?

Remember, viruses need us to survive. They jump at the chance to enter any body orifice (eyes, nose, mouth, anus, vagina, urethra). Most often, they are spread via the nose or through cough droplets, saliva, poop, or sexual relations.

Garden-variety viruses enter our body, replicate, and leave. This makes it hard to detect a virus or use a medicine to stop a viral infection—by the time you realize you have been attacked by a virus, the virus itself may have moved on.

The symptoms we experience are due to our immune response to the infection. For example, the common cold virus (rhinovirus) attacks the nose. Our immune system sends white blood cells there to fight the infection. The result of the bug/white blood cell battle is mucus production.

Once we have symptoms, the virus has already replicated numerous times in our body. It's usually too late to do anything. Fortunately, most viral infections are not serious and our bodies recover from the invasion.

BOTTOM LINE: Think of a virus as a speedboat. It zips in and out of our body.

Q. How do doctors know that a child has a viral infection?

Your baby's doctor will make a diagnosis based on symptoms (the problems/complaints you describe) and the signs of infection (the abnormal findings on physical examination). *Most experienced physicians are able to accurately make the diagnosis of a typical viral infection on this information alone.*

Q. Are there any tests that can detect a viral infection?

For the most part, no. Most testing looks for signs of a *bacterial* infection. The problem with viruses is that they are extremely small. We can't see them with a regular microscope. And often, the virus is already out of the body so it can't be caught. Lab work that tests for specific viral infections look for an immune response to a particular virus (antibody levels).

Can't your doctor just do a blood test to see if your baby has a virus? If a complete blood count is done on a child with a viral infection, the results are usually normal. The white blood cell count does not rise in response to a virus. In fact, some viruses cause a decrease in the number of cells that fight infection (termed *viral bone marrow suppression*). Influenza is classic for causing a low white blood cell count. White blood cells can be further differentiated by their shape under a microscope. The types of white blood cells that mount an immune attack to viruses are predominantly *lymphocytes*. Seeing a high number of lymphocytes is one of the only useful bits of information in a blood count to diagnose a viral infection.

BOTTOM LINE

Lab work and x-rays are rarely necessary to diagnose a virus in your baby. If a child does not improve as expected, though, doctors need you to call or follow up to explore things further.

Q. Are there any anti-viral medications?

Yes. There are a few available. But, all of these medicines must be given within the first 24 to 48 hours of symptoms because they act by inhibiting the replication of the virus. It is useless to take an anti-viral medicine more than three days into a viral illness.

For most viruses, there is no anti-viral medication available to clear the infection. The ones that ARE available include:

1. Tamiflu (Oseltamivir) for influenza A and B
2. Symmetrel (Amantadine) for influenza A
3. Zovirax (Acyclovir) for chicken pox, shingles, or herpes
4. AZT, Abacavir for HIV infections
5. Formvirisen for CMV eye infections

Q. How long do most viral infections last?

You can expect a typical virus to cause symptoms for seven to 14 days.

Usually a fever is present for the first two to four days of illness. While there is a fever, your child is contagious. The virus is actively growing/replicating. The fever stops when the virus stops replicating. But, our bodies will feel the impact of the infection for about a week.

Q. Is there any way to prevent a viral infection?

Yes—with vaccination.

We are fortunate to have vaccinations to prevent some of the most serious viral infections known to civilization: smallpox, polio, hepatitis B, measles, mumps, rubella, and chickenpox.

The Common Cold

Q. What is the common cold?

A. A viral infection usually caused by our friend, rhinovirus ("rhino" is the Latin word for nose.)

Here is what you need to know:

1. The virus enters the host body through the nose and goes to work.
2. Fever and body aches occur when the virus starts reproducing.
3. Snot (mucus production), cough, with or without sore throat follows.
4. Symptoms last for up to 14 days, with day three or four being the worst.
5. The snot can change from clear to green and still be just the same old virus (not a sinus infection, which we'll discuss in Appendix D).

So, how long with cold and flu symptoms last?

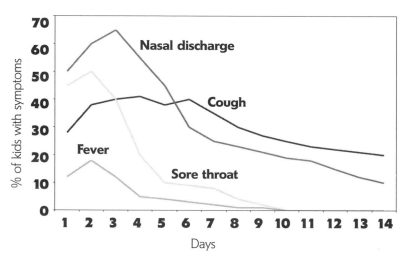

Source: Dr. S. Michael Marcy & Kaiser Permanente from data presented in JAMA

Q. How is the common cold diagnosed and treated?

A cold virus or upper respiratory infection is diagnosed based on the symptoms that the patient has. There is currently no test for it.

For babies, the best treatment is to use saline nose drops as much as needed. Saline is salt water. (See home remedies in medications, Appendix A.) A mist or two in each nostril before feedings and bed helps loosen the

**DR B'S OPINION:
COLD MEDS AND INFANTS**

I do not recommend using over-the-counter cough and cold preparations for babies under six months of age. Infants under six months of age can have a paradoxical reaction to antihistamines (instead of sedating a baby, these medicines can leave your child wired). Pseudoephedrine, the decongestant used in most of these medicines, can act similarly to caffeine. I personally would rather deal with a snotty sleeping baby than a snotty awake baby.

mucus and often makes babies sneeze. The beauty of saline is that it is safe and nearly impossible to overdose on it!

Remember, antibiotics will not cure a cold.

Top Remedies to Treat a Cold

- ◆ Saline nose drops.
- ◆ Running a humidifier in baby's room to help loosen the mucus.
- ◆ Having baby sleep in car seat or with head of mattress elevated (place a pillow or wedge *under* the mattress).

DR B'S OPINION: VAPO-RUBS

Some parents love to use this stuff. There is no proven scientific benefit and it makes the baby smell stinky! But if it makes you feel better doing something for your baby, go for it. It is not harmful to place it on the baby's chest. See Appendix B "Alternative medicine" for information on menthols/peppermint oil.

Reality Check

There are over 100 rhinoviruses. Once your child has a rhinovirus infection, he is immune to that one. But there are 99 more that he isn't immune to. Get the picture?

Q. I can feel a rattling in my baby's chest. Are you sure the infection isn't in his lungs?

Yes. It's air moving through snot that you hear and feel. See transmitted upper airway noise info in Chapter 15, "First Aid."

Q. How long is a baby contagious with a cold virus?

In general, the first three days of illness.

With viruses in general, people are contagious while they have a fever. The infection is spread via hand-to-hand contact with snot (mucus). It is also spread from cough and sneeze droplets.

Q. When my baby has a cold, he has a runny nose for almost two weeks. I'm afraid to take him back to playgroup because the other moms seem upset. When is he no longer contagious?

With the common cold virus or upper respiratory infection, the virus is spread in the first three or four days of illness (usually when kids have a fever). After that, it's just snot. You can return to playgroup.

Q. My baby has swollen glands. What are swollen glands?

Lymph nodes. Our bodies have chains of lymph nodes that look like a

infections

HUMIDIFIERS & VAPORIZERS: COLD VS WARM MIST DEBATE

A humidifier and vaporizer both do the same thing—they add humidity to dry air. Vaporizers have a place to add medicine to the mist but this feature is rarely used today. Kids who have asthma and need breathing treatments have a high-tech machine called a nebulizer.

Warm mist humidifiers are unnecessary and they make the nursery feel like the Bahamas. There is also a risk of an older baby burning his hand on a warm mist machine.

Bottom Line: Buy a cheap, cool-mist humidifier. It loosens up mucus so babies can sleep when they have a cold.

For a discussion of which humidifier models are best, ratings and buying advice, see our other book *Baby Bargains* (the back of this book has more details).

string of pearls. These chains are located throughout the body, but mostly in the neck, armpits, and groin. Each area works to protect a particular body area. For instance, the neck nodes are dedicated to the head, ears, nose, and throat. These tiny glands are jam packed with the cells that fight off infection. When there is an active infection in the body, these glands rise to the occasion, swelling to several times their normal size. They can be tender and can remain enlarged for up to six weeks after the infection is gone.

Swollen lymph nodes point us in the direction of where an infection is located.

Q. What is the significance of green snot? I always thought that it meant a bacterial infection.

Bacterial sinus infections cause green nasal secretions, but green snot alone does not diagnose sinusitis. The nasal secretions are a result of our immune system (white blood cells) fighting with either a virus or bacteria. The discoloration tells us that the battle has been going on for a while.

The change from clear secretions to yellow/green secretions WHEN ACCOMPANIED by fever, headache, fussiness, or prolonged symptoms (over two weeks of illness) is suspicious for a bacterial sinus infection.

The difference between a cold and a sinus infection

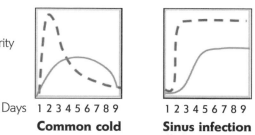

Key: --- Fever — Green Snot

Severity

Days 1 2 3 4 5 6 7 8 9   1 2 3 4 5 6 7 8 9

Common cold   **Sinus infection**

The common cold causes a short lived fever with several days of snot. A sinus infection causes prolonged fever and prolonged snot.

Bacteria

Q. What are bacteria?

These are much larger germs than viruses. These bugs can live on their own without a host. Most bacteria do not cause illness, and live in harmony with us. Some bacteria cause infection in only susceptible humans (those that are "immune compromised"), or when they end up in places they don't belong (e.g. intestinal bacteria in the urinary tract causes a bladder infection). And there are only a few bacteria that live to hurt us.

Q. I have heard about "good bacteria." What are they?

The bacteria that live in and on our bodies are called *normal flora.*

These bacteria live on our skin, and in our mouths, nostrils, vagina, and intestines. Babies are born relatively sterile (bacteria free). But it only takes a day or two in the real world to become colonized with bacteria. Here are the typical bacteria that are in you and your baby's body:

- ◆ *Skin bacteria:* Staph and Strep
- ◆ *Nostril bacteria:* Staph and Strep
- ◆ *Gut bacteria:* lactobacillus and E coli, among many others
- ◆ *Vagina and gut bacteria:* Group B Strep
- ◆ *Mouth bacteria:* too numerous to mention here

Q. How do bacteria cause infection?

They enter through any body opening under favorable conditions. These conditions include open wounds, mucus in the nose from viral infection, fluid in Eustachian tubes with a common cold virus, poop and bacteria pushed into the urethra/bladder opening. Other bacteria get in via respiratory secretions, saliva, or sexual activity.

Then they grow and fester in our bodies. Unlike viruses, they like to stick around.

Bacteria either invade our body tissues or produce a toxin (poison) that injures our bodies. Each bug has a particular body part they prefer to hang out in (throat, intestine, bladder, eye, etc)

Q. I have heard the term "secondary bacterial infection." What does it mean?

Bacteria often capitalize on a person who already has an active viral infection.

The viral infection is the *primary* infection. The bacteria that come in later are termed *secondary* infections. This is an important concept to understand why a) you are at risk for bacterial infections when you have a cold or flu, b) you don't often get bacterial infections when you are well, and c) why many bacterial infections are not contagious to others.

BOTTOM LINE: Think of bacteria as tugboats. They are slower moving than viruses. Their lack of speed and tendency to stick around make them susceptible to antibiotics.

Old Wives Tales

◆ **Going out in the rain causes pneumonia.**

The truth: Having a viral infection (cold or flu virus) predisposes a person to getting a secondary bacterial infection (pneumonia is a bacterial infection in the lungs). The weather has nothing to do with it.

◆ The wind or ceiling fans cause ear infections.

The truth: If your baby has a cold (or any viral infection), she is more susceptible to getting an ear infection (or another bacterial infection). Like the old wives tale about the rain and pneumonia, the wind has nothing to do with ear infections.

Q. Are bacterial infections contagious?

It depends on the bug and the host.

Not all bacteria jump from person to person. Some just set up shop in one body and grow until they are killed off.

And some bacteria will only cause infection in people who are susceptible (either because they already have a viral infection or their immune systems are compromised—such as premature infants, the elderly, people on chemotherapy, AIDS).

As a general rule, assume your child is contagious if he has a fever. The fever tells you that the body's immune system is actively fighting the bug.

But, your doctor can tell you if the particular bacterial infection is contagious to others (or read the final section of this chapter) For example,

HOW A DOC CAN TELL A BACTERIAL INFECTION FROM A VIRUS

1. **Your child is sicker.** Bacterial infections, in general, make people sicker than viruses.
2. **Your child's fever lasts longer than four days.** Viral illnesses usually cause fever for three to four days maximum (except influenza which last up to a week).
3. **Your child's fever is really high (over 105).** Viruses cause high fevers, too. But there is a greater chance it's a bacterial infection when you could fry an egg on your child's back.
4. **Your child has a localized area of infection.** Bacteria pick a body part to live in. The most common bacterial infections in childhood include: ear, sinus, throat, eye, lung, bladder/kidney, lymph node, intestine, blood, or the brain.
5. **Your child has abnormal lab work.** If there is not an obvious source of infection on examination, and he looks really sick with or without prolonged or high fever, some tests will be done. A complete blood count shows an elevation of the cells that fight infection (total white blood cell count over 15,000, and a high percentage of **NEUTROPHILS**—see lab section in Appendix C for details). Or, white blood cells in urine, spinal fluid, etc. indicate that infection is there (white blood cells are never found in normal urine or spinal fluid).

Strep throat (Group A Strep) infection IS contagious. An ear infection caused by Strep pneumoniae is NOT contagious.

Q. Can you find out which bacterium is causing an infection?

Yes.

Because bacteria don't leave the body, doctors can potentially catch the bacteria and identify them under a microscope or grow them on a culture plate. Blood, urine, stool, spinal fluid, eye discharge, ear discharge, throat pus, sputum (mucus coughed up), and vaginal discharge to name a few, can be examined.

> ### DR B'S OPINION
>
> *"If you can get a child over three months old to smile at you, he isn't that sick. There is a scientific study that has proven this. In practice, I can tell you it's true."*

Bacteria living in our bodies can grow on a culture plate in about 48 hours.

The only problem is that we can't always get a specimen from the location of the infection (like an ear infection). Fortunately, a limited number of bacteria cause certain infections. Once the source of the infection is identified (eye, ear, sinus, lung, etc.), doctors have a pretty good idea which bacterium is wreaking havoc.

Q. How do doctors know which antibiotic will kill a bacterial infection?

Doctors select an antibiotic that kills the bacteria most likely causing the infection. Antibiotics are not all the same. They are each potent against specific families of bacteria. (See Appendix A, "Medications.")

If bacteria grow on a culture plate (from an available specimen), doctors get exact information for antibiotic selection. The growing bacteria are placed on several "sensitivity" plates. These plates contain a growth medium and an antibiotic. If the bacteria can't grow on a particular antibiotic plate, the right medication to keep the infection from growing in the body is found.

Antibiotic Resistance

Q. I've heard a lot about drug resistant bacteria/antibiotic resistance. What is it?

Darwin's Survival of the Fittest.

Bacteria adapt to survive. There is a constant challenge to create more anti-microbials (antibiotics) to kill off the smart drug-resistant bugs.

Many people don't understand the concept of antibiotic resistance. They think that a *person* who is taking antibiotics will develop a drug resistance. *Drug resistance refers to the bugs.* When so many antibiotics are being used in the community, the bugs know our ammunition. Those that survive are drug resistant. The idea is that we can't overuse our weapons—otherwise we will be left with no defense. We need to use our antibiotic weapons judiciously.

Reality Check

Penicillin resistant strains of bacteria, particularly one called Strep pneumoniae (see Prevnar in the last chapter on vaccines) began emerging in 1991. Now, 20% of Strep pneumoniae strains are resistant to Penicillin and 10% are resistant to at least three types of antibiotics. Strep pneumoniae cause five to seven million ear infections annually.[2]

Q. What can be done to reduce the number of drug resistant bacteria?

◆ Give the Prevnar vaccine to children at high risk of getting Strep pneumoniae infection (children under age two)
◆ Use a higher dose of the first-line antibiotic (Amoxicillin).
◆ Save the big gun, broader spectrum antibiotics for persistent infections.
◆ Only use antibiotics when it is really necessary.

Q. When should antibiotics NOT be prescribed?

1. The common cold or "upper respiratory infection."
2. A sore throat caused by a virus (as opposed to Strep throat which is caused by a bacteria).
3. Green snot (see the common cold section earlier in ths chapter).
4. Because someone else in the house is on antibiotics.

The abuse of antibiotics

Here are a couple of startling stats: In 1980, four million prescriptions were written for Amoxicillin (a popular antibiotic).

In 1992, over 12 million prescriptions were written for Amoxicillin.

It is clear that doctors over-prescribe antibiotics. Want to know the number one reason doctors site for over-prescribing? Parent expectation that an antibiotic will be prescribed!

Truth be told, it's not just the parents' fault. A recent study showed that doctors often misperceive what a parent expects at an office visit (and try to satisfy them).[3]

Old Wives Tale

I am on an antibiotic for an upper respiratory infection. My child is sick, too. He needs antibiotics.

DR B'S OPINION: CAN WE TALK?

Parents and doctors need to communicate better. If a bacterial infection is diagnosed, an antibiotic is in order. Viruses are not cured by antibiotics.

Doctors need to do a better job of explaining viruses. Parents need to do a better job of accepting the fact that their child will get better on their own. And this may mean missing work to take care of a sick child. A miracle "pill" isn't always available to restore your child to perfect health in mere hours.

The truth: Not everyone with a cold develops a sinus infection. That is probably why you are taking an antibiotic. Your child should be checked for a secondary bacterial infection if he has a fever, crankiness, or prolonged symptoms (beyond ten to 14 days). It was common 15 to 20 years ago that if one person in a house had a strep infection, then doctors prescribed antibiotics for the ENITRE family, Now, we realize that is NOT the answer. Giving antibiotics to healthy folks only strengthens the bugs' resistance to drugs.

When can Johnny go back to childcare/playgroup?

DISEASE	TREATMENT	RETURN TO CHILDCARE?
Common cold	None	When fever is gone.
Influenza	+/- Anti-viral Rx	When fever is gone.
Croup	+/- Steroid Rx	When fever is gone.
Hand-foot-mouth	None	When fever is gone.
Herpes stomatitis	None	When lesions are healed.
Conjunctivitis/Pink eye	None it viral infection	When eyes are clear
Bacterial conjunctivitis	Antibiotic eye drops Rx	After 24 hrs. of treatment.
Stomach virus	None	When poop is formed.
Viral rashes	None	Depends on the infection
Chickenpox	+/- Antiviral Rx	When all lesions crusted (1 wk.)
Fifth disease	None	Not contagious once rash appears
Impetigo	Antibiotic Rx	After 24 hours of treatment.
Food poisoning	Depends on the bug	When poop is formed.
Giardia	Anti-parasitic Rx	When poop is formed.
Ringworm	Anti-fungal Rx	After 24 hours of treatment.
Scabies	Body wash rx	After 1 treatment.
Head lice	OTC shampoo	After 1 treatment.
Pinworms	Anti-parasitic Rx	After 1 treatment.[4]

KEY—Rx: prescription medicine; OTC: over-the-counter medicine

Putting it all together...

Now you know the usual suspects. Here is how doctors put it all together. When a child has a fever, your doctor looks for infection. (There are other causes for fever, but infection tops the list). The symptoms IN ADDITION TO the fever are what lead to the diagnosis. (Vomiting, diarrhea, cough, runny nose, decreased appetite, rash...) The constellation of symptoms and findings on physical examination are often enough information to make the call. Lab work and x-rays are sometimes needed to help figure out the source of infection.

Viral infections for the most part do not require any medication and are fought off by our body's immune systems. Bacteria, fungi, mites, and parasites require medication to eliminate the infection. The medication selection is often based on the usual suspects for a particular illness. If an infection doesn't clear up or the patient is pretty sick, cultures can help identify the particular bug and the right medication.

Bacterial infections are frequently secondary infections that capitalize on a weakened immune system that is fighting a virus (ear infections, sinus infections/adenoiditis, pneumonia). Doctors worry about secondary infections when a child with a viral infection suddenly gets worse (i.e. new fever, new green snot, new irritability, new respiratory distress).

NEW PARENT 411: ANTIBIOTICS

Just because YOU are on an antibiotic, does not mean your child needs to be on one. Whole families can get infected with a virus. But not everyone gets a secondary bacterial infection from the virus. Remember that secondary infections are not contagious. So, even if you now have a sinus infection, your baby most likely will still have just a cold.

Special Feature: Ear Infections

Is your child earning frequent flier miles at the doctor's office? Are you exhausted by the constant ear infections your poor baby has had to endure? Then this section is for you.

Q. Why is my baby prone to getting ear infections?

Thanks to your baby's facial structure, her Eustachian tubes are not working right.

The Eustachian tubes equalize pressure changes in the ear and clear the fluid created from infection or allergies. Babies are born with round heads to get through the birth canal. As a result, the Eustachian tubes (connection between the ears and the back of the nose) *lie horizontally* in kids until three years of age. This keeps the tubes from draining effectively. As a child grows, his head and face elongate. The Eustachian tubes ultimately slant downwards (and work better).

When a child gets a cold or upper respiratory infection, the virus causes the lining of the Eustachian tubes to swell, making the tubes even more inefficient. Bacteria like to grow if the fluid sits there long enough. The body's immune response to the bacteria creates pus, and that is the definition of a middle ear infection (**ACUTE OTITIS MEDIA**). Older children and adults rarely get ear infections because their Eustachian tubes drain more effectively.

Your Baby's Ear, in a nutshell

Middle ear
Inner ear
Adenoids (in back of nose)

Ear canal   Eardrum   Eustachian tube

Notes:

1. The ear is divided into three parts—the inner, middle, and outer areas.
2. The Eustachian tubes attach to the middle part of the ear.
3. The eardrum (tympanic membrane) is a piece of tissue that separates the middle and outer ear.
4. The eardrum protects the delicate middle ear bones and nerves.

Ear Infection Facts

◆ By the age of three, 75% of all children have had at least one ear infection.

◆ 40% of all antibiotics prescribed for children are for ear infections.

◆ The peak age of ear infections is six to 18 months of age.

◆ 90% of ear infections are caused by bacteria. 10% are caused by viruses.

Q. What is the difference between an ear infection and swimmer's ear?

An "ear infection" generally refers to a *middle* ear infection (**ACUTE OTI-TIS MEDIA**). The pus/infection sits behind the eardrum (see diagram on the previous page). A "swimmer's ear" (**OTITIS EXTERNA**) refers to an infection of the skin lining the *outer* ear (the canal where Q-tips don't belong!).

TOP 7 RISK FACTORS FOR EAR INFECTIONS

Parents often ask if there is anything that can be done to prevent an ear infection from happening. Here are the risk factors:

1. **The common cold/ upper respiratory infection.** By definition, fluid must be present in the Eustachian tubes to allow bacteria to grow. Having a cold is the perfect set up for fluid accumulation in the sinuses and Eustachian tubes.

2. **Daycare.** Children get more cold viruses when they are around other kids. Naturally, kids in daycare will get more colds, thus more ear infections. And, the bacteria that live there are more likely to be drug resistant bacteria.

3. **Second hand smoke.** Smoke is irritating to the whole respiratory tract, from the nose down to the lungs. Irritation of the Eustachian tubes causes swelling of the tissues, and inefficiency in clearing fluid.

4. **Pacifier use.** Constant sucking seems to create a backup of fluid in the back of the throat and Eustachian tubes.

5. **Bottle propping.** Babies who lie down and hold their own bottles allow fluid from the back of the throat to end up in the Eustachian tubes. The fluid is a set up for infection.

6. **Native American.** The facial structure of this ethnic group predisposes them to Eustachian tube dysfunction.

7. **Cleft lip/palate.** This facial structure predisposes them to Eustachian tube dysfunction.

If you're looking for more information on common ear, nose and throat problems in childhood, check out the web site of the American Academy of Otolaryngology Head and Neck Surgery at www.EntNet.org/kidsent/.

Middle Ear Infection (Acute Otitis Media)

A normal looking eardrum is grayish and translucent. The bones that control hearing (the ones you learned about in junior high science class) are visible behind it. An infected eardrum has pus behind it and is swollen and red. The pus and swelling obscure the view of the middle ear. *Think of the infection as being a zit.* It has to drain before it gets better. It can either rupture the eardrum and drain (undesirable) or drain down the Eustachian tube (desirable). The use of antibiotics taken by mouth clears the pus and decreases the chance of the zit bursting (**PERFORATED EAR DRUM:** see more below).

Swimmer's Ear (External Otitis)

This is a skin infection caused by either water that chronically collects in the ear canal or skin irritation from being scratched (from a Q-tip). Both situations allow bacteria to penetrate the skin and cause infection. *Swimmer's ear causes extreme pain with touch or movement of the outer ear* (the part you can see). There is swelling, redness, and sometimes debris in the canal. The eardrum is normal. These infections usually clear up with antibiotic eardrops.

Q. My baby's eardrum popped! Will he have permanent hearing damage?

No. Perforated eardrums heal like a piece of skin that has been cut.

Remember the zit analogy? The eardrum is under pressure with all that pus behind it. When the pimple pops, it lets the pus drain out. The perforation hole is usually small and not completely ruptured. The ear feels better if this happens. The infection still needs to be treated, though. The doctor may prescribe antibiotic drops and oral antibiotics if this occurs. It should heal up without any long-term consequences as long as the infection is treated.

Q. Will my child get an ear infection from lying in bath water?

No.

Bath water is fairly clean and very little collects in the outer ear canal. But it's a good idea to wipe the water out of the ears. It's not a major player in causing swimmer's ear. And it has absolutely nothing to do with middle ear infections (which happen on the other side of the eardrum).

Q. My child was just in the doctor's office two days ago. Now he has an ear infection. Didn't the doctor see it then?

Back to the zit thing. Ears can go from normal to bulging with pus in a matter of hours.

Q. Can I buy one of those ear scopes (otoscope) and examine my own child's ears?

Sure. But you might not know what you are looking at.

An acute middle ear infection may present itself in one of several ways.

The obvious bulging red ear is one you'd be able to diagnose. But not all of them look like that. They are more subtle. It doesn't just take the light of an otoscope to make the diagnosis. It takes the experience of looking at thousands of ears for comparison.

Don't be disappointed if you buy an otoscope, feel sure that you have diagnosed an ear infection, and find that your pediatrician has a different opinion.

Q. I've heard that not all ear infections require antibiotics to go away. Do we have to treat every ear infection with antibiotics?

Not all middle ear infections require antibiotics.

A small percentage (10%) of ear infections are caused by viruses. And some bacterial ear infections will clear on their own without any consequences. However, bacterial ear infections clear more quickly with antibiotics.

In Denmark, ear infections are treated differently than in the United States. Doctors in Denmark diagnose an ear infection and send a child home without a prescription. They tell the parent to give their child a pain medication and come back the next day for a re-check. If the ear looks worse or unchanged, they prescribe antibiotics. If the ear is improved, no therapy is required.

Q. What happened in the days before antibiotics when children had ear infections?

Some children did just fine. Others did not.

DR B'S OPINION:
WHY THE DENMARK PLAN IS A HARD SELL

Let's look at the reasons why the "Denmark Plan" (described above) just doesn't work well here in the U.S.:

1. **Most parents want to do something ASAP.** Ear infections hurt a lot. Parents don't want to stay up all night (again) with a sick child when something could be done about it.
2. **Dual-career families.** Coming back the next day for a second appointment means another lost workday for a parent.
3. **Health insurance plans with high co-payments for office visits.** A second office visit means a second co-payment.

If I diagnose a child with a mild ear infection, I offer the Denmark Plan to the family. I have no problem with this approach. But, most families don't choose this option.

This goes back to the discussion on antibiotic-resistant bacteria. These are the pressures that pediatricians, like myself, perceive from parents. If pediatricians and parents embrace this "wait and see" approach, we could reduce the number of antibiotic resistant bacteria.

INFECTIONS

? ?

Untreated bacterial infections can lead to *hearing loss* (from chronic fluid accumulation, chronic infection, and chronic ear drum perforations), *mastoiditis* (infection invades the skull bone), and *brain abscesses/meningitis* (infection extends to brain and spinal fluid). In the old days before antibiotics, 80% of ear infections would go away on their own. But the last 20% of ear infections that were untreated lead to these significant complications.[5]

Q. What antibiotics are typically used to treat ear infections?

The right drug for the bug.
The most common bacteria that cause middle ear infections are:

◆ Strep pneumoniae (of Prevnar vaccine fame, discussed earlier).
◆ Moraxella
◆ H. Influenza *non-typable* (a cause of pink eye with an ear infection)
◆ Group A Strep

There are basically four antibiotic classes that kill all of these bugs. As a general rule, doctors prescribe Amoxicillin (in the Penicillin class) as their first choice. It is a broad-spectrum antibiotic that is well tolerated by most kids, has been around for a long time, and is relatively inexpensive (about $10 for generic). It works about 85% of the time, depending on the amount of drug resistant bacteria living in your neighborhood. That's a pretty good track record.

If it has been *less* than 30 days since a previous ear infection, doctors may select a different class of antibiotics because the bacteria may be resistant to the Amoxicillin (that is, the same bug may have grown back after being off medication).

If there is pink eye associated with an ear infection, there is a good chance that H. influenza is the bug. This bug is resistant to Amoxicillin about 50% of the time (again, depending on your neighborhood). So, a doctor may choose a different antibiotic in this situation.

Q. My child was on Amoxicillin before and it never works.

Your child is not resistant to Amoxicillin—the bacterium he is being infected with is resistant. Children in daycare settings tend to have more ear and sinus infections with drug-resistant bacteria. That doesn't mean that Amoxicillin will *never* work. For instance, Group A Strep (which causes Strep throat) is almost always cured with Amoxicillin.

Q. My child is pulling on his ears. Should I be worried about an ear infection?

No. It's not a reliable indicator.
Parents frequently rely on ear pulling as a sign of an ear infection. There was an excellent study done on this suspicious behavior

DR B'S OPINION

"I always pick the least potent antibiotic that will work in a given situation. The only way to have the 'big gun' when you need it is to avoid using it when you don't need it."

that showed ear pulling predicted ear infections only 5% of the time. 95% of the time, babies pull on their ears because they can![6]

Q. Why do I have to bring my child back for an "ear check" after he has been treated?

Because infants can't tell you that their ears are better.

The antibiotic prescribed should kill the bacteria. But, there are smart, resistant bugs that will survive. That's one reason why the doctor wants to see your child back two to three weeks after the diagnosis.

The other reason is that residual sterile fluid (**SEROUS OTITIS MEDIA**) can remain for a long time after the bacteria is gone. This is basically pus that is dissolved, but not dried up. The fluid is not infected, but can create two problems:

◆ It puts a child at risk for getting another middle ear infection down the road.

◆ It inhibits sound waves from getting through the middle ear (**CONDUCTIVE HEARING LOSS**). It's like walking around with earplugs in all day long. Chronic fluid (more than three months duration) is a problem for a child who is trying to learn his native language (**EXPRESSIVE LANGUAGE DELAYS**).

Q. My child feels better after just a couple of days taking Amoxicillin for his ear infection. Why do we have to continue the medicine for ten days?

Antibiotics start to clear an infection within 48-72 hours. However, it can take five to ten days to kill off all of the bacteria. Stopping an antibiotic early allows a germ to re-grow and cause infection (and pain) to return. Doctors are trying to shorten the course of antibiotics because of the growing number of antibiotic resistant bacteria. If you doctor prescribes a shorter course (five days) of medicine, be sure to follow up with an appointment to make sure the infection has cleared.

RESIDUAL EAR FLUID

The pus from the ear infection gradually dissolves and gets reabsorbed by the body. The name for this sterile (bug-free) fluid is called **SEROUS FLUID** or serous otitis. 70% of children will still have serous fluid two weeks after an ear infection. Up to 40% of kids will still have serous fluid one month later, and 10% have fluid three months after infection.[7]

The serous fluid does NOT need to be treated with antibiotics to clear up. However, kids with residual fluid need to be re-evaluated to make sure the fluid goes away. As mentioned earlier, chronic fluid in the ears interferes with language development (in the short term).

If a child has chronic fluid in the ears, over three months duration, an Ear/Nose/Throat specialist may want to drain the fluid by popping the eardrum with a needle. Frequently, if the drum is popped, a PE tube is inserted to prevent further accumulations of fluid.

Q. We are flying with our baby tomorrow and he was just diagnosed with an ear infection. Should we cancel our trip?

No. Go have fun.

As anyone who's traveled on a plane knows, the pressurized air in the cabin requires you to "clear" your ears (by chewing gum, yawning, etc). Babies have the same needs—their middle ear must accommodate to the pressure change. When a child has an acute ear infection, pus fills in the middle ear space and the eardrum cannot move. The ear won't hurt. In fact, the pressure change might make the drum pop to release the pressure (and that's okay—see perforated eardrum later in this chapter).

It is more problematic when an ear infection is starting to clear up. Then there is both air (normal) and fluid (not normal) in the middle ear. The eardrum will try to accommodate to the pressure change and will be only partially successful. This HURTS. Don't cancel your trip; just be prepared for some discomfort on take off and landing. Nursing, feeding your child a bottle or sucking on a pacifier can help relieve the pressure.

Q. How many ear infections are too many?

Great question. For this answer, we've recruited Dr. Brown's husband, Mr. Dr. Brown (an Ear, Nose, and Throat specialist) for some advice:

"Most kids outgrow the problem of ear infections by about three years of age. (See earlier for information on why this is). So theoretically, we can all wait until your child turns three. But, there are some important considerations that compel doctors to take a more active approach. Here are some key questions:

1. How many courses of antibiotics are too many? Antibiotics can have unpleasant side effects like diarrhea and yeast infections. Being on antibiotics frequently leaves a child susceptible to bacteria that are smarter (the drug-resistant strains) and allows bacteria in the community to see our weapons. From an economic standpoint, every ear infection costs parents a visit to the pediatrician, missed work, and another round of antibiotics.

2. How old is the child? If a child is in the midst of language acquisition (nine months to age two), it's critical for him to hear what people are saying to him. Otherwise, the infections can contribute to short-term expressive language delays. In the long run, these kids do catch up and have normal language skills.

3. How miserable is the child? Ear infections hurt. That leads to disrupted sleep for the whole family. This important point tends to get overlooked by both parents and doctors.

Reality Check

It's important to look at what is in the best interest of the child. There is some variability amongst doctors, but a reasonable answer to what is "too many" is the following:

◆ Four infections in the peak (winter) season
◆ Three infections in the off peak (summer) season

◆ Three months of persistent residual fluid (serous otitis media)

◆ Three back-to-back courses of antibiotics for the same ear infection.

Too many ear infections buy your child a trip to see the Ear, Nose, and Throat specialist. These doctors assist in decision making for children with recurrent ear infections. If necessary, they can place pressure equalization tubes in the eardrum to reduce the number of ear infections (we'll discuss this more in detail later in this chapter).

Ear infections occur mostly in cold and flu season. (Remember, bacteria are secondary infections for a child with fluid in his ears already). So, it's expected that more infections will happen then. Kids who get middle ear infections in the off-season are time bombs for the winter.

Q. How can I prevent ear infections from happening?

There are a few things you can do:

1. **Feed your baby in an upright position.** Milk can get into the Eustachian tubes if a baby is lying horizontally while eating.

2. **Avoid pacifiers after three months of age.** There is some good data to suggest this is a risk factor for ear infections.[8]

3. **Don't smoke.** Smoking is a respiratory irritant—both to the smoker and his family. It causes swelling of the Eustachian tubes, which can lead to infection.

4. **Infection control during the cold and flu season.** Good hand-washing and flu shots for the family are helpful. The Prevnar vaccine for your child helps limit some (not all) infections.

5. **Reconsider your childcare options.** There is no question that children in daycare settings get more infections (and with drug-resistant bugs). When families have reached the end of their ropes, doctors may discuss this subject with you.

DR B'S OPINION:
WHEN TO CALL IN AN ENT

Here is how I would approach making a referral to an Ear/Nose/Throat Specialist for a child with recurrent ear infections (other than the "too many" criteria above).

Scenario 1: If a child already has had three ear infections by Thanksgiving, that doesn't bode well for the rest of the season (cold and flu season will continue through March). Refer now to an ENT.

Scenario 2: If a child gets ear infection sporadically through the winter and gets his fourth infection in April, wait and see if the ear infections stop as the season ends.

Scenario 3: If a child gets two ear infections during the summer months and a third in September, the child gets one more chance before referring. But, I prepare the family for the possibility.

Q. Can we just start an antibiotic when my child has a cold? What about preventative antibiotics through the winter months?

Doctors used both of these methods in the past. And to a certain degree, they worked. However, the price paid is too great. This approach created drug-resistant bacteria.

Q. Can I prevent an ear infection from happening by using a decongestant or antihistamine to dry up all that snot?

No.

You would think that if you got rid of the fluid, the ear infection could be prevented. This idea was studied about 30 years ago and it didn't prevent ear infections. There is a reason it doesn't work. When there is infection, the Eustachian tubes are full of fluid *and* get swollen. This prevents them from draining effectively.

Q. What are "tubes"?

The official term is Pressure Equalization (PE) Tube.

The alternative to antibiotics for recurrent ear infections is to insert PE tubes into the eardrums. These tubes are the length of a pencil point and the diameter of angel hair pasta (i.e. really small). The procedure is relatively simple. An ENT Specialist makes a tiny hole in the eardrum, cleans out any fluid/pus, and inserts the tube. The tube falls out on its own after a lifespan of 6-18 months. The eardrum heals beautifully 99% of the time.

Children have this procedure done in a day-surgery facility. They do require anesthesia, but don't require an IV, breathing tube, or ventilator. Why anesthesia? It's helpful not to have a squirming child when someone is poking a hole into the eardrum. The procedure takes about five minutes. Kids are usually back to themselves again later that day.

Many parents are incredibly fearful of having PE tubes placed. They are afraid of the procedure, the anesthesia, or the risk of having an opening in the eardrum (you have to keep water out of the ear). Most of these concerns should be clearly addressed by your ENT doctor.

Helpful Hints: Understanding PE Tubes

Think of PE tube placement as a *procedure* and not surgery. I think the word surgery really freaks people out.

◆ This is a simple, quick procedure. For adults, it could be performed in an office setting.

◆ The risk of anesthesia is no greater than the risk of all the antibiotics your child has been taking.

◆ You'll stop needing to see the pediatrician. My frequent fliers stop visiting my office after they have PE tubes placed. I always enjoy seeing my patients, but I see some kids too often.

THE INFECTION HIT PARADE: VIRUSES AND BACTERIA

So, let's sum up this chapter. Here is a list of the top infections, as caused by viruses and bacteria:

Viruses That Cause Infection

Here is a list of the most common VIRUSES that cause infection in babies ages birth to age one. For details on these infections, see Appendix D.

Viral Respiratory Infections
1. The Common Cold or upper respiratory infection (Rhinovirus)
2. The Flu (Influenza)
3. Bronchiolitis (RSV)
4. Croup (numerous viruses)

Viral Mouth And Tonsil Infections
1. Hand-Foot-and-Mouth (Coxsackievirus)
2. Herpes Stomatitis (Herpes Type-1)
3. Sore throat virus (Adenovirus)

Gastrointestinal Viruses
1. Stomach virus, or "stomach flu" (Rotavirus)

Viral Exanthems (Viruses That Cause Skin Rashes)
1. Roseola (Herpesvirus-6)
2. Chickenpox (Varicella)
3. Slapped Cheek or Fifth Disease (Parvovirus)

Bacteria That Cause Infection

Here are some of the bacterial infections in babies birth to age one. For details, please see Appendix D.

1. **Ear Infections** (Strep pneumoniae, H. Influenza, And others)
2. **Sinus Infections** (Strep pneumoniae H. Influenza, and others)
3. **Eye Infections** (H. Influenza, Strep pneumoniae, and others)
4. **Throat Infections** (Group A Strep)
5. **Lung Infections** (Strep pneumoniae, Staph, and others)
6. **Food Poisoning** (E. Coli, Salmonella)
7. **Bladder Infections** (E. Coli, and others)
8. **Meningitis** (Group B Strep, Strep pneumoniae)

Things That Make You Itchy Just Thinking About Them

These infections are discussed in detail in Appendix D.

1. **Fungus:** Ringworm, Thrush, Yeast diaper rash
2. **Mites:** Scabies
3. **Lice:** Head lice
4. **Parasites:** Giardia
5. **Worms:** Pinworms

infections

BOTTOM LINE

As a general rule, PE tubes are a life changing experience for the whole family. Even the most anxious parents report how "easy" the experience is, how much better their child feels, and wonder why they waited so long to do it.

Q. I've heard that a chiropractor can do a manipulation to clear up or prevent ear infections. What do you think about it?

Explain why it works and show me a good scientific study. Then I'll give it some consideration.

To date, I have not seen any of this. I have some families who go to extreme measures to keep their child from getting PE tubes. I, personally, feel safer putting my child in the hands of a skilled surgeon and anesthesiologist.

Having a neck manipulation to clear pus from a Eustachian tube just doesn't work. I'd also be afraid of a child being injured by a neck manipulation.

Whew! That was a load of viruses and bacteria. Now, it's on to other medical problems that are NOT caused by infectious bugs. The next chapter explores the most common diseases that affect babies.

Chapter 14

Common Diseases

This chapter is devoted to the most common medical problems in infants ages birth to one. Some topics have been discussed in other chapters. (See the index if you can't find the disease you are looking for in this chapter). The common thread of these medical problems is that they are not caused by an infectious bug.

We've organized this discussion by body system—first up, it's the eyes.

WHAT'S IN THIS CHAPTER

- ◆ **EYES: LAZY EYE**
- ◆ **LUNGS: ASTHMA, BRONCHIOLITIS**
- ◆ **HEART: MURMURS**
- ◆ **BLOOD: ANEMIA, SICKLE CELL DISEASE, IRON DEFICIENCY, LEAD EXPOSURE**
- ◆ **SKIN: ECZEMA**
- ◆ **MUSCLES/BONES: INTOEING, BOW-LEGGED, FLAT FEET**
- ◆ **ENDOCRINE: DIABETES**
- ◆ **ALLERGIES: SEASONAL, ENVIRONMENTAL**
- ◆ **WHAT'S THAT SMELL? UNUSUAL ODORS**

Eyes

Q. I'm worried my baby has a lazy eye. How do you check for that?

By examining the eyes every time you visit your doctor.

Under three months of age, babies can looked cross-eyed occasionally. The muscles of both eyes aren't working together yet.

After three months, both eyes should move together. There are two medical reasons for why they don't:

1. Strabismus. The muscles that move the eye are weak.

2. Amblyopia. The eye itself is weak or injured.

Often a parent will notice this at home. Doctors check by covering up one eye and checking that the other eye can focus on an object. A child looks away or tries to remove the examiner's hand when the unaffected eye is covered.

Regardless of the reason, these kids need to see an eye specialist (ophthalmologist). If a lazy eye goes untreated, permanent problems can occur. Eye doctors prefer to assess these problems before three years of age.

Helpful Hint

There is a benign condition called **PSEUDOSTRABISMUS** where kids just have narrowly set eyes. This is not a medical problem.

RED FLAG

If your child has a dramatic new problem with an eye turning in, go see your doctor ASAP. This can be a sign of a brain tumor.

Lungs

Q. What is asthma?

In short, it's like hay fever in the lungs.

Asthma is a process of swelling, muscle tightening, obstruction, destruction, and mucus production in the big and little airways of the lungs. This chain of events occurs due to a revved up immunologic/allergic response to *infections, allergies, weather, and emotions.*

The narrowed airways interfere with the air exchange (getting clean air in and dirty air out) that occurs with each breath. As a result, children are "air hungry." Their bodies try to get more air in by breathing fast and pulling the rib muscles in when breathing. The characteristic wheeze comes from air traveling through a narrowed passageway.

Asthma attacks (termed exacerbations) occur intermittently depending on what a child is hypersensitive to. Often, kids with asthma have flare ups with upper respiratory infections. This makes for a bad winter.

Q. How do you diagnose asthma?

Asthma is a diagnosis made by physical examination.

If a child is caught wheezing three or more times in his life, he carries a diagnosis of asthma. The first and second time a child wheezes, it might be bad luck. The third time, it's a trend.

There are reasons other than asthma that make children wheeze. Babies can get RSV Bronchiolitis (see more below) or another infection that results in wheezing. Older babies can get a raisin (or other small object) stuck in their airway and wheeze, too.

Your doctor can get a chest x-ray to rule out an infection or a foreign body in the airway. Blood tests aren't particularly helpful. Probably the best information to confirm a diagnosis is a child's response to asthma medication. If their lungs clear up with asthma medication, they likely have the diagnosis.

Q. My doctor said my child has "Reactive Airway Disease." Is that asthma?

Basically, yes. It's just a nicer term to use for a younger child who has not been diagnosed asthmatic.

Doctors tend to hedge on the diagnosis of asthma in a child before the first birthday. Some infants get hit really hard with an RSV infection and wheeze for what seems like months. By definition, they have airways that are "reacting" to infection—by getting swollen and full of mucus. Doctors use this term for little ones who haven't proven themselves to be true asthmatics yet.

Q. My husband had asthma as a child. What are the chances that my baby will have it?

There is definitely a genetic predisposition to asthma and other allergic disorders.

There is probably a 25% chance your child will have asthma. That means there is a 75% chance he won't. Given the odds, it doesn't pay to worry.

Q. My baby had RSV Bronchiolitis this winter. What are the chances that he will have asthma?

Thirty to forty percent.

This is a chicken or the egg dilemma. We just don't know which came first. But it is true that kids who wheeze with RSV tend to wheeze again in their lifetimes.

Interestingly, not all kids who get RSV wheeze. And of the kids who do wheeze with RSV, not all of them respond to asthma medication. So, there may be just a subset of kids who would have wheezed anyway who have trouble with RSV infection. See the RSV section in Appendix D for more details.

Q. How do you treat asthma?

Are you old enough to remember those old Primatene mist commecials?

◆ *For immediate rescue:* A **BRONCHODILATOR** (albuterol) very quickly relaxes the airways. This can be administered by liquid taken by mouth or inhaled via an inhaler device or a nebulizer machine (a souped-up vaporizer). For infants, the nebulizer provides the most immediate, effective relief. This medication can be given for prolonged periods in an office or emergency room setting. It can be administered every four to six hours at home.

◆ *For prevention of attacks:* Kids who wheeze more than twice a week need a medication to keep their asthma in check. Persistent symptoms mean chronic destruction to the lungs, which we now know, can be permanent. An **INHALED STEROID** (Budesonide/Pulmicort) is administered via nebulizer daily for these high-risk kids.[1] (See common medications Appendix A for more info.)

Reality Check

Most insurance plans cover the cost of a nebulizer machine for a patient who needs one. They know it's less expensive to buy a $100 machine than to pay for an ER visit or hospitalization.

Q. What are the chances my child will outgrow asthma?

50/50.

Those odds aren't bad for a chronic illness. Unfortunately, no one can predict if and when your child will outgrow it. As a general rule, kids who have asthma before the age of five tend to outgrow it. Children who are diagnosed with asthma when they are older are more likely to have it in adulthood.[2]

Q. What are the long-term consequences of asthma?

Asthma can cause permanent airway damage. This is a recent discovery in the medical world.

Kids who have occasional asthma flare-ups do fine in the long term. If a child has *chronic* airway reactivity, destruction of the normal structures occurs and don't recover. So, doctors are more aggressive about treatment for a child with persistent symptoms. Chronic obstructed airways also decrease the amount of oxygen getting to the body on a daily basis.

Q. My child has eczema. My doctor told me he has a higher risk of developing asthma. Why?

Because allergic diseases can occur as a group. This particular problem is called **ATOPY**.

Atopy or atopic disease refers to a classic triad of asthma, eczema, and seasonal allergies. Of the kids who have eczema, 30% get either asthma or seasonal allergies (but 70% won't get either).[3]

Q. My child wheezes. Could he have Cystic Fibrosis?

Yes, but it is very unlikely. Cystic Fibrosis is a genetically inherited disorder that affects one in 1600 children. It causes an abnormality in body cells that impair absorption of chloride. The result of this is that the lungs pull in too much sodium. Normal airway secretions get thick and don't move. Chronic lung infections develop. Other body systems are affected by this cell abnormality, particularly the intestines, pancreas, and reproductive system.

If your baby wheezes chronically, and especially if he is having trouble gaining weight, a screening test for cystic fibrosis may be in order. A simple assessment of a baby's sweat will give the answer.[4]

Heart

Q. What is a heart murmur?

A murmur is an extra noise that is heard when your doctor listens to the heartbeat with a stethoscope. The normal heartbeat is actually a series of sounds best described as "lub-dub". A murmur is an extra noise that may sound like rushing water ("p-ssh") or a squeak ("eek"). The quality, duration, and location of that noise help your doctor determine what is producing it.

If the cause isn't obvious by physical examination, your doctor may order a chest x-ray, electrocardiogram (EKG), or an echocardiogram (ultrasound of the heart) to get a better idea of what is going on.

Q. My doctor heard an "innocent" heart murmur in my baby. Should I be worried?

No.

There are innocent murmurs and there are pathologic murmurs. Innocent murmurs are caused by the turbulence of blood flowing through a valve or vessel in the cardiovascular system. These unique sounds come and go and may have a typical location where they can be heard. Many innocent murmurs are detected in the first 24 hours of life as the baby's circulation is changing from life in the womb to the outside world. Other innocent murmurs are detected after six months of age.

Doctors refer a child to a pediatric cardiologist if they have any uncertainty about whether the murmur is innocent or pathologic (see below).

Q. My baby has a heart murmur and is going to see a specialist. Should I be worried?

Be appropriately concerned, but the murmur may still not be a problem.

Again, most doctors err on the side of checking things out to be sure everything is okay. The term for a murmur caused by a defect in the heart is a **PATHOLOGIC MURMUR**. Most pathologic murmurs are caused by a problem with the way the heart developed before a baby was born (**CONGENITAL HEART DISEASE**). A congenital heart defect occurs in about one in 1000 newborns. The most common cause for an *acquired heart defect* is rheumatic fever from an untreated Strep infection. Fortunately, this is rarely seen anymore thanks to the development of Penicillin.

Even if your child does turn out to have a pathologic murmur, it may be caused by something that will go away on its own. The most common congenital heart defect (30% of all defects) is called a **VENTRICULAR SEPTAL DEFECT** (**VSD**). This means there is a small hole in the heart wall that separates the large chambers (ventricles). Some oxygen rich blood gets mixed into the oxygen poor blood, but it usually has no dramatic effect on the child. A vast majority of these holes will close on their own by five years of age. So, children with VSD's are followed closely by both their primary doctor and cardiologist to be sure they outgrow this condition.[5]

Other, less common defects may require either a procedure or surgery to correct. These defects are beyond the scope of this book. But, if you are looking for more information, check out www.cincinnatichildrens.org/heartcenter/encyclopedia

Blood

Q. What is anemia?

Let's discuss what red blood cells are first.

Red blood cells carry oxygen to our body tissues and remove carbon dioxide. Hemoglobin is the name of the protein that performs this function in each red blood cell. And, the key ingredient of hemoglobin is iron.

"Anemia" means there are not enough red blood cells circulating in the bloodstream. The causes of anemia are either *excessive destruction* or *inadequate production of red blood cells*.

Examples of *excessive destruction* of red blood cells include:

- ♦ More blood is being lost than made (such as menstruating women).
- ♦ Abnormal red blood cells are made and destroyed (such as sickle cell disease).

Examples of *inadequate production* of red blood cells include:

- ♦ Bone marrow production slows (such as bone marrow suppression by virus).
- ♦ Iron deficiency limits production due to lack of a key ingredient (that is, iron-deficiency anemia).
- ♦ Lead poisoning (technically, this is competition for iron's place in the red blood cell).
- ♦ Poor nutritional intake of key vitamins like B12/ Folate.

The number one cause of anemia in childhood is iron deficiency. Kids who are severely anemic are pale and fatigue easily.

Q. My baby had an abnormal newborn screen. We found out he has "sickle cell trait." What does that mean?

Let's be geneticists for a moment. Babies get one set of genes/DNA from Mom, and one set from Dad. Some diseases require one defective gene to affect someone (**AUTOSOMAL DOMINANT**). Some diseases require *both* genes to be abnormal to manifest themselves (**AUTOSOMAL RECESSIVE**).

Sickle cell disease is an autosomal recessive disease. People with one defective gene and one normal gene are called carriers. They carry the trait (gene) for the disease but are not affected by it. About 8% of the African-American population are sickle cell carriers.

Both sickle cell trait and disease can be detected by that first newborn blood test sent to the state laboratory (see Newborn Screening Tests in Chapter 1). It's detected by the type of protein chain that makes up red blood cells.

This is only a problem when your child gets married. If he marries a woman who also has sickle cell *trait*, his children are at a high risk for having sickle cell *disease*.[6]

Q. My baby has sickle cell disease. Can you explain what that means and what I should worry about?

Sickle cell disease is caused by abnormal protein (hemoglobin) in red blood cells. This protein causes the red blood cell shape to be deformed. Instead of an oval shaped cell, these cells look like half moons (like the 'sickle' on the Russian flag).

Sickle cells die more quickly, have trouble carrying oxygen, and clog up blood vessels. This blood vessel clogging kills the tissues that the blood vessel supplies (muscle, bones, spleen, lung, kidney, intestine).

The consequences in infancy and early childhood are the following:

1. **Chronic Anemia:** This shows up by age three months. Folate supplements are given to promote red blood cell formation.

2. **Dactylitis:** Infants get hand and foot swelling from clogged blood vessels.

3. **Non-functional spleen:** The spleen filters red blood cells as well as white blood cells (infection fighters). Because of the spleen's job, it takes the greatest hit as far as clogged vessels. We can't rely on the spleen being a functional organ in a child with sickle cell disease. This leaves children prone to infection, particularly with Strep pneumoniae and H. influenza bacteria. These kids need Prevnar vaccine, flu vaccine, and the Pneumonia (pneumo-coccal) vaccine that elderly people get.

4. **Failure to thrive:** Because of a chronic lack of oxygen to the tissues, these children are shorter and smaller than their peers.

There are a variety of medical problems associated with sickle cell disease as a child gets older. For more information, see www.sicklecelldisease.org.

Q. My nine month old had a routine blood test performed. He has iron-deficiency anemia. What did I do wrong?

You probably haven't done anything wrong.
However, there are some parent mistakes that can cause this problem:

1. **Exclusively breastfeeding** without introducing cereal after six months of age.

2. **Using low iron formula**—we have already warned you about this one.

3. **Replacing breast milk or iron-containing formula with regular cow's milk before the first birthday.**

Q. How is iron deficiency anemia treated?

With a high iron diet and an iron supplement (we discuss this in detail in Chapter 7, "Solids").

If your child is diagnosed with iron-deficiency anemia, your doctor will prescribe an iron supplement. Don't try to treat anemia by yourself without professional help. Why? Because iron, in high doses, can be toxic.

As a result, although vitamins containing iron are available without a prescription, the infant drops are located at the pharmacist's counter. The pharmacist dispenses these medications so he can counsel you on the correct dosage.

Also: there is a difference between the recommend daily allowance for iron (*maintenance iron dosage)* and the dose required for *replacement therapy* for those with low iron stores (iron-deficiency anemia). Doctors usually treat a child with iron-replacement therapy and then recheck their blood counts in three months.

Helpful Hints
Getting your child to take his iron supplement.
◆ Iron supplements universally taste bad. The brand name products taste a little better. Icar and Feostat brands taste best.

◆ It's okay to mix the medicine in juice. Just make sure your child drinks *all* the juice. Vitamin C actually helps the iron get absorbed into the bloodstream.

◆ DO NOT MIX WITH MILK. The calcium in milk competes with iron and can block absorption.

◆ Iron can cause a temporary gray/brown stain on the teeth. You can use baking soda on a toothbrush to remove it.

◆ Iron can make poop look black. It's not blood. Don't worry.

Q. We live in an old house. I'm worried about lead exposure. When should I get my child tested?

The appropriate time to get tested depends on when your child becomes mobile.

Most children who have lead poisoning live in homes built before 1978. These older homes have lead paint and lead pipes. Chipping paint is a very popular item for kids to pick up and eat. There is also lead in the soil surrounding these homes.

Screening for lead exposure is usually performed at nine to 12 months of age. In high-risk areas (urban, older homes), all children have a blood test done routinely. In low risk areas, doctors will screen with a risk-factor question list. If there is a possible exposure, a blood test is performed.

For more information, check out the Environmental Protection Agency's website at www.epa.gov/lead/index.html or call the National Lead Information Center (NLIC) at 800-424-5323.

While the Environmental Protection Agency recommends consumers turn to professionals to have their homes tested for lead, there are also a number of home tests available on the market. For under $10, you can purchase a lead test kit that includes swabs with a chemical that changes colors when it comes in contact with lead. Unfortunately, the accuracy of these tests has not been proven independently. If you're looking for a reputable professional testing lab in your state, check out the EPA's state-by-state listings of certification officers at epa.gov/safewater/privatewells/labs.html. Once you contact a certification officer in your state, he will be able to provide a list of certified labs.

Feedback from the Real World

I cared for a family who carefully de-leaded their home built in 1910 before moving in with their young children. Unfortunately, a central air conditioning unit was installed AFTER the move and it spewed old dust from the attic into all of the children's rooms. The children required medication to remove the lead from their bloodstreams. They are all doing fine now.

Skin

Q. What is eczema?

This falls into the allergic disease category. Eczema is a broad term to describe dry, scaly, itchy skin that appears in patches. It is often referred to as "the itch that rashes". In other words, kids have particularly sensitive, itchy skin. The itching is what produces the rash that you see.

The sensitive skin flares up with *dryness, exposure to perfumes/dyes,* or *allergies to metals/plants.*

The rash appears in different places depending on the age of the child. Younger kids tend to get it on their elbows, knees, and face. Older kids get it in their elbow and knee creases. We have more on managing eczema in Chapter 4, "Hygiene" and below.

Q. How do you get rid of eczema?

You don't. You may win the battle, but you won't win the war.

The key to managing eczema is to keep the skin moist. Eczema always flares up in the wintertime because of cold, dry air.

LIVING WITH ECZEMA: 7 TIPS & TRICKS

As a parent of a child with severe eczema, we've been there, done that. Here are our tips:

1. Moisturizing soap: The cheapest in this category is good old Dove soap. Other options are Cetaphil, Aveeno, and Neutrogena. Avoid anti-bacterial soaps—the alcohol will sting cracked skin.

2. Avoid perfumes and dyes: If it smells good, don't use it on your child. That goes for laundry detergent too. Use All Free and Clear or an equivalent product.

3. The thicker and greasier moisturizing cream, the better: My personal favorite is Creamy Vaseline. Eucerin creme, Aveeno, and Cetaphil are also popular choices among dermatologists. You need to lube your child up several times a day. As soon as you get your child out of the bathtub, apply the moisturizer (I'm serious—have the tube ready).

4. Apply 1% hydrocortisone cream to really red areas twice daily: 1% hydrocortisone cream is a low-potency steroid cream available without a prescription. It is very safe to use on a daily basis when flare-ups occur.

5. Give Benadryl at bedtime (for babies over six months): Benadryl will help reduce the amount of scratching that goes on when you aren't watching your child.

6. No bubble bath—most contain dyes and perfumes that can aggravate eczema. Instead, consider oatmeal bath treatments (Aveeno makes one). And don't bathe your child every night, especially in winter. The combination of frequent baths and dry heated air can cause flare-ups.

7. If you have tried all of this and your child is still miserable, it's time to check in with your pediatrician. They can recommend prescription products that are safe and effective. Don't hesitate to see a dermatologist if you and your pediatrician can't keep your baby's eczema under control.

Q. I'm worried about using steroids all the time to treat eczema. Are there any other options?

Yes.

If your child has become a professional scratcher, there are some other options for treatment.

In the past, the only option was to use a prescription-strength steroid cream. Steroids are extremely good anti-inflammatory medicines. They act by reducing the irritation of the skin, thereby reducing the itching. These products range from low to high potency. Doctors move up on the strength level until they find one that works, and taper back down when the eczema improves.

Now there is another option. A new class of medications (by prescription only) is an immunoregulator. The brand names are Elidel and Protopic. They also work on eczema but are safer to use long term and can be used on the face (high-potency steroids should not be used on the face).

Q. Is there a link between eczema and asthma?

Yes, for some people.

Eczema is an allergic disorder. About 70% of kids who have eczema have a parent, brother or sister who has some type of allergy (hay fever/seasonal allergies, eczema, asthma).

About 30% of kids with eczema will have the classic triad of **ATOPY** (eczema, seasonal allergies, and asthma). But, 70% of kids have eczema without any other type of allergic disease.[7]

It's just something to pay particular attention to.

Q. Will my baby outgrow eczema?

Chances are, yes.

About 70% of kids will outgrow eczema. But no one can predict if and when your child will outgrow it. Chances are better if your child gets eczema as a baby. Kids who get eczema later in life have a greater chance of having it into adulthood.

Muscles/Bones

Q. My baby's feet turn in. Will he need to wear special shoes or a brace?

No.

The official term for this is called **INTOEING**. This is very common and usually corrects itself as your child becomes a good walker.

Old Wives Tale
Pigeon toed children need to wear corrective shoes.
The truth: It was trendy 30 to 40 years ago to have kids wear corrective shoes or braces (for example Forrest Gump) if they turned their feet in while walking. Since then, doctors discovered feet get

better whether a child wears this apparatus or not—so why put a child through the trauma of special shoes or braces.

Q. My one year old is bow-legged. Will he always walk like this?

No.

Kids have some trouble finding their center of gravity. When they first start walking, they bend their knees to support their body weight. As they get older, they often go the opposite direction and look knock-kneed. It's nothing to worry about unless one leg is misshapen or both legs look severely deformed.

Q. My baby seems to have flat feet. My husband has flat feet, too. Do we need to see a podiatrist?

Your child can thank your husband for his feet. And no, you don't need to see a podiatrist yet.

The term "flat feet" refers to a lack of a natural arch in the bones of the feet. Some flat feet are flexible (the arch is seen when standing on tip-toe) and some are rigid (always flat). The feet that are always flat can cause some discomfort when kids become teenagers and adults. But placing a shoe insert (**ORTHOTIC**) into a toddler's shoes is not going to change the results down the line. The American Academy of Pediatrics feels orthotics are not necessary for kids with flat feet.

Endocrine

Q. Diabetes runs in my family. How can I get my baby tested for it?

Let's discuss diabetes first.

Diabetes mellitus is a chronic disease due to impaired sugar metabolism. There are two types (Type 1 and Type 2). They are divided by the cause of the disorder and the treatment. Although both can be inherited diseases, Type 2 tends to "run in families" more often.

Here is a brief explanation of the malfunction:

Since a person with diabetes doesn't breakdown sugar properly, the sugar ends up in vast quantities in the bloodstream. The body tries to eliminate the sugar by filtering it through the kidneys and into the urine. The sugar pulls excessive amounts of water with it into the urine. The result?

◆ Elevated blood sugar level.
◆ Excessive urination (with sugar found in the urine).
◆ Excessive thirst to keep up with fluid loss in the urine.
◆ Weight loss (from poor metabolism and fluid losses).

Type 1 Diabetes is also known as *Juvenile Diabetes*, or *Insulin Dependent Diabetes*. This is an autoimmune disease—that means the cells in the pancreas that make insulin get killed off by a person's own body. Insulin is the chemical in our body that metabolizes sugars.

There are some genes that have been identified in people with Type 1 diabetes and genetic defects can be passed on to offspring. Treatment is life-long with insulin injections and dietary modifications. Onset of Type 1 Diabetes is usually around school age (six to seven years old). It is extraordinarily rare to be diagnosed with diabetes while a child is still in diapers.

Type 2 Diabetes is also known as *Adult Onset Diabetes*. This type of diabetes is caused by the body's impaired response to insulin—this impairment is related to obesity.

As you can tell by the name, this USED to be an adult disease. Unfortunately, there is a virtual "epidemic" today of Type 2 Diabetes in pre-teens and teens. Children at risk are obese (defined as a Body Mass Index greater than 85%—see Chapter 5, "Nutrition and Growth" for details on the BMI) as well as other family members with Type 2 diabetes. Treatment includes dietary modifications and medications taken by mouth. FYI: There is a higher risk of developing this disorder among African-Americans, Hispanics, and Native Americans.[8]

BOTTOM LINE
Diabetes is not a disorder of infancy. But, if you have a family history of diabetes it's a good idea to watch your child's growth. Eating a healthy diet and avoiding obesity is even more important in your family.

As your child gets older, a screening test for diabetes can be done by obtaining a urine and blood sample.

For more information, check out this web site: diabetes.org.

Allergies

Q. My husband and I both have seasonal allergies. What are the chances that our baby will have allergies?

50%.

For each parent who has allergies, a child has a 25% risk of developing them himself. This refers to seasonal allergies, asthma and eczema. Some doctors might also put food allergies on this list, too. The earliest manifestations of an allergic child are eczema and food allergies. Asthma is usually diagnosed after a year of age. Seasonal allergies come even later.

Reality Check
The hereditary patterns of allergies do *not* apply to *drug* allergies. Just because you have an allergy to Penicillin doesn't mean your child will have one too.

Q. My baby seems to have a runny nose all of the time. Does he have seasonal allergies?

No.

Allergies ("hay fever") that cause a runny nose can be divided into perennial (all year long) or seasonal categories.

◆ **Perennial allergies.** These are year round allergies caused by something a child is exposed to on a daily basis. This is something inside your house, not outside your house. The most common causes are dust mites or cat dander. Molds are found both inside and outside the house year round.

◆ **Seasonal allergies.** These are allergies caused by something that's in the air outside of your house. These pollens include weeds, trees, and grasses that come in seasonal patterns. Most children under one year of age do not get *seasonal* allergies. Allergies, by definition, are a body's hyper-response to an allergen they have seen before. In the first year of life, a child has never seen these pollens before so there is no response.

BOTTOM LINE

Newborns do not have seasonal allergies when they are congested for the first six weeks of life. Nor does a nine month old have a ragweed allergy.

Most of the time, a chronic runny nose is caused by one viral upper respiratory infection after another. Although there are conflicting viewpoints, some doctors feel that perennial allergies or food allergies may cause a chronic runny nose year round in kids under age two.

Helpful hint

For perennial allergies (for example, dust mites), allergists often recommend plastic bedding covers, air filters, etc. These products are available through medical supply companies. Check out the following resources for a product catalog: National Allergy Supply, Inc. (800-522-1448, web: natlallergy.com) or Allergy Asthma Technology Ltd. (800-621-5545, web: allergyasthmatech.com).

What's that smell?

Have you ever gone to a wine tasting and tried to describe the 'nose' of a wine? When babies smell unusual, parents go to great lengths to come up with adjectives to explain the odor to their doctor.

We hesitate to explain this category of disorders in a chapter entitled "Common" diseases. But, there are some very rare metabolic disorders that are associated with unusual body odors. It is important that you are aware of them, and seek medical care if you notice any of the following smells:

FELINES ARE OUR FRIENDS

Although most people have heard that having a cat causes allergies, recent research shows that early exposure (first year of life) to cats and dogs may actually *prevent* allergies. Kids who grow up on farms have significantly less problems with allergies, presumably due to their constant exposure to animals and the germs they carry.[9]

◆ **Body odor**s: Barn-like, mousy, musty, horsey, wolf-like, sweaty socks, cheesy

◆ **Breath odors:** fruity/sweet, fishy, ammonia-like, clover, musty fish, raw liver, foul

◆ **Urine (pee) odors:** mousy, musty, horsey, wolf-like, barn-like, maple syrup, caramel, boiled Chinese Herbal medicine, yeast, celery, malt, brewery, sweaty feet/socks, ripe cheese, tomcat urine, dead fish, cabbage

◆ **Stool (poop) odors:** foul, vile

Note that other problems may cause you to turn your nose: poisonings and infections.

BOTTOM LINE: Bad odors are worth checking out.[10]

Now that you've been briefed on the most common diseases that affect children, let's talk First Aid. The next chapter covers the 12 most common calls that doctors get about babies—and what you can do to treat the problems.

Baby 411

First Aid:
The Top 12 Problems & Solutions

Chapter 15

First Aid: The Top 12 Problems & Solutions

"It's no longer a question of staying healthy. It's a question of finding a sickness you like."
~ Jackie Mason

What's in this Chapter

Did you see the *Friends* episode where Rachel's pediatrician fires her for calling too much? Although doctors entertain this thought occasionally, we never act on it (well, almost never). Phone calls are a part of the job. Most phone calls come from new parents. You are not alone.

The purpose of this chapter is to help you troubleshoot the most common problems you will encounter on the front line of your baby's medical care. It should help you determine when to call the doctor. It also prepares you for what the doctor will ask when you call.

This chapter does not replace the need to check in with your doctor. Pick up the phone if you are worried. But, being educated helps you worry less and trust your instincts more.

Helpful Hints
On Call Etiquette

How can you make the most of a call to your baby's doctor? As a doctor who has spent one third of her life on call, here are some important points to consider:

1 **The on-call doctor is not in the office.** Doctors leave the office at the end of the workday and carry a beeper to receive after hours calls. Doctors also go to sleep. (It's often disrupted sleep—but we try). If you call about your child's diaper rash at 2am, the doctor won't be as perky as when you call during office hours.

2 **TELL THE ON-CALL DOCTOR ABOUT PAST MEDICAL PROBLEMS.** Most pediatric and family doctor practices have SEVERAL doctors on staff. After hours, there is usually one doctor (who picks the short straw) that is on-call. This may or may NOT be your regular doctor. As a result, the on-call doctor may not know your child and does not have your child's medical chart. Explain any previous medical problems, surgeries, or hospitalizations. It might have a bearing on the particular problem at hand.

3 **TELL THE ON-CALL DOCTOR ABOUT ALLERGIES TO MEDICATIONS.** If your child has an allergic reaction to a medication, put it in YOUR family medical records. Don't rely on an on-call doctor or your pharmacy to know this information.

"The pink medicine" or "some antibiotic" is not adequate. Most doctors inquire about drug allergies before any medicine is prescribed—but we appreciate it if you tell us.

4 **HAVE A PHARMACY PHONE NUMBER READY.** True confession: I call patients back on my cell phone when I am driving. I don't have the yellow pages sitting in my glove compartment. And, frequently, there is more than one Walgreen's on a major street in town. Please have a phone number of a pharmacy near you that is open when you are calling. That way, I can call in your prescription after I talk with you.

5 **DON'T CALL FOR REFILLS, REFERRALS, OR APPOINTMENTS AFTER HOURS.** Universal doctor rule—we don't do these things without patient charts or schedules available. Medical emergencies are the only exception to this rule.

6 **DON'T LEAVE YOUR HOUSE OR GET ON THE PHONE AFTER PAGING US.** Believe it or not, this happens. If it's truly an emergency, keep your phone line clear. During cold and flu season, it may take a while for the doctor to return your call (the on-call doctor may get several calls per hour). But, we appreciate it if we can get through to you when we call you back.

7 **DON'T USE CALLER ID TO CALL THE ON-CALL DOCTOR BACK WITH ANOTHER QUESTION.** Okay, for the doctor, this is just creepy. If you call back through the appropriate answering service or voicemail system, you will always get your call returned. There is a protocol for a reason, folks—there is often a queue of patients who may need callbacks. If you use caller ID to find the doctor's home or cell phone number, don't use it.

8 **DON'T EXPECT OR DEMAND THAT ANTIBIOTICS BE PRESCRIBED OVER THE PHONE.** There is a good reason why antibiotics aren't available over the counter. A child needs to be seen to make a diagnosis of a bacterial infection. Remember the drug-resistant bacteria problem. (This is mentioned in Chapter 13, "Infections"). Doctors usually prescribe "supportive relief" (such as acetaminophen (Tylenol)) until your child can be evaluated.

9 **IF YOU HAVE A QUESTION ABOUT A MEDICATION, HAVE THE BOTTLE IN HAND WHEN YOU CALL.** Just common sense here. We will probably ask you to read the information on the bottle to us.

Q. What should I have in our first aid kit at home?

Here is your grocery list:
◆ Band-Aids (lots of them—they become badges of courage)
◆ sterile, nonstick dressing and tape
◆ "butterfly" bandages or thin adhesive strips
◆ Ace wrap
◆ a roll of gauze dressing
◆ rectal thermometer
◆ petroleum jelly
◆ Syrup of Ipecac
◆ acetaminophen (Tylenol)
◆ ibuprofen (Motrin, Advil)
◆ antibiotic ointment
◆ diphenhydramine liquid (Benadryl)
◆ saline nose drops (home made or store bought)
◆ Afrin nose spray
◆ 1% Hydrocortisone cream
◆ A list of emergency phone numbers, including the National Poison Control Center (800-222-1222) or your local poison control number.
◆ baking soda
◆ tweezers
◆ measuring spoon, cup or dropper; you'll want one with cc/ml measurements for those tiny infant doses. (See Chapter 5, "Nutrition & Growth" for a list of common measurements)

Q. Should I take a CPR course?

Yes!

Learn how to handle emergencies before they happen. Even if you can't remember exactly what to do, you will be more prepared to take action if something bad happens.

It's also helpful to learn how to take your child's vital signs. This information is very useful for when you call your doctor for advice.

Q. How do I take my child's vital signs?

Vital signs include the heart rate (pulse), respiratory rate (breaths per minute), temperature, and blood pressure. The only thing you cannot do at home is the blood pressure.

1. **Temperature:** Know how to take a rectal temperature. (See fever section later in this chapter for details.)

2. **Pulse:** Feel your baby's pulse in the inner part of the elbow or in the groin. Count the number of pulsations for 15 seconds and multiply by four. This gives you the beats per minute. Below is a list of average heart rates for your baby's age:

first aid

Average heart rates for babies, birth to three years of age:
Birth to one week: 95-160
One week to six months: 110-180
Six to 12 months: 110-170
One to three years: 90-150
(Compare these to an adult's heart rate of 60-100 beats per minute.)

3. **Respiratory Rate:** Watch your baby's chest as it moves in and out. Count one breath for each time he breathes in for 30 seconds and multiply by two. This gives you the number of breaths per minute. Babies have very erratic breathing, so you won't get an accurate count if you only look for ten or 15 seconds. Below are the details.

Average respiratory rates by age:
Newborns: 25-50
One week to one year: 24-38
One to three years: 22-30
(Compare to an adult's respiratory rates of 12-16 breaths per minute.)[1]

Helpful Hint

When a child runs a fever, all the other vital signs are elevated, too. Parents worry about the heart racing when children run a fever. That is to be expected and normal.

How Can Docs Make a Diagnosis Over the Phone Without Examining a Child?

Your doctor will rely on you to provide the signs and symptoms (the clues).

Doctors are very systematic in the way they make a diagnosis. A professor once told me that 90% of the time, a diagnosis can be made purely on the history of the problem. Only 10% of the time will the physical examination of the patient be necessary to make the diagnosis. It's true. I usually know what I will find when I examine the patient just by listening to the story. But, this requires some detective work. I always ask the same questions for each complaint to get a history of signs and symptoms (that is, location/type of pain, length of fever, appetite or lack of, sleep disruption, runny nose, cough, vomiting, etc.) When you call, expect to be interrogated.

Nervous parents often focus on one particular aspect of a disease process while doctors are trying to figure out the big picture. (See fever section later in this chapter). Doctors need to know about various symptoms to put the puzzle together. Let the doctor direct the conversation and point you in the right direction!

The Most Frequent Phone Calls

First, here's some doctor lingo: ever heard the guys on the old M*A*S*H television series say a patient was "in triage?" Triage just means to sort out by severity of the condition. The point: phone calls are triaged by the doctor into the following categories:

- ◆ **Priority 1:** Needs immediate evaluation and treatment—NOW.
- ◆ **Priority 2:** Needs appointment the next day.
- ◆ **Priority 3:** Watch and wait. Needs appointment if there is no improvement or worsening of symptoms.
- ◆ **Red flags:** Denote symptoms that are medical emergencies.

We've adopted this system in this chapter to give you a general idea of how problems are managed. But every problem is unique. If you have concerns, call your doctor.

Abdominal Pain

Q. My baby has a stomachache. When do I need to worry?

It's hard to tell when an infant has a stomachache, unless he has vomiting or has diarrhea. Some reliable signs include irritability during/after feedings, pulling up of the legs, or a tense, full belly. There are also medical problems that have nothing to do with the stomach that cause abdominal pain (such as bladder infections).

Abdominal pain is divided into acute (a new event as of yesterday or today) or chronic pain (the problem has been going on for over a week). Acute issues *only* are discussed below.

first aid

Priority 1: Needs immediate evaluation and treatment—NOW:

The most serious problems are called surgical emergencies or an "acute abdomen." A piece of bowel may be kinked, blocked, or infected. Babies with these problems look sick and are often inconsolable. Concerning symptoms include: swollen and/or tender belly, lack of interest in eating, persistent vomiting, unusual looking diarrhea, and difficulty settling down. These problems need to be addressed quickly. See the Red Flags on the next page. Diagnoses include: **INTESTINAL OBSTRUCTION, INTUSSUSCEPTION, INCARCERATED HERNIA, APPENDICITIS, PYLORIC STENOSIS**

Priority 2: Needs appointment the next day.

Most problems fall into the non-urgent category. These symptoms are less severe and babies are consolable. Symptoms include: gas, trouble settling after a feeding, crying/straining while attempting to poop, and one or two episodes of vomiting. Observation and medical evaluation is in order if things are not improving. NOTE: In babies under a year of age, it's better to be cautious and contact your doctor if you are worried.

Diagnoses include: **GAS, CONSTIPATION,EARLY VIRAL GASTROENTERITIS**

What the doctor will ask you about ABDOMINAL PAIN:
1. Does your baby have a fever?
2. Is your baby vomiting? What does the vomit look like?
3. Does your baby have diarrhea? Is it watery, bloody, mucousy, look like grape jelly?
4. Does your baby's tummy look like he is pregnant? Does it hurt to touch?
5. How long has the pain/vomiting/diarrhea been going on?
6. Does your baby have at least three wet diapers (urine) a day?
7. Is your son's scrotum swollen?

RED FLAGS
Call your doctor immediately if you see the following symptoms with abdominal pain:

◆ Fever and pain without diarrhea.
◆ Projectile vomiting or bright green/yellow vomit.
◆ Diarrhea that is bloody/mucousy/grape-jelly like.
◆ Tense, distended belly.
◆ Pain more than two hours in duration.
◆ Prolonged vomiting (see vomiting section later in this chapter).
◆ Prolonged diarrhea (see diarrhea section later in this chapter).
◆ Less than three wet diapers a day.
◆ Swollen scrotum.
◆ Crying with urination.

Feedback from the Real World
My four-year-old daughter slept for 12 hours once and awakened with the tensest belly I had ever seen. She was very uncomfortable and was having difficulty walking. She screamed when I tried to touch her belly. She had no interest in eating. Being quite convinced that she had an acute abdomen, I called one of my pediatric surgeon friends to evaluate her in the ER. As we drove to the hospital, she proclaimed that she needed to pee NOW. I pulled off the highway onto the shoulder. She urinated in my portable car trashcan. She had had a full bladder. She felt much better and asked if we could go out to lunch after visiting the doctor. We sheepishly walked into the ER together. She skipped to the exam room. I apologized for calling my friend to look at my perfectly normal child. His comment was, "Well, she does have a *cute* abdomen!"
Lessons learned here:
1. Sometimes benign processes (like a full bladder, constipation, etc.) can look like an acute abdomen. Doctors prefer to check out suspicious patients rather than wait.
2. It's hard to be objective when dealing with your own child.

Allergic Reaction

Q. I think my child is having an allergic reaction. Do I need to go to the ER?

Clarify the reaction. Do you see a rash or is he having difficulty breathing?

Priority 1: Needs immediate evaluation and treatment—NOW:

RED FLAGS
Anaphylactic Reaction
Call 911 for a child who is drooling, anxious, having obvious labored breathing (stridor), lip swelling, sweating. Another serious allergic reaction is called Stevens Johnson Syndrome. This is an extensive rash accompanied by mouth ulcers. This requires immediate medical attention.

If your child is having an anaphylactic reaction, do not attempt to drive to the hospital. Unless you can see the hospital from your front door, call 911 and get immediate help. Most ambulances are equipped with medicine to handle these reactions immediately.

Diagnoses: **ANAPHYLACTIC REACTION, STEVENS-JOHNSON SYNDROME**

Priority 2: Needs appointment the next day.

Most rashes are less of an emergency. (See details of other rashes in the rash section later in this chapter). Allergic reaction rashes can have various configurations. They are all itchy. Rashes (except Stevens Johnson Syndrome, see above) can be evaluated by a doctor when their office is open. These include:

♦ *Hives:* raised mosquito bites with flat red circles around them or large flat red areas with raised edges (for example, a drug allergy).
♦ *Erythema multiforme:* extensive, small, flat, red patches with raised edges (for example, a drug allergy).
♦ *Eczema:* red plaques with a scaly rough appearance overlying it (for example, a food allergy).
♦ *Contact dermatitis:* red pimples or blisters in a patch or streak (for example, poison ivy).

See our web site at Baby411.com for a visual library of common rashes.

Reality Check
Have your child in front of you when you speak to the doctor on the phone. You will be asked to describe what you see over the phone.

What the doctor will ask you about ALLERGIC REACTIONS:
1. Is your baby having any trouble breathing?
2. What does the rash look like? Where is it on the body?
3. When did you first see the rash?
4. Is the rash itchy?
5. Is your baby currently taking any medication?
6. Has your baby been exposed to any new foods, laundry detergents, clothing, or soaps?

Helpful Hints

◆ Unless your child is having an anaphylactic reaction (see above), give diphenhydramine (Benadryl) and schedule an appointment.

◆ Stop any other medication until a doctor sees your child.

◆ Don't give diphenhydramine (Benadryl) in the morning before your appointment—otherwise the rash will be gone.

◆ Try to think of any new medication or food your child may have had recently.

Reality Check

FYI: An allergic reaction is caused by a release of a chemical called histamine. Diphenhydramine (Benadryl), an anti-histamine, effectively clears the results of histamine (the rash) until the medicine wears off (about six hours). Histamine levels stay elevated for several DAYS. So, don't be surprised to see the rash "come back" after the medicine wears off. You will need to use the antihistamine medicine for a few days.

Causes of allergic reactions: Food allergy, medication allergy, bug bites, poison ivy (rhus dermatitis).

Bleeding And Bruising

Q. My child bruises easily. Should I be worried?

No, not usually.

Bruising in high trauma areas is not worrisome (shins, knees, elbows, forehead). We worry much more about bruising on the torso—most falls do not cause bruising to this area.

Easy bruisability can be a sign of low platelet count (platelets help your blood clot). Bruising is much more worrisome when it is seen with **PETECHI-AE**. (pe-teek-ee-ay). See box on the next page. Bruising accompanied by excessive bleeding can indicate a blood clotting disorder.

See our web site at Baby411.com (click on Bonus Material) for a picture.

Common Diagnoses include: Trauma/injury, temporary bone marrow suppression from a viral infection.

Uncommon Diagnoses include: Hemophilia, Von Willebrand's disease Leukemia, Idiopathic Thrombocytopenic Purpura, Henoch-Schonlein Purpura, Meningitis.

Priority 1: Needs immediate evaluation and treatment—NOW:

1. A fever with petechiae rash
2. Petechiae AND bruising, with or without a fever
3. Bruising and lethargy
4. Excessive bruising (beyond the knees/elbows)
5. Uncontrollable bleeding

Priority 2: Needs appointment the next day.

1. Bruising with no other symptoms
2. Recurrent nosebleeds

NEW PARENT 411: ALL YOU EVER WANTED TO KNOW ABOUT PETECHIAE BUT WERE AFRAID TO ASK

Petechiae are flat, purplish, pinpoint dots that almost look like freckles. When you push down on them, they remain colored (that is, they do not blanch). Petechiae are caused by broken blood vessels. They arise for the following reasons:

1. Pressure: Straining while pooping, giving birth, coughing, or vomiting forcefully.
2. Infection: Strep, meningitis, Rocky Mountain Spotted Fever.
3. Low platelet count: Leukemia, Idiopathic Thrombocytopenic Purpura, temporary bone marrow suppression from a viral infection.

If there is a good reason to have petechiae (such as repeated coughing), and they are located above the level of the chest only, you can relax a bit, but still call your doctor.

If there is *not* a good reason, your baby needs to be seen quickly to rule out the serious medical problems on this list.

What the doctor will ask you about BRUISING OR BLEEDING:
1. Where are the bruises?
2. Are there any other rashes on his body?
3. Does he bleed excessively? Does anyone in the family have bleeding problems?
4. Has he been unusually tired or been running a fever with no explanation?

Q. My child is having a nosebleed. What do I do about it?

Lean your child's head *forward*, not backwards. Apply pressure to the base (soft part) of the nose for ten minutes. If this doesn't work, you can spray some medicated decongestant nose drops into the nostrils (Little Noses or Children's Afrin are two brand names). This causes the blood vessels to shrink and stop bleeding.

Most nosebleeds stop in about ten minutes. If it goes beyond that, call your doctor.

Q. My child just vomited blood. Where is it coming from and should I be worried?

If it looks like fresh red blood, it can't be coming too far from the mouth. Blood that comes from the stomach is partially digested and will look like coffee grounds. Be prepared to describe the vomit. Lack of an obvious explanation for the blood needs an evaluation.

What the doctor will ask you about VOMITING BLOOD:
1. How old is your baby?
2. Are you breastfeeding? Are your nipples cracked and raw?
3. Have you been suctioning your baby's nose with a bulb syringe?

first aid

4. Has your baby been vomiting forcefully?
5. What does the vomit look like? Are there streaks of blood? Coffee grounds? Mucus?

The most common cause of *Upper GI Bleeding* (official term for vomiting blood) in a newborn is Mom's cracked nipples. The blood in the spit up is really Mom's. There is a test to prove it, but one look at Mom's nipples is a dead give-away.

The next likely culprit is that dreaded bulb syringe we told you to throw away in Chapter 4. It causes an irritation in the lining of the nose, making it raw to the point of bleeding. Nasal secretions are swallowed and then spit up.

As your baby gets older, he will explore his body. His finger will find his nostrils and cause trauma. The number one cause of bloody vomit in an older child is a nosepicker's nosebleed.

Now, for more serious causes. Forceful vomiting can cause a small tear in the lining of the esophagus. A child with persistent blood in vomit needs to be examined.

Vomit that looks like coffee grounds also needs to be evaluated. In older babies, doctors worry about a toxic ingestion/poison that irritates the esophagus or stomach, ulcers, gastritis, or esophagitis . If the vomit looks like Folger's coffee, call your doctor.

Diagnoses of an upper GI bleed include: Mom's cracked nipples, esophagitis, toxic ingestion/poisoning, gastritis, ulcers

Priority 1: Needs immediate evaluation and treatment—NOW:

1. No obvious source for bleeding
2. Vomit that looks like Folger's coffee.
3. Persistent bleeding.

Q. My baby has blood in his poop. Should I worry?

No, but Lower GI bleeding *always needs to be evaluated by a doctor*. If you see blood in the diaper, save the diaper. It's helpful to bring a fresh specimen to the office visit. If your baby doesn't cooperate, doctors have other ways to get what they need (via a rectal exam).

You will describe every detail of that poop to the On-Call Doctor. If the blood looks red and fresh, the source is close to the anus. If the blood looks darker or the poop looks like meconium, it comes from further up the pipes (small or large intestine). The age of the child partially determines the cause of the problem.

◆ **Newborns:** Bad *diaper rash* is often the explanation. Blood is usually found on the diaper wipe more than in the poop with an obvious raw bottom. Babies under four months of age with streaks of blood often have a *milk protein allergy*. Even exclusively breast fed babies can encounter this because the cow's milk protein can enter the breast milk. It often takes six weeks for the blood to clear once babies eliminate the cow's milk from their diets. Even if this is what the working diagnosis is, bacterial stool cultures are in order to rule out infection.

Diagnoses include: diaper rash, milk protein allergy, food poisoning (Bacterial gastroenteritis).

◆ *Older babies:* Babies who have started solids, often get constipated. If your baby looks like he is giving birth when he pushes out a solid poop ball, he might bleed with it. An *anal tear or fissure* can be seen if you look for it. This is not serious. Put some Vaseline on the area and check out fiber facts in Chapter 8, "The Other End."

Now for more serious causes. Babies can get *food poisoning*—even those who aren't eating off the Chinese buffet line yet. Where do babies get it? Human carriers, pets, and food exposure. Babies in daycare are at higher risk of parasite infections. Your doctor can test for all of these bugs with cultures (see bacterial infections and parasites in Appendix D: Common Infections in Infants). Symptoms include diarrhea with streaks of blood and mucus.

Finally, poop that looks like grape jelly (currant jelly stool) is a medical emergency. The diagnosis is *intussusception*, where the bowel telescopes on itself and creates an obstruction. Symptoms include abdominal pain (pulling up of the legs), irritability, and grape jelly stool.

Diagnoses: Anal fissure/tear (caused by constipation), food allergy, food poisoning (bacterial gastroenteritis), parasite infection, antibiotic induced colitis (C difficile infection), intussusception

What the doctor will ask you about BLOOD IN POOP:

1. How old is your baby? Was your baby premature?
2. What did you see in the diaper? Streaks of blood mixed in poop? Solid poop with blood on the diaper wipe? Explosive bloody diarrhea? Mucus also? Grape jelly?
3. Is there a diaper rash?
4. What is your baby eating?
5. Has anyone in the house had diarrhea?
6. Does your baby look sick or well? Fever?
7. Is your baby's belly full and distended?
8. Is your baby interested in eating? Is he vomiting?
9. Has your baby been on antibiotics recently?

Priority 1: Needs immediate evaluation and treatment—NOW:

◆ Bloody diarrhea
◆ Grape jelly poop
◆ No obvious diaper rash or anal tear
◆ Former premature baby

Priority 2: Needs appointment the next day.

◆ Streak of blood with normal looking stool and well appearing child

Priority 3: Watch and wait. Needs appointment if there is no improvement or worsening of symptoms:

◆ Obvious constipation
◆ Obvious diaper rash

Feedback from the Real World
Dr. Brown's TRUE STORIES about food poisoning:

1. One mother was a short order cook who discovered she was

a carrier of Salmonella when her newborn had it. She truly was "Typhoid Mary" (named for a woman who was a cook and a carrier of typhoid fever—a cousin of Salmonella). Sometimes parents are carriers who have had a previous infection and don't know it.

2. Unusual pets can be carriers of Salmonella. One of my patient's uncles had a pet iguana that roamed freely on the family's kitchen counter.

3. Raw eggs and chicken are also known to have Salmonella. I had a patient who acquired Salmonella when Grandma was preparing chicken gizzards next to Mom preparing a bottle for the baby.

Feedback from the Real World

There was an outbreak of the deadly E. coli 0157 bacteria (hemolytic uremic syndrome) on the East Coast several years back. It was traced to an apple cider producer in New Hampshire. It had been a bad apple season, so the producer used apples that had already fallen off the trees to press for cider. Unfortunately, the cows that lived on the farm pooped on those apples and contaminated them with the E.coli. There are new regulations for cider production now. Moral of the story: Never drink unpasteurized apple cider.

A similar outbreak happened with Odwalla apple juice in 1996—a small batch of unpasteurized juice contained E.coli bacteria, sickening more than a dozen children. This juice was blended with other products as well. Be sure to look for these products—make sure ALL the ingredients in a blended juice product are pasteurized.

HOW TO AVOID FOOD POISONING

Many of these foods are off limits to infants under a year anyway, but it's good to know about. Remember to clean cutting boards, knives, and countertops when dealing with these products, too. Keep a spray bottle of bleach handy in the kitchen to clean these items.

◆ unpasteurized dairy products
◆ unpasteurized juices (fresh squeezed OJ, apple cider)
◆ alfalfa sprouts
◆ raw shellfish
◆ oysters
◆ undercooked and raw meat or seafood
◆ unwashed fruit and vegetables
◆ undercooked eggs (sunny side up, raw cookie dough, fresh Caesar salad dressing, homemade ice cream, homemade mayonnaise)

Natural food warning: while it doesn't seem likely that you and your baby would come across the above items, think for a moment about unpasteurized juices. These are common in health food stores and some vegetarian/vegan restaurants. It can be easy to pick up a bottle of such juice without thinking about it. The same goes for unpasteurized dairy products—gourmet cheeses at health food stores sometimes fall into this category. While adults might be able to eat these products without a problem, they are much more dangerous to infants and children. Check the labels: raw milk cheese, for example, should be clearly labeled as such.

Burns: Water, Sun, Hot Drinks, Appliances, BBQ

Q. My child got a burn from _____. What do I do? Does he need an appointment?

Don't get out the butter, and maybe.

First rule: If it blisters, it should be looked at.

Second rule: Apply cool water, not butter.

Third rule: Don't pop a blister.

Any type of burn damages the top layer of skin. This causes redness (first degree). Burns that go deeper than that create blisters (second degree) or damage to the full thickness of the skin. Your skin is your body's protection from foreign invaders such as infection. Without the skin, the body is defenseless. To help combat infection, it's always a good idea to use an antibiotic ointment (such as Neosporin) on a burn and cover it with a non-stick dressing.

For second-degree burns, a prescription product called Silvadene may be needed. Second degree burns (or worse) need to be seen by your doctor to assess the damage, look for infection, and clean away any dead skin (this debris inhibits healing and promotes infection). Any burns on the hands, genitals, and on large areas should also be seen.

Priority 1: Needs immediate evaluation and treatment—NOW:

◆ Extensive areas burned.

◆ Area looks infected (red, weeping pus, fever)

Priority 2: Needs appointment the next day.

◆ Second degree burns (blisters).

◆ Burns on the hands or genitals.

Priority 3: Watch and wait. Needs appointment if there is no improvement or worsening of symptoms:

◆ First degree burns.

Breathing Problems (Respiratory Distress)

Q. My baby is having trouble breathing. What do I do?

Knowing what true respiratory distress looks and sounds like is very important. Read the section below and then, how calls are triaged. The short answer is—if your child is having labored breathing, call your doctor immediately.

Understanding the Respiratory System

Think of the respiratory system as one big tube. The opening of the tube starts at the nose. The bottom end branches into tiny tubes in the lungs. Air goes in and out of this tube with each breath.

What is an UPPER respiratory infection?

The common cold or flu viruses live in the top of the tube (nose and sinuses).The body forms mucus or snot as a result of it. A person coughs because that mucus drips down the tube towards the lungs. Coughing protects our lungs. The cough brings the mucus up so it can be swallowed (into the stomach) instead of collecting in the lungs. Upper respiratory infections rarely cause labored breathing. They do cause noisy breathing, though, as air travels through the snot in the nasal passages.

Diagnoses include: Common cold, the Flu (influenza)

What is a LOWER respiratory infection?

Bronchiolitis (RSV), bronchitis, or pneumonia are infections (viral or bacterial) that live in the lungs or tubes in the lungs. Because there is swelling or mucus in the tiny tubes and lung tissue, it is hard to exchange air effectively (remember that oxygen/carbon dioxide thing you learned about in science class). A person with a LOWER respiratory infection may become *air hungry*. We'll discuss this more in detail later in this section.

Diagnoses include: RSV Bronchiolitis, bronchitis, pneumonia

Any others?

There are also infections that attack the middle of the tube (larynx and trachea) where the voicebox (vocal cords) is located. The tube swells in this area. Because children's tubes are smaller than adults, they are more compromised by these infections. The younger the child, the more problematic.

Diagnoses include: croup, whooping cough (pertussis)

Now that you understand the tube analogy, here is what you will encounter. **Rattling in the chest** or **hearing wheezing** are NOT usually signs of a lower respiratory infection.

Think about the tube. You know how your pipes are all attached in your home? When you flush your toilet upstairs, you can hear it in the kitchen. Here is the analogy: nose is to toilet as lung is to kitchen. The water is in the nose, not the lung—but it can be heard and felt down there. This is called **transmitted upper airway noise.** The wheezing noise is **air passing through snot—it whistles.**

A child who is really wheezing enough to be audible to the naked ear is in such severe distress that you will *see it* in his chest (**AIR HUNGRY**).

WHAT AN AIR HUNGRY CHILD LOOKS LIKE: A MUST READ

The diagnosis of an air hungry child can be made without a stethoscope. It's not what is heard—it's what is seen. A baby or child who is air hungry breathes rapidly and shallowly (**elevated respiratory rate**), sucks in his rib cage (**retractions**), and flares his nostrils (**flaring**). A child may also make a grunting noise at the end of each breath. These are the body's way of using every muscle to pull in more air with each breath.The number of breaths taken per minute (respiratory rate) is much higher than normal. (See guide to vital signs earlier in this chapter). If a child is air hungry, call your doctor immediately.

Helpful Hints

◆ Sometimes your doctor can tell what the problem is just by listening to the baby breathing on the phone. If the breathing noises are dramatic, have the baby handy when you call.

◆ When a person lies down, the snot from the nose drips down the back of the throat. Our body's job is to cough and keep it out of the lungs. The cough is likely coming from nasal secretions when the "cough is worse at night."

Red Flags

◆ Air hungry.
◆ Croup under age two. (See below).
◆ Repeated coughing spasms, followed by reddening of face, possibly a 'whoop', or vomiting.
◆ Episodes of not being able to catch one's breath.

What the doctor will ask you about RESPIRATORY DISTRESS:

1. How long has he been having trouble breathing?
2. Could he have swallowed something?
3. Does he have a fever?
4. Is he barking like a seal? Any high-pitched squeals?
5. Look at his chest. Is he sucking in his ribcage with each breath (retractions)? Is he panting or breathing fast? Are his nostrils flaring? Is he grunting at the end of each breath?
6. Has he wheezed before? Ever stayed in the hospital overnight for it?
7. Are there coughing spasms? Any gasping for breath? Vomiting or turning red with cough?

Priority 1: Needs immediate evaluation and treatment—NOW:

◆ Signs of air hunger.
◆ Any stridor noise (see croup box below).
◆ Trouble catching breath.
◆ Child who has asthma.
◆ Child who is a former premature infant.
◆ Choking (see choking emergencies on the next page).

Priority 2: Needs appointment the next day.

◆ Barking like a seal, but no squeal.

EVERYTHING YOU EVER WANTED TO KNOW ABOUT CROUP

A virus causes croup. It appears in epidemics every winter. A croup cough has a characteristic bark that sounds like a seal. Although impressive, this can be managed by quality time spent in your bathroom with a steamy shower running all night. When the airway tube is markedly swollen, the bark changes to a high-pitched squeal, called **STRIDOR**. Stridor requires an emergency breathing treatment and steroids to reduce the swelling or the airway. FYI: Croup is always worse at night.

Priority 3: Watch and wait. Needs appointment if there is no improvement or worsening of symptoms:

◆ Chest rattling.
◆ Intermittent wheezing noises WITHOUT labored breathing.

Red Flag

When your child stops breathing. Call 911 immediately if your baby has any episode of true apnea (lack of breathing over 15 seconds).

Reality Check

There is a difference between apnea (not breathing) and **PERI-ODIC BREATHING**. Newborns frequently pause for several seconds between breaths. It is your child's job in life to give you grey hairs. Adults breathe 12 times a minute at a nice regular rate. Newborns breathe 30-60 times per minute at an irregular rate. *Newborns can pause for up to ten seconds and be feeling just fine.* To monitor the respiratory rate of a newborn, count the breaths for a whole minute.

What the doctor will ask about APNEA:
1. Is your child breathing okay now or is he having labored breathing?
2. Does he have a fever?
3. Has he had a problem with acid reflux?
4. Was he born prematurely?
5. Any recent trauma or injuries?

Babies with apnea get admitted to the hospital to be evaluated. *Diagnoses include:*
1. Near Sudden Infant Death Syndrome (SIDS) event or acute life threatening event (ALTE).
2. Gastroesophageal reflux.
3. Infection (whooping cough, RSV bronchiolitis).
4. Metabolism problem.
5. Head trauma.

Choking Emergencies: 4 Tips

1 **DO NOTHING IF YOUR CHILD IS ALERT AND MAKING NOISES (CRYING, GAGGING, COUGHING).** He is effectively attempting to clear his airway.

2 **IF YOUR CHILD IS IN DISTRESS AND NOT MAKING ANY NOISE, ATTEMPT TO GET THE ITEM OUT OF HIS MOUTH.** Only put your finger in if you can see the item—do not blindly sweep his mouth with your finger; it can lodge the item in his throat.

3 **IF YOUR CHILD BECOMES UNCONSCIOUS,** put his belly on your forearm, face down (hold him like a football). Push forcefully between the shoulder blades with the lower part of your palm five times (called back blows). DO NOT PERFORM THE HEIMLICH MANEUVER ON INFANTS UNDER ONE YEAR OF AGE.

4 **IF THAT'S NOT WORKING, CALL 911.**

Feedback from the Real World
Another True Story from Dr. Brown

I was on-call and answering a page. While I was on the phone, my nine-month old son crawled over to our dog's food bowl and did a taste test. In my panic, the first thing I did was to put my finger in his mouth to pull the food out. I ended up pushing it down and he swallowed it. He never touched the dog's food again! And I never made the mistake again of ignoring my own advice.

Cough And Congestion

Q. My baby's nose is so congested that he can't eat or sleep. What do I do?

This is the second most popular phone call. (Fever is number one). Nasal congestion happens for many reasons:

◆ Newborns all have nasal congestion for the first four to six weeks of life. They ALL sneeze and snort and snore. They do not have allergies (and rarely have a cold).

◆ Babies with acid reflux can have congestion from the milk that heads upwards behind the nose.

◆ Mucus pouring out the nose suggests an upper respiratory infection.

Diagnoses include: Common cold, the flu (influenza), RSV bronchiolitis

Tricks of the trade: How To Make (And Use) Saline Nose Drops

The most safe and effective way to clear the mucus is to flush the nostrils with saline nose drops. Saline is just a salt-water solution. You can't overdose it. You can make your own concoction (1/2 tsp salt to eight oz water). Or, you can buy it for about a dollar at the grocery store. Shoot several drops in each nostril before feedings. *You don't need to suck it out with a bulb syringe.* The saline will either make your baby sneeze or loosen the mucus enough to swallow it.

There are other methods of reducing the amount of mucus, but doctors always suggest saline first. Over the counter cough and cold medicines are *not recommended* under six months of age.

What the doctor will ask you about NASAL CONGESTION
1. Has he ever breathed through his nose?
2. Does he have a fever?
3. Is anyone else in the house sick? Is he in childcare?
4. Is he fussy or having disrupted sleep?
5. Does he have goopy eyes and/or green snot?

Helpful Hint
If a baby under age two has an upper respiratory infection, the flu, or especially RSV, he is at risk of getting an ear infection.

Nasal discharge with fever, goopy eyes, and/or fussiness deserves a visit to the doctor to check for an ear infection.

Priority 1: Needs immediate evaluation and treatment—NOW:

◆ Has labored breathing or appears air hungry.
◆ Under four weeks of age and has a fever of 100.4 or greater (see fever section later in this chapter).
◆ Irritable and inconsolable.

Priority 2: Needs appointment the next day.

◆ Never breathes through the nose.
◆ Under four weeks of age, WITHOUT fever.
◆ Four weeks old to six months old, nasal congestion with or without fever.
◆ Fussy mood or disrupted sleep.
◆ Goopy eyes or red eyes.
◆ New appearance of green nasal discharge after clear discharge for at least one week.

Priority 3: Watch and wait. Needs appointment if there is no improvement or worsening of symptoms:

◆ Over six months of age with nasal congestion, runny nose, and cough for less than one week's duration (see fever section for other reasons to call).

Q. My child is keeping up the whole house with his cough! Make it go away.

Doctors are not miracle workers.

Nighttime coughs cause sleep deprivation for the child *and the parent.* Take a moment to review the respiratory system lecture. Coughing is a protective mechanism to keep the nasal discharge from collecting in the lungs. So, for an upper respiratory infection (cold), let the cough happen during the day. The cough is worse at night because your baby is lying down. Always try saline nose drops first. Stopping the drip may stop the cough.

If the cough is keeping the baby awake, your doctor may recommend an infant cough suppressant—check first. Letting your baby sleep in an upright position (such as in a car seat) is also helpful.

If the cough is keeping YOU awake, turn off the baby monitor!

What the doctor will ask you about COUGHING:
1. How long has he had the cough? (Over three weeks deserves an appointment).
2. Is it worse at night or in the daytime?
3. Is he having any breathing difficulties? (See that section).
4. Is he barking like a seal? Squealing?
5. Is he panting or breathing shallowly?
6. Any apnea (no breathing for 15 seconds or more)?
7. Any concern for having swallowed a foreign body?
8. Any new fever?

? ?

Priority 1: Needs immediate evaluation and treatment—NOW:

◆ Breathing appears labored—grunting, flaring, retractions, stridor, or elevated respiratory rate.
◆ Trouble catching breath with coughing episodes.
◆ Foreign object known to be swallowed.
◆ Known asthma, and not responding to medication.

Priority 2: Needs appointment the next day.

◆ Persistent cough.
◆ Cough sounds productive (wet or juicy).
◆ Vomiting or turning red with coughing episodes, but no apnea.
◆ Barking like a seal, but no squeal.
◆ New fever with a cough and NO labored breathing.

Priority 3: Watch and wait. Needs appointment if there is no improvement or worsening of symptoms:

◆ Cough under three weeks duration.
◆ Exposure to someone with a chronic cough.

Chronic Coughs

Not all coughs are caused by infection. Prolonged coughing (over three weeks) should be evaluated. Occasionally, we discover something interesting that has ended up in a branch of the lung airway. Mr. Dr. Brown (the Ear/Nose/Throat specialist) removes toy jacks, beads, peanuts, teeth, and popcorn kernels in the airways of small children on a regular basis.

The major causes of chronic cough include: foreign object in airway asthma, sinusitis, whooping cough, tuberculosis (rare).

Red Flags

◆ Cough with breathing difficulties.
◆ Chronic cough over three weeks.
◆ New fever with worsening cough.
◆ Possible foreign body (swallowed object).

Diarrhea

Q. My baby is having diarrhea. What do I do and when do I worry?

Most of the time, diarrhea is a sign of a *stomach virus* (**VIRAL GAS-TROENTERITIS**). Some people call it the stomach flu. It's not THE flu. (The flu that we can get vaccinated for is influenza—a respiratory virus.) At best, your baby vomits once and the diarrhea continues for three to five days. At worst, your child vomits for 12-18 hours and has diarrhea 25 times a day for ten days (see rotavirus infection in Chapter 13, "Infections"). Those "24 hour bugs" don't really exist.

Food poisoning (**BACTERIAL GASTROENTERITIS**) is a concern when there is mucus or streaks of blood in the diarrhea. (See abdominal pain section earlier for details). Bacteria will cause only 10% of intestinal infections. Of those 10%, the most common culprit is **SALMONELLA**. *Other diagnoses include:* Shigella infection (bacteria), Yersinia infection (bacteria), Campylobacter infection (bacteria), C. difficile (bacteria, after an antibiotic) Giardia (parasite), Cryptosporidium (parasite), food allergy.

FYI: Chronic diarrhea (over two weeks duration) is a different problem More on this next.

Diarrhea for more than two weeks

If the diarrhea has been going on this long, your baby needs to see his doctor. Most commonly, chronic diarrhea is the result of an acute stomach virus.

Stomach viruses tear up the intestine's normal "flora" of good bacteria that help digest food. Stomach viruses can also break up a digestive enzyme called lactase, which helps the body digest milk sugar (lactose). Occasionally, infants and children can get a temporary lactose intolerance for up to six weeks after a stomach virus. Diarrhea results from repeated dairy intake and inability to digest it.

Another culprit is high juice intake. This is more of a problem with toddlers who become juice-a-holics. The high sugar content pulls water into the poop, causing increased frequency and watery stools.

Causes of chronic diarrhea include: Lactose intolerance (Post-stomach virus), high juice intake, food intolerance, celiac disease, parasite infection, Inflammatory Bowel Disease.

What the doctor will ask you about DIARRHEA:

1. How old is your baby?
2. How long has the diarrhea been going on?
3. Has there been vomiting or fever?
4. What does the diarrhea look like? Watery, bloody, mucus or blood streaked?
5. Is your baby still urinating?
6. Has your baby eaten any new foods?

Priority 1: Needs immediate evaluation and treatment—NOW:

◆ Under three months of age.
◆ Blood or mucus in diarrhea.
◆ Grape jelly diarrhea.
◆ Not urinating at least three times in 24 hours.
◆ Unsure about frequency of urination.
◆ Lethargy.

Priority 2: Needs appointment the next day.

◆ Diarrhea more than one week.
◆ Age over three months and fever more than three days.

Priority 3: Watch and wait. Needs appointment if there is no improvement or worsening of symptoms:

◆ Watery diarrhea for less than one week, with frequent wet diapers, and over three months of age.

Q. I'm worried about my baby getting dehydrated. Should I be?

Yes.

Babies under a year old are at higher risk of getting dehydrated. *Contrary to popular belief, dehydration is caused more by diarrhea than vomiting.* The vomiting part of an illness usually stops within about 12 hours. There is only a limited amount of fluid lost from vomiting (once the stomach is empty, there's not much left to throw up). As long as the vomiting is short lived, dehydration is not a problem. Diarrhea is another story. Frequent, explosive, watery diarrhea for a week causes a tremendous amount of water loss. Your baby needs to keep up with these losses with fluid intake.

BOTTOM LINE: Although vomiting is scary, persistent diarrhea is more likely to cause dehydration.

Helpful Hint
How to tell if there is urine in the diaper:
Put a tissue in the front part of the diaper. The urine looks yellow on the tissue because it is concentrated.

HOW TO TELL IF YOUR BABY IS DEHYDRATED—A MUST READ

1 URINE OUTPUT: When our body needs fluid, less water is released as urine. If your baby pees (urinates) at least three times in 24 hours, he is doing okay. It's sometimes hard to tell if there is pee in the diaper, though, when there is explosive poop in it. (See Helpful hint above).

2 WEIGHT LOSS: If your baby has lost 10% of his body weight, he is severely dehydrated. This is an emergency.

3 SUNKEN FONTANELLE: Babies under a year still have a soft spot in their skull. That is their oil gauge equivalent. If the tank is low, the soft spot is sunken. That's the first place a doctor will touch when he examines your baby.

4 SKIN TURGOR: You know what your skin looks like when you have been in the bathtub too long? That prune like appearance is a clue to dehydration. Nice doughy skin has plenty of water in it.

5 DRY LIPS AND MOUTH: When you're dry, you stop making saliva.

6 CAPILLARY REFILL: Press down gently on your fingernail. You will see the pink color turn white. When you release the pressure, the pink color returns in less than two seconds. In severe dehydration, that refill will take more than two seconds because the blood supply is sluggish.

7 LETHARGY: This is a difficult one to assess. If your baby looks like a wet noodle, it's time to visit the doctor.

Q. What can I give my baby to eat and drink to prevent dehydration?

Start with liquids, then slowly add solids.

Presuming that vomiting has come first in this scenario, make sure that fluids stay down before going back to solid food (if baby is over four months old). *Liquids are much more important than solids.* It's the fluid that replaces the losses. Babies make up for lost time and will eat when they are feeling better.

Your doctor may recommend Pedialyte (see page 315) to treat dehydration—see the vomiting section later for details. Once your baby has kept Pedialyte down, return to regular formula or breast milk.

Here are some other suggestions:

1. *Try Isomil DF formula* for severe or prolonged diarrhea. (see formula section in liquid nutrition, Chapter 6) The DF stands for Diarrhea Formula. But it also stands for Dietary Fiber. The formula is lactose free and has a high fiber content that helps bulk up the poop.

2. *Try a high fat, high fiber diet* for babies over four months old. Resume solids when a baby is interested in food again. Depending on the age and what foods your baby has tried, look for high fiber foods (prunes, oatmeal, beans) and high fat foods (whole milk yogurt, avocados) to feed your baby.

3. *Try acidophilus/lactobacillus,* the bacteria that lives in yogurt. Stomach viruses kill off the "good germs" that live in the intestines and help digest food. Replenishing the gut with good germs improves digestion. If your baby is over six months, offer four oz. yogurt daily during the illness. Another option: acidophilus chewable tablets and powder packets are available over the counter. Use half of a packet or crush up half of a tablet daily and mix into food.

4. *Try a lactose (dairy) free diet* for diarrhea lasting over one or two weeks. If the diarrhea is prolonged, a secondary lactose intolerance may be the culprit (see chronic diarrhea section earlier).

BOTTOM LINE: Liquids are the priority in re-hydration. Your baby will eat solid food again when he is well.

Old Wives Tales

1. Avoid milk when your baby has diarrhea.

The truth: Your baby will have diarrhea no matter what he is eating or drinking. Give him what he is willing to drink. If the diarrhea has been going on for *over a week*, however, dairy restriction may be in order to avoid a lactose intolerance (see earlier section on chronic diarrhea).

2. Use the BRAT diet for a baby with diarrhea (Bananas, Rice, Applesauce, Toast)

The Truth: Fat and fiber are more effective in bulking up the poop than these foods. The old school of thought was called the BRAT diet. It was thought that a bland, carbohydrate diet was best for infants with diarrhea. The latest research (1999) suggests that fat and fiber are actually more effective in reducing water loss in diarrhea.

Q. Can I give my baby any anti-diarrhea medications?

No.

Some doctors feel uncomfortable using Pepto-Bismol and similar medications for babies under a year of age. Check with your doctor for her opinion.

These medicines slow down the intestines, which can actually prolong the length of some illnesses.

The American Academy of Pediatrics issued a policy statement in 1996 that advises against using anti-diarrhea medications in infants.[2] However, more recent studies suggest that these products are probably safe and somewhat beneficial for babies over four months of age.[3]

Vomiting

There is spit up, and then there is vomit. All babies spit up (see acid reflux in Chapter 8, "The Other End"). Vomiting is the forceful elimination of food and fluid that is in the stomach.

There is only a fixed amount of stomach contents. So, if a child is vomiting repeatedly, eventually he will have "dry heaves" (vomiting with nothing coming out). If a child is vomiting *bile* (fluorescent green/yellow fluid), that is coming from the small intestine and may be a concern for an intestinal blockage.

In the strictest sense, repeated vomiting causes dehydration. If your child is vomiting more than 18 hours straight, he is unable to maintain adequate fluid intake. *This rarely happens.* With most garden-variety stomach viruses, the vomiting stops within 12 hours and kids are drinking again. The greater risk of dehydration is the water lost in the diarrhea that accompanies the vomiting. Dehydration usually occurs later in the course of the illness.

All vomiting is not due to stomach upset. Babies and young children have active gag reflexes. *Forceful coughing* can result in vomiting (see **POST-TUSSIVE EMESIS**). So, a baby with the common cold might vomit after coughing. Headaches can also be accompanied by vomiting. This category includes ear infections, head injury, brain tumors, meningitis. That's why unexplained vomiting needs to be checked out.

BOTTOM LINE: Persistent vomiting with no obvious cause should be evaluated.

Causes of vomiting include:

Gastroesophageal reflux | Early viral gastroenteritis
Pyloric stenosis | Intestinal obstruction (rare)
After coughing (post-tussive emesis) | Ear infection
Head injury | Brain tumor (rare)
Meningitis | Metabolic disorders (rare)
Bladder/ kidney infections | Food poisoning (bacterial gastroenteritis)

What the doctor will ask you about VOMITING
1. How old is your baby?
2. How long has he been vomiting?
3. Is it projectile (Exorcist-like) or just coming up effortlessly?
4. What does the vomit look like? Any fluorescent green or yellow color? Any blood or coffee grounds?
5. Does he have a fever?
6. Does he have diarrhea?
7. Is he around other children/anyone sick in the house?
8. Does he look like his stomach hurts?
9. Is he still urinating?
10. Any recent head injuries?

Priority 1: Needs immediate evaluation and treatment—NOW:
◆ Vomiting with a head injury.
◆ Vomiting bile (bright green or yellow).
◆ Vomiting over 12 hours straight.
◆ Projectile vomiting more than three times in a row.
◆ Vomiting only in the mornings.
◆ Vomiting blood or coffee grounds.
◆ Appears dehydrated (see section earlier on this topic).

Priority 2: Needs appointment the next day.
◆ Large volume spit ups frequently.
◆ Recurrent vomiting.

Priority 3: Watch and wait. Needs appointment if there is no improvement or worsening of symptoms:
◆ Isolated episode of vomiting in well appearing child.

WHAT TO DO WHEN YOUR BABY VOMITS

1. While your baby is actively vomiting, DO NOT GIVE HIM ANY FOOD OR DRINK. Parents are often so afraid that their baby will get dehydrated, they offer fluids immediately. And it comes right back at them. Don't give fluids on an unsettled stomach.

2. If it has been at least one hour since your child has vomited, offer a few sips of Pedialyte (see below). The goal is one teaspoon every five minutes for an hour. *Do not offer a whole bottle to your child.* He is thirsty and will drink the whole thing—only to vomit again because his stomach isn't ready for that much. If this plan fails (that is, your baby vomits again), call your doctor.

3. If the Pedialyte stays down, you can add to the volume one to two ounces every time your baby wants to drink. If this plan fails, call your doctor.

4. If your child has four hours vomit free, return to breast-feeding or formula.

5. After eight hours of success, babies who are already eating solid foods can return to eating again.

Q. What is Pedialyte?

Pedialyte is kind of a Gatorade equivalent for babies. It is made especially for babies ages birth to one year. Parents often ask if it's okay to use for babies that young—this is exactly who it is made for! It has a high salt and moderate sugar content and tastes like salt water. Usually babies under a year don't mind the flavor. (Kids over a year are pretty smart and will refuse it.) If you want to make your own Pedialyte, check out Appendix B for a recipe you can make at home.

Do NOT give plain water to babies when they have vomiting or diarrhea. Their body salts are already depleted and giving plain water messes up the delicate electrolyte balance even more.

For older kids, try Pedialyte popsicles, Sprite, or clear chicken broth.

Reality Check

Regular Pedialyte is a clear fluid. But, it also comes in "flavored" varieties which contain food coloring. Stick with the clear version. Why would you give a child who is vomiting a purple drink?

Eye Problems

Q. My newborn has goop draining from his eyes. Does he have pink eye?

No. It's a blocked tear duct.

Babies are born with narrow canals that let the tears flow out of them. Until the canals widen, the tears can get clogged. This can happen intermittently through the first year of life. (See glossary for **NASOLACRIMAL DUCT OBSTRUCTION**). Just wipe away the goop with warm water.

Call your doctor if the white of the eye is red, or if the eyelids are swollen.

Q. My nine month old has goop draining from his eyes and has a cold. Does he have pink eye?

Probably.

When the eye goop is accompanied by other symptoms (runny nose, cough, fever), it's more likely to be an infection called conjunctivitis or pink eye.

Conjunctivitis can be caused by either a virus or bacteria. Bacterial infections cause goopy eye discharge (eye boogers) and viral infections cause watery eye discharge. Both are extremely contagious. Bacterial infections can be treated with antibiotic eye drops or oral antibiotics. Viruses cannot be treated and can last up to a week.

Children under age two years with bacterial conjunctivitis (goop) should see a doctor. About 30% have an ear infection or sinus infection to go along with it. The bug is usually Haemophilus influenza non-typable (a cousin of the HIB we vaccinate against). This is a smart bug often resistant to first line antibiotics.

HOW TO AVOID HAVING THE WHOLE FAMILY GET PINK EYE

Pink eye is spread by the sick person touching the infected eye and leaving the germs for someone else to touch (doorknobs, hand towels, toys). The best approach if you have pink eye in your house is to wash hands frequently and make a concerted effort not to touch your face.

BOTTOM LINE: A child under age two with goopy eyes needs to be seen by a doctor. There is an association of pink eye with ear infections and sinus infections.

Q. My baby's eye is red. Does he have allergies?

Unlikely.

As a general rule, babies under one year do not have seasonal allergies. A red eye is either caused by *trauma, irritation,* or *infection.* If just one eye is red, consider trauma (corneal abrasion—see below, foreign body) or irritation (soap, sun block). If it is bothersome to your baby, try flushing the eye with some lukewarm water.

If your baby looks uncomfortable, he needs to be evaluated.

Causes of red eyes: trauma, irritation, infection—viral or bacterial.

Q. My baby's eye is swollen shut. Should I worry?

Yes— if she has a fever.

Usually the cause of impressive swelling is a local allergic reaction. If a bug bite or poison ivy occurs on an eyelid, the reaction can be impressive. Proof of a bite or rash is helpful.

The concern is a serious infection called **ORBITAL CELLULITIS**. This is a sinus infection that extends into the area where the eye rests in the skull (orbit). It happens in stages, and the prognosis is obviously better if caught early. The first sign is redness and swelling of the eyelid. It then progresses to a bulging eye, with limited motion of the eye itself.

If you see this, call your doctor NOW. This is a medical emergency. See our web site at Baby411.com for a visual library picture.

Q. My baby's eye is tearing constantly today. What is wrong?

Probably a corneal abrasion.

Babies can scratch their eyes accidentally. This is a superficial scratch that takes a day or two to heal. Foreign bodies (dust, etc.) can also cause similar symptoms. Doctors check for abrasions using a purple light and fluorescein dye. If a scratch is found, antibiotic eye drops are prescribed. If a foreign body is found, it can be flushed out.

What the doctor will ask you about RED EYES
1. How old is your baby?
2. Is there eye discharge? Is it watery or goopy?
3. Is there fever, runny nose, or fussiness?
4. If the eyelid is swollen, is there any bug bite or rash visible? Any fever?

Priority 1: Needs immediate evaluation and treatment—NOW:

◆ Eyelid swollen shut with fever.
◆ Question of foreign body in the eye.
◆ Very uncomfortable child with a red eye.

Priority 2: Needs appointment the next day.

◆ Goopy eyes with a cold, with or without fever

Priority 3: Watch and wait. Needs appointment if there is no improvement or worsening of symptoms:

◆ Newborn with eye that waters frequently, without redness.

Fever: Special Section

Fever is the number one reason pediatricians get called at night. At some point in your baby's life, he will have his first fever. And, like every new parent that has come before you, you will have some anxiety. Read this section in its entirety! (Note: all temperatures are in degrees Fahrenheit).

Q. What is the definition of a fever?

Fever is an elevation of the body's regular temperature.

Contrary to what you learned in junior high science class, our body temperature is not 98.6 for 24 hours a day. It varies on a daily rhythm based on hormone levels. Our body is the coolest at 7am (as low as 97.6) and the hottest at 7pm (as high as 100). *The true definition of fever is a body temperature of 100.4 or higher taken rectally.*

When an infection (most common reason for fever) enters the body, the body mounts a defense via the immune system. The immune system revs up all other body systems into attack mode. This raises all vital signs (temperature, heart rate/pulse, respiratory rate, blood pressure). A warmer body temperature actually helps fight infection. FEVER IS NOT BAD.

Because the normal body temperature is lowest in the morning and highest at night, our fever will be lower in the morning and higher at night. With a typical viral infection, we may have a temperature of 99 in the morning and be 102 at night. This is why pediatricians get phone calls about fever at night. *The fever doesn't go away and come back. It's always there. It's just lower in the morning. Fevers often last for three to four days for a viral infection.*

Fever, in and of itself, does not do any harm to the body. But it is an indicator that something (usually infection) is going on in the body. *Parents tend to focus and worry about the fever. Pediatricians worry about what the diagnosis/infection is.* Body temperatures over 108 cause brain damage. Infections do not cause body temperatures over the 106 range. (Hyperthermia, the term for body temperatures over 107, are usually caused accidentally—for example, someone locked in a car in the middle of August).

Fever is often the first sign of illness. It can take several hours to see the other symptoms blossom from the infection. So, unless a baby is under three months of age (see protocol below), you may need to watch and see how things evolve.

DR B'S OPINION: FEVER-PHOBIC PARENTS

Here is a typical phone encounter on fevers:

Parent: "Doctor, my baby has a fever."
Doctor: "Yes, but what else is going on?"
Parent: "But, doctor, he has a fever."
Doctor: "I understand, but can you tell me if he has any other symptoms?"

You get the picture. I heard you. I know your baby has a fever. I need to figure out WHY he has the fever. Help me. Don't fixate on the fever. *The fever is not the problem—it's a clue for the real problem.* Be a good detective and help me look for clues. It will make for a much more productive conversation!

Fever Phobia

A recent study looked at parent misconceptions of fever:[4]

- ◆ 91% believed fever could cause harmful effects (death, brain damage).
- ◆ 44% believed that a fever over 102 was a "high" fever.
- ◆ 7% believed that a fever could rise to 110 if left untreated.
- ◆ 25% gave fever reducing medicine for temperatures less than 100.
- ◆ 85% said they awaken their child to give fever-reducing medicine.
- ◆ 44% dosed the fever reducing medicine incorrectly.
- ◆ 52% said they checked their child's temperature at least every hour when they had a fever.

BOTTOM LINE

The body is coolest at 7am (as low as 97.6) and hottest at 7pm (as high as 100). So, the true definition of fever is a body temperature of 100.4 or higher taken rectally.

Fever is the body's immune response to infection. The immune system revs up all other body systems and raises all vital signs. A warmer body temperature actually helps fight infection. Therefore, fever is *not* bad.

Remember, fever is not the problem, rather it is a clue to finding the problem. And, fever is often the first sign of illness.

Don't be fooled that your child is fever-free in the morning if he had a fever the night before. It's just naturally lower in the morning. If you send him to childcare, you will get called to take him home when his fever spikes in the afternoon. Prepare to stay at home next day if your child has a fever at night.

Q. At what temperature should I be worried?

This is a protocol for fever in infants. A management plan is based on a child's age. The protocol is fairly universal for all babies under three months.

Reality Check

Most of the time, newborns have a virus they picked up from a family member. But your doctor doesn't want to take any chances. Now you know why the standard advice is to limit visitors during the first four weeks after birth.

Helpful Hint

Newborns can also have problems if they have LOW body temperatures. If your newborn has a persistently low body temperature (under 97.6 taken rectally), it's best to check in with your doctor.

Priority 1: Needs Immediate Evaluation And Treatment—NOW

◆ *Age zero to four weeks: any fever in this age group is an emergency!*

1. A rectal temperature of 100.4 or greater requires hospitalization ASAP.
2. Newborns have a unique risk of serious bacterial infections due to delivery and congenital urinary tract defects (Group B strep meningitis, pneumonia, sepsis, urinary tract infections/kidney infections). They are tested for all of these potential infections and treated with antibiotics until bacterial cultures are clear of growth. (see sepsis workup in Appendix C, "Lab Tests").
3. *Never give acetaminophen (Tylenol) to your feverish newborn. Call your doctor.*

◆ *Age four weeks to three months: any fever in this age group is an emergency!*

1. A rectal temperature 100.4 or greater requires examination and lab evaluation.
2. These infants need to be seen either in the doctor's office or in an emergency room depending on the hour. They still run the risk of having those bacterial infections that newborns get.
3. If there is an obvious source of infection (e.g. a cold), and the baby's lab work looks reassuring, hospitalization is unnecessary.
4. *Never give acetaminophen (Tylenol) without calling the doctor.*

◆ *Age three months to six months: a fever AND these problems in this age group is an emergency.*

1. A fever over 102.
2. A fever lasting more than three days.
3. A new fever, after a recent illness.
4. No obvious symptoms of viral infection (cough, runny nose, diarrhea)
5. Fussy mood/inconsolable.
6. Petechiae rash (See bleeding section earlier).

◆ *Age six months to one year:*

1. A fever of 104 or above deserves a phone call. (We know that's way beyond *your* comfort level)
2. A fever lasting more than three days.
3. A new fever, after a recent illness.
4. No obvious symptoms of viral infection (cough, runny nose, diarrhea).

5. Fussy mood/inconsolable.
6. Petechiae rash (see bleeding section earlier in this chapter.)

Priority 2: Needs appointment the next day.

◆ *Age three months to six months*
1. If everyone in the house has the flu and your baby has the same symptoms, make an appointment if the fever persists longer than three days (or something else is concerning—i.e. dehydration, labored breathing).
2. *You can give acetaminophen (Tylenol) for the fever. Just make sure you have figured out why your baby has the fever first.*

Priority 3: Watch and wait. Needs appointment if there is no improvement or worsening of symptoms

◆ *Age six months to one year:*
1. Obvious symptoms of a virus (cough, runny nose, vomiting, diarrhea), you can probably manage the infection without a doctor's visit.
2. *You can give acetaminophen (Tylenol) or ibuprofen (Motrin) when your baby has a fever. Just make sure you know why your baby has the fever.*

Reality Check

After six months of age, it's not the degree of the fever that is concerning, it's what the baby looks like. Everyone looks sick when they are running a fever. If a baby still looks sick after taking a fever reducing medicine, it's time to call the doctor.

Insider Tip: Roseola

Children usually get the common childhood infection, **ROSEOLA**, between nine to 12 months of age. It causes a high fever (103 to 104) for about three days with no other symptoms. These kids look perfectly happy and go about their daily routines. On day four, when they are fever free, the classic roseola rash (flat red patches on the chest and arms) comes out. They are not contagious with the rash. High fevers (104 or above) deserve to be evaluated, but roseola is often the culprit.

See our web site at Baby411.com for a visual library of rashes.

Q. My baby is running a 'low grade' fever. Should I be worried?

Who started this urban legend? What is a low-grade fever? It's not in the doctor dictionary.

Parents worry about body temperatures of 99 to 100. This is not, by definition, a fever. It has no association with an infection unless your baby is 100 at 7am. In that case, it does not bode well for what the night will bring.

Q. My baby has had a fever "on and off" for several days. I thought he broke the fever. Why does it keep coming back?

Let's review. A typical viral infection will cause a fever for three or four days.

Remember, it may look like your baby doesn't have a fever in the morning, but it always comes back at night. If there is a fever at any point in a 24-hour day, your child still has fever on a daily basis. This is helpful when you are reporting symptoms to the doctor. Doctors want a record of how many days in a row your child has had a fever. It helps make diagnostic decisions.

Fever reducing medicine (acetaminophen—Tylenol), ibuprofen—Motrin) will help bring the body temperature down for four to six hours. But once the medicine wears off, the fever will return. The medicine does not make the infection go away. (See later questions on fever-reducing medications).

BOTTOM LINE: A truly NEW fever after being fever free for a period of at least 24 hours is concerning for a bacterial infection that has capitalized on a sick person (such as ear infection, sinus infection, pneumonia). Make an appointment to see your doctor.

Helpful Hint
On Fever curves
Another important trend doctors watch is the fever curve over a period of days. At the beginning of an infection, the fever is the highest. As the body effectively fights off the infection, the maximum fever spikes should be lower. If a fever curve trends up instead of down (fevers are getting higher on a day to day basis), this is more concerning and may prompt an evaluation.

Q. How do you recommend taking a baby's temperature?

For the target age of this book (birth to age one), you need to take the temperature with a rectal thermometer.

Most parents cringe just thinking about this task. Are you cringing? Don't. Babies really don't mind. It does not hurt or make them feel like you've invaded their space. In fact, it's a good trick to make them poop. But, back to the subject at hand.

Rectal temperatures are the most accurate way to check a human's body temperature. And for infants under three months of age, one tenth of a degree will make the difference between whether you stay at home in your nice warm bed or head out for an evening of fun at your local emergency room.

If you call the doctor at 2 am and tell her that your six week old has a fever, the first thing she will ask is, "How did you take the temperature?" If you took it any way other than rectally, we make you get a rectal thermometer and call us back. Invest in one now—digital rectal thermometers cost about $5.

After one year of age, there is more flexibility about how to take your child's temperature. Trendy products on the market for toddler temperatures include a pacifier thermometer, ear thermometer, temporal artery scanners, and plastic skin stickers. Using an oral thermometer in the armpit is also okay. None of these are as accurate as a rectal temperature. But after a year of age, the actual degree of fever is much less important to making a management plan for your child. That is, a child with 101 or 103 is managed based on the *other symptoms* they have in addition to the fever.

FIRST AID

DR B'S OPINION: THERMOMETERS

Ear thermometers are not my friend. Their reliability is based upon the ability of the user to line the tip up with the eardrum. If you compare your own two ears and get two different readings, you will understand what I mean. They are very pricey, too. Not to mention that they can also overestimate the degree of fever and create parent panic. I've received frantic calls regarding kids with fevers of 107 taken with an ear thermometer that turned out to be 102 or 103 when taken rectally.

Except for the ear thermometers (which OVER estimate fever), alternative methods to check temperature UNDER estimate the degree of fever. Parents often ask, "Do you add or subtract a degree from the non-rectal measurement?" My response is, "If you ever get an actual reading that is 100 or over, you know your child has a fever. That is all the information I need."

Mom Knows Best

There was a great study that tested Mom's method of temperature taking (placing the hand on the forehead). Guess what? Mom is usually right—at least 80% of the time—with this method. Some thoughts on this:

1. After six months of age, if you say your child "feels hot," that's often enough proof of fever.
2. Trust yourself! Parents think they need to take their baby's temperature periodically to make sure he is okay. You hold your baby 24 hours a day. You will know when he feels hot. Then you can get out the thermometer.

New Parent 411: How to take a baby's rectal temperature.

Don't be embarrassed. You've never done this before. Get out your digital rectal thermometer. Place some Vaseline on the tip. With one hand lift up your baby's feet, holding them together. With your other hand, insert the tip of the thermometer into his anus about one inch. Leave the thermometer in there for one minute (or until it beeps at you). See, you and baby did just fine.

FYI: The American Academy of Pediatrics now recommends using digital (rectal/oral) thermometers as opposed to glass mercury thermometers. The latter are dangerous if broken.

Q. What is the correct dose of medication? It says on the box to consult a physician.

Ever wonder why it says this on the box? It's to make sure that you call the doctor when your newborn has a fever. Now that you know when you need to call, we will tell you how to dose these medicines. Both acetaminophen (Tylenol) and ibuprofen (Motrin) are dosed at five milligram per pound per dose. See the dosing chart on page 324.

Treating a Fever: Dr. B's 10 Commandments

1 If you have your doctor's blessing (see age question earlier), it's okay to give a fever reducing medication.

2 Babies from three to six months can use acetaminophen (Tylenol).

3 Babies over six months of age can use ibuprofen (Motrin/Advil) or acetaminophen (Tylenol).

4 I prefer ibuprofen for older babies because the medication lasts for six hours instead of four. Since the fever will climb at night, this will buy everyone two extra hours of sleep.

5 Acetaminophen is preferred if a child is dehydrated or has a stomach virus (ibuprofen can upset an empty stomach).

6 Be forewarned: these medications are called fever *reducers* not fever eliminators. At best, these medications will bring the body temperature down by two degrees. If your baby is cooking at 104, he will be feeling more comfortable at 102. That's as good as it gets.

7 I don't routinely instruct parents to alternate acetaminophen and ibuprofen. If a baby is old enough for the ibuprofen, stick with that. I only alternate medicines in babies prone to febrile seizures (see glossary for details). There is no proven benefit of alternating medicines.

8 Don't bother putting baby in a tepid bath. If you had the chills, would you want to sit in cold water? This cooling technique is only necessary in an emergency situation (such as extreme hyperthermia, a 107 degree temperature). Bring your child's temperature down with this technique is not only unpleasant, but a waste of time and effort.

9 Never give your child ASPIRIN. It can cause liver failure when given with particular viral infections.

10 Always use the medicine dropper that comes with the package. The term "one dropperful" refers to the dropper that comes with the medicine.

How to avoid overdosing your baby

1. Acetaminophen is the generic name for Tylenol, Feverall, and Tempra.

2. Ibuprofen is the generic name for Motrin and Advil.

3. Both acetaminophen and ibuprofen are effective fever reducers and pain medications.

4. Acetaminophen is dosed every four hours. Ibuprofen is dosed every six hours.

5. *As we've said earlier, always use the medicine dropper that comes in the package.* The dropper size varies between products. (The Tylenol dropper is a 0.8 ml one. The Motrin dropper is 1.875 ml.).

6. There is a difference in the concentration of medicine in the *infant drops* and the *children's syrup.* The infant drops are much more concentrated so you won't have to force a large volume of medicine into your baby.

7. Acetaminophen suppositories (medicine bullets inserted in the anus) are available for babies who resist taking medicine or are actively vomiting.

8. *When your doctor tell you to use "one dropperful," it routinely means the dropper that comes with the package, with the medicine drawn up to the line marked on the dropper.* A mother requested that we share this with you because she mistakenly thought it meant to fill the *whole* dropper up with medicine (look at a medicine dropper and you'll understand).

9. When you graduate to the syrup medicine, use a medicine cup to dispense. Silverware teaspoons are not an exact teaspoon measurement. They can be larger or smaller depending on your set. Medicine syringes are also helpful—they make it easier to measure and dispense medicine.

DR B'S OPINION

"I have too many stories about Tylenol overdoses to share in this book. It's just not as easy to figure these medicines out as it should be."

Dosing Chart

Acetaminophen:

BABY'S WEIGHT IN LBS.	6-11LBS	12-17LBS	18-23LBS	24-35LBS
Dose in mg	40mg	80mg	120mg	160mg
Infant drops	0.4ml	0.8ml	0.8+0.4ml	0.8+0.8ml
(80mg per 0.8 ml)				
in dropperfuls	1/2	1	1 1/2	2
Children's syrup		1/2 tsp	3/4 tsp	1 tsp
(160 mg per tsp)				
Suppositories (80mg)		1 suppository	1 1/2	2
Suppositories (120mg)			1	1 1/3

Ibuprofen:

BABY'S WEIGHT IN LBS.	6-11LBS	12-17LBS	18-23LBS	24-35LBS
Dose in mg	*	50mg	75mg	100mg
Infant drops				
(50mg per 1.25 ml)	*	1.25ml	1.25+0.625	1.25+1.25
1.875ml is a dropperful	*	1	1 1/2	2
Children's syrup (100mg per tsp)		1/2 tsp	3/4 tsp	1 tsp

*Note: Ibuprofen is NOT for babies under six months of age

Q. Is it safe to give a fever reducing medicine longer than five days? It says on the box to consult a physician.

The medicine itself is safe to give. This warning is a way to make sure you have checked in with your doctor if your baby has a prolonged fever. A child with a fever more than four days straight should be seen by her doctor.

Q. I have given my baby acetaminophen(Tylenol) and he still has a fever.

This one is on the Top 10 List of most asked questions for any pediatrician. *The most common reason this happens is that your child has outgrown the dose of medicine you have given him.* Fever reducing medicines (as well as most other types) are dosed based on the weight of a child. A few pounds can make a difference for the correct dosing.

Look at the chart above. When your doctor tells you the dose of acetaminophen(Tylenol) at your child's two-month well check, don't think that the dose will never change.

BOTTOM LINE: Acetaminophen and Ibuprofen are fever reducers (not eliminators). If your child has a high fever, it won't be completely eliminated by the medicine. The fact that the fever does not go down with medication has no implication on the severity of the illness.

Q. I've heard that fevers can cause seizures in babies. Is this true?

Yes, babies can have febrile seizures or convulsions.

A few children—less than 5% (ages six months to five years) are prone to having a seizure/convulsion as a fever is shooting up. "Febrile seizures" do not cause brain damage or lead to a seizure disorder such as epilepsy.

The seizure happens when the body temperature rises quickly. If your child's temperature is at 104, you don't have to worry about him having a seizure.

Yes, it is terrifying to watch a child have a full-blown seizure in your living room. Fortunately, febrile seizures last less than five minutes. And children are fine afterwards.

About 30% of children who are prone to febrile seizures have more than one episode in their lives. But after the first time, parents are much more comfortable about managing it. Parents will give fever medicine around the clock so that the temperature elevation can never rise rapidly during the course of an illness.

The first time a child has a febrile seizure, he needs to be evaluated thoroughly. Once this diagnosis is determined, evaluation and treatment focuses on the cause of the fever.

Old Wives Tales

Don't give your baby a bath while he has a fever.
Don't let your baby drink milk while he has a fever.
Fevers cause brain damage.
Teething causes fever.

The Truth: None of these statements are remotely true. Keep feeding your baby breast milk or formula, go ahead and give him a bath, and unless his fever reaches the extreme temperatures mentioned earlier, relax a bit. Oh, and teething has *nothing* to do with fever; remember fever is caused by viral or bacterial invaders.

What the doctor will ask you about FEVER:
1. How old is your baby?
2. How did you take the temperature?
3. What other new symptoms are you seeing?
4. Is anyone else in the household sick?
5. Is your child exposed to other children?
6. How many days has the fever been going on?
7. Any recent illnesses prior to the fever?
8. Any rashes?
9. Have you given any fever reducing medicines?
10. What dose of medicine did you give?
11. What does your baby look like after giving the medicine?

Red Flags
◆ Fever under three months of age.
◆ Fever over 102 in three to six-month-old.
◆ Fever of 104 or above in six months and older.
◆ Fever lasting over three days.
◆ Fever without obvious source of infection.
◆ Fever with petechiae rash.
◆ Fever with irritability or lethargy.
◆ Febrile seizure.
◆ Fever with a limp or limb pain.

Poisonings/Ingestions

If your child accidentally swallows a household product, call poison control immediately.

Have the phone number at each of your telephones. Have syrup of ipecac (induces vomiting) in your first aid kit but don't ever use it unless you are instructed to by poison control. In fact, inducing vomiting with ipecac is used LESS as a treatment of poisonings today, as doctors have realized that other treatments are more effective (and vomiting can, in some cases, causes MORE harm than good). Yet, to be on the safe side, we'd still stock ipecac in your first aid kit.

Poison Control is an amazing resource of information on any product a curious child might ingest. They will tell you whether the product can do potential harm to the body or not. And they know the antidotes.

Occasionally, a parent is not even aware of the ingestion happening. They only know that their child is acting unusual. *Some clues to ingestion include: mouth burns, drooling, rapid or shallow breathing, vomiting without fever, seizures, extreme lethargy, or body/breath odor.*

Helpful hint

If Poison Control directs you to an emergency room, take the poison/medication with you if you have it. It helps determine the ingredients and the amount that was swallowed.

Feedback form the Real World
Dr. B True Story

I cared for a patient once who ate part of a necklace a mother had brought back from traveling abroad. The beads were made of ricin, the active ingredient of poison darts (think Bond, James Bond). **Bottom Line:** Be careful. Babies are programmed to taste everything.

What the doctor will ask you about POISONING:
1. Is the product toxic vs. non-toxic?
2. Do you have the bottle/container?
3. Is your child having trouble breathing?

THE MOST DANGEROUS HOUSEHOLD PRODUCTS

Here is a list of childhood favorites to keep out of reach. (place items in high cabinets or in places with cabinet locks or out of reach).

Chemicals
- ◆ cleaning products
- ◆ paint thinner
- ◆ dishwashing detergent
- ◆ gasoline

Medications
- ◆ especially Mom's prenatal vitamins (iron)
- ◆ especially visiting grandparents (heart or blood pressure medications)

Plants (some of these are common houseplants).
- ◆ Christmas favorites: poinsettas, mistletoe, holly
- ◆ wild mushrooms
- ◆ hyacinth, narcissus, daffodil, elephant ear, rosary pea, larkspur, Lily-of-the-Valley, iris, foxglove, bleeding heart, daphne, wisteria, golden chain, laurels, azaleas, jasmine, lantana

Hygiene products
- ◆ mouthwash
- ◆ nail polish remover
- ◆ rubbing alcohol
- ◆ hair dye

Food and wine
- ◆ liquor
- ◆ pottery from foreign countries (lead)

When to call:

All poisonings and ingestions are Priority 1: Needs immediate evaluation and treatment—NOW!

Rashes

Until we have videophones, you need to be the eyes for your doctor. Trying to diagnose a rash over the phone is always a challenge. At best, we can figure out whether the rash fits into the worrisome or the non-worrisome categories. Worrisome rashes need prompt attention. Non-worrisome ones can wait until the office opens the next day. Causes of rashes include:

◆ **Infection:** viruses, bacteria, funguses, mites
◆ **Allergy:** eczema, contact allergy (poison ivy, sensitivity to a skin care product), food/medication allergy
◆ **Newborn rashes:** due to hormonal changes
◆ **Blood cell abnormalities**

See our website at Baby411.com for a visual library of rashes.

What the doctor will ask you about RASHES:
1. How long has the rash been there?
2. Where on the body did the rash start? Is it spreading? Where?
3. Is there a fever?
4. Is it itchy? Really really itchy?
5. Anyone else in the house with a rash?
6. Is the rash flat or raised? (Can you feel it with your eyes closed?)
7. Is it scaly on top?
8. What color is the rash?
9. How big are the spots?
10. When you press on the rash, does the color turn white? Or, does it remain discolored?
11. Is your child taking any medications?
12. Has your child eaten any new foods?
13. Have you used any new skin products? (sun block, lotion, soap, detergents)
14. How old is your child?

Q. Which rashes are worrisome?

Petechiae with or without bruising. (See bleeding section earlier for details on petechiae). Petechiae are small flat freckle or pinpoint dots, purplish in color, that stay purple when you push on them.

This is really the only rash that needs immediate attention. Petechiae can be caused by forceful coughing or vomiting. But, this rash can also indicate meningitis, Rocky Mountain Spotted Fever, idiopathic thrombocytopenic purpura (ITP), or leukemia. Petechiae are *Priority 1: Needs immediate evaluation and treatment—NOW.*

Q. What are hives and what causes them?

A rash that appears due to release of a chemical called histamine. 20% of the population will get hives once in their lives. But 75% of the time, the cause is never found.[5]

Hives look like mosquito bites with red circles around them. Or, they look like a flat red area with a raised border. Hives vary in size and shape. They are itchy and occur anywhere on the body. The individual lesions come and go. See the Chapter 14, "Diseases" for causes of hives.

What to do if your child breaks out in hives

◆ **Relax.** If your child is not having any trouble breathing, this can be managed at home.

◆ **Try to figure out what caused the hives** (foods, medications, illness).

◆ **Stop any medications until seeing the doctor.**

◆ **Give diphenhydramine (Benadryl).** Liquid Benadryl comes in 12.5mg per teaspoon syrup. A 20 lb baby can have 3/4 tsp. If your baby is smaller than 20 lbs, call your doctor before giving it.

Q. What does a drug allergy rash look like?

True drug allergies will cause hives or erythema multiforme. Any other rash does not require avoidance of a particular medication.

Erythema multiforme basically means "redness in multiple forms." What you see is a full body rash of red flat patches and raised borders. Many of the patches run into each other.

If you see a concerning rash while your child is on medication, hold the dose of medicine and bring the child in to be seen. A particular medication class should not be avoided unless there is a documented allergy.

Q. What does a food allergy rash look like?

Food allergies can cause hives and lip swelling if the reaction is severe. But, it can also cause a flare up of a rash called eczema. Eczema is an allergic skin disorder—the equivalent of hay fever. Eczema looks like a scaly plaque lying on top of a red base. With a food allergy, the eczema can cover huge body surface areas.

Food allergies do NOT cause mild diaper rash, a few patches on the face, or heat rashes.

Q. My child has a scaly rash on his elbows and knees. What is it?

Eczema. It is sensitive skin. In infants, it likes the elbows and knees because these areas get chewed up from crawling. It also ends up in the skin folds of the elbows and knees from rubbing. See Chapter 14 "Common Diseases" for more details on this.

Q. Which rashes are likely to be contagious/due to infection?

Most of them. Kids have wonderful immune systems (much better than ours). And rashes are created from an immune response to a particular infection.

The diseases listed below are The Classics. There are also a variety of non-descript rashes that fit in the category of "viral and non-worrisome".

RASH-O-RAMA: COMMON RASHES SEEN WITH

Viral exanthems: (rashes caused by viruses)

	Rash looks like	**Where?**
Chickenpox	fluid filled blisters come up in crops	all over avg. 350 lesions
Shingles	fluid filled blisters	1 patch
Measles	red, raised pimply	face to body
German measles	red, raised	face to body
Roseola	FLAT red ovals/ lace	chest, arms, neck, +/- face
Parvovirus (Fifth disease)	"slapped cheeks" Flat, red, lacy on body	chest, arms
Coxsackievirus (hand, foot, and mouth)	red dots or blisters +/- buttocks	palms, soles,
Unilateral Latero-thoracic Exanthem	raised red bumps, scaly on top	one armpit
Pityriasis rosea	raised red streaks a little scaly	back, angled like a fir tree

Special viral rashes:

Herpetic Whitlow	blister, red around	thumb, finger
Molluscum Contagiosum	pinpoint blisters	anywhere

Bacterial infections:

Impetigo*	red, raised with weeping golden crust	anywhere
Scarlet fever* (usually over 2 yrs old)	red, sandpaper feel, rough raised dots	armpit, groin, neck, body
Meningitis	petechiae (purple freckles)	spreads head to toe

Fungal infections:

Ringworm*	circle, red raised edge +/- overlying scale	anywhere
Yeast diaper rash*	raw meat red with surrounding pimples	diaper area

Tick borne illness:

Lyme Disease*	bullseye with bite in the center	bite site
Rocky Mountain Spotted Fever*	starts out flat, red then petechiae (purple freckles)	wrist, ankles palms, soles

Mites:

Scabies*	lines of red raised bumps (burrows) blisters in babies	head, neck, palms, soles, armpits, finger webs

Other:

Kawasaki Disease*	red cracked lips peeling skin on fingers flat/mildly raised red spots	lips, palms, soles of feet

*Denotes an infection that needs treatment

INFECTIONS, HOW LONG THEY LAST AND MORE!

Duration	Other symptoms
1 week	fever, itchy
1 week	painful
1 week	fever, pink eye
3 days	swollen glands
1 day	high fever that breaks then rash appears
2-40 days	mildly itchy, joint pains
1 week with ulcers	fever, sore throat
4-6 weeks	mildly itchy
6 weeks	mildly itchy
1 week	very painful
1-2 years	
gets worse until treated	very itchy
3-4 days	sore throat, fever
hours	fever, irritability, light sensitivity
gets worse until treated	very itchy
gets worse until treated	itchy
enlarging diameter	fever, fatigue
1-6 days	fever, vomiting irritability light sensitivity
worse until treated	ITCHIEST RASH EVER!
Over five days	Fever for more than 5 days pink eye swollen lymph nodes in neck

first aid

Q. I know that all newborns get rashes. Are there any I need to be worried about?

Yes. Herpes.

Moms with genital herpes have a chance of spreading it to their newborn during a vaginal delivery. (If Mom has an obvious outbreak a Caesarian section is performed.) A herpes rash in a newborn shows up within two weeks of life. The lesions look like little blisters either alone or in crops. This is *Priority 1: Needs immediate evaluation and treatment—NOW!*

Q. My four week old has a pimply rash all over his face and chest. What do I do?

It's acne, but don't break out the Oxy 10. This rash is caused by a hormonal change in the baby. Leave it alone and it goes away by eight weeks of age.

Feedback from the Real World
Dr. Brown True Story

My son woke up one morning with three distinct red circles on his chest. I thought he had ringworm until I realized the circles matched the snaps on his sleeper pajamas. He had an allergy to the metal snaps.

Necklaces, earrings, and snaps on jeans can cause a similar reaction in people with sensitive skin.

Q. My one year old looks like he has the measles! Does he?

No. Did he come in for his one-year well check recently? That rash is the response to the MMR vaccination. (the same thing happens with the chickenpox vaccine). Be happy. This means he has formed a good response.

These rashes usually appear one to four weeks after being vaccinated.

Q. My baby has a diaper rash. What do I do about it?

See Chapter 4, "Hygiene" for details on how to treat diaper rash.

Priority 1: Needs immediate evaluation and treatment—NOW:

◆ Hives that occur while taking medication or trying a new food.
◆ Hives with difficulty breathing (Call 911).
◆ Petechiae rash.
◆ Newborn with a blistery rash.
◆ Any rash with a fever.

Priority 2: Needs appointment the next day.

◆ Rashes that are scaly, without fever.
◆ Rashes that are not going away after being treated by a doctor.

Priority 3: Watch and wait. Needs appointment if there is no improvement or worsening of symptoms:

◆ Newborn (birth to eight weeks) with a non-blistery rash, acting well.
◆ Diaper rashes.
◆ One year old with rash after being in for his one year well check.

Seizures

Seizures are scary to watch. If your child has a seizure, **dial 911.** Once the episode is over, you can review this information.

Q. What is a seizure?

Involuntary muscle (motor) activity is the definition of a seizure. This is caused by an electrical brainwave that has fired incorrectly. In kids under age one, the most common type of seizure is associated with a fever that is rising quickly (See febrile seizure in the fever section of this chapter).

Causes of new onset seizures include: Febrile seizure (convulsion), head trauma/ injury, Meningitis, poisoning/ingestion, metabolic disorder, seizure disorder

What To Do If Your Baby Has A Seizure

◆ *Call 911.*
◆ Put him in a safe place (a carpeted floor)
◆ Make sure he can breathe.
◆ Do not put anything in his mouth to hold his tongue (contrary to what you see on TV).
◆ Start CPR—do mouth-to-mouth resuscitation if baby looks blue.

What the doctor will ask you about SEIZURES:
1. Has your baby ever had a seizure before?
2. How old is your baby?
3. Does the baby have a fever?
4. Anyone in the family prone to febrile seizures as a child?
5. Any history of head trauma?
6. Any history of poisoning or ingestion?

Priority 1: Needs immediate evaluation and treatment—NOW

◆ Known history of febrile seizures, with another episode
◆ Has a known seizure disorder.

Stitches (Sutures)

The key point to remember: *Stitches (sutures) need to be placed within 12 hours of the injury. So they are always considered Priority 1.* Any later than that, the wound has a much higher chance of getting infected. If your child has a wound that might need stitches, call your doctor now.

What the doctor will ask you about NEEDING STITCHES:
1. What happened? For example, animal bites usually are not stitched because of infection risk.
2. How long ago did the injury happen? If over 12 hours, wound can't be sutured.
3. Where on the body is the cut (laceration)? Location of the wound makes a difference because of cosmetic issues (face) and poten-

tial nerve damage (hands).

4. If on the face, is it crossing the lip/skin line or the eyebrow line? (It may need stitches for better cosmetic result)

5. How deep is it? (If you can see fat, it needs stitches—anything deeper than 1/4 inch).

6. Is the bleeding under control? (If not, it needs stitches).

7. For older wounds: Is there any pus, redness around the wound, streaks of red from the wound, or fever? (Needs to be seen for possible wound infection).

8. Are your child's immunizations current? (Needs tetanus shot if not up to date).

9. Does your child have any bleeding disorders? (There is a risk of large volume of blood loss).

Q. Are there any body parts that always need stitches?

Yes. Eyebrows and lip lines. The lip line means the area where the lip meets the skin. If a wound crosses this line, the lip will not line up correctly without stitches. The same is true for the eyebrow line. Cosmetically, this is a big deal.

Q. Are there any body parts that never need stitches?

It is RARE to need stitches on the lip itself, tongue, or gums. The blood flow to these areas is tremendous (which is why they bleed so much). This blood flow allows very rapid healing.

Q. How can I tell if the wound is infected?

Pus (white/yellow/green discharge) will start to ooze out of the wound. There will be red and tender skin around the wound site, and maybe even a streak of redness starting from the wound. There may also be a fever.

HOW TO CLEAN AND CARE FOR MINOR WOUNDS

It's not what you use, it's how you use it. Plain old soap and water is fine. You don't have to get high tech here. The key is to flush the wound and repeat this several times. Wash the wound every day until it heals. Here's how to care for minor wounds:

1. Apply pressure to the wound with a gauze pad or towel for ten minutes.
2. Thoroughly clean wound with soap and water. The most important part of the cleaning process is flushing with water repeatedly—especially with puncture wounds (bites, sharp objects). Your doctor will use a mechanism much like a water pik to clean "road rash" scrapes.
3. Apply antibiotic ointment for two or three days. This prevents infection and improves cosmetic results.
4. Look for signs of infection. (Redness, pus, fever).
5. For cuts in the mouth or tongue, try popsicles or ice cream (if age appropriate) to help control bleeding.

Q. Is my child's tetanus shot up to date?

If your child is receiving his immunizations regularly at well baby checks, he is well protected. He gets a tetanus shot at two, four, six, fifteen months and again at five years old. Your child is probably better protected than you.

Q. Can I get water near the stitches?

YES!

This is a common misconception. Clean the wound, even if it has stitches in it. The uncleaned ones have crust around them, making it a challenge for the doctor to remove the stitches.

Q. When should the stitches be removed?

It depends on the location. Skin heals at different rates on the body. The doctor who puts the stitches in will tell you when they need to come out. Try to do it when suggested— a delay in suture removal can not only impair the cosmetic result, but can also be very painful if the stitches are imbedded in the skin.

To give you an idea of the variability of suture removal, stitches on the face come out in four days. Stitches on the palm of the hand come out in 14 days.

Q. What is that new glue to close wounds? Can we use that instead of stitches?

It's called Dermabond. It's like superglue. It dissolves on its own and does not need any removal. Sounds great, right?

Well, it is only useful for a limited number of wounds. If the skin is under any tension (gets pulled frequently), the glue won't be able to hold the wound together. The glue is also not intended for use near the eyes.

Q. I've also heard about using staples instead of stitches. Is this better than stitches?

It's easier than stitches for placement, but they are painful to remove. For noncosmetic areas such as the head, it is a reasonable option.

Helpful Hint

Cuts on the scalp and face bleed a lot. The blood flow to these body parts is much greater than any other areas. Don't be alarmed. It is only a problem if you can't get the bleeding under control.

Priority 1: Needs immediate evaluation and treatment—NOW:
- ◆ Any skin wound that you think might need stitches.
- ◆ Unable to control the bleeding after ten minutes of pressure to the wound.
- ◆ Wound in a cosmetically undesirable location.
- ◆ Looks like it is getting infected (redness, pus, fever).
- ◆ If immunizations are not current.

Priority 3: Watch and wait. Needs appointment if there is no improvement or worsening of symptoms:

◆ Making an appointment for suture removal.

Trauma (Accidental Injury)

No matter how good of a parent you are and how safety proofed your house is, your child will find a way to hurt himself. Welcome to parenthood—this is only one of the many reasons that your child will give you grey hairs.

This section is body part specific. The section on skin trauma/injury is covered in the Stitches section.

What the doctor will ask you about TRAUMA/ ACCIDENTAL INJURIES

1. What happened?
2. Any loss of consciousness or did he cry immediately?
3. With head injury: Any vomiting or confusion?
4. With head injury: How far did the child fall and what surface did he fall onto?
4. Any bleeding or fluid draining from the nose or ears?
5. Are there any obvious broken bones—sticking out of the skin?
6. Any pain with touching or movement of a body part?
7. Any bruising or swelling?
8. Can you check the eye pupils. Are they equal?

Helpful Hint
The mechanism of injury (that is, what happened) is the most reliable factor in determining the severity of a body injury.

I. Head injury

Once babies are mobile, they run into things like the coffee table and fireplace hearth. The result is a big bruise (a.k.a. "goose egg") on the forehead. It is an impressive bump because of that vast blood supply to the head and face. Despite the appearance, goose eggs are not too worrisome.

The mechanism of injury is much more concerning. Here are the red flags for head injuries:

Priority 1: Needs immediate evaluation and treatment—NOW!

Concerning injuries for a concussion or bleeding in the head.

◆ Child falls a distance greater than his own height.
◆ Child falls onto hardwood floors, tile, or concrete.
◆ Child loses consciousness (blacks out) after the injury.
◆ Child vomits more than once after the injury.
◆ Baby's soft spot is bulging.
◆ Seizure after head injury.
◆ Acting abnormal or confused.
◆ Bruising behind the ear or bleeding from the ear.
◆ Clear fluid draining from the nose.

Priority 2: Needs appointment the next day.

◆ Child falls a distance less than his height, onto a padded surface, no loss of consciousness.

Priority 3: Watch and wait. Needs appointment if there is no improvement or worsening of symptoms:

◆ Child has a minor accident resulting in a large bruise on the head (goose egg), no loss of consciousness, no vomiting, and is acting normally.

BOTTOM LINE

Every child who has rolled off a bed onto a carpeted floor does not need to be rushed to an emergency room. (And yes, this will happen to you!)

Which head injuries require a CAT scan?

When there is a concern for a severe head injury (bleeding inside the skull), a CT scan (Computer Tomography) is helpful to check it out. Here are the criteria:

◆ loss of consciousness for over one minute
◆ trauma (knife, bullet)
◆ abnormal neurologic examination (weakness, abnormal reflexes..)
◆ vomiting
◆ seizures
◆ bulging soft spot (fontanelle)
◆ bruising behind the ear or bleeding from the ear
◆ clear fluid draining from the nose
◆ depressed skull fracture (i.e. a break in the skull detected on a plain x-ray)

Reality Check

Walkers cause over 6000 head injuries in the U.S. annually. Yes, the newer models have more "safety features" that keep them from rolling down stairs. But we say save your money or buy some other really cool toy.

New Parent 411: Handling Minor Head Inuries

◆ Put a bag of frozen vegetables on the goose egg, if your child lets you. It will be less swollen in the morning, but will change into a rainbow of colors for a week or two.
◆ Watch for signs of concussion for the next two days (vomiting, irritability from headache, confusion, lethargy)
◆ Let your child go to bed. Invariably, it's nap or bedtime when these events happen (probably because your child is tired and clumsy then). You can monitor him every few hours by watching his breathing and gently touching him to see if he stirs. Vomiting or seizure activity happens whether he is awake or asleep.

2. Neck and back injuries

CALL 911 and do not try to move your child. He will be immobilized on a straight board until x-rays can prove that no spine damage has occurred.

3. Eye injuries

All eye injuries should be evaluated by a doctor immediately. Here are the most common problems:

♦ **Corneal abrasion:** surface of the eye is scratched. It heals in a day or two. Frequent tearing is a clue to this diagnosis.

♦ **Hyphema:** bleeding that occurs beneath the surface of the eye (a doctor sees it with special equipment). If the blood is not removed, vision can be lost. This is fairly uncommon, but it is the reason that all eye injuries need a medical evaluation.

♦ **Subconjunctival hemorrhage:** bleeding occurs on the surface of the eye. It can be seen on the white part of the eye. Although it looks dramatic, it's not serious.

4. Ear injuries

Outer ear: (the part you can see) can be bruised and cause permanent cartilage damage. If you see bruising, this is a *Priority 1: Needs immediate evaluation and treatment* call—the blood might need to be drained.

Inner ear: (the inside) can be injured when curious kids put things in their ears. Usually they don't get anywhere near the eardrum. If you see bleeding, it's likely from scratching the lining of the canal. Doctors need to see these kids, but it can wait until the office opens (*a priority 2 call*). The only emergency is if your child had a head injury and you notice blood draining out of the ear or a bruise behind the outer ear. This is a sign of a skull fracture.

5. Nose injuries

Priority 1: Needs immediate evaluation and treatment—NOW:

♦ A nosebleed after a nose injury increases the chances of it being broken.

♦ A clear drainage or bloody nose after a head injury increases the chances of a skull fracture.

♦ Inability to breathe through the nose after an injury may mean a severe bruise in the nose (septal hematoma)

♦ Nose is obviously crooked (displaced nose fracture).

Priority 2: Needs appointment the next day.

♦ Nose injury without bleeding or obvious fracture.

6. Mouth injuries

See stitches section for details. The bottom line: Very few injuries to the mouth require stitches. They bleed a lot but heal quickly and beautifully. Injuries that go through the inside of the mouth to the outside of the skin, or full thickness through the tongue need to be seen (*Priority 1: Needs immediate evaluation and treatment—NOW*).

? ?

7. Tooth injuries

Injuries to baby teeth rarely need intervention. Worry only if the tooth was 'knocked out' and you can't find it anywhere. That is a sign of a tooth intrusion. The tooth can get pushed back into the gums *(Priority 1: Needs immediate evaluation and treatment–NOW call to the dentist).*

FYI: You may know about the trick of placing a knocked out tooth in milk and rushing to the dentist to re-implant it. They only do this for permanent teeth, not baby teeth.

8. Bone injuries

Q. Is it BROKEN?

The best way to tell over the phone is to know the mechanism of injury and what your child is doing with the limb. The list of red flags is below.

If there is a break (fracture), your child needs a cast. Some specialists prefer to see kids with broken bones 48 hours after the injury so the swelling will be down before casting. As long as the bone is immobilized, it is fine. A temporary (splint) cast can be applied to keep the bone fixed and comfortable.

RED FLAGS
Does it need an x-ray?
All of these are *Priority 1: Needs immediate evaluation and treatment–NOW:*

1. Unable to move a limb without crying.
2. Limping or refusing to bear weight.
3. Impressive bruising or swelling.

BOTTOM LINE
Broken bones hurt. If you can distract your child and move or touch the area without pain, it may just be bruised.

Helpful hint
Kids have areas in their bones called growth plates. This area is located at the end of each bone that gives it growing room. These plates fuse when children go through puberty (hormone levels cause them to close). A normal x-ray of a child's bone shows a gap where the growth plate is. Occasionally, if there is a fracture along the line of the growth plate, it may not be seen when the x-ray is read. So, even if an x-ray is read as "no fracture," call the doctor if there is no improvement in your child's symptoms in five to seven days.

HOW TO IMMOBILIZE AN INJURED LIMB

◆ Use a scarf or large towel and wrap it around the shoulder to keep an arm in place. Pinning a long arm sleeve to the shoulder also works.

◆ Use a piece of cardboard and an Ace wrap to form a makeshift splint for an arm or leg.

Q. My child was walking and put his hand out to break his fall. Is the wrist broken?

Probably. Your wrist joint is not intended to sustain your body weight. Your baby needs an x-ray.

Q. I was walking with my child and holding his hand. He pulled away from me and now he won't use his arm. Is it broken?

No—it's probably dislocated.

This is called a nursemaid's elbow. The elbow joint has gotten pulled out of its socket. Some children are repeat offenders. It can be easily fixed by your doctor in a matter of seconds. For frequent fliers, Mom and Dad can learn how to do it at home. It's a good idea not to pull your kids up by their arms, or jerk their arms when they resist motion. (And obviously, kids with frequent dislocations shouldn't play on the monkey bars!).

9. Fingers and toes

The classic injury here is the finger that gets slammed in a car door. If there is bruising or swelling, it needs an x-ray (*Priority 1: Needs immediate evaluation and treatment—NOW*). If there is a blood blister/collection of blood under the fingernail (subungual hematoma), it may need to be lanced by a doctor to relieve the pressure (*Priority 1 or 2*).

The fingers and toes are an exception for casting of broken bones. Some of these breaks only require stabilization (buddy taping) to the finger or toe next to it.

So, how do you immobilize a finger or toe? Tape fingers or toes together (buddy tape) for an injured digit. The neighbor of the injured digit gets taped to it for support.

RED FLAGS

A recap:
- ◆ head injury with loss of consciousness
- ◆ head injury with vomiting
- ◆ head injury with confusion
- ◆ significant height of fall or to a hard surface
- ◆ any eye injury
- ◆ head injury with nosebleed or ear drainage
- ◆ ear injury with bruising
- ◆ limb injury with swelling/bruising and discomfort
- ◆ fall onto an outstretched arm
- ◆ jerked elbow
- ◆ neck or spine injury—call 911
- ◆ bone injury with exposed bone

BOTTOM LINE

If you are ever in doubt, call your doctor.

SECTION 6

Baby 411

Reference Library

Appendix A

Medications

Here's a look at the most common medications used by children.[1] Obviously, with the huge universe of possible medications, this chapter is by no means comprehensive. Instead, we focus on the most popular and widely used meds in children. We will cover both over the counter products and prescription medications. FYI: We have also designated products that are safe for moms who are breastfeeding. Let's begin with some general questions regarding administering medicine to your child.

Q. If my child throws up right after I give him medicine, do I re-dose the medicine or wait until the next dose is due?

If your child throws up less than 20 minutes after administering medicine, give the dose again. It didn't have time to get through the stomach and be absorbed into the blood stream.

Q. Is a generic medication as good as a brand name?

For the most part, yes.

When a pharmaceutical company develops a medication, the company obtains a patent for it, which lasts for 17 years. Because it takes several years of research before a medication is approved for use, a medication may be on the market for an average of eight years before the patent runs out. Once the patent runs out, any pharmaceutical company can make their own product, which is the exact duplicate of the original brand.

The potency is the same, but sometimes the taste is not. And the cost is definitely not the same. Generic medications are often much cheaper than the brand name.

Q. If my doctor prescribes an expensive antibiotic, can I ask for a generic brand at the pharmacy?

Yes, but it might not be available.

In the case of antibiotics, we have been forced to develop new medications to keep up with the drug resistant bacteria. If an antibiotic is less than 17 years old, only the brand name is available—which usually means it's pretty expensive.

Helpful Hint

If you are paying out-of-pocket for prescription medications, speak up! Don't be shy about inquiring about the cost of the medication. Your doctor may have free samples available in the office. Or she will be able to prescribe a less-expensive generic drug if available.

Q. How do I get my baby to take her medicine?

Here are a few tricks to getting all the medicine down:

1. Give small amounts over several minutes, instead of the whole dose at once.

2. It is okay to mix certain medications in with formula or juice—but check with your pharmacist for the particulars. The only problem with this plan is that your child has to drink the whole thing. Be sure to mix the medicine in a small volume of fluid (less than an ounce).

3. Some pharmacies offer a service called Flavor RX (www.flavorx.com or 1-800-884-5771). For a relatively small fee (often worth it), a choice of 25 different flavorings is available—these can be added to your child's prescription to make it more palatable.

4. Taking a prescription medicine is not optional. It may take two parents to administer medicine to one strong-willed child.

Q. Is it okay to use a medicine if it is past the expiration date?

No.

For the most part, medications start to lose their potency after the listed expiration date. So, the medication may be less effective (for example, Albuterol for an asthma attack).

Q. The prescription medicine was supposed to be given for ten days. We ran out of it after eight days. What happened?

Most of the time, this happens when a "teaspoon" dose is administered with an actual teaspoon from your kitchen. Your silverware spoon may hold anywhere from 4-8 ml of fluid. Buy a medicine syringe that lists both cc/mls and teaspoons on it.

Q. I have some leftover antibiotic from a prescription. Can I save it and use it for another time?

No.

First of all, you should never have leftover antibiotics. Your doctor wanted your child to have a specific length of therapy for that medication. If your child stops taking an antibiotic "because he feels better," you run the risk of the bacteria growing back. This is particularly true of Group A Strep (of Strep throat fame). Yes, people often forget to give all of the doses of antibiotic—we're human. But try to finish a prescription as it was intended to be used.

Second of all, antibiotics that are in liquid form will only stay potent for about two weeks. They come as a powder from the manufacturer and the pharmacist mixes it with water when he fills the prescription order. If you have any medicine leftover—toss it.

Q. Are all medications administered to children of all ages?

No.

Many medications are not approved for infants under six months of age. Doctors' choices are more limited for these patients. There are also some medications that are purely for adult usage (for example, Tetracycline).

Q. How do I know if there is a problem taking more than one medicine at a time?

The official term is "drug interactions".

Your doctor or pharmacist can answer this question. Don't assume that your doctor knows all the medications your child is taking. If your child received a prescription from another doctor/specialist, it might not be recorded in your child's chart.

Reality Check

Tell your doctor if your child is taking any herbal remedies. There can be overlap in effects of herbal and over-the-counter products. For instance, a medical student recently made national news for taking ephedra (an herbal decongestant) and sudafed (a traditional decongestant) at the same time. He ended up in the ER with a heart rhythm disturbance. It pays to ask.

Q. Can you use Tylenol and an antibiotic at the same time?

It is okay to use Tylenol/Motrin, cough/cold medicine, and an antibiotic simultaneously.

Q. What does the term "off-label" mean?

It means that a pharmaceutical company has not received FDA (Food and Drug Administration) approval for a medication to be used for a particular problem or age group.

Medications are approved for use based on research studies for particular medical problems. Once a drug is available for use, doctors may find it useful to treat other ailments. In this case, a doctor might prescribe a medicine to a patient and explain that it is being used "off label."

What frequently happens in pediatric medicine is that clinical research studies are done on adults, so a medication is approved for use only in adults. When it appears to be a safe product, the medication is used in pediatric patients as well. Pediatricians feel relatively comfortable using these medications for children, but your doctor should always explain to you if he prescribes a medicine that does not have FDA approval for use in a particular age group. This problem has been a topic addressed on Capitol Hill recently. (Pediatricians support more research studies of medicines for children!)

Q. How can I find out if a generic equivalent is available for the medicine my doctor has prescribed?

Ask your doctor or pharmacist. For the medication tables below, generic availability is noted with an (*) asterisk. Note: while all medications have a generic name, not all of them are available to be purchased in generic form.

Q. How do I read a doctor's prescription? I've always wondered what they really mean.

It's written in medical abbreviations, so here's how to read it. You'll need this for the medication tables later in this appendix..

How often to take a medicine
QD: once daily
BID: twice daily
TID: three times daily (preferably every eight hours)
QID: four times daily (preferably every six hours)
QHS: once daily, at bedtime
QOD: once, every other day
PRN: as needed

How medicine is given
po: taken by mouth
pr: insert in rectum
ou: put into each eye
au: put into each ear

How medicine is dosed
1 cc (cubic centimeter) : 1ml (milliliter)
tsp: teaspoon (1 tsp is 5 cc or 5ml)
T.: tablespoon (1 T. is 3 tsp or 15cc or 15 ml)
tab: tablet
gtt: drop

Q. How do I know which medications require a prescription?

We've included some handy tables later in this chapter with information on common medicines used for treating babies. In the tables, you'll note the following symbols.
  ◆ Rx: Denotes that a product is available with a doctor's prescription only. If nothing is designated, assume the product in question is prescription-only.
  ◆ OTC: Denotes that a product is available Over The Counter (that is, without a prescription).

Q. How do I know if a medication is safe for me to take while I am pregnant or breastfeeding?

Some information is listed in the medication tables later in this appendix. Your obstetrician, pediatrician, pharmacist, and lactation consultant all have reference books in their offices with this information—if you have doubts, call them.

Breastfeeding Categories
Category 1: Okay to use while nursing.
Category 2: Okay, but use with caution.
Category 3: Unknown whether there is a risk.
NO: Definitely harmful to baby.

Pregnancy Categories
Category A: Studies have been done with first-trimester pregnancies and show no risk to fetus.
Category B: Animal studies prove medicine to be safe, but not enough data in humans yet.
Category C: Animal studies prove medicine to be harmful, but no data in humans.
Category D: Known risk to fetus, but benefit of medicine to mother may outweigh the risk.
NO: Known risk to fetus outweighs any benefit to the mother.

Drugs Of Abuse: Not To Be Used While Breastfeeding (And not recommended otherwise)
Amphetamines, Cocaine, Heroin, Marijuana, Nicotine, Phenylcyclidine[2]

Category 3 Medications (Unknown Risk)[3]
Medications in the following classes of drugs have potentially concerning effects on babies who are breastfed.
Antianxiety drugs
Antidepressant drugs
Antipsychotic drugs

Category 2 Medications (Okay, But Use With Caution)[4]
Acyclovir (Zovirax)
Cetirizine (Zyrtec)
Diphenhydramine (Benadryl)
Fluconazole (Diflucan)
Ketorolac (Toradol, Acular)
Loratidine (Claritin)
Omeprazole (Prilosec)

Category 1 Medications (Okay To Use While Breastfeeding)[5]
Acetaminophen (Tempra, Tylenol)
Albuterol (Proventil, Xopenex)
Alcohol**
Allergy injections
Amoxicillin (Amoxil)
Amoxicillin + Clavulanate (Augmentin)
Atenolol (Tenoretic, Tenormin)
Captopril (Capoten)
Cefadroxil (Duricef, Ultracef)
Cefazolin (Ancef, Kefzol)

Cefotaxime (Claforan)
Cefoxitin (Mefoxin)
Cefprozil (Cefzil)
Ceftazidime (Fortaz, Tazidime)
Ceftriaxone (Rocephin)
Chloroquine (Aralen, Novo-chloroquine)
Chlorothiazide (Hydro-Diuril)
Cimetidine (Tagamet)
Cisapride (Propulsid)
Clindamycin (Cleocin)
Codeine (Tylenol #3, Empirin #3)
Contraceptive pills
Dextromethorphan ("DM" products- Delsym, Robitussin DM)
Digoxin (Lanoxin)
Diltiazem (Cardizem, Dilacor-XR)
Enalapril (Vasotec)
Erythromycin* (E-mycin, Ery-tab)
Hydralazine (Apresoline)
Ibuprofen (Advil, Ibuprofen, Motrin, Nuprin)
Magnesium sulfate
Prednisone (Deltasone, Meticorten, Orasone)
Propranolol (Inderal)
Pseudoephedrine* (Sudafed, Actifed)
Trimethoprim/ Sulfamethoxazole (Bactrim, Septra)
Valproic Acid (Depakote, Depakene)
Verapamil (Calan, Covera-HS)
Warfarin (Coumadin)
*Medication concentrates in breast milk, but is still acceptable to use while nursing.
**Acceptable in moderation.

Medication Index

- ◆ antihelminthics (for pinworms)
- ◆ amebicides (for Giardia infection)
- ◆ antivirals (for viral infections)
8. Nutrition
    - ◆ iron supplements
    - ◆ vitamins
9. Respiratory
    - ◆ asthma
    - ◆ cough and cold preparations
10. Skin
    - ◆ antibiotic creams
    - ◆ antifungal creams
    - ◆ scabies/ head lice medications
    - ◆ steroids
    - ◆ anti-inflammatory (immunomodulators)
    - ◆ diaper rash creams

Medications

1. Allergy Medicines

These medications are used for allergic reactions, itching, and nasal congestion. For skin allergy products, see skin section (10).

Antihistamines have been around for decades. They are classified by their "generation." The first generation products are very effective but also have more side effects (drowsiness, dry mouth). Second and third generation products do not cause nearly as much sedation and can be dosed once every 24 hours. These newer products are approved for children over the age of two years, with the exception of Zyrtec, which is approved for age six months and up.

Under six months of age, doctors use all medications with caution. Antihistamines, which are usually sedating, can cause an opposite effect of excitability in infants. Consult your doctor before using any of these products.

GENERIC	BRAND	DOSE	RX?	AGE LIMIT	BREAST
Brompheniramine	Dimetapp*	QID	OTC	over 2 years	1
Cetirizine	Zyrtec	QD	Rx	over 6 months	2
Clemastine	Tavist*	BID	Rx	over 6 months	2
Chlorpheniramine	Chlor-Trimeton*	QID	OTC	over 2 years	No
Diphenhydramine	Benadryl*	QID	OTC	Infants ok	2
Fexofenadine	Allegra	QD	Rx	over 6 years	1
Hydroxyzine	Atarax*	QID	Rx	Infants ok	?
Loratidine	Claritin, Alavert	QD	OTC	over 2 yrs	1

KEY: Dose—see page 346 for an explanation of doses. Rx? Rx medications are available by prescription only; OTC is over-the-counter. Breast—see page 347 for an explanation of the safety of using these medications while breastfeeding. * A generic is available for this brand-name medicine.
Side effects: Drowsiness, dry mouth, headache, paradoxical excitability
Serious Adverse effects: tremors, convulsions

2. Dental/Mouth

Fluoride Supplements

Fluoride is a mineral well known to prevent cavities. Infants need daily fluoride intake from six months of age until age 16 years to significantly reduce cavities in both primary (baby) and secondary (adult) teeth. Fluoride is added to tap water in many cities and counties in the United States. Find out if your city has added fluoride to its water supply. If your child drinks a pint a day of water, he does not need a fluoride supplement.

So, who does need a fluoride supplement? There are four situations that call for a fluoride supplement:

1. A household that uses well water, baby is over six months old, and has no source of tap water (such as a childcare facility).
2. Baby over six months of age, exclusively breast fed, and does not drink tap water.
3. Baby over six months of age, formula is prepared with bottled water or uses ready-to-feed formula, and does not drink tap water.
4. Baby over six months of age and county water supply does not add fluoride.

If you fall into one of those categories above, the American Academy of Pediatrics and American Dental Association recommends the following dosages of fluoride (these are based on age and the amount of fluoride in your drinking water):

How much extra fluoride does your baby need?

Age	Amount of flouride in your community's water supply (in parts per million- ppm)		
	LESS THAN 0.3 PPM	0.3-0.6 PPM	GREATER THAN 0.6 PPM
0-6 months	None	None	None
6 months-3 yrs	0.25 mg	None	None
3-6 years	0.5 mg	0.25mg	None
6-16 years	1 mg	0.5 mg	None

Flouride supplments include: Luride*, Fluoritab, Pediaflor*, Poly-Vi-Flor*, Tri-Vi-Flor*. These are all available by prescription only and dosed once daily.

Possible side effects: Overuse of fluoride can cause white spots on the teeth (fluorosis). This occurs in daily doses of greater than 2 mg of fluoride /day.

Reality Check

Fluoride containing toothpaste has about 1 mg of fluoride per ribbon. Kids tend to eat toothpaste instead of spitting it out. For this reason, it is suggested NOT to use toothpaste until your child can spit (around age three). It's also a good idea to limit the volume to a pea-sized ration.

Q. Is fluoride safe? I've heard it can cause bone cancer in lab rats.

Yes it is safe. If you give toxic mega-doses of any product to rats, you will create medical problems. So, just how much flouridated water would you have to drink each day to equal the volume that the rats drank? Answer: 42 gallons a day!

Helpful Hint
Give fluoride drops on an empty stomach. Milk prevents the absorption of the medication.

3. Teething

Teething medications are topical numbing products. They are rubbed on the gums to provide temporary relief of gum pain due to tooth eruption. They are dosed four times daily. Their active ingredient is Benzocaine. The brand names are: Baby Anbesol, Baby Numz-it, Baby Oragel, and Zilactin Baby.

DR B'S OPINION: TEETHING PAIN

A dose of Tylenol (acetaminophen) is more likely to provide relief than any of the topical products. At best, the topical products provide about one hour of relief.

I do not recommend herbal teething tablets. Natural remedies for teething may contain belladonna (a neurotoxin that causes blindness) and caffeine (known to keep humans awake, not asleep).

4. Ear Medication

Antibiotic Ear Drops
For swimmer's ear (otitis externa) or for children who have ear infections with PE tubes, antibiotic eardrops are used. Because the medicine is not absorbed into the bloodstream, there are more antibiotic family choices. Below are the most popular antibiotic eardrops. Note: most products also contain a steroid. The steroid reduces the inflammation and swelling of the ear canal so the antibiotic can work more effectively.

GENERIC	BRAND	DOSE	RX
Acetic Acid	Vosol*	QID	yes
Acetic Acid + Hydrocortisone	Vosol-HC*	QID	yes
Chloroxylenol +Pramoxine + Hydrocortisone	Zoto-HC	QID	yes
Ciprofloxacin + Hydrocortisone	Cipro HC	BID	yes
Ofloxin	Floxin Otic	BID	yes
Polymyxin B + Neomycin + + steroid	Cortisporin* Pediotic	TID	yes

KEY: Dose—see page 346 for an explanation of doses. Rx? Rx medications are available by prescription only; OTC is over-the-counter. * A generic is available for this brand-name medicine.

Side Effects: Irritation of the ear canal such as itching and stinging.

Swimmer's Ear Prevention Drops

These drops dry up any left over water in the ear canal after swimming. Drops are placed in the ears immediately after swimming. These are used primarily for older kids, not infants.

You can make your own concoction: 2 drops of rubbing alcohol and 2 drops of vinegar per ear.

Brand names: Auro-Dri, Swim Ear. Both products are OTC. Active ingredient: Rubbing Alcohol

Ear Pain Drops

These are topical numbing medications, in the same mindset as using teething gels for gum pain. They have a modest effect in providing temporary relief of pain in the ear canal. (Remember that middle ear infections occur behind the eardrum.)

Numbing drops are absolutely not intended for use if a child has PE tubes (see Chapter 11 "Infections" for more details) or has ruptured the eardrum with infection.

Brand names are: Americaine, Auralgan*, Tympagesic.* Active ingredient: Benzocaine
Dosing: 2-3 drops to affected ear, QID
Rx only.

Reality Check

Although we don't find them helpful, some doctors will prescribe numbing drops for pain relief. But do NOT use the drops prior to your doctor's appointment. It makes it hard for the doctor to see the eardrum!

DR B'S OPINION

"These drops do not reach the real location of the pain (which is why many ear, nose, and throat specialists don't find these drops very helpful). Acetaminophen (Tylenol) and a heating pad (low setting) placed on the ear are more effective pain reducers than ear pain drops."

Ear Wax Drops

These drops help loosen or dissolve earwax. Earwax rarely is a problem unless it is hard and stuck in the canal (impacted). If the earwax is impacted, earwax drops loosen up and break down the earwax.

Brand names are: Auro, Debrox, and Murine eardrops. OTC Active ingredient: carbamine peroxide *Dosing: 3 drops per ear, TID, for 3 days*

Cerumenex is an earwax drop available by Rx only. Colace, a stool softener, also works nicely to soften up earwax. It's available OTC.

BOTTOM LINE

We don't recommend routine cleaning with Q-tips. Q-tips can irritate the ear canal and push the earwax backwards, creating wax that is hard and stuck (impacted).

Helpful Hints

◆ Rub the eardrop bottle in your hands for a minute or two before administering the drops. Warm drops in the ear are less bothersome than cold ones.

◆ If a child has a perforated eardrum or PE tubes, many types of eardrops should NOT be used (exception: approved antibiotic drops). Check with your doctor.

Reality Check

ENT specialists frequently use antibiotic eye drops for the ears. If you get a prescription filled for your child's ear infection and it turns out to be eye drops, don't think we have lost our minds.

One caveat here: It's okay to use *eye drops* for the ears, but you cannot use eardrops for the eyes!

6. Eye Problems

Antibiotic Eye Drops/Ointment

These are used primarily for conjunctivitis (pink eye) and corneal abrasions.

Generic	Family	Brand	Dose	Rx Only?
Ciprofloxacin	Quinolone	Ciloxan	BID/QID	yes
Erythromycin	Erythromycin	(many)*	BID/QID	yes
Gentamicin	Aminoglycoside	(many)*	QID	yes
Ofloxin	Quinolone	Ocuflox	BID/QID	yes
Tobramycin	Aminoglycoside	Tobrex*	QID	yes

KEY: Dose—see page 346 for an explanation of doses. Rx? Rx medications are available by prescription only; OTC is over-the-counter. * A generic is available for this brand-name medicine.

Side effects: Burning, itching, local irritation

7. Fever And Pain Medications

Please keep in mind the following points about fever medication:

1. If your baby is less than four weeks old and has a fever, do NOT give a fever reducing medicine—call your doctor immediately.
2. Never give aspirin to a child unless directed by a doctor. Aspirin use is associated with Reye's syndrome (liver failure) when taken during an influenza or chickenpox infection.
3. Ibuprofen is not recommended for babies under six months of age.

medications

4. Tylenol is the brand name. The generic name is acetaminophen (other brand names include Tempra, Feverall)
5. Ibuprofen: brand names are Motrin, Advil
6. Do not use more than one fever reducing medicine at a time, unless your doctor specifically recommends it.
7. REMEMBER TO USE THE DROPPER THAT COMES WITH THE PACKAGE OF MEDICINE. See Chapter 15, "First Aid" for details on fever and when to administer medication (as well as a dosing chart).

DR B'S OPINION: ALTERNATING FEVER MEDS

Unless your child is prone to febrile seizures, I do not recommend alternating fever medications during the day to keep the body temperature down. I also prefer to use acetaminophen (Tylenol) for children who are dehydrated or not eating. Ibuprofen is more likely to cause stomach upset when taken on an empty stomach.

---

8. Gastrointestinal Problems

Antacids/Gastroesophageal Reflux

GENERIC	BRAND NAME	DOSE	RX?	AGE LIMIT	BREAST
Aluminum Hydroxide	Gaviscon	QID	OTC	ask Dr.	?
Calcium Carbonate	Mylanta, Tums	TID/QID	OTC	ask Dr.	?
Lansoprazole	Prevacid	QD	Rx	ask Dr.	No
Metoclopramide	Reglan*	QID	Rx	None	3
Omeprazole	Prilosec*	QD/BID	Rx	None	2
Ranitidine	Zantac*	BID/QID	Rx	over 1 mo.	1

KEY: Dose—see page 346 for an explanation of doses. Rx? Rx medications are available by prescription only; OTC is over-the-counter. Breast—see page 347 for an explanation of the safety of using these medications while breastfeeding. * A generic is available for this brand-name medicine.

Side effects:

Aluminum hydroxide and calcium carbonate both can cause constipation and decrease absorption of other medications.

Ranitidine (Zantac) is often used first-line for gastroesophageal reflux because it has been around the longest. Most common side effects are headache and stomach upset.

Lansoprazole (Prevacid) and Omeprazole (Prilosec) are newer medications approved for children with acid reflux. Both can cause stomach upset and headaches.

Metoclopramide (Reglan) can cause sedation, headaches, and diarrhea.

 Helpful Hint
It is more effective to give these medications 30 minutes before a meal if you can.

Constipation

GENERIC	BRAND NAME	DOSE	RX?	AGE LIMIT	BREAST
Docusate	Colace	QD/QID	OTC	over 1 year	?
Glycerin	(suppository)	1 dose	OTC	None	?
Guar gum	Benefiber	QD	OTC	over 6 mos	?
Lactulose	Duphalac, Chronulac*	QD	Rx	Ask Dr.	?
Malt soup	Maltsupex	BID	OTC	over 1 month	?
Mineral oil	Kondremul	QD/ TID	OTC	over 5 years	?
Polyethylene glycol	Miralax	QD	Rx	Ask Dr.	?
Senna	Senokot	QD	OTC	over 1 mo	1

Side effects: diarrhea, bloating, gas, body salt (electrolyte) disturbances with excessive or prolonged use.

Diarrhea

GENERIC	BRAND NAME	DOSE	RX?	AGE LIMIT	BREAST
Acidophilus	Lactinex	QD	OTC	Ask Dr.	?
Bismuth subsalicylate	Pepto-Bismol*	up to 6x day	OTC	Ask Dr.	2
Loperamide	Imodium AD*	QID	OTC	over 2 yrs	1

KEY: Dose—see page 346 for an explanation of doses. Rx? Rx medications are available by prescription only; OTC is over-the-counter. Breast—see page 347 for an explanation of the safely of using these medications while breastfeeding. * A generic is available for this brand-name medicine.

Helpful Hint
Fat and fiber intake both help bulk up the stools.

Reality Check
Pepto-Bismol has a common side effect of causing a temporary blackened tongue and black poop. Because it contains an ingredient similar to aspirin, some doctors have concerns about use when a child has chickenpox or an influenza-like illness (there is a risk of Reye's syndrome).

BOTTOM LINE
If diarrhea has been going on more than a week, check in with your doctor. Doctors also want to know about blood or mucus in the stools. (See Chapter 15 First Aid for more).

DR B'S OPINION

"In general, the only product I recommend is acidophilus. The other products have the potential to create problems by impairing the motility of the intestines to remove the infection."

medications

Gas/Colic

GENERIC	BRAND NAME	DOSE	RX?	AGE LIMIT	BREAST
Hyoscyamine	Levsin*	QID	Rx	None	?
Simethicone	Mylicon, Phazyme*	up to 12x day	OTC	None	?

Reality Check

Remember, there is no miracle cure for either gas or colic. These products are okay to try, but they may not work.

Vomiting

GENERIC	BRAND	DOSE	RX?	AGE LIMIT	BREAST
Dimenhydrinate	Dramamine*	QID	OTC	over 2 yrs	No
Diphenhydramine	Benadryl*	QID	OTC	over 6 mos.	2
Phosphorated-Carbohydrate	Emetrol*	QID	OTC	Ask Dr.	?
Promethazine	Phenergan*	QID	Rx	over 2 yrs	?

KEY: Dose—see page 346 for an explanation of doses. Rx? Rx medications are available by prescription only; OTC is over-the-counter. Breast—see page 347 for an explanation of the safety of using these medications while breastfeeding. * A generic is available for this brand-name medicine.

Helpful Hint

Home remedy: The equivalent of Emetrol is to give 1-2 teaspoons of heavy fruit syrup (fruit cocktail juice) every 20-30 minutes. This occasionally works to relieve nausea.

Rehydration Solutions

These products are the Gatorade equivalent for babies. They are designed to replace water, body salts, and sugar lost when a child has vomiting and diarrhea. They are most helpful in the early phase of a stomach virus when a child is just starting to take fluids after actively vomiting. Doctors prefer rehydration solutions instead of plain water, juice, milk, or soda for infants. Once a child is keeping down this clear fluid, we usually suggest that your child resume breastfeeding or formula. All products are available over the counter. See Chapter 15 "First Aid" for more information on using this product. See Appendix B "Alternative Medicine" for a recipe you can make at home.

Brand Names: Enfalyte, Gerber Pediatric Electrolyte, Kao-electrolyte, Pedialyte.*

9. Infections

Antibiotics (Bacterial infections)

This list contains the most popular choices of antibiotics (taken by mouth).

There are basically four classes of medications approved for pediatric use. There are more classes available to adults. Take special note of the class or family each medicine belongs to. If a person develops an allergic reaction to a medication, ANY antibiotic that belongs to that class is to be avoided.

In this chart, we note what these medications are typically used for (usage): Ear and sinus infections (1), Pneumonia (2), Skin infections (3), Bladder infections-UTI (4), Strep throat (5).

Note: all products are available by prescription only.

GENERIC NAME	BRAND NAME	FORM	DOSE	USAGE	PREG/BREAST
PENICILLIN FAMILY					
Amoxicillin	Amoxil, Polymox, Trimox, Wymox*	Liq/Chew	BID	1,2,4,5	B, 1
Amoxicillin+ Clavulanate	Augmentin* Augmentin ES-600	Liq/Chew	BID	1,2,3,4,5	B, 1
(Clavulanate kills resistant bacteria strains)					
Dicloxacillin	Dycill Dynapen, Pathocil	Liquid	QID	3, 5	B, ?
Penicillin V-K	Pen VeeK, V-cillinK*	Liquid	BID-QID	5	B, ?
CEPHALOSPORINS					
Cefaclor	Ceclor	Liquid	BID	1,2,5	B, ?
Cefadroxil	Duricef, Ultracef	Liquid	BID	3, 5	B, 1
Cefdinir	Omnicef	Liquid	QD/BID	1,2,3,5	B, 1
Cefpodoxime	Vantin	Liquid	QD/BID	1,2	B, 1
Cefprozil	Cefzil	Liquid	BID	1,2,3,4,5	B, 1
Ceftibuten	Cedax	Liquid	QD	1,2,5	B, 1
Ceftriaxone	Rocephin	injection	QD	1,2,3,4,5	B, 1
Cefuroxime	Ceftin	Liquid	BID	1,2,3,5	B, 1
Cephalexin	Keflex*	Liquid	TID/QID	3,5	B, 1
MACROLIDES					
Azithromycin	Zithromax	Liquid	QD	1,2,3,5	B, ?
Clarithromycin	Biaxin	Liquid	BID	1,2,3,5	C, 2
Erythromycin	E.E.S., Eryped*	Liq/chew	BID/QID	2,3,5	B, 1
Erythromycin + Sulfisoxazole	Pediazole*	Liquid	TID	1,2	C, 1
SULFONAMIDES (SULFA)					
Sulfisoxazole	Gantrisin	Liquid	QD	1,4	B/D, 2
	Used as preventative therapy only				
Sulfamethoxazole + Trimethoprim	Bactrim, Septra* Sulfatrim, TMP-SMX	Liquid	BID	1,4	C, 1

KEY: Dose—see page 346 for an explanation of doses. Rx? Rx medications are available by prescription only; OTC is over-the-counter. Breast—see page 347 for an explanation of the safety of using these medications while breastfeeding.
* A generic is available for this brand-name medicine.

Side Effects:

The most common side effects include:

1. *Diarrhea.* The antibiotic kills the bacteria causing infection, but also some normal bacterial "flora" that helps us digest food in our intestines. Lack of bacterial flora can cause malabsorption (i.e. upset stomach). ANY antibiotic can cause this problem.

2. *Yeast Infections.* Again, the antibiotic kills both bad bacteria and certain bacterial flora that live in our mouths and on our skin. Lack of normal bacteria predisposes a person to yeast infections in the mouth (thrush) and in the genital area (yeast diaper rash).

Allergic Reactions:

A true allergic reaction to these medications includes hives, lip swelling, or difficulty breathing. About 25% of patients who are allergic to the Penicillin family will also be allergic to the Cephalosporin family.

Rare Adverse Reactions:

1. Stevens-Johnson syndrome (severe allergic reaction)
2. C. difficile colitis (bacterial superinfection in intestines)

Antifungals:

GENERIC	BRAND	DOSE	USAGE	AGE LIMIT	RX	BREAST
Fluconazole	Diflucan	QD x 2 wks	Thrush	None	RX	1
Griseofulvin*	Grifulvin Grisactin Fulvicin	QD x 1month	Ringworm of Scalp	None	RX	?

Side effects: nausea, headache, rash, stomach upset

Griseofulvin can cause skin sensitivity to sunlight. Used with caution in patients with Penicillin allergy.

Helpful Hint

Griseofulvin is absorbed better when taken with something rich in fat (milk, ice cream...)

Antihelminthics (For Pinworm Infections):

GENERIC	BRAND	DOSE	AGE LIMIT	RX	BREAST
Mebendazole	Vermox*	2 doses, 2 weeks apart	over 2 years	RX	1
Pyrantel	Pin-X	2 doses, 2 weeks apart	over 2 years	OTC	?

Side effects: stomach upset, headache

KEY: Dose—see page 346 for an explanation of doses. Rx? Rx medications are available by prescription only; OTC is over-the-counter. Breast—see page 347 for an explanation of the safety of using these medications while breastfeeding. * A generic is available for this brand-name medicine.

Reality Check

Often the whole family gets treated when one child has pinworms.

Amebicides (For Giardia Infection):

GENERIC	BRAND	DOSE	AGE LIMIT	RX	BREAST
Metronidazole	Flagyl	TID for 10 days	None	RX	3

Side effects: nausea, diarrhea, hives, metallic taste, dizziness

Antivirals:

GENERIC	BRAND	DOSE	USED FOR	AGE LIMIT	RX	BREAST
Acyclovir	Zovirax	4-5x daily	Varicella Oral herpes, Zoster	None	RX	1
Amantadine*		BID	Influenza A	over 1 year	RX	1
Oseltamivir	Tamiflu	BID	Influenza	over 1 year	RX	?

Side effects: stomach upset, insomnia, headache

Adverse reactions: kidney failure with acyclovir—patient needs to be well hydrated

KEY: Dose—see page 346 for an explanation of doses. Rx? Rx medications are available by prescription only; OTC is over-the-counter. Breast—see page 347 for an explanation of the safety of using these medications while breastfeeding.
* A generic is available for this brand-name medicine.

BOTTOM LINE

Because antiviral medications work by preventing replication of the virus, the medication must be started within 48 hours of when the illness began. Otherwise, it will have no effect on the course of the illness.

10. Nutrition

Vitamin supplements for children aged birth to one are used for specific situations. These include Vitamin D for exclusively breastfed infants, and iron for children with iron deficiency anemia. A multivitamin for general well being of infants is not routinely prescribed.

Vitamins

Vitamin D supplements:

BRAND NAME	INGREDIENTS	DOSE	RX?
Tri-Vi-Sol	Vitamins A, D, C	1 ml/day	OTC
Vi-Daylin	Vitamins A, D, C	1 ml/day	OTC

Other products containing Vitamin D are multivitamins and you should consult your doctor before purchasing.

Iron Supplements:

Iron is a necessary ingredient to carry oxygen on red blood cells. Babies are born with a stockpile of iron from their mothers. However, by six months of age, they need to consume iron in their diets to meet their daily needs (11mg/day for ages six to 12 months). Some babies need an iron supplement in addition to their food intake (see Chapter 5 "Nutrition & Growth" for details of iron containing foods).

Multivitamins often contain iron (see chart above). The dose of iron in multivitamins made for infants is 9-10 mg of iron per daily dose. This meets the daily nutritional needs of a six to12 month old. If a child has iron deficiency anemia, he needs daily nutritional iron requirements PLUS an additional amount to fill back up his depleted iron stores. The only way to get the higher dose of iron is to use the specific products listed below.

Iron Replacement Therapy

Brand Names: Fer-In-Sol*, Feosol*, Icar, Niferex
Dose: Comes in drops 15mg iron per 0.6 ml. Dose is based on weight. Your doctor will calculate it for you. There are also syrups for older kids, which can be confusing!
Rx: These drugs are OTC, but are behind your pharmacist's counter so they can help you select the appropriate product.
Side effects: constipation, black looking poop, nausea, stomachache, temporary teeth staining

Helpful Hints

◆ You can avoid staining the teeth by shooting the medicine in the back of the throat. If the teeth do become stained, use baking soda on a toothbrush to remove the stains.

◆ Vitamin C improves the absorption of iron. Calcium interferes with the absorption of iron. So, if you are offering a drink with the iron medicine, offer juice—not milk.

◆ If you give the iron AFTER a meal, there is less stomach upset.

11. Respiratory Problems

Asthma

Asthma medications are divided into rescue medications and preventative/long term control medications. The rescue medicines are used as needed (with a certain interval between doses). A child is placed on preventative medicine if he:
  1. needs rescue medicine more than twice a week
  2. has his activity affected by asthma flare-ups
  3. has problems at night more than twice a month
The idea is to get the asthma under control, then cut back on the amount of medications needed to minimize flare ups.

For information on asthma and home nebulizers, see the common diseases chapter.

Rescue medicines

GENERIC	BRAND	DOSE	RX	BREAST
Albuterol	Proventil, Ventolin Accuneb*	Syrup TID Rx Nebulizer solution Q4 hrs Inhaler Q4 hrs		2
Levalbuterol	Xopenex	Nebulizer Rx solution TID		3

This class of medication is called a Beta agonist. There can be effects on the body similar to caffeine. More side effects are seen with the dose given orally (syrup) than with the doses that are inhaled (nebulizer machine, inhaler). Levalbuterol is a newer product that seems to have fewer side effects than the older albuterol product.

Side effects: Increased heart rate, palpitations, nervousness, insomnia, nausea, headache.

Preventative/Long term control medicines

GENERIC	BRAND	DOSE	RX	AGE LIMIT	BREAST
Mast cell stabilizer					
Cromolyn	Intal*	Nebulizer TID	Rx	None	?
Inhaled corticosteroid					
Budesonide	Pulmicort	Nebulizer BID	Rx	over 1yr/ask Dr.	?
Fluticasone	Flovent	Inhaler BID	Rx	over 4yrs	?
Leukotriene antagonist					
Montelukast	Singulair	Chew tab QHS	Rx	over 2 yrs	?
Long acting beta agonist					
Salmeterol	Serevent	Inhaler BID	Rx	over 4 yrs	?
Combination product					
Fluticasone + + Salmeterol	Advair	Inhaler BID	Rx	over 4yrs	?

KEY: Dose—see page 346 for an explanation of doses. Rx—Rx medications are available by prescription only; OTC is over-the-counter. Breast—see page 347

MAKE THE CALL: ASTHMA CONCERNS

If your child needs his rescue medicine more frequently than it has been prescribed, CALL YOUR DOCTOR. Here are some important points to consider:

1. Your child is air hungry and needs to be evaluated by a doctor See Chapter 15, "First Aid."

2. Administering asthma medicine more frequently than recommended can be dangerous. A doctor's office or hospital can administer asthma medicine more often than prescribed because a medical provider can be monitoring a patient for side effects of the medicine.

3. If a child is having that much trouble breathing, it is likely that he needs to receive oxygen in addition to medication, which is only available in a medical facility.

medications

for an explanation of the safety of using these medications while breastfeeding.
* A generic is available for this brand-name medicine.

Side effects:
Mast cell stabilizer: bad taste, cough, nasal congestion, wheezing.
Inhaled corticosteroid: sore throat, nosebleeds, cough, thrush (see below for more information).
Leukotriene antagonist: stomach upset, headache, dizziness.

 Helpful Hint
◆ In the past, there were no inhaled steroid options for children under four years of age. We would use oral steroids (Prednisone) to get a severe flare up under control. We now have Pulmicort respules (a grainy substance dissolved in liquid), which can be administered in a nebulizer machine. Pulmicort is very effective for younger children and has significantly fewer side effects than its oral counterpart. Many doctors feel comfortable using this product in infants even though the product is approved for ages one year and up.

◆ Always rinse your child's mouth after he has taken an inhaled steroid. It reduces the incidence of thrush.

◆ Steroid medications are always used cautiously. Steroids given by mouth (liquid/pill) are more likely to cause systemic side effects if given for a long time (more than one to two weeks). Inhaled steroids (nebulizer or inhaler) have significantly fewer side effects because only a small amount is absorbed into the bloodstream. As with any medication, the risks of taking these medications are weighed against the potential benefit of therapy for the disease.

Risks of long-term steroid use:
1. Mood change
2. Stomach upset
3. Intestinal bleeding
4. Impaired body's stress responses (HPA axis suppression: hypothalamic-pituitary-adrenal)
5. Bone demineralization (Osteopenia)
6. Weight gain, hair growth (Cushingoid features)
7. Cataracts
8. Growth suppression. There is data which shows some evidence of decreased height curves while a pre-pubertal child is taking steroids chronically. However, children with chronic problems with asthma also have poor growth. Studies have not concluded whether or not these children have 'catch up growth' when steroids are discontinued.[6]

Preventing RSV infection in premature babies
If you have a baby who has graduated from a Neonatal Intensive Care Unit, you may already know that RSV (bronchiolitis) can be a serious lung infection for a premature infant.

A new product to prevent RSV infection is called Synagis (generic name is palivizumab). This is a synthetic antibody given by a monthly injection during the peak of RSV season (November to April). The antibody provides immunity for a period of 30 days.

Children who are at risk for more severe cases of RSV are:
1. Babies born prematurely, prior to 35 weeks gestation.
2. Children with chronic lung disease under age two years.
3. Children with congenital heart disease.
4. Children with certain immune deficiencies.
5. Weight under ten pounds.
6. Children of lower socioeconomic status.
7. Males.

Children who are more likely to get RSV infection include:
1. Babies under age six months when RSV season begins.
2. Babies in daycare.
3. Multiple births.
4. Babies with school age siblings.
5. Babies exposed to smoking.

The American Academy of Pediatrics recommends monthly Synagis injections during RSV season for the following babies:
1. Children under age two years with chronic lung disease (requiring treatment within six months of RSV season)
2. Babies born at or less than 28 weeks gestation and at or less than one year of age at the start of RSV season.
3. Babies born at 29-32 weeks gestation and at or less than six months of age at the start of RSV season.
4. Babies born 32-35 weeks gestation, at or less than six months of age at the start of RSV season, AND another risk factor for likelihood of infection.

Cough And Cold Medicines

Decongestant
These medications reduce or relieve congestion in the nose. They can be taken by mouth (absorbed into bloodstream) or sprayed into the nose.
Oral decongestants: Pseudoephedrine, phenylephrine, ephedrine.
Side effects: Insomnia, restlessness, dizziness, high blood pressure, heart rhythm disturbances.

Nasal spray: Oxymetazoline (Afrin), Phenylephrine (Neosynephrine)
Side effects: stinging, burning, nosebleed, rebound nasal congestion with prolonged use (>4 days)

Nasal spray: Saline
Side effects: None! Saline is salt water. It is effective in loosening mucus and can be used as often as needed.

FYI: A very effective decongestant, phenylpropanolamine or PPA, was taken off the market a few years back because it was similar to a product used in diet pills that was also taken off the market. There are no products containing PPA available today.

Antihistamine

These medications combat the effect of histamine in the body. Histamine is released as an allergy response and causes nasal congestion. Antihistamines are frequently found in cough and cold medicines because they are sedating, improve the cough suppressant effect, and dry up a runny nose.

Common ingredients: brompheniramine, chlorpheniramine, diphenhydramine, (promethazine- Rx only), carbinoxamine

Side effects: sedation, dry mouth, blurred vision, stomach upset, paradoxical excitement in infants

Expectorant

These medications make thick mucus looser. By doing this, the mucus in the bronchial tubes (lungs) can be coughed up more easily. These medications do not suppress the cough.

Common ingredients: guaifenesin

Side effects: sedation, stomach upset, headache

DR B'S OPINION: COUGH & COLD MEDICINE

I don't like to use any of these products in children under six months of age because there is a higher chance of side effects. I usually stick with saline nose drops.

I am also not very excited about the combination products that contain a fever reducing medication. Your child may not need all of the ingredients in a particular product. Sometimes it's better to get single-ingredient medication and use what you need.

Cough Suppressant

These medications reduce the brain's "cough center" activity. These products are not recommended when someone has pneumonia. For common cold and flu bugs, this is the type of cough medicine you want to give for your child to stop coughing at night.

Common ingredients: Dextromethorphan, (codeine-Rx only), carbetapentane

Side effects: drug interactions with psychiatric medications.

FYI: A table that compares common cough suppresant and cold medicines is on our web site, Baby411.com. Click on "Bonus Material."

Helpful Hint

As you probably know, there are many cough and cold products on the market. And the table on our web site even a complete list. Most doctors become familiar with a few products and use/recommend them regularly. So, if you call us about a dose of a particular medicine, we might ask you to read the package to us so we know what is in it.

Cold Medicines For Breastfeeding Moms

Cold medicines and breastfeeding: As a general rule, products containing pseudoephedrine (decongestant) are fine. Decongestant nose sprays (like Afrin) are also okay. Antihistamines are usually okay. Some cough medicines are NOT okay.

12. Skin (Dermatologic) Products

1. Antibiotic creams are used for wound care and minor bacterial infections (impetigo, mild cellulitis).
2. Antifungal creams are used for fungus infections (ringworm, yeast infection, jock itch, athlete's foot) on the skin.
3. Scabicides and pediculocides are used for scabies and head lice.
4. Steroids are used for contact irritations (bug bites, poison ivy, local allergic reactions), seborrhea, cradle cap, and eczema. Steroids are divided into classes by their potency. Doctors always try to use the lowest potency if possible. The higher the potency, the more the risk of side effects (the high potency products can get absorbed into the bloodstream).
5. Anti-inflammatories are a sexy new product used currently only for eczema.
6. Diaper rash creams form a barrier between the irritated skin and recurrent insults caused by pee and poop.

Antibiotic Cream

GENERIC	BRAND	RX?
Bacitracin, Polymyxin B Used for minor cuts, scrapes, irritations	Polysporin	OTC
Mupirocin Used for impetigo and cellulitis	Bactroban	Rx
Neomycin Used for minor cuts, scrapes, irritations, and superficial burns	Neosporin*	OTC
Silver Sulfadiazine Antibiotic salve used for second-degree burns	Silvadene*	Rx

Side effects: Burning, stinging, itching.

Antifungal Cream

Uses:
1. Yeast diaper rash (monilial dermatitis)
2. Ringworm of skin (tinea corporis)
3. Athlete's foot (tinea pedis)
4. Jock itch (tinea cruris)

GENERIC	BRAND	USED FOR	AGE LIMIT	RX
Clotrimazole 1%	Lotrimin AF*	1, 2, 3, 4	None	OTC
Ketoconazole 2%	Nizoral*	1,2,3,4	Over 2 yrs	Rx
Nystatin	Mycostatin, Nilstat*	1	None	Rx
Econazole	Spectazole*	1,2,3,4	None	Rx

KEY: Rx—Rx medications are available by prescription only; OTC is over-the-counter. * A generic is available for this brand-name medicine.

Reality Check

Ringworm of the scalp (called tinea capitis) requires an antifungal medication by mouth for four to eight weeks. The fungus gets imbedded in the hair follicles and will not respond to an antifungal cream.

Scabicides And Pediculocides

Generic	Brand	Dose	Used for	Age limit	Rx
Acetic acid	Klout	No limit	Head lice	None	OTC
Lindane1%**	Lindane	1 dose	Head lice, scabies	Over 1 yr	RX
Malathion	Ovide	2 doses, 1 week apart	Head lice	Over 6 yrs	RX
Permethrin 1%	NIX	1-2 doses, 1 week apart	Head lice	None	OTC
Permethrin 5%	Elimite*, Acticin	1-2 doses 1 week apart	Head lice scabies	None	RX
Pyrethrum***	A-200* Pyrinyl* RID, Pronto*	2 doses, 1 week apart	Head Lice	None	OTC

**Medication has significant side effects/potential for seizures. Other medications are better alternatives.
***Medication is derived from the chrysanthemum flower. Avoid use with a ragweed allergy.

Side effects: burning, itching, redness, rash

Helpful Hints for Head Lice

1. Use OTC products as directed. I know you are grossed out, but don't overdose the medicine.
2. Don't use more than one medicine at a time.
3. Use the nit combs religiously every three days.
4. Wash clothing and bed linens in hot water and dry on the hot cycle.
5. Soak combs and hairbrushes in rubbing alcohol for one hour.

Reality Check

◆ When head lice enters your home, treat any family member who has an itchy scalp.

◆ When scabies enters your home, treat *all* family members, regardless of whether they have symptoms or not.

Steroids

◆ Low potency: can be used for longer periods (months) of time without side effects, okay to use on the face

◆ Mid potency: okay to use for short periods (weeks) of time without side effects, use with doctor's recommendation on the face

◆ High potency: okay to use for limited period (days) of time without side effects, do not use on the face

GENERIC	BRAND	POTENCY	DOSE	Rx/OTC
Hydrocortisone 0.5%	Cortaid, etc*	Low	BID	OTC
Hydrocortisone 1%	Cortaid, etc*	Low	BID	OTC
Hydrocortisone 2.5%	Hytone*	Low	BID	Rx
Triamcinolone 0.025%	Aristocort, Kenalog*	Low	BID	Rx
Desonide 0.05%	Desowen*	Mid	BID	Rx
Hydrocortisone valerate	Westcort*	Mid	BID	Rx
Hydrocortisone butyrate	Locoid	Mid	BID	Rx
Mometosone furoate	Elocon	Mid	QD	Rx
Triamcinolone 0.1%	Aristocort, Kenalog*	Mid	BID	Rx
Betamethasone	Diprolene*	High	BID	Rx
Diflorasone diacetate	Psorcon*	High	BID	Rx
Fluocinonide	Lidex*	High	BID	Rx
Triamcinolone 0.5%	Aristocort, Kenalog*	High	BID	Rx

KEY: Dose—see page 346 for an explanation of doses. Rx? Rx medications are available by prescription only; OTC is over-the-counter. * A generic is available for this brand-name medicine.

Side effects: skin irritation, decreased pigmentation, thinning of skin
Rare adverse reactions:
HPA axis (adrenal gland suppression)—only with high potency steroids

Anti-inflammatory cream

GENERIC	BRAND	DOSE	Rx/OTC
Pimecrolimus	Elidel	BID	Rx
Tacrolimus -.03%, 0.1 %	Protopic	BID	Rx

Side effects: burning, redness, itching
Rare adverse reactions: worsens warts, herpes, and chicken pox infections

Diaper rash creams

The idea behind all of the products listed below is to provide a barrier between the skin and moisture (pee and poop). When applying these creams and ointments, it is key to apply liberally and frequently.

Dr. B's opinion: I prefer creams to powders. When powder is applied, there is a risk that the baby will inhale the powder.

Diaper rash creams

A+D ointment	OTC
Boudreaux's Butt Paste	OTC
Dr. Smith's Diaper Ointment	OTC
Silvadene	Available by Rx only.
	Used for diaper that looks like a burn.
Triple Paste	OTC
Vaseline	OTC
Zinc Oxide (brands: Desitin, Balmex)	OTC

BOTTOM LINE

Many pediatricians have a secret recipe of salves and barrier creams that pharmacies will make especially for them. If none of these over the counter products are working, it's time to visit your pediatrician for some help.

Appendix B

Alternative Medicines

Have you ever asked your doctor about an alternative medical therapy and gotten an odd reply? Traditional doctors frequently have a negative attitude about herbs, and often with just cause. Here are the concerns:

1. There are very few scientific studies that prove with statistical significance that an herbal remedy will work.
2. There are no required clinical research trials that test herbal products on humans to prove that they are safe before they are sold to the public.
3. Herbal remedies fall into the category of "foods" by the FDA (Food and Drug Administration). This is a convenient loophole for herbal product manufacturers. This means that they do not need to do any of the scientific research that a pharmaceutical company does to market their medications. This is based on federal legislation from 1994.
4. Production is not standardized. The potency and purity of the product may vary tremendously. This is especially true for products that contain expensive herbs (e.g. ginseng).
5. The claims on the label for marketing purposes do not require scientific evidence that the information is accurate. So, consumers don't have any protection against misleading information.

FYI: Herbs produced in China are often laced with unlabeled products such as steroids and antibiotics to make them more potent. Also know that

DR B'S OPINION: HERBAL REMEDIES

Disclaimer: I am a medical doctor trained in the art and science of traditional medicine. My training did not include acupuncture, spinal manipulations, or education about over the counter 'natural' products. So, like many other physicians, I have a certain degree of skepticism about both their usefulness and their safety—particularly when used in children.

developing countries may sell products that are contaminated with mercury, arsenic, and lead.[1]

What you see may not be what you get

This is a reprint of a scientific paper's abstract that demonstrates the lack of uniformity in herbal products on the market:

Echinacea and Truth in Labeling[2]

"Herbal medications are big business in the United States, given that the touted uses of herbal remedies are considerable. However, their effectiveness in preventing and treating disease remains largely unknown due to lack of prospective, placebo-controlled trials. More than $5 billion are spent on herbal medicines each year in the US, and Echinacea sales represent 10% of this herbal market. Because the FDA does not currently require formal evaluation and approval of herbal medicines, labels on these products may not only represent inaccurate claims of efficacy but may have absent or erroneous information as to the content in the medication. Many labels on herbal remedies use the term "standardization" to imply that an herb is uniformly comparable with other preparations of the same herb. These authors examined 59 Echinacea single herb preparations bought within a two-day period from a range of stores in a major metropolitan area to examine whether the labeling claim "standardized" indicated a more accurate account in milligrams of that herb. In addition, these investigators used current FDA recommendations in labeling to assess the products. These included the inclusion of a Dietary Supplement Statement, a Supplemental Facts Box, FDA Disclaimer, and Nutrition Facts. Of the samples, only 7% met all four of the FDA's labeling requirements. *Six of the samples contained no measurable Echinacea.* The measured content of 31 of the samples (53%) agreed with the labeling. The non-standardized group had almost twice the labeled milligrams as compared with the standardized group. However, the degree of inaccuracy of labeled to measured milligrams was not statistically significant between the two groups."

Despite physicians' concerns, herbal remedies have captured a significant market share of health care spending. It's no wonder that even the most traditional American companies are jumping on the bandwagon to make their products more "natural" (such as Johnson and Johnson's Herbal Baby Shampoo).

So, if herbs are so popular, why doesn't the government to regulate their contents like medications? Because the dietary supplement industry has a very powerful lobbying group. They have contributed a great deal of money to both political parties. The Dietary Supplements Health and Education Act of 1994 (co-authored by Iowa Democrat Tom Harkin and Utah Republican Orrin Hatch) protects the dietary supplement industry and lets the consumer use these products at their own risk. Both Harkin and Hatch recently received awards from the National Nutritional Foods Association for supporting their cause. These and other politicians have also received donations from this group to their political campaigns.

DR B'S OPINION:
TELL YOUR DOCTOR

A recent article in a parenting magazine stated that 12% of all children have been given alternative therapies. Patients are using these products—most of the time without their doctor's knowledge. Parents don't tell the doctor they are trying herbals because a) they fear that their decision will not be respected or b) think the doctor won't know anything about the product.

The truth is, I respect parents' decisions even though I may not agree with them. As far as my knowledge about herbal remedies, I am learning as I go along. *But it is very important to tell your doctor if you are giving your child an herbal remedy. Some herbal products have significant drug interactions with other medications your doctor might be prescribing.*

Attempts to revise this act have failed in the past due to political pressure (and money) from this lobbying group. There are renewed discussions of changing this act in the current legislature, however.[3]

Why do people choose herbal therapies? Two reasons: first, because it is a "natural" product, people *think* it is safe. And secondly, because traditional medications are not solving the medical problem.

Compare herbs to traditional medicine. Many traditional medications are based on naturally occurring products. Penicillin is derived from a mold. Digoxin, a popular heart drug, is based on the digitalis plant. It is true that certain naturally occurring products have medical value. The difference between herbs and medications is *how they are tested and regulated.* Some herbs have absolutely no therapeutic value. And some herbs are so potent, they can be harmful.

Consider alcohol and tobacco. Both have known effects on the body. Both are legal for use. But long term, chronic use of these products also can cause problems. These products are as natural as the herbs you are trying. No one knows what long-term problems *some* herbs can create.

Herbs: A review of uses and precautions

Aloe Vera

Uses: Minor burns, eczema, constipation
Scientific Data: Good evidence that it promotes wound healing.
Precautions: Overusing aloe as a laxative has been linked to increased cancer risk.
Not safe for use as a laxative in children under 12 yrs of age.[4]

Calendula

(calendula officinalis)
Uses: Acne, allergies, burns, conjunctivitis
Scientific Data: Some evidence that it promotes wound healing in rats.

alternatives

Precautions: Allergic reactions can occur, and can cause eye irritation. Not recommended for use in the eye.[5]

Chamomile

(anthemis nobilis)
Uses: acne, allergies, colds, colic, diaper rash, ear infections, eczema, sleep problems, sore throats, vomiting.
Scientific Data: Some data shows 3-4 oz per day of a combination (chamomile, fennel, vervain, licorice, balm mint) herbal tea improves symptoms of colic. Some evidence of improved wound healing.
Precautions: Infant botulism has been reported from contaminated home-grown chamomile tea. Allergic reactions.[6]

Echinacea

Uses: allergies, colds, sore throats
Scientific data: Clinical studies show NO benefit in reducing length and severity of cold symptoms.
Precautions: It can cause allergic reactions in some people.[7]

Ephedra

Found in: Ma Huang: Mexican, Mormon or Miner's Tea; Desert Herb (original source of ephedrine)
Uses: colds, allergies, bodybuilding, weight loss
Scientific Data: There is proven benefit for use as a decongestant.
Precautions: Over 1000 cases of toxicity and over 100 deaths have been reported while using this product (including Baltimore Orioles pitcher Steve Bechler). A majority of these cases occur in children and adolescents. The Metabolife company received 13,000 consumer complaints about health related issues as of August 2002.

Evening Primrose Oil

(Oenothera biennis)
Uses: allergies, eczema, attention deficit disorder
Scientific Data: Some evidence of benefit for eczema.
Precautions: Stomachache, headaches reported.[8]

Fennel

(foeniculum vulgare)
Uses: colic, gas, diarrhea, colds, conjunctivitis
Scientific Data: Only one study has been done which shows some benefit for colic, in combination with other herbs.
Precautions: None[9]

Garlic

(allium sativum)
Uses: ear infections, colds, high cholesterol, high blood pressure
Scientific Data: NO benefit has been proven in reducing risk factors for heart disease in children who had hereditary high fat (lipid) levels.
Precautions: Gas and heartburn side effects. Interferes with platelet activity (blood clotting cells) if taken with anti-coagulant medicine.[10]

Ginger

(Zingiber officinale)
Uses: colds, diarrhea, headaches, nausea, vomiting, colic
Scientific Data: Some evidence for use in motion sickness. No studies done in children.
Precautions: heartburn. Not for use if prone to gallstones[11]

Golden seal

(Hydratis canadensis)
Contains Berberine
Uses: allergies, diarrhea, sore throats, nausea, vomiting, wound healing
Scientific Data: Some evidence of anti-bacterial properties against Salmonella (1).
Precautions: NOT for use in pregnancy, breastfeeding, or in infants. Berberine can cause jaundice by affecting bilirubin metabolism.[12]

Licorice

(glycyrrhiza glabra)
Uses: allergies, asthma, cough, eczema, sore throats, canker sores
Scientific Data: Minimal data on canker sores done on 20 patients, one study on eczema.
Precautions: Long-term use has similar effects to steroids (high blood pressure, altered body salts). Heart rhythm disturbances possible. Not for use with diabetes, liver, kidney disease.[13]

Peppermint

(Mentha piperita)
Uses: decongestant, cough, irritable bowel syndrome, headaches, itching
Scientific Data: Data shows that peppermint actually INCREASES nasal congestion but people subjectively report that they can breathe better.
Precautions: Heartburn. Peppermint oil should not be placed in nasal passages of babies as it increases risk of apnea (cease of breath)[14]

Slippery Elm Bark

(Ulmus fulva)
Uses: colds, diaper rash
Scientific Data: NONE
Precautions: Can cause skin rashes[15]

DR B'S OPINION: NEW STUDIES MAY SHED LIGHT ON ALT MEDS

By looking at this section, you can see why doctors hesitate to use many of these remedies, particularly in children.

The NIH (National Institutes of Health) has numerous scientific trials ongoing to study the effects and safety of herbal medicines. Hopefully, this will provide the data that physicians need to feel comfortable prescribing these products to their patients.

BOTTOM LINE

Just because it's natural doesn't mean it's safe. Get educated about these products before using them.

DR B'S OPINION

Many people want to use homeopathic teething remedies. Some of these products contain belladonna, a neurotoxin that causes blindness. I feel very uncomfortable giving belladonna to anyone, particularly a baby.

What is *probably* safe to use on your baby (with several disclaimers via our attorneys):

1. Calendula based diaper rash cream (although Lanolin cream is just as "natural").
2. One or two ounces of chamomile tea daily for colic.
3. Baby's Bliss Gripe Water (made of ginger and fennel) for gas and colic.
4. Acidophilus/Lactobacillus supplements for babies over six months of age with diarrhea.

For more information on this topic, check out *The Holistic Pediatrician*, by Kathi J. Kemper, M.D. (see Appendix G). She is a well-respected pediatrician who has done a great deal of research on alternative therapies.

Check out her website at www.mcp.edu/herbal.

Complementary Therapies

DR B'S OPINION

Again, I did not go to massage therapy or chiropractor school. So, I can only call it as I see it, folks.

I think that infant, child, and spouse massage all have therapeutic benefits. The laying on of hands, for most people, is very soothing and comforting.

Spinal manipulations are another story. I can see how an adult with chronic back pain might benefit from this therapy. I cannot support this therapy in children. There are no scientific studies to prove this treats any ailment. And chiropractors receive no special training in the care of children.

Home Remedies

Not every ailment requires a trip to the pharmacy. Here is a list of household items and remedies that often provide symptomatic relief for various problems.

Abdominal pain/gas/colic

Give your child a bath. The warm water is soothing. Playing in the bathtub is also a nice distraction technique.

Bruises

Pull out a bag of frozen vegetables and place on the site.

Common Cold (URI)

Make your own saline (salt water) nose drops. Take 1/2 teaspoon of salt and add to 8 oz. of water. Use as much as needed.

Chicken soup. Every culture has their own recipe, and for good reason. The high salt and water content is good for hydrating a child with a fever.

Pull out the humidifier. This moistens the air your child breathes, and loosens the mucus in his nose.

Cradle cap

Massage olive oil into the scalp. Then lift off the plaques.

Croup

Take your child into the bathroom. Close the door. Turn on the shower for ten to 15 minutes. The warm mist will help relax the airway.

If this technique doesn't work, walk outside with your child. The cold night air will often shrink up the swollen airway. It also changes the scenery for your child, which has a therapeutic effect too.

Croup usually occurs in the wintertime. If you live in a warm climate, this might not work for you.

Diaper rash

Good old Vaseline works well. It provides a barrier between the skin and moisture.

Leave your baby open to air (diaper-less) in a safe place inside or outside your house.

Use a blow dryer on the lowest setting to dry baby's bottom.

Some doctors recommend applying liquid antacids (milk of magnesia, kaopectate) to the diaper rash. It might be worth a try.

Vomiting and Diarrhea

Make your own Pedialyte solution. Here is the recipe:

4 cups of water
1/2 tsp of salt
2 Tbsp. of sugar
1/2 tsp of instant Jell-O powder for flavor

Ear infections

Use a heating pad on low setting up to the ear.

Want to prevent your child's ear infections? Stop smoking.

To prevent swimmer's ear, you can make your own "Swim-ear" drops. The alcohol will dry up the water left in the ear canal. The vinegar changes the pH of the ear canal so bugs won't want to grow there. Here's the recipe:

2 drops rubbing alcohol
2 drops of vinegar

Eczema

Keeping the skin moist is the key. The best moisturizer (although not very practical) is good old Vaseline. Lube your child up head to toe.

Eye stye

Place a warm tea bag over the eyelid. It is soothing and reduces the swelling.

Lice

Put mayonnaise on your child's hair at bedtime. Cover with a shower cap. Rinse off in the morning. There seems to be limited success in smothering the lice with this technique. I used to tell people to use Vaseline instead of mayonnaise until I received too many phone calls about getting the Vaseline out!

Sore throat

Make a milkshake or smoothie (depending on the age of your child). Cold drinks feel good and are a nice way to get the fluid intake in. This idea makes me very popular with my patients.

Warts

Try duct tape. A recent study showed that smothering the warts suppresses the growth of the virus that causes them. Apply a new piece of duct tape to the wart nightly and leave on for the day. It takes about six weeks.

Appendix C

Lab Work & Tests

When The Parent Wants Tests Done

Parents frequently ask their doctor to order lab work on their child. Doctors are less interested in getting lab work done if they are comfortable in making a diagnosis. But, doctors also know that a parent may bring their child in for the common cold and are actually concerned that the child has leukemia or some other devastating diagnosis. In medical terms, this is called "The Hidden Agenda." It's perfectly fine to have that agenda—you are a parent. But, don't keep it a secret. Your doctor won't laugh at you. What we will do is make sure that your child does not have the problem that is keeping you up at night worrying.

What you need to know is that there is no one "test" that will uncover every disease that you have concerns about (like a total body CAT scan or a comprehensive blood test panel). In the past, doctors would perform annual blood metabolic panels on adults to go on a fishing expedition for abnormalities. This is out of vogue for adults and has never been standard practice for children.

What we might do is order a particular test that would help to diagnose or rule out the concern you have.

When The Doctor Wants Tests Done

Pediatricians can frequently make a correct diagnosis of illness in a child without any tests. I wish I could say it's because we are so much smarter than our other doctor colleagues. The truth is, childhood illnesses are often infections that follow classic patterns. And rashes, which occur more in kids than adults, are helpful in determining the cause of illness.

When do doctors order a test?

1. When there is something about the child's illness history or examination that may indicate a bacterial infection.
2. When there is a concern infection is bacterial and cultures are needed to know what bug the patient has (so it can be treated appropriately).
3. When a child has a fever with no obvious source.
4. When a baby under three months has a fever.
5. When your doctor thinks your child has a broken bone.

6. When your doctor feels a hip "click" in a newborn. Testing will verify he doesn't have a congenitally dislocated hip.

7. When a child is vomiting bile or has intractable vomiting.

8. When a child has blood in his poop.

9. When a child has pain when he urinates.

10. When a child's head size is enlarging across percentiles (in other words, the head is growing much faster than the rest of the body).

11. When a child's head size is *not* enlarging.

12. When a child is failing to thrive (not gaining weight).

13. When a child wheezes for the first time and it doesn't sound like RSV bronchiolitis.

14. If an abnormality is found during a regular exam (such as distended abdomen, swollen testes).

15. When a child is drinking or urinating excessively.

16. When a child has excessive bruising.

17. When a child has petechiae.

18. When a child has a persistent fever (five days or more).

19. When a newborn is jaundiced to the level below the belly button.

20. When a child is disoriented.

21. When a child has a seizure for the first time.

22. When a child appears dehydrated and the doctor needs to decide how dehydrated he is (that is, does he need to be admitted to the hospital and get IV fluids).

23. When a child bleeds excessively—with cuts or nosebleeds.

24. When a mother has Blood Type O. Your doctor needs to know the baby's blood type so the doctor can be prepared for potential newborn jaundice problems.

25. When your doctor thinks a child has pneumonia and want to confirm it.

26. When a parent is worried.

27. When a child is limping.

28. When a child has recurrent bacterial infections (not just ear infections) such as pneumonia, sinus infections, skin infections.

29. When a child has chronic or severe problems with wheezing.

30. Anytime a child is jaundiced out of the newborn period.

31. When a child has a heart murmur that does not sound like an innocent heart murmur.

32. When a child has an irregular heartbeat.

33. When a child has a bladder or kidney infection.

34. When a child has swallowed a non-food object.

With that said, here are the most common tests we order and what they mean.

Imaging Studies

Ultrasound

The beauty of ultrasonography is that no radiation is used. The technology involves use of sonar waves and computer imaging. Doppler flow studies in addition to ultrasound pictures are helpful in looking at blood flow. Ultrasound pictures can be limited, however. Gas and fat obstructs the view.

Abdominal. Looks at the anatomy of the liver, gallbladder, spleen. Not as good at looking at intestines. Detects pyloric stenosis, intussusception, gallstones, masses.

Head. Looks for bleeding inside the skull. Wand is placed on top of the anterior fontanelle (soft spot) to see inside. Not used once fontanelle has closed. Detects intraventricular hemorrhage (IVH), a problem that can occur in babies born prematurely.

Hip. Looks at the hip joint. Detects congenital hip dislocations in infants under four months of age.

Heart (echocardiogram with Doppler). Looks at the anatomy of the heart and the great blood vessels coming off of the heart. Detects heart defects.

Kidney (renal). Looks at the anatomy of the kidneys. Detects evidence of enlargement, fluid collection (hydronephrosis), and infection.

Pelvic. Looks at anatomy of the ovaries, uterus, bladder. Detects ovarian cysts, masses. Also detects location of a testes if it has not descended into the scrotum.

Spine. Looks for spina bifida, an abnormal formation of the spine

Testicular, with Doppler flow. Looks at the anatomy of the testes. Detects a twisted testes and can assess blood flow to the testes. Also detects some hernias.

Plain x-rays

X-rays use diffraction of low doses of high-speed electrons (radiation) to project an image. Solid or fluid filled objects appear white and air appears clear. As a general rule, plain x-rays are better at detecting bone problems, and less helpful at assessing problems with "soft tissues."

Abdomen. Looks at the anatomy of the intestines, liver, spleen. Detects intestinal obstructions, malrotations, constipation. Can detect some foreign bodies (swallowed objects that are metal).

Chest. Looks at the anatomy of the heart, lungs, ribs. Detects fluid (blood, pus) in lungs, masses in lungs, enlargement of the heart, rib fractures, foreign inhaled objects.

Extremities. Looks at the bones of the arms and legs. Detects fractures (broken bones), fluid or swelling occasionally. Less helpful in detecting problems with muscles, tendons, and joints.

Neck. Looks at the anatomy of the throat (epiglottis, tonsils, adenoid, trachea). Detects swelling of these areas, location of some swallowed objects.

Skull. Looks at the anatomy of the skull bones. Detects craniosynostosis, fractures.

Sinus. Looks at the anatomy of the sinus cavities of the face. Detects *acute* sinus infections by identifying an air/fluid level. Not helpful in detecting chronic sinus infections.

Spine. Looks at the anatomy of the vertebrae from the neck to the buttocks. Detects fractures, slipped discs, scoliosis.

CT/MRI with or without contrast

Computerized Tomography (CT) uses x-ray technology (radiation) to look at cross sectional slices of the body in a two-dimensional picture. Magnetic Resonance Imaging (MRI) uses a magnetic field to detect the body's electromagnetic transmissions. MRI's produce narrow slices of the body without radiation.

As a general rule, these studies are better at detecting abnormalities with soft body tissues and less helpful with bone problems. The decision to perform a CT versus an MRI is based on the particular problem that is being assessed.

Abdomen. Looks at the anatomy of the liver, spleen, pancreas, gallbladder, intestines, kidneys. Detects masses, tumors, abscesses—including appendicitis, fluid collections, trauma.

Chest. Looks at the anatomy of the lungs and heart. Detects masses, tumors, fluid collections, congenital abnormalities, trauma.

Extremity. Looks at the anatomy of the arm or leg. Detects fractures, torn ligaments, masses, tumors, osteomyelitis (infection).

Head. Looks at the anatomy of the brain. Detects masses, tumors, obstruction of spinal fluid flow (hydrocephalus), evidence of stroke (cerebrovascular accident), evidence of trauma, bleeding.

Lymph node. Looks at the anatomy of a concerning (swollen) lymph node. Detects pus (infection), masses, congenital cysts.

Pelvic. Looks at the anatomy of the ovary, uterus, bladder. Detects masses, tumors, fluid collections.

Sinus. Looks at the anatomy of the sinus cavities. More helpful imaging study than plain x-rays. Detects obstruction to flow in the sinuses, chronic sinus infections, masses/polyps.

Special studies

Barium swallow/Upper GI. Looks at the anatomy of the upper gastrointestinal tract (esophagus, stomach, upper small intestine). Detects anatomic abnormalities, hiatal hernias, pyloric stenosis, ulcerations, narrowings. Although gastroesophageal reflux may be seen (barium goes backwards), it doesn't tell you the severity of the reflux. It also does not rule out reflux as a diagnosis.

Bone scan. Nuclear medicine study (uses a radio-isotope to be visualized on x-ray). Looks at the all of the bones of the body in one study. Hot and cold "spots" detect areas of inflammation. Detects: infection, tumors, avascular necrosis, child abuse.

Voiding Cystourethrogram. Looks at the flow of urine from kidney to ureters to bladder to urethra. Detects vesicoureteral reflux in children prone to bladder infections.[1]

Laboratory Tests

Blood tests

Amylase. This test looks at the level of an enzyme that the pancreas makes. Detects: pancreatitis

Basic Metabolic Panel. This is a battery of tests that includes *sodium, potassium, chloride, bicarbonate, blood urea nitrogen, creatinine, glucose.* This combination of tests assesses body fluid and salt (electrolyte) balance as well as kidney and adrenal function.
Detects: Dehydration, kidney dysfunction, diabetes, hypoglycemia, adrenal dysfunction

Bilirubin. This test assesses the level of this substance circulating in the bloodstream. Newborns uniquely have higher levels than any other time in life because:
1. newborn metabolism is not functioning at 100%
2. newborns are not eliminating bilirubin in their stool yet
3. newborns have bilirubin load due to prematurity, birth trauma, or blood type incompatibility.
A total level is assessed as well as *direct* and *indirect* levels. These indicate the cause of the total elevation.
Beyond the newborn period, any evidence of jaundice prompts a lab evaluation.
Detects: Hyperbilirubinemia, Hepatitis, Biliary Atresia, gallstones, hemolytic anemia

Blood culture. see below

Blood sugar (glucose). This test assesses the body's metabolism of sugar. A random level above 110 is concerning for diabetes. In newborns, a level less than 40 is concerning for hypoglycemia. Levels less than 60 in children is concerning for hypoglycemia.
Detects in newborns: Hypoglycemia in large birth weights, babies whose mothers have gestational diabetes or diabetes, body temperature irregularities, lethargy
Detects in children: Diabetes, hypoglycemia

Blood type. This test determines what proteins sit on the surface of a patient's red blood cells. There are A and B proteins. The AB blood type means both A and B protein are present. The O blood type means there

lab tests

are no proteins present. Rh typing refers to the presence (+) or absence (-) of another type of protein that sits on the red blood cell surface. These tests are necessary when a blood transfusion is needed. In an emergency situation, however, everyone gets O (-) negative blood. Most hospitals no longer test a newborn's blood type on a routine basis.

Cholesterol level. See lipid panel

Complete Blood Count (CBC). This refers to a test that looks at the number of white blood cells, red blood cells, and platelets that are circulating in the bloodstream.

1. *White blood cell count (WBC).* These cells fight infection, but also rise with inflammation. An elevated count is concerning for a bacterial infection. A depressed count is due to decreased bone marrow production (where white blood cells are made)—usually caused by viral infections (e.g. influenza, mononucleosis).

2. *White blood cell count differential.* Not only is the number of white blood cells counted, but the types of white blood cells are identified in a CBC. The types of cells also give your doctor clues as to the disease process going on.

◆ *Neutrophils (PMN's)-* Cells that fight bacteria. If more than 50% of the WBC's are this type, the likelihood of a bacterial infection is greater.

◆ *Lymphocytes:* Cells that fight viruses. If more than 50% of the WBC's are this type, the likelihood of viral infection is greater.

◆ *Eosinophils:* Cells that fight parasites. Also revved up by allergies. If more than 10-15% of these cells are present, it prompts an investigation.*

3. *Hematocrit/Hemoglobin.* These measurements assess the amount of red blood cells in the circulation. Low levels detect anemia.

4. *Platelet count.* These cells help clot the blood. A low level detects a cause for bleeding problems. A low level can also suggest bone marrow suppression (where platelets are made) or an autoimmune disorder. Platelet counts can be elevated with infection or inflammation.

*When all thee cell lines (white, red, platelet) are depressed, there is a concern for leukemia.
Uses: infection, inflammation, leukemia, anemia, bleeding disorder

Comprehensive Metabolic Panel. This is a large battery of tests that assesses adrenal, kidney, liver, gallbladder, fluid and electrolyte balance, and a measure of general nutrition. Many physicians pick a select number of these tests and not the whole panel. These tests include:

Albumin
Alkaline phospatase
Alanine Aminotransferase (ALT)
Aspartate Aminotransferase (AST)
Bicarbonate
Bilirubin
Blood Urea Nitrogen (BUN)
Calcium

Chloride
Creatinine
Glucose
Phosporous
Potassium
Sodium
Total Protein

Detects: Liver dysfunction, hepatitis, gallbladder dysfunction, kidney dysfunction, dehydration, diabetes, adrenal dysfunction, malnutrition.

Chromosome analysis. This test assesses a patient's chromosomes, the part of each cell that contains genes. Blood, tissue, or an amniotic fluid sample can be tested.

Detects: Chromosomal abnormalities related to developmental delays/congenital defects; determines the sex of a baby born with ambiguous genitalia.

Coagulation studies. These tests detect an abnormality in the clotting "cascade" or chain of events that allow blood to clot. These tests include:
Bleeding Time, Factor levels, Prothrombin time(PT), Partial thromboplastin time(PTT)

Detects: Bleeding disorders—such as Hemophilia, von Willebrand's disease

Coombs test. This test looks for antibodies (reaction) to a person's blood type. In newborns whose mothers have O Blood type, many hospitals perform a Coombs test on the baby routinely. There is some mixing of mother's and fetus's blood in the placenta, which can cause a Type O mother's blood to create antibodies to a type A or B baby. These antibodies can potentially kill some of the baby's red blood cells creating an extra bilirubin load in the newborn.

Detects: Blood type incompatibility in newborns

Electrolytes. See Basic Metabolic Panel

Erythrocyte Sedimentation Rate (ESR). This test looks at how fast it takes for red blood cells to settle at the bottom of a test tube. It is a very nonspecific test, but an elevated level suggests further testing. It is a non-specific sign of inflammation.

Detects: inflammation, infection, pregnancy, malignancy, anemia

Liver function tests. This is a battery of tests that evaluates how the liver is working. It looks at products the liver is in charge of metabolizing and producing. Some tests look at the breakdown product of liver cells (but these products are also seen in muscle breakdown) so they are not specific in detecting liver disorders.
Alanine Aminotransferase (ALT)
Albumin
Aspartate Aminotransferase (AST)
Bilirubin
Total protein

Detects: Hepatitis, liver failure, drug toxicity, heart attack.

Monospot/EBV titers. For monospot, see rapid assays below.
Epstein-Barr Virus (EBV) titers detect a person's immune response (anti-bodies) to an EBV infection (mononucleosis). Because different types of antibodies are formed through the course of infection, this test differenti-ates a recent infection and a prior one.
Detects: Acute mononucleosis, prior mononucleosis.

Lipid panel/ cholesterol. This battery of tests looks at how the body metab-olizes fat. Poor fat metabolism is associated with coronary artery disease (heart disease) in later life. In children, often a random (non-fasting) choles-terol level is obtained for those at risk (family history, obesity). If that level is elevated, a full panel is done with the child fasting prior to the test.
Cholesterol
HDL
LDL
Triglyceride level
Detects: Hypercholesterolemia, hepatitis, metabolic disorders, bile duct obstruction, nephrotic syndrome, pancreatitis, hypothyroidism

Reticulocyte count. Reticulocytes are baby red blood cells. They circulate in the bloodstream while they mature. This test looks at the number of these present in the blood. A high level suggests good bone marrow produc-tion in response to anemia.
Detects: Body's response to anemia

Thyroid function tests. This is a battery of tests that assesses the function of the thyroid gland. An indirect way of testing thyroid gland function is to look at a Thyroid Stimulating Hormone (TSH) level, a hormone produced by the pituitary gland. If the thyroid gland is not functioning well (hypothy-roidism), the TSH level is elevated to stimulate the gland to work harder. This is a test included in all state metabolic screens to detect congenital hypothyroidism.
T3 (triiodothyronine)level
Thyroxine Binding Globulin
T4 (thyroxine) level
Free T3, Free T4 levels
TSH
Detects: Hypothyroidism, Hyperthyroidism

Viral titers. There are a few viruses for which a patient's antibody response can be detected. These tests are useful to make a diagnosis or confirm immunity to a particular virus.
CMV
Hepatitis A, B,C
HIV
Parvovirus
Rubella
Syphilis
Toxoplasmosis
Varicella

Urine tests

Urinalysis. This is a test that looks at the components of urine and detects any abnormal components. Urine is normally a sterile fluid, thus should not contain any bacteria or white blood cells (which fight infection). Urine does not breakdown sugar or protein, so it should not contain any of those substances. Urine is produced in the kidneys, so some abnormalities will point to a kidney dysfunction.

In children, obtaining a urine specimen can be challenging. A urine specimen needs to be clean to be able to make any decisions based on its findings. The preferred method of obtaining this specimen is to insert a small catheter in the urethra of a non-toilet trained child. If the reason for testing urine is not to look for infection, a collection bag may be placed over the urethra.

Specific gravity
pH
Color, odor
White Blood Cells
Red Blood Cells
Glucose
Protein
Nitrite
Microscopic analysis for bacteria
Detects: Bladder infection, dehydration, kidney disease, diabetes, adrenal dysfunction, metabolic disorder, kidney stones

Skin tests

PPD. This is the preferred test for exposure to tuberculosis. PPD stands for purified protein derivative, which refers to a synthetic protein "signature" that belongs to the tuberculosis bacteria. If a person has had an exposure to tuberculosis, their antibodies will also respond to this skin test. A positive test requires further evaluation and testing.

Stool tests

Occult blood. This test detects blood in the stool. A small amount of stool (poop) is placed on a special developing card. When a processing fluid is added to the specimen, it turns blue in the presence of blood.
Detects: Gastrointestinal bleeding (e.g. food allergy, infection, ulcer, inflammatory bowel disease, polyp)

Spinal fluid (CSF) tests

Cerebrospinal fluid (CSF) is a liquid that bathes the brain and spinal cord. It transports important chemicals through the central nervous system. A specimen of this fluid helps diagnose viral and bacterial infection, and tuberculosis meningitis (infection of the tissues protecting the brain), brain infection, and obstruction of the spinal fluid collecting system.

CSF is obtained by performing a lumbar puncture or "spinal tap." This sounds scary, but it is a similar concept to having an epidural placed in childbirth. A small needle is inserted between two vertebrae in the back. A small amount of fluid is collected, and then the needle is removed.

We look at the pressure of the fluid, the appearance of the fluid (should be clear/watery), the sugar/protein levels, and if there are any cells in the fluid (white, red, bacteria).

A culture of the fluid is also done (see below).

Sweat test

A specimen of sweat is obtained by warming the skin on the arm or thigh and obtaining a small amount of sweat.
Detects: Cystic Fibrosis

Cultures

This group of tests takes a particular body fluid and incubates it (creates ideal growing conditions for bugs). If there is a germ in a specimen, there is a chance to identify it. Germs that grow are very accurate for infection growing in the patient (except for contaminated/dirty specimens). But, lack of growth in culture does not necessarily rule out an infection.

Most germs will grow out in a culture within three days. Fungus infections, however, may take up to one month to grow.

Blood. Detects BACTERIAL infections
Urine. Detects bacterial infections
Spinal fluid. Detects primarily BACTERIAL infections, some VIRAL infections
Stool. Detects BACTERIAL, PARASITE, AMOEBA infections
Throat. Detects BACTERIAL infection
Sputum. Detects BACTERIAL infection
Abscess. Detects BACTERIAL infection
Viral. Detects limited number of VIRAL infections (such as Herpes, Varicella, Chlamydia)
Fungal. Detects FUNGUS infections

Rapid Antigen Assays

As a group, these tests identify responses that infections have to certain chemicals. You might think of them in a similar way to a home pregnancy test. A positive test accurately confirms infection. But a negative test does not rule *out* infection. These "assay kits" also look like a home pregnancy test. The earlier these tests are done in the course of an illness, the less accurate they are.

Strep. Throat swab specimen
Monospot. Blood specimen
Influenza. Nasal secretion specimen (not covered on many insurance plans—not in widespread use in pediatric offices)
RSV. Nasal secretion specimen. Not offered in pediatric offices. Used routinely in a hospital setting to isolate and treat patients who have this infection.
Rotavirus. Stool specimen[2]

Appendix D

Infections: The Details

Viral Infections

I. Respiratory Viruses

The Flu (Influenza)

Disease: Respiratory illness caused by either influenza A or B. A different strain causes epidemics every year. Influenza causes more severe respiratory illness than the common cold. Higher risk of secondary bacterial infections in infants, people with chronic lung disease, or other chronic diseases.

Symptoms: High fever, body aches, and chills. Then runny nose, cough and sore throat.

Diagnosis: Based on symptoms. White blood cell count is low (less than 4,000) with mostly lymphocytes. Rapid flu assay is available, but may not be covered by insurance.

Treatment: Amantadine or Tamiflu, anti-virals, can be given to children over one year old if diagnosis is made within 48 hours of becoming ill.

Contagious: From 24 hours before symptoms start, and while person has symptoms. Spread via respiratory droplets, fomites.

Incubation period: 1-3 days after exposure

Season: Winter

Prevention: Annual flu vaccine offered each November. Now recommended for children ages 6 months to 24 months old, and other high risk groups.[1]

Bronchiolitis (RSV)

Disease: RSV stands for Respiratory Syncytial Virus. It can infect anyone, but causes more severe illness in infants (especially babies born prematurely). As opposed to the common cold (upper respiratory infection), RSV attacks the tiny branches of the lower lung airways (bronchioles). Swollen bronchioles make the air flow turbulent through them, creating a wheeze with inspiration (similar to the mechanism of asthma).

Symptoms: Fever, runny nose, breathing faster than normal and wheeze, but no "distress." Infants and premature babies may have more "**RESPIRA-**

TORY DISTRESS" (see glossary). *About 30% of children who wheeze with an RSV infection will have asthma.* The cause is debatable. Does the RSV infection causes long term damage to the airways, predisposing to asthma; or are the kids who wheeze with RSV really asthmatics with sensitive airways? Regardless, damage to the bronchioles from RSV takes a long time to heal. Symptoms can go on for *weeks*.

Diagnosis: Based on symptoms. A rapid assay test is available, usually only in hospitals.

Treatment: Some kids respond to asthma medication (Albuterol) via a nebulizer machine to aerosolize the medication. Some kids need oxygen, which requires hospitalization.

Contagious: 3 to 8 days, but sometimes up to 3 weeks. Spread by fomites, respiratory droplets.

Incubation period: 2 to 8 days.

Season: Winter, early spring

Prevention: For children under age 2 who were born prematurely (less than 32 weeks gestation) or who have chronic lung disease, RSV-Antibody (Synagis) provides immunity for one month. The medication is a shot given monthly through RSV season. (It's about $1000 a shot, and the series is usually six injections). (See Appendix A "Medications" for details on Synagis.)[2]

Croup

Disease: A viral infection that attacks the voice box area. The smaller the child, the smaller the airway tube, the more problematic when the airway is swollen.

Symptoms: Fever. Cough is a classic "bark", like a seal. Always worse at night when lying down. This is a 3 *night* illness. With babies, significant swelling can occur. A squeal is heard. Persistent squealing (**STRIDOR**) more than 5 to 10 minutes is a medical emergency. Adults with croup have laryngitis instead of a bark because adults' airway tubes are larger.

Diagnosis: The bark is usually enough to prove it. A neck x-ray is occasionally done to identify the swollen area.

Treatment: Turn on the shower in a closed bathroom. The steam works well. Humidifier in room. For more severe cases, steroids (taken by mouth or a shot) help reduce the airway swelling. A breathing treatment (racemic epinephrine) also relaxes the airway for kids with stridor.

Contagious: 4 to 7 days. Spread via direct contact, fomites, respiratory droplets.

Incubation period: 2 to 6 days.

Season: Fall.[3]

2. Mouth And Tonsil Viruses

Hand-Foot-and-Mouth (Coxsackievirus)

Disease: A virus that causes ulcers in the back of the mouth, and sometimes a rash on the palms, soles, and around the anus.

Symptoms: Fever, lack of interest in eating. Rash can be flat red dots or raised like pimples. Ulcers in the *back of mouth.*

Diagnosis: The ulcers in the back of the mouth are classic. No diagnostic testing is done.

Treatment: Avoid citrus and salt. Acetaminophen (Tylenol) or Ibuprofen (Motrin) for discomfort. Make up a concoction of Benadryl and Maalox (1 tsp of each), then give about 0.8 ml of the mixture before feedings. This coats the ulcers.

Contagious: Up to 7 days. Spread through saliva, poop, and fomites. Incubation period: 3 to 6 days.

Season: Summer, fall.[4]

Oral Herpes Stomatitis

Disease: Viral infection caused by HSV Type 1. (Type 2 is genital herpes— a completely different infection). Once a person is infected, the HSV-1 lies dormant for life and can re-activate as a cold sore. Cold sores appear on the outer lip and last for a week. Cold sores spread HSV-1 to others.

The worst case scenario is a newborn who contracts HSV infection (75% of these are from genital herpes type 2, but 25% are HSV-1). These babies are at high risk of getting an infection of the brain (**ENCEPHALITIS**) from HSV.

Symptoms: Fever over 102 for a week. VERY poor fluid and food intake (at risk of dehydration). Numerous ulcers in mouth, gums, tongue called **GINGIVOSTOMATITIS.** The pain is so severe, some children avoid swallowing their saliva. These kids feel awful.

Diagnosis: Can be made just by looking at the mouth lesions (very impressive looking). Can also be grown (takes 3 days) in a culture by taking a specimen from the ulcer base. It's not always cultured because by the time the culture grows out, it's too late to treat the infection.

Treatment: FLUIDS. Acyclovir, an antiviral, is used for newborns. The gingivostomatitis is usually diagnosed too late (after two days of illness) to use an antiviral medication. Cold sores can be treated with anti-virals.

Contagious: VERY! For 7 days. Spread via saliva and direct contact with the lesions.

Incubation period: 2 to 14 days.

Season: Year round.

Prevention: Avoid contact with child if someone has an active cold sore.[5]

3. Viral Sore Throat

Disease: A viral infection that causes the tonsils to be swollen. Caused by many different viruses. Adenovirus often causes pink eye (***viral conjunctivitis***), runny nose, and ear infections in addition to a sore throat.

Symptoms: Fever, decreased appetite, redness or pus (white patches) on tonsils.

Diagnosis: Based on age group and associated symptoms. No lab test. Strep test rarely done because it is rare for babies under age two. It is extremely rare for babies under age two to get Strep (bacterial) Throat.

Treatment: To treat the symptoms only. Acetaminophen(Tylenol) or Ibuprofen(Motrin), lots to drink.

Contagious: While child has a fever. Spread by direct contact, respiratory droplets, fomites.

Incubation period: 2 to 14 days.

Season: Winter, spring, summer.[6]

4. Gastrointestinal Viruses

There are many types of viruses that are known collectively as the "stomach virus". They are all treated the same way—lots of fluids to prevent dehydration. The most notorious one of all is Rotavirus. It comes every winter.

Viral gastroenteritis (Rotavirus)

Disease: Rotavirus enters the stomach and intestines. Almost all kids get this infection by three years old. (And you can get it more than once). The kids at greatest risk are infants. They lose so much water in the diarrhea. It is hard to keep the fluid intake greater than the losses. That's why some babies get admitted to the hospital for IV fluids.

Symptoms: Fever, vomiting, and extremely watery diarrhea (often more than 20 times a day). This lasts for about a week.

Diagnosis: Usually obvious by the volume of diarrhea! Assay test is available.

Treatment: Lots of fluids. See Diarrhea section in Chapter 15, "First Aid."

Contagious: VERY. FOR THE WHOLE TIME YOUR CHILD HAS DIARRHEA. Spread via contact with infected poop, fomites. Spreads like wildfire through childcare centers and households.

Incubation period: 1 to 3 days.

Season: Winter (starts southwest and moves northeast every year-the opposite of birds)

Prevention: There was a vaccine that came out (Rotashield), but then was taken off the market. We are hopeful that there may be another vaccine in the future.

5. Viral Exanthems (viruses that cause rashes)

See Viral rash section in Chapter 15, "First Aid."

Roseola (Herpes virus 6)

Disease: A virus that the entire world population over one year of age has had. Because it is a Herpes virus (this is NOT genital herpes HSV 2), it stays in our bodies forever. We all shed this virus in saliva and respiratory droplets daily. Mom's antibodies (immunity) are passed to baby and provide protection against illness for 9 to 12 months. When immunity wanes, babies get this infection. The only time you see a roseola 'epidemic' is if you hang out with a bunch of one year olds.

Symptoms: Fever over 102 for about four days with no other signs of infection. Kids are usually in good spirits. *When the fever breaks, the rash comes out.* The rash can be subtle or dramatic. It is mostly flat, with some raised areas. Red, blotchy. On chest, back, arms. Not itchy, goes away within hours to a few days.

Diagnosis: Obvious after the rash comes out. The fever often prompts lab work (CBC, urinalysis) to prove that there is not a bacteria causing the fever.

Treatment: None. Acetaminophen (Tylenol) or Ibuprofen (Motrin) for the fever.

Contagious: We are all contagious because we shed the virus for a lifetime once we are infected.

Incubation period: Ten days.

Season: When is your baby's first birthday?

Chicken pox (Varicella)

Disease: Caused by Varicella-Zoster virus, another type of Herpes virus. Like all Herpes viruses, it lies dormant forever in previously infected people. Because chicken pox can cause serious infection and death, vaccination became standard of care in 1995. The vaccine is given to all children at one year of age and anyone (including adults) who has never had chickenpox. The vaccine is not 100% effective in preventing infection. But, people who get infection despite vaccination have a very mild form of the disease. Babies under three months of age are usually protected via Mom's immunity (as long as she had chickenpox). Both immunized and infected kids can get Zoster (shingles) infection later in life (reactivation of Varicella). Shingles infects only one group of nerves (called a dermatome). A group of lesions come up in one patch. These blisters are more painful than itchy. They contain the virus and are contagious.

Symptoms: A full blown case causes fever, body aches, and a rash of tiny fluid filled blisters (called **VESICLES**) that appear in crops. New crops come up over a period of 3 to 4 days. The average number of pox is 350. Very itchy. Secondary Strep skin infections can occur. Watch for red areas surrounding pox, or a new fever after the initial fever breaks.

Diagnosis: Classic rash. Virus (found in vesicle fluid) will grow in culture in 2 to 3 days.

Treatment: Acyclovir, an anti-viral, can be given within 48 hours of illness. It will shorten the course of illness by a couple of days and reduces the total number of lesions (not dramatically though)

Contagious: VERY. FOR ONE WEEK. Child is contagious for 24 hours before the rash comes out and until all lesions (which contain the virus) are crusted over. Spread via respiratory droplets and direct contact.

Incubation period: 10 to 21 days. If you know when your child has been exposed, look for infection 10 days later and for the next 11 days. If you make it out of that window, you are safe.

Season: Winter, early spring

Prevention: Vaccination.

Slapped Cheek (Parvovirus)

Disease: Also known as **FIFTH DISEASE** or **ERYTHEMA INFECTIOSUM**. Occurs more in school age children. Questions arise more with exposure in pregnancy than anything else. The biggest problem with this infection is that it can cause miscarriage (fetal demise). If a pregnant woman (usually in the first 20 weeks) is not immune to parvovirus and gets the infection, her fetus is at risk. Unfortunately, by the time we know a child has had parvovirus (i.e. the rash appears), he has already exposed everyone.

Symptoms: Mild or even undetectable when a child is contagious. Low fever, body aches, or headache. Ten days after the infection is gone, a classic rash erupts. The red cheeks look as if someone slapped them plus a lacy, mostly flat, red rash on chest, arms, and legs. The rash can last several weeks. When older kids and adults get infected, they may get joint pains that last for weeks.

Diagnosis: Easy once the rash has erupted. Antibody levels can be checked for evidence of recent infection.

Treatment: None.

Contagious: Hard to know when contagious because often there are no

symptoms. Spread via respiratory droplets, blood products.
Incubation period: 4 to 21 days.
Season: Winter, spring.

Bacterial Infections

1. Sinus Infections

Disease: Caused by the same bacteria that cause ear infections. Sinus infections are a secondary bacterial infection after a person has a common cold or flu. The virus sets up fluid in the sinus cavities behind the cheeks and above the eyes. More common in older children.
Symptoms: Prolonged runny nose over 14 days. New onset of discolored nasal secretions (snot) after 10 to 14 days of illness. New fever. Nighttime cough.
Diagnosis: Mostly by examination. Occasionally sinus x-ray is helpful.
Treatment: Same antibiotic choices as for ear infections, but often needs longer course.
Contagious: No.

2. Lung Infections (pneumonia)

Disease: Lung tissue inflammation that can be caused by bacteria or a virus. Bacterial pneumonia is a secondary infection after a viral illness (cold or flu).
Symptoms: High fever, wet cough, respiratory distress, vomiting. Child is getting worse instead of better with an illness, or new fever after initial fever resolved from an upper respiratory infection.
Diagnosis: Abnormal lung exam, chest x-ray, elevated white blood cell count
Treatment: Antibiotics. Rarely hospital admission—for respiratory distress, need for oxygen.
Contagious: Depends on the bug.

3. Skin Infection (Impetigo and cellulitis)

Disease: Skin infection caused by bacteria that normally live on the skin that get under the skin. Bacteria capitalize on open wounds (bug bites, raw nostrils, burns).
Symptoms: Wound gets red with a golden, crusty, weeping discharge over it with impetigo. The skin is red, warm, and tender with cellulitis.
Diagnosis: Based on symptoms. Bugs can also grow in a culture of the wound.
Treatment: Impetigo can be treated with prescription antibiotic cream. Extensive impetigo and cellulitis are treated with antibiotics given by mouth.
Contagious: Impetigo-yes. Spread by direct contact with wound. Not contagious after 24 hours of antibiotic therapy. Cellulitis is not contagious.
Incubation period: 7 to 10 days.
Season: Year round.

4. Eye Infections "Pink Eye" (Bacterial conjunctivitis)

Disease: Infection of the eye lining. Can be caused by either viruses or bacteria. Bacterial infections usually cause yellow or green eye discharge. Viral infections usually cause watery eye discharge. One bacteria, Haemophilus influenza, causes pink eye, sinus infections, and ear infections at the same time. About 30% of babies under age two with bacterial pink eye will also have an ear infection to go with it.

Symptoms: Red, itchy eyes with discolored thick fluid draining or matting the eyes shut.

Diagnosis: Based on exam. Occasionally, a culture is done of the fluid.

Treatment: Antibiotic eye drops if infection is bacterial. No treatment for viral pink eye.

Contagious: VERY. Spread by direct contact with eye discharge. Use separate hand towels.

Incubation period: Varies. For viral pink eye, 2 to 14 days.

Season: Year round.

5. Food Poisoning (E. coli, Salmonella, Shigella, and others)

Disease: Bacterial infection spread through contaminated food (and infected people's mouths and poop). Salmonella bacteria is the most common cause of food poisoning (80% of the time). E. coli Type 0157: H7, although less common, can be particularly serious. This bug releases a toxin/poison that causes **HEMOLYTIC UREMIC SYNDROME** (HUS). HUS causes severe anemia, low platelet count, and kidney failure. It is a reversible condition, but can be fatal. These kids are *really* sick with abdominal distention, pain, bloody diarrhea, and **PETECHIAE.** E. coli 0157 comes from cow and deer poop. Ground meat can have bacterial contamination throughout. Because of that, the meat needs to be cooked thoroughly to kill any of these bugs. Whole muscle cuts are only contaminated on the surface of the meat, which are always cooked well. (the poop gets spread to the meat during hide removal or evisceration).[7]

Symptoms: Vomiting, diarrhea mixed with blood or mucus. Fever. Body aches. Abdominal pain.

Diagnosis: Stool culture, blood and white blood cells in poop, some blood test abnormalities.

Treatment: FLUIDS to avoid dehydration. Some bacterial infections need antibiotics to clear. Some bacterial infections should NOT be treated with antibiotics as it causes the person to remain a "carrier" of the infection.

Contagious: Spread through contaminated food/water (poultry, undercooked eggs, alfalfa sprouts, unpasteurized milk, undercooked hamburgers), breast milk, fomites (e.g. raw meat on countertop), direct contact with infected poop, saliva . Salmonella is also spread via pet iguanas and turtles, who are carriers. People, especially infants, who get Salmonella will often remain carriers for months after the infection.

Incubation Period: Varies on the bug, usually 6 to 72 hours.

Season: Year round.

Prevention: Never eat a hamburger that can moo back at you (it needs to be well done). Avoid fresh fruit/vegetables and water when traveling to developing countries. Drink only pasteurized milk and apple cider. Be careful in the kitchen. Food preparation and baby products (bottles, nipples...) need to be separated. Avoid owning a pet iguana or turtle.

6. Bladder Infections or Urinary Tract Infections (E. coli and others)

Disease: A bacterial infection caused by intestinal bacteria that get into the bladder. Bacteria (e.g. E. coli) routinely come out in our poop. They only cause infection when they creep into our bladders. Babies who are in diapers are susceptible to bladder infections (especially girls) because the poop sits where the opening to the bladder sits (urethra). Some babies are prone to bladder infections because of an abnormality called **VESI-COURETERAL REFLUX.**

Symptoms: Fever, fussy mood, lack of other symptoms to explain fever

Diagnosis: Abnormal urinalysis, urine culture grows bacteria. All pre-pubertal kids with bladder infections have an evaluation done of their urinary tract system to rule out abnormality.

Treatment: Depends on the age and severity of infection. Babies under six months of age are hospitalized because of a higher risk of kidney infection and meningitis from infection.

Contagious: No.

Prevention: Clean poopie diapers as soon as possible. Wipe girls front to back.

7. Meningitis

Disease: Inflammation of the tissues that line the brain. This can be caused by viruses or bacteria. Bacterial meningitis is a life threatening illness. There are different bacteria that cause meningitis in various age groups.

Meningitis can be caused by more than one type of bacteria. The top two that you need to know about are discuss below:

Group B Strep

In the newborn period, the bacteria you will hear the most about is **Group B Strep.** This bacteria is normal flora in the intestines, bladder, and the vagina of mothers. It uniquely causes infection in newborns as they pass through the birth canal. Pregnant women are routinely screened at 35 to 37 weeks to check for the presence of Group B Strep (GBS). If Mom is a carrier, she is given IV antibiotics during labor to suppress the growth of this bacteria. If Mom goes into labor before 37 weeks, has broken her water more than 18 hours, or has a fever greater than 100.4, she also gets IV antibiotics because of the risk of Group B Strep infection. (Women who have planned C-sections don't have to worry about this stuff.) Doctors watch all newborns closely, but those with GBS-positive Moms get watched even more closely.

A standard protocol is to get a complete blood count and blood culture on a newborn if Mom is GBS-positive and didn't get pretreated with antibiotics (i.e. a quick labor), baby is born less than 35 weeks gestation, or if a baby starts misbehaving (temperature instability, respiratory distress).

There is also potential for a late onset GBS infection up to three months after delivery.

Diagnosis: Bacteria can be seen in blood or spinal fluid under a microscope (see Gram stain in lab section). Blood or spinal fluid cultures give the definitive answer in 2 to 3 days.

Treatment: IV antibiotics. Penicillin works well.

Contagious: Spread via birth canal.

Incubation period: 0-3 months.

Season: N/A.

Prevention: Prophylactic antibiotics to Mom while in labor.

Strep pneumoniae

Disease: This type of Strep is also known as *pneumococcus* (very confusing). This bacteria is THE number-one cause of bacterial meningitis in infants. (It also causes ear infections, blood infections, sinus infections and pneumonia). Strep pneumoniae has developed resistance to many antibiotics. This is why the Prevnar vaccine (for Strep pneumoniae) has been a welcome arrival. Since the vaccine was introduced in February 2000, we have seen an 87% disease reduction in bloodstream (bacteremia) infections and meningitis.

Symptoms: High fevers (usually more than 103), *without obvious symptoms*, irritability. If the infection is caught early while it is in the blood, treatment prevents travel to the brain (meningitis).

Diagnosis: Blood infections (bacteremia) by an elevated white blood cell count over 15,000 (often over 20,000) and a blood culture which may grow the bug. Meningitis is diagnosed by an abnormal spinal fluid (white blood cells in it) and a culture that grows bacteria.

Treatment: Blood infections get treated with an antibiotic shot initially, then oral antibiotics. Meningitis requires IV antibiotics and hospitalization.

Contagious: Spread by respiratory droplets. Strep pneumoniae lives everywhere. Some people are carriers. Children get infected when they already have a viral upper respiratory infection.

Incubation period: 1 to 3 days.

Season: Winter mostly

Prevention: Prevnar (PCV-7 strains) vaccine for infants and children under five who are high risk. There is also a Pneumococcus vaccine (23 strains) for high risk children and elderly people. High risk: sickle cell disease, children with no spleen, kidney disease, immune compromised, HIV.[8]

Things That Make You Itch Just Thinking About: Fungal Infections

Disease: Fungi are plant relatives (yeast, mold) that don't need light to live. Fungi prefer places where there is little competition (i.e. low bacteria levels). And, some fungi thrive on people whose defenses are down (i.e. immune compromised). We get infected in the following ways:

1. Fungus infestation. These are the accidental tourists. These fungi thrive on our skin, but don't go any deeper than that (**RINGWORM, ATHLETE'S FOOT, JOCK ITCH**). They are passed from person to person, or via a pet. These fungi just happen to be at the right place at the right time.

2. Opportunistic infection. These fungi grow when other factors alter our body defenses to fungi. Infants are susceptible to fungal infections (**THRUSH, YEAST DIAPER RASH**) because their bodies are relatively free of bacteria flora. Kids are also at risk for yeast diaper rash after having a course of antibiotics because the antibiotic not only kills the bad bacteria, but also the good normal flora.

Other fungal opportunities include people on chronic steroids or with diabetes.

3. Invasive infection. This virtually never happens to normal, healthy people. A fungus invades the blood or lungs after its spores are inhaled.

Diagnosis:

Ringworm. Classic circular area with raised red border, and central scale. Fungus visible under microscope. Culture will grow in 2 to 3 weeks.

Ringworm of scalp. Patch of hair loss with overlying scale, or dots of hair loss with stubs of broken hair, or big ugly pus pockets (kerion) in the scalp. More in African American kids (fungus likes the hair texture). Culture grows in 2 to 3 weeks.

Thrush. Classic white plaques on a red base in the cheeks, gums, tongue. Looks like milk you can't wipe off. Diagnosis based on examination.

Yeast diaper rash. Raw meat red area with satellite pimply dots. Won't improve with Desitin. Found often when thrush is present in the mouth.

Treatment:

Ringworm. Anti-fungal cream for 2 to 4 weeks.

Ringworm of scalp. Anti-fungal medicine by mouth for 1-2 months. (cream won't kill it). The fungus imbeds in the hair follicle and is very hardy. We see some drug resistant strains.

Thrush. Anti-fungal mouthwash for 1 to 2 weeks. Sterilize all nipples, pacifiers.

Yeast diaper rash. Anti-fungal cream for 1 to 2 weeks.

Contagious: Until treated for 24 hours with anti-fungal medicine.

Ringworm. Direct contact with infected person or animal (itchy dogs). Fomites too.

Ringworm of scalp. Direct contact with combs, hairbrushes, bed sheets.

Thrush. Direct contact with infant's mouth (spreads to Mom's nipples)

Yeast diaper rash. Opportunistic infection. Not particularly contagious.[9]

Scabies (Mite Infection)

Disease: An infection caused by mites. Mites are tiny bugs that are somewhere between parasites and ticks. The female scabies mite burrows into our skin and lays her eggs. She lays 200 eggs in eight weeks. When the eggs hatch, the babies burrow into our skin and start eating. This is the ITCHIEST rash ever. Even after treatment, people are itchy for weeks afterwards.

Symptoms: The mites usually burrow between our fingers, elbow creases, armpits, belly button area, and genitals. In infected kids under two years old, they prefer the neck, palms, and soles. What you will see is a streak made out tiny bumps—they start out gray, but are usually red by the time medical attention is sought.

Diagnosis: If the rash is classic, diagnosis is made on examination alone. For unclear cases, a scraping of a burrow can be done. It may reveal the mite, mite egg, or mite poop under the microscope.

Treatment: A scabicidal body wash (Elimite-5% Permethrin) is available by prescription. ALL FAMILY MEMBERS GET TREATED. Clothing and bedding used for four days before treatment need to be washed and dried on the hot cycle. Disinfecting the house is a waste of time.

Contagious: Until treated with Elimite. Spread by direct contact, especially by holding hands. Co-sleeping is also an easy way for the whole family to get infected with scabies. Mites cannot survive off of humans for more than 24 hours.

Incubation period: 4 to 6 weeks.

More mite facts:

Chiggers are mites who like pores and hair follicles of people. These are self-limited infestations, but are also very itchy.

Dust mites do not cause infection. They feed off of the dead skin that we slough off on a daily basis. Some people are allergic to dust mite poop and have chronic nasal congestion as a result of it (see environmental allergies).[10]

Lice

Disease: Infection by a human louse. Head lice enjoy feeding on us via human hair. They don't have wings. They migrate from one head to the next by crawling over. They can't survive away from hair for more than 24 hours. The adult females lay eggs (nits) in the hair shafts (less than 1/4 inch from the scalp). Adults live about one month. The eggs become thriving nymphs in about one week. Head lice prefer the straighter hair of Caucasian people. Outbreaks happen more in school age children, but younger kids can acquire lice at childcare centers.

Symptoms: Itchy scalp, white flakes that are firmly adherent to the hair shaft.

Diagnosis: Adult lice are brown and visible with the naked eye-but they move quickly. The diagnosis is made most often by finding the nits. Nits are white and stick firmly to the hair shaft close to the scalp. Dandruff is rubbed off easily, nits are not.

Treatment: An over the counter shampoo called Nix (1% permethrin) kills adult lice and the eggs. Two treatments, one week apart (to kill any baby lice that survived the first round). Since babies in the eggs (nits) are either killed or not contagious yet, removing nits is more of a cosmetic issue than a therapeutic one. The phrase "nit-picking" comes from the tedious task of removing the sticky nits that are close to the scalp. Some little lice are resistant to treatment.

Contagious: Until treated. "No-nit" policies in childcare facilities are not necessary.

Incubation period: 6 to 10 days.

Creative treatment for resistant head lice: If living *adult* lice are found (not nits), then re-treatment is in order. The list of alternatives include prescription 5% Permethrin (Elimite), Malathion (a pesticide), Bactrim (an antibiotic), and products that smother the lice (Vaseline, olive oil, mayonnaise).

For more information on lice: www.headlice.org

Pinworms

Disease: Pinworms live in our intestines and lay eggs on the outside of the anus. Infection is spread when worm-ridden Johnny scratches his bottom and plays in the sandbox. Suzie plays in the sandbox later and picks up the eggs on her fingers. Her fingers go in her mouth, and voila! Suzie has pinworms too!

Symptoms: The female pinworm comes out to the anus at night and lays her eggs. This causes a symptom called pruritus ani (Latin for itchy tushie). Itchy vagina also happens from pinworms.

Diagnosis: Often based on symptoms alone. Parents can go on a worm hunt. The female comes out of the anus about two hours after a child is sleeping. Put clear Scotch tape on a toothpick and obtain a specimen.

Treatment: Two doses of Vermox (Latin for worm-out) prescription, given two weeks apart. Doctors often treat the whole family. Bathing in morning helps remove the eggs.

Contagious: Until treated. Infected people often re-infect themselves by scratching their anus and ingesting more eggs.

Incubation period: 1 to 2 months (egg is ingested, then matures into an adult egg-laying female in 1 to 2 months).[11]

Parasites

Another stomach infection is called Giardia. This is a parasite spread via water. Yes, this includes swimming pools, hot tubs, and area lakes. Someone with the infection who is swimming in the water can share it. It frequently haunts childcare centers. Prolonged or foul-smelling diarrhea deserves to be tested for parasites.

Abdominal tumors. There are some solid tumors that occur more frequently in children than adults. These include Wilm's tumor and neuroblastoma. Patients with these tumors may (not always) have enlarged, firm bellies with a mass that can be felt. Other symptoms include weight loss, lack of appetite, or unexplained fevers.

ABO incompatibility. See Coombs test in Lab section.

Acholic stool. Official term for a clay colored poop. In isolation, it may have no significance. But, it can indicate a problem with the biliary system (liver, gallbladder, pancreas) if it is associated with other symptoms—particularly jaundice (yellowing) of the skin. Diagnoses can include hepatitis infection and biliary atresia. If you see this, check in with your doctor.

Acne (neonatal). Skin inflammation due to hormonal changes in the newborn period. Onset is usually by four weeks of age and lasts until about eight weeks of age.

Acute abdomen. Term that refers to an emergency requiring surgical intervention to alleviate an intestinal problem. Examples of these problems include: appendicitis, intussusception, intestinal obstruction.

Acute life threatening event (ALTE). The term that describes an episode of lack of breathing (apnea) that requires intervention to resume spontaneous breathing. If an event like this happens, a thorough evaluation is done to determine the cause of the event.

Acute otitis media. Infection in the middle ear space. This is primarily caused by bacteria. When the infection comes up quickly, it is called "acute." Symptoms include fever, cranky mood, and vomiting. Occasionally, children may also seem dizzy. Ear infections that smolder for a long period of time are called "chronic" and do not have the same symptoms.

Acrocyanosis. The blue discoloration frequently seen on the hands and feet of newborns. This is due to the body circulation transitioning from fetal to newborn. It doe not indicate any problem with the heart or circulatory system. Blue discoloration only on the feet or legs (not hands) can be a sign of a circulation problem (Coarctation of the Aorta) and needs to be evaluated.

Air hungry. The inability of a person to get enough oxygen in with each breath. The person then tries to get more air in with each breath by using chest wall muscles and increasing the number of breaths taken per minute. This is also known as **respiratory distress**.

Ambiguous Genitalia. It's hard to tell whether the baby has boy parts or girl parts. We'll test chromosomes, hormone levels, and get an ultrasound to look for internal genitalia (ovaries/uterus or undescended testes).

Amblyopia. (Known as lazy eye). A reduction of vision in an eye that is not correctable with glasses. This problem can be caused by a weakness of an eye muscle (strabismus). It is important to detect this eye problem early (under age two or three years) so it can be treated.

Anal fissure. A crack in the anus opening usually due to passage of a hard poop. The crack causes discomfort and occasionally blood in the diaper or on a diaper wipe.

Anaphylactic reaction. An allergic response to exposure to a particular item (that is, medication, food). The response is extremely serious and life-threatening. These body responses include: difficulty breathing, heart failure, loss of blood pressure.

Anemia. A reduced number of the product (hemoglobin) that carries oxygen on red blood cells. Because the body is less capable of getting oxygen, symptoms include tiredness, pale appearance, and quick fatigue.

Ankyloglossia (tongue tie). The tongue is attached to the base of the mouth too close to the tip. Not all babies with tongue tie need intervention. If it is so tight that it interferes with feeding or talking, the tissue band can be clipped. This is more likely to be a problem if the tip of the tongue is forked.

Anomaly. Fancy word for abnormality, usually malformed prior to birth (congenital anomaly).

Antibiotic induced colitis. Inflammation of the lower part of the intestine which, rarely, can be caused by antibiotics. Symptoms of colitis include blood and mucus in the poop, diarrhea, and cramping. If someone has been on an antibiotic just prior to the onset of these symptoms, a specimen of poop can be checked for this problem.

Apnea. Pause, or temporary absence in breathing. Frequently babies born prematurely have these events when they just plain forget to breathe. This is called **apnea of prematurity**. Preemies eventually outgrow this problem. Until they do, they are placed on an apnea monitor which alarms with lack of breathing. Some babies also need caffeine (in medication form) to stimulate them to breathe.

Appendicitis. Inflammation of a small piece of the intestine called the appendix. The appendix is usually located in the lower RIGHT side of the belly, but this varies occasionally. When the appendix gets swollen, symptoms include: vomiting, diarrhea, fever, and abdominal pain that worsens over time. Appendicitis is extremely rare in the birth age one group.

Asperger's Syndrome. A developmental disorder that is part of the Autism Spectrum Disorders. Children with Asperger's have more social and language skills than those more severely affected.

Asthma. The swelling of the big and little airways in the lungs. The swelling can occur due to allergic response. The episodes happen intermittently. Symptoms include: coughing and labored breathing (respiratory distress).

Atopy. A classic triad of allergic disorders: eczema, asthma, and seasonal allergies (termed "allergic rhinitis"). Not everyone is unlucky enough to have all three problems, but some people are.

Atresia. Means that something is completely absent or is significantly narrowed
Anal atresia. anus (opening of the intestines to the outside)
Biliary atresia. Bile ducts
Choanal atresia. Nasal/throat
Duodenal atresia. Small intestine
Esophageal atresia. Esophagus
Ileal atresia. Small intestine
Tricuspid atresia. Heart valve

Autism. A developmental disorder that is characterized by poor or no language development, lack of normal social skills and repetitive self-soothing behaviors. The disorder likely has a genetic basis, as seen by research done on twins. There is a broad range of this disorder from mild to severely affected. Thus, Autism Spectrum Disorder is a new term used to describe it.

Autosomal dominant. A genetically inherited trait that requires only one parent to have an abnormal gene to pass it on to a child. If one parent carries an autosomal dominant gene, the chances are 50% that a child inherits the gene.

Autosomal recessive. A genetically inherited trait that requires both parents to have the gene to pass it on to a child. If both parents are carriers of the autosomal recessive gene, the chances are 25% that they will have an affected child. If both parents have the disease, chances are nearly 100% that they will have an affected child.

Bacterial gastroenteritis. (See gastroenteritis)

BAER. Brainstem Audio Evoked Response. An objective hearing test that measures the electrical activity of the inner ear in response to sound. This is a universal screening test done on newborns. It is recommended by the American Academy of Pediatrics and currently mandated by law in 37 states.

Bladder infection (see UTI)

Blood in stool. A symptom that may be caused by a variety of reasons. Blood can be found in poop due to skin irritation (diaper rash), a crack or tear in the anus (see anal fissure), inflammation in the intestine (milk protein allergy), intestinal infection (see gastroenteritis), or intestinal obstruction (intussusception). As you can see, the problem may be a minor or serious one. It always should be checked out by your doctor.

Brain tumor. Abnormal mass of cells that grow in the brain tissue. Although not all tumors are malignant (fast growing, aggressive), even benign tumors can be life threatening depending on the location that it arises. Symptoms in infants and young children include morning headaches accompanied by vomiting, increasing head size, behavior changes, imbalance, seizures, and new onset eye abnormalities.

Branchial cleft cyst. An abnormality in fetal development of the throat that results in a cyst that occurs on the neck

Breath-holding spell. An episode where a child holds his breath when upset or angry. Usually occurs after one year of age. The episode ultimately results in a child losing consciousness and regaining normal breathing. Rarely, these episodes are due to anemia—but worth checking out if the episodes occur frequently.

Bronchiolitis. Swelling in the tiny airways in the lungs (bronchioles). In children, this is caused primarily by a virus called RSV (respiratory syncytial virus). When the little airways are swollen, it can be difficult to exchange oxygen poor air with oxygen rich air. In severe cases, particularly infants under a year of age or those born prematurely, some children need medication to reduce the swelling (see bronchodilators in medication appendix) and supplemental oxygen.

Bronchitis. Swelling in the larger airways of the lungs (bronchi). In children, this swelling is usually caused by a virus or bacterial infection.

Cafe au lait spots. As the name implies, these are light brown (coffee with milk) colored birthmarks. They occur in babies of all races. Most of the time, there is no significance to these marks. When a child has more than five of these birthmarks, there may be an association with a disorder called **neurofibromatosis.**

Carotinemia. A benign yellow discoloration of the skin due to a large dietary intake of carotene containing foods (carrots, sweet potatoes). The whites of the eyes remain white, as opposed to what is seen with jaundice—**see jaundice**.

Cataracts. A clouding of the eye's lens. This can occur at birth (congenital cataracts). If a newborn has cataracts, it can be detected by the lack of a 'red reflex' on an eye examination. A referral to a pediatric ophthalmologist is made.

Celiac disease. A disorder of the intestines which causes poor digestion and absorption of foods. The underlying problem is due to an abnormal response to 'gluten' containing foods (e.g. wheat, oat, rye grains). The classic symptoms of this disorder include foul smelling, chronic diarrhea and failure to thrive (lack of weight gain). Treatment is a lifelong gluten-free diet.

Cephalhematoma. Literally, a head bruise. This often occurs in newborns as a result of birth trauma. Some of these bruises are quite large and take one to two months to completely go away. In the process of healing, these areas can become very hard and firm. Since the bruise is a collection of blood, it sometimes creates an additional bilirubin load and can lead to jaundice in some newborns.

Cerebral palsy. An abnormality of the brain center that controls muscle tone and movement. Cerebral palsy does not cause any abnormalities in IQ. However, there are children who have *both* mental retardation AND cerebral palsy.

Choanal atresia. Lack of communication between the back of the nasal passages and the throat. This can occur in one or both sides of the nose. If both sides are blocked, a newborn will have severe breathing problems. Newborns only know how to breathe through their noses for the first four months of life.

Clavicle (collar bone) fracture. When Mom is small and baby is big, it can be difficult to get the baby out of the birth canal. The baby's shoulder pulls out and can break the clavicle (collar bone) in the process. It heals nicely without a cast. The area can feel crunchy under the skin, then it feels like a hard lump. The lump is healing bone and goes away after several weeks.

Cleft lip and palate. The roof of the mouth and/or the upper lip does not completely form in a fetus. These defects can occur together or separately in 1 in 1000 births. There is some hereditary predisposition. Rarely, this defect is associated with other congenital defects. Frequently, a team of providers manage babies with these defects (Ear, Nose, and Throat doctors, Plastic Surgeons, Dentist, and Occupational Therapists). See Appendix F for web sites on this issue.

Club foot. An abnormality in the formation of the foot of the fetus. The result is a stiff foot that turns markedly inwards. Pediatric orthopedic surgeons are consulted and a cast is made to correct the position of the foot.

Coarctation of the Aorta. A narrowing or kink in the great artery (aorta) that leaves the heart and supplies the body with oxygen rich blood. This is a defect that occurs during fetal development (prior to birth). If the

glossary

abnormality is severe, it is diagnosed in newborns who have weakened/no pulse in the legs. If the abnormality is small, it may go undetected until later in life. It is repaired by surgery.

Colostrum. A first "milk" that a mother produces. This product is rich in antibodies and cells. It has fewer calories than mature milk which arrives on about the fourth day after birth.

Conductive hearing loss. Difficulty hearing due to a problem with the transmission of sound waves to the part of the ear that controls hearing. Sound waves can be blocked due to fluid sitting behind the eardrum (see serous obits media) or a significant amount of earwax sitting in the ear canal. The good news about conductive hearing loss is that the problem can usually be fixed and normal hearing is restored.

Congenital. This refers to an abnormality in the *formation* of a certain organ/body part that occurs in the development of an unborn fetus. These abnormalities may be due to either hereditary problems or environmental exposures during pregnancy. The lay term for these disorders is **birth defect.**

Congenital Adrenal Hyperplasia. An abnormality in the gland that produces steroids in the body (adrenal gland). This can cause severe metabolism problems of body salts. This abnormality is routinely tested in the newborn metabolic screen.

Congenital heart disease. A defect in the structural development of the heart or the great vessels that attach to the heart. Because heart development occurs in the first trimester of pregnancy, many congenital defects can be identified on a prenatal ultrasound. Some abnormalities will resolve on their own. Some require surgical repair. The disease incidence is 1:1000. The most common defects are the least serious ones. Remember, there is a difference between an innocent heart murmur (no defect) and a pathologic murmur (caused by congenital heart disease).

Congenital nevus. (Known as moles, birthmarks) A mark on the skin which is present at birth, or appears within the first year of life. The most concerning moles are ones larger than 10 to 20 cm (really big) that are present at birth. These have more potential risk of skin cancer and removal is usually advised.

Congestive heart failure. When the heart is unable to perform adequately, the blood flow accumulates in the lungs and liver. So, symptoms of heart failure include shortness of breath and enlarged liver size. In children, symptoms include failure to thrive, sweating with feedings, shortness of breath, and excessive fatigue.

Conjunctivitis. An inflammation of the lining of the eyelid. Otherwise known as "pink eye." The inflammation can be caused by a virus, bacteria, allergies, or irritation. All types of conjunctivitis cause redness and some discomfort. Here are the major types of conjunctivitis:

Allergic. An allergic response usually due to a sensitivity to something in the air (e.g. pollens). Usually causes watery, somewhat itchy eyes. Antihistamines treat the symptoms.

Bacterial. A bacterial infection in the eye (often accompanied by ear and sinus infection). Causes thick yellowish eye discharge and may even cause the eyes to be caked over or "matted." Antibiotic eye drops treat the infection.

Viral. A viral infection in the eye (that may be accompanied by a sore throat). Causes watery and very itchy eyes.

Irritation. Eyes become inflamed because of a chemical irritant (e.g. shampoo).

Constipation. The texture of poop is significantly hard, and is passed either in small pieces or in a very large mass of small pieces stuck together. Contrary to popular belief, constipation is NOT defined by the infrequency of poop (although this can contribute to the problem). There is no defined length of interval for which a person needs to poop—it can vary considerably. If the poop is soft when it comes out, your baby is unlikely to be constipated.

Craniosynostosis. A baby's skull bones have gaps that allow for the brain's growth in the first one to two years of life. This abnormality is a premature closure of the gaps (sutures). We detect this problem by finding a closed fontanelle (soft spot) or lack of head growth. This requires surgery to repair.

Cystic Fibrosis (CF). This is a genetic disease that causes body glands to produce abnormal secretions. Lung, sinus, pancreas, intestine, and reproductive organ problems occur because of it. One in 20 Caucasians are carriers of this genetic abnormality. The disease incidence is 1:1600 for Caucasian babies (it is much less common in other races). Many women now receive genetic testing during pregnancy for CF, although it is not a routine screening test.

Diarrhea. Frequent passage of watery or very soft poop. In a breast fed baby, diarrhea is defined more by the dramatic increase in frequency of poop than by the texture.

Duodenal atresia. Congenital abnormality of the first part of the small intestine to form. It's often associated with other abnormalities. Babies are diagnosed with this disorder before birth by an abnormal ultrasound (extra amniotic fluid found) or shortly after birth when they start vomiting bile. This requires surgical repair.

Eczema. A skin disorder that causes redness and scaling. The underlying problem seems to be allergic in nature, and children with eczema have flare-ups with exposure to perfumed products and certain chemicals. Eczema can be associated with other allergic disorders such as asthma, seasonal allergies, and food allergies but it can also occur without any other problems.

glossary

Egocentric. The inability to see things from someone else's point of view. This is a child's view of the world from age two to about seven years.

Emesis. The technical term for vomit.

Encephalitis. Brain inflammation usually caused by a virus or a bacterial infection.

Engorgement. The Milkman Cometh. Period of excessive breast milk production around three to five days after childbirth. Women's breasts feel full and often uncomfortable until milk demand and milk supply equilibrate.

Epispadias. Congenital abnormality of the formation of a boy's urethra (tube connecting the bladder to the outside). The hole is located on the top side of the penis, instead of in the center. This requires surgical repair.

Epstein's pearls. Tiny cysts (white bumps) found on the roof of the mouth in newborns. These are common, non-problematic, and go away on their own.

Erb's palsy. An injury to the nerves that supply the arm. This occurs as a result of a difficult delivery requiring the baby's head to be pulled forcefully. On examination, the arm will hang limp. The nerve injury usually heals in a year, but may require surgery or physical therapy.

Erythema toxicum. A normal newborn rash that looks like flea bites (white pimple with red around it). These tiny bumps come and go.

Esophagitis. The inflammation of the upper part of the gastrointestinal system (esophagus).

Expressive language delays. A child whose ability to speak words is behind his peers. A child with this delay may have completely normal ability to understand and process language that he hears (see receptive language).

Failure to thrive. When a baby or child falls below the 3rd percentile on the weight curve. When the problem is a chronic one, height and head size also drop on the growth curves. Failure to thrive prompts a thorough medical evaluation.

Fat necrosis. An occasional complication from vaccination injection. As a needle goes through the fat under the skin, it can injure it and create a firm lump. This lump may be present for several weeks after the injection is given. It is painless and not harmful.

Flaring (nostrils). When an infant or young child is having trouble breathing (respiratory distress), he will use any additional methods his body can to get in more air. Nostrils will flare with each breath to try to capture more air. Thus, this is a red flag for respiratory distress.

Flat angiomata. Official term for an "angel kiss" birthmark on the forehead or eyelids. These are flat, reddish colored marks that eventually fade. The color becomes more dramatic with crying or anger.

Fomites. Objects handled by a person with an infection that subsequently allows passage of the germs to someone else.

Fontanelle. A space between the bones of the skull that allows room for the baby's head to pass through the birth canal and room for the baby's brain to grow after birth. The main fontanelle is on top of the head (anterior) and is sometimes called the baby's "soft spot." There is a smaller fontanelle in the back of the head (posterior). The anterior fontanelle closes between nine to 18 months of age.

Food poisoning (see gastroenteritis)

Foreign body/object. Term used to describe an object which has no place being where it is in someone's body. Kids have a way of putting objects like small toys in their noses, ears, etc. as well as swallowing them.

Foremilk. A breastfeeding term used to describe the milk that is released in the first several minutes of nursing. It is less fatty than what comes out later (see **hindmilk**). If your breastfed baby is a snacker, he may not be getting the richer milk. For these babies, its better to nurse on one breast per feeding.

Frenulum. The tissue that connects the tongue to the base of the mouth. (see **ankyloglossia**)

Galactosemia. A rare metabolic disorder that makes a baby unable to digest galactose, a milk sugar. Newborns are routinely tested for this disorder in the state metabolic screen. If present, a baby needs a special formula diet. Breastmilk contains galactose, so it is not possible to breastfeed. Babies who have galactosemia and continue a normal diet can become mentally retarded.

Gastroenteritis. An inflammation of the stomach and intestines caused by either a virus or bacteria. The inflammation can cause both vomiting and diarrhea. Viral gastroenteritis is commonly known as the "stomach flu" and tends to cause watery diarrhea. Bacterial gastroenteritis is commonly known as "food poisoning" and tends to cause diarrhea mixed with blood or mucus.

Gastroesophageal reflux (GER, acid reflux). The backflow of food and liquids from the stomach into the esophagus (and often all the way to the mouth). This is a common problem for newborns up to age one year. The muscle that separates the esophagus and the stomach (lower esophageal sphincter) is relatively loose in infants, allowing food to travel down to the stomach (good) and back up to the esophagus (not good). Once food contents make it to the stomach, they are mixed with stomach acid. So, when this partially digested food goes backwards, the

glossary

stomach acid can irritate the esophagus (i.e. acid reflux). Most babies outgrow this problem by age one.

Gingivostomatitis. Inflammation and irritation of the gums and lining of the mouth caused by the Oral Herpes virus. The amount of inflammation is usually extensive and may lead to refusal to eat or drink anything.

Glaucoma. Increased pressure behind the eye. Babies with hemangiomas near the eye need to be evaluated by an ophthalmologist because they are at risk for glaucoma.

Heart murmur. A noise heard in addition to the normal heart sounds audible with a stethoscope. The murmur can be due to normal heart function (termed innocent, benign, or transitional). Or, it can be due to a structural defect of the heart or great blood vessels coming off of the heart (termed pathologic). The type of noise, location of the noise, and other abnormalities found on physical examination help determine the cause of the murmur. All murmurs do not require an echocardiogram and a cardiologist evaluation to determine the cause.

Hemolytic Uremic Syndrome. (Also known as HUS). A group of medical problems caused by some food poisoning (E coli, Shigella) infections. The problems include severe anemia, low platelet count, and kidney failure. HUS typically occurs in children ages four months to four years of age.

Hemophilia. A genetically inherited blood clotting disorder. People with this disorder lack a chemical clotting "factor" that impairs the body's chain reaction to clot blood when bleeding occurs. In general, this is a disease of males and women are only carriers (i.e. not affected) because the gene for the disorder is on the "X" chromosome.

Henoch-Schonlein Purpura. (Also known as HSP) Inflammation of the blood vessels (vasculitis) after a viral illness. Symptoms include a dramatic rash of raised bruised areas on the legs. Joint pain, abdominal pain, and blood in the urine also occur. Although the disease sounds and looks serious, 90% of children recover completely without any treatment. Occurs mostly in children aged four to 10 years.

Hernia. The term used to describe a bulging out of tissue or organ where it is not supposed to be. It occurs due to a weakness of a muscle wall. The most common types include:
Diaphragmatic hernia—abdominal organs protrude into chest
Femoral hernia—intestines protrude into thigh
Inguinal hernia—intestines protrude into groin
Umbilical hernia—intestines protrude into belly button
The risk of all hernias is that the organ that is bulging out will get stuck in that position and cut off the blood supply to it. Umbilical hernias rarely get stuck (incarcerate), thus rarely require any treatment.

Hemorrhagic disease of the newborn. A relatively common (one in 200) problem of newborns who have a Vitamin K deficiency. Infants with this disorder can have severe bleeding. Because of this risk, all newborns receive a shot of Vitamin K shortly after they are born.

Hindmilk. Another breastfeeding term. This refers to the fattier milk that comes out after several minutes of nursing. This milk can actually look yellow (like fat). Don't be alarmed—it's good stuff.

Hip dysplasia. Also known as congenital hip dyplasia, or developmental dysplasia of the hip. This is a congenital abnormality where the leg bone is out of its socket at the hip. It is easily treated with a brace if detected in the first few months of life. Babies who are **breech** have a slightly higher risk of having this disorder.

Hirschprung's disease. A congenital abnormality where the nerves of the rectum (intestinal exit) don't form. As a result, newborns cannot poop (stool) without assistance. Infants with severe constipation may have a partial defect and are also tested for this disorder. Treatment is surgical.

Histamine. A chemical compound the body produces in an allergic response. Histamine causes the characteristic "allergy symptoms" that people experience such as hives, itchy eyes, and congestion.

Human Papilloma Virus (HPV). A virus that is transmitted through sexual contact. HPV can live in the undersurface of the foreskin of an uncircumcised man. HPV is also a known factor in the development of cervical cancer in women.

Hydrocele. A fluid collection in a boy's scrotum. Rarely, it is associated with a **hernia**. Most of the time, the fluid is present at birth and goes away on its own by six months of life. It makes the boy's scrotum look unusually large.

Hydrocephalus. An abnormally large collection of cerebrospinal fluid (CSF), the fluid that bathes the brain and spinal cord. This can be caused by excessive production, blockage of the collection pathway, or decreased absorption in the body. Symptoms include: bulging fontanelle (soft spot), headache, vomiting, enlarged head size, loss of developmental milestones, and abnormal neurologic exam.

Hypospadias. A congenital abnormality where the urethra (tube that connects the bladder to the outside) opening is on the underside of the penis instead of in the middle. This requires surgical repair, usually after six months of age. Because the foreskin is used to perform the repair, these babies are not circumcised.

Hypothyroidism. A poorly functioning thyroid gland produces a suboptimal level of thyroid hormone. Thyroid hormone is an essential chemical needed for body metabolism. Babies with congenital hypothyroidism can become mentally retarded (cretins) if they are not treated. This is one of the screening tests performed in the state metabolic screen. The incidence of congenital hypothyroidism is one in 4000 newborns.

Idiopathic Thrombocytopenic Purpura (ITP). The destruction of platelets due to an autoimmune response in the body. Can occur after a viral illness. Because platelets are needed to clot blood, a low count causes bruising and **petechiae**. Some children need medication to help the body increase platelet production in the body, others bounce back on their own. The good news is that almost 90% of kids do beautifully and have no further problems after the one episode.

Imperforate Anus. A congenital abnormality where the anus (opening of the intestines to the outside) does not form completely. This abnormality is often associated with a combination of abnormalities called VATER syndrome. It is repaired surgically.

Inflammatory Bowel Disease (IBD). Chronic swelling of the intestinal lining that results in bloody diarrhea. Crohn's Disease and Ulcerative Colitis are types of IBD. It is rare for a child under age two years to be diagnosed with this disorder.

Inguinal hernia. (see **hernia**)

Inhaled steroid. Medication used to control chronic asthma symptoms. The medication is administered via a machine that aerosolizes it (nebulizer) or via a hand-held "inhaler." The inhaled method is preferable because most of the medication goes to the location it is intended to help (i.e. the lungs). Very little of the medicine gets absorbed into the bloodstream—this means there is less of the unwanted side effects and more therapeutic benefit.

Intestinal obstruction. This is a general term to describe the blockage of the intestine. The gastrointestinal tract is like a big pipe, and in these terms, obstruction is a clogged pipe. This can occur due to intussusception, volvulus, malrotation (congenital defect), and hernias. Because the area is blocked, blood flow to the intestines decreases and may cause death of that tissue. This is a surgical emergency or an "acute abdomen." Symptoms include distended belly, vomiting bile.

Intussusception. When a piece of intestine telescopes upon itself creating an intestinal obstruction. The most common time this occurs is between six and 18 months of age. Symptoms include intermittent abdominal pain with pulling up of the legs. Vomiting, and poop that looks like "currant jelly" also occur. This is an emergency. Diagnosis (and treatment) can be done with a special radiological study.

Jaundice. Yellowing of the skin and the whites of the eyes due to a collection of body garbage called bilirubin. The newborn period is a unique time in life that causes a "normal" jaundice. Outside of the newborn period, jaundice is NOT normal. It requires a thorough medical evaluation to look for the cause.

Kawasaki Disease. An illness that causes the body's blood vessels to swell (vasculitis). The cause is unknown. Occurs mostly in children under two years of age. Symptoms include: fever for five or more days straight, rash on the palms and soles, peeling skin on the fingertips, pink eye, bright red lips/tongue, swollen lymph nodes in the neck, general body rash, and irritable mood. The most severe complication is swelling of the arteries that supply the heart (coronary artery aneurysm). This disease is one of the reasons that doctors want to see a child who has had a fever for five consecutive days or more.

Labial adhesion. A condition where the labia minora (smaller lips) of the vaginal opening get stuck together. This happens in little girls because they do not make estrogen hormone yet (pre-puberty). The amount of tissue that is stuck can vary. The problem is that the urethra (opening for the bladder) is located beneath the labia. If the lips are almost completely fused shut, estrogen cream (RX) is applied so that the urine can flow out more easily. Once the labia are unstuck, it is prudent to put Vaseline on the area at diaper changes to prevent them from re-sticking. All girls outgrow this condition once they hit puberty.

Laryngomalacia. A floppy airway. Some babies are born with relaxed throat tissue. When they breathe in, they make a high pitched squeaky noise (**stridor**). Babies outgrow this condition, often by age one. These babies get evaluated by an ear, nose, and throat specialist just to confirm the diagnosis. It does not affect their breathing and no treatment is needed.

Leukemia. Abnormal production of body's blood cells which then leads to failure of the bone marrow to produce normal blood cells necessary for body functioning. Symptoms include: fever, fatigue, paleness of the skin, excessive bruising, **petechiae**, and joint pain.

Macrocephaly. Official term to describe a big head. Most of the time, a child's big head is due to his genes (i.e. someone else in the family has a big head). But, if the head size percentile is enlarging or if there are other concerning symptoms, a doctor may evaluate the head with an imaging study to rule out **hydrocephalus** or a **brain tumor**.

Malabsorption. When the intestine is not performing its job of digesting food. The result is a watery, foul smelling diarrhea. Some causes of chronic malabsorption are **celiac disease** and **cystic fibrosis**. This deserves to be checked out.

Malrotation. A congenital abnormality in the development of the intestines. The abnormal position creates a problem with blood flow to the intestines as well as potential for obstruction of food transit. Newborns with this problem have vomiting, constipation, and abdominal pain. Treatment is surgical.

Masturbation. A normal behavior of exploring one's sexual organs. Both boys and girls do it.

Meconium. The first poop a newborn passes. Black, tarry, sticky. Some

glossary

babies will pass this first poop before birth during a stressful labor. If the meconium is seen prior to birth, a baby will have his nose, mouth, and throat suctioned at delivery to prevent passage of this stuff into the lungs (called **meconium aspiration syndrome**).

Meconium ileus. A failure of the newborn's poop (**meconium**) to pass because of abnormally thick intestinal secretions. This condition is associated with **cystic fibrosis**.

Meconium plug. A delay in passing of the newborn's first poop (**meconium**). This usually responds to rectal stimulation (e.g. taking a rectal temperature).

Meningitis. Inflammation of the tissues that line the brain and the spinal cord. This can be caused by a virus, bacteria, or by tuberculosis. Symptoms include: headache, vomiting, TRUE IRRITABILITY (i.e. unconsolable), bulging fontanelle (soft spot), fever, neck stiffness, seizures, **petechiae**. This is a medical emergency.

Metabolic disorder. A broad term that describes disorders in breaking down foods (see metabolic storage disease below). These disorders are different than endocrine disorders, which involve abnormal levels of body hormones (e.g. thyroid disease, diabetes, adrenal disease).

Metabolic Storage Disease (Inborn Errors of Metabolism). A group of diseases that all cause an inability to break down certain food products. As a result, byproducts of metabolism accumulate. In some of these disorders this accumulation goes to body parts (liver, heart, brain, kidney, eye) causing permanent damage or even death. The more common storage diseases are tested for on the state metabolic screens (**PKU, galactosemia**). Some of the less common disorders can be tested in the optional **supplemental newborn screens**.

Microcephaly. The technical term for a small head. Head size is often hereditary. Families with small heads have small headed babies. However, if a child's head size percentile is plateauing or decreasing, an imaging study may be done to look for **craniosynostosis**.

Milk protein allergy. Milk contains protein, sugar, and fat. Some babies (about 1%) have an allergy to the protein component that causes inflammation and irritation of the intestine lining. This leads to diarrhea that can be mixed with blood or mucus. A significant percentage of babies who are allergic to milk protein are also allergic to soy protein. The good news—most kids outgrow this problem.

Milia. A normal newborn rash on the nose that look like pinpoint white dots. These go away on their own.

Miliaria. A normal newborn rash that looks like prickly heat. This goes away on its own.

Mongolian Spots. A bruise like discoloration found on the buttocks of darker pigmented newborns. These spots fade over several years. No treatment is needed.

Murmur. (see heart murmur)

Nasolacrimal Duct Obstruction (blocked tear duct). Babies have narrow tear ducts that lead out to the corner of the eyes. Occasionally, the tube gets clogged. Tears, which are usually watery, get thick from being backed up. The result—goopy fluid that comes out of the eyes. This can happen intermittently for the first year of life. You can help open up the duct by massaging gently just below the corner of the eye near the nose. I usually refer patients to an eye doctor if this is happening beyond a year of age. The difference between blocked tear ducts and pink eye (infection) is that the eye is not red or irritated.

Nevus Flammeus (Stork bite, angel kiss). These are newborn birthmarks located at the nape of the neck, eyelids, and forehead. They are bright pink in color. The marks on the face fade over the first year of life. The marks on the neck can last forever. These marks are not associated with cancer.

Neural tube defects. A congenital abnormality of the brain/spinal cord development. Many of these disorders can be detected prenatally via an abnormal AFP test or an ultrasound. These disorders vary in severity. The most severe form is lack of brain formation (anencephaly). The least severe form is **spina bifida occulta** (see **sacral dimple**), where there is completely normal nerve function.

Neurofibromatosis (NF). A genetic disorder (gene defect) that causes tumors of the tissue covering nerves. Babies are often born without symptoms, although some will have three or more **cafe au lait spots** at birth. As a child grows, he develops numerous (more than five) cafe au lait spots and freckles in the armpit and groin areas. The tumors on the nerves grow later and can be seen as large bumps under the skin. Most of these tumors are benign (not cancerous), but can occur in dangerous places (e.g. eye, ear, brain, kidney). Children with this disorder are seen regularly by a number of doctors. FYI: The diagnosis of NF is not made on the presence of cafe au lait spots alone—this is only one of several symptoms and signs. Most children with a few cafe au lait spots do not have NF.

Newborn acne. (see acne)

Newborn nasal congestion. All newborns have snotty noses. They will sneeze, snort, cough, and snore. This lasts for four to six weeks. If it does not interfere with feedings or sleep, do nothing. If it is causing a problem, use saline nose drops to flush the nose before feedings or bedtime.

Omphalitis. A belly button infection. The umbilical stump and skin surrounding it looks red and swollen. There is a foul odor coming from it. If this occurs in a newborn, it usually requires admission to a hospital for intravenous (IV) antibiotics.

Orbital cellulitis. A serious infection that involves the tissue surrounding the eye. It is caused by a sinus infection that spreads into the area. Symptoms include: limited eye motion, bulging of the eyeball, eyelid swelling, eye pain, and fever. This is the reason that doctors want to see children who have eyelid swelling and a fever.

Orthotic. A custom made shoe insert designed by a podiatrist to provide arch support for people who are flat-footed. The AAP does not currently recommend orthotics for babies and young children.

Otitis media. Literally, middle ear inflammation. Acute otitis media refers to an active infection that came up shortly before it is diagnosed in the office. Serous otitis media (or otitis media with effusion) refers to residual fluid that remains after the active infection is over.

Otitis externa. (Otherwise known as swimmer's ear) Literally, external ear inflammation. This is really an infection of the skin that lines the ear canal. It is caused by water that pools in the ear canal and allows germs to grow. Symptoms include pain with touching the ear itself, swelling and redness of the canal, and sometimes a fever. This is uncommon in the under one age group.

Paraphimosis. The foreskin gets stuck behind the head of the penis in an uncircumcised boy. This causes lots of swelling and pain.

Pathologic Heart Murmur. (see Heart Murmur)

Penile adhesions. The head of the penis sticks to the shaft skin. In boys who are circumcised, it is important to visualize the edge of the head at diaper changes and clean the area of any debris (smegma). If the skin starts to get stuck together, try gently pulling down at the base of the penis to separate the area.

Perforated eardrum. The natural occurrence of a middle ear infection that causes a small hole in the eardrum to evacuate the pus that is under pressure. It is the equivalent of a pimple popping and draining. Pus and blood will be seen draining out of the ear canal.

Periodic breathing. Newborns do not breathe in a regular pattern. They breathe 30 to 60 times a minute, but very erratically. There may be a stretch of several pants in a row, then a long p-a-u-s-e, then a big breath. That is normal, as long as that pause is less than ten seconds.

Pervasive Developmental Delay (PDD). A disorder of development that falls into the category of Autism Spectrum Disorders. Children with PDD are higher functioning and capable of limited social interactions. They may also have more language skills than those who are severely affected.

Phenylketonuria (PKU). A metabolic disorder routinely tested on the state metabolic screen. It is a genetic defect in an enzyme that breaks down phenylalanine. The incidence is one in 10,000. People with this disorder need to have a special diet. See **metabolic storage disease**.

Phimosis. Inability to pull the foreskin of an uncircumcised boy's penis back. In severe cases, circumcision is necessary to fix the problem.

Phototherapy. The term used for treatment of moderate-severe jaundice (hyperbilirubinemia). A jaundiced baby is placed in a blue light source (either via "bili" blanket or bank of lights). The lights help to breakdown the bilirubin. For babies who are mildly jaundiced, we do NOT recommend placing an undressed baby near a sunny window in the house. It doesn't help and makes the baby uncomfortable.

Pneumonia. Lung inflammation caused primarily by infection. Both viruses and bacteria can cause pneumonia. The tiny air sacs (alveoli) fill up with pus and prevent air exchange. Symptoms include fever, cough, chest pain, and respiratory distress.

Polydactyly. When there are more than five fingers or toes on a hand or a foot. The extra digit can be removed.

Port wine stain. This is a large, red/purple, flat birthmark that occurs on one side of the face or limb. These do not fade over time and are mostly a cosmetic issue. If the birthmark covers the eyelid, a child is evaluated for glaucoma. Any time it occurs on the forehead or eye, a child is also evaluated for a brain abnormality (**Sturge-Weber syndrome**).

Posterior urethral valves. A congenital defect of the formation of the urethra (tube that connects the bladder to the outside). There are valves that normally push the urine (pee) outwards. In this condition, the valves push the urine backwards into the urinary tract. This is rare, and only occurs in boys.

Post-tussive emesis. The Latin words for 'after-cough' vomiting. Babies and young children have overactive gag reflexes. So a forceful cough might bring up lunch. All vomiting in children is not due to an upset stomach.

Preauricular pits and tags. Minor congenital defects of the formation of the external ear. The pits are due to remnants of a cyst that occurred prior to birth. Pits are rarely associated with hearing disorders. The tags are extra pieces of skin. If severe, these can be removed for cosmetic reasons.

Pseudostrabismus. The false appearance that a child looks cross-eyed or has a lazy eye due to the child's facial structure. Babies and young children are often referred to a pediatric ophthalmologist for concerns of a lazy eye (**esotropia, amblyopia**) and are ultimately diagnosed with this benign entity. But, it is better to be on the safe side and check out any concerns.

Pustular melanosis. A normal newborn rash found in darker pigmented babies. The original rash looks like little pimples. As the lesions fade, they leave a temporary brown freckle. Some babies have hundreds of these freckles. They go away on their own.

Pyelonephritis. An infection of the kidneys. In an acute infection, a child has fever, back pain, and pain with urination. Infants under six months of age with a bladder infection routinely get admitted to the hospital because there is a greater risk of the infection extending into the kidneys.

Pyloric stenosis. A narrowing of the outlet from the stomach to the small intestine due to a congenital abnormality in the muscle (pylorus). Babies (more commonly males) will have projectile (REALLY IMPRESSIVE) vomiting at every feeding starting between two and four weeks of life. The vomiting may start out in a small way, but progressively gets worse and more projectile. Delay in seeking medical attention results in dehydration. Treatment is surgical, by making a cut in the muscle.

Respiratory Distress. This is the term used to describe a child who is air-hungry. If a child cannot successfully get enough oxygen in with each breath, he will breathe faster, heavier, and use chest wall muscles to get as much air in as possible. This equates to a child who is panting, grunting, flaring his nostrils, and retracting (sucking in of the ribcage).

Retinoblastoma. A malignant tumor of the eye that occurs in babies. Fortunately, this is quite rare. This is one of the important reasons we do an eye exam in the nursery.

Retractions. The term used to describe the sucking in of the ribcage when a child has **respiratory distress**. Retractions occur when the body starts using the chest wall muscles to pull more air in with each breath. With phone encounters, we will ask you to look at how your child is breathing to tell us if he has retractions.

Rickets. Malformation of growing bones in children most commonly due to Vitamin D deficiency. Vitamin D is necessary for calcium to be deposited into the bone (which makes them hard). Bones will form with a bent shape because they are softer than they should be.

Ringworm. (see fungal infections in Appendix D)

Rooting reflex. This is a newborn 'primitive' reflex that causes a baby to turn his head if you stroke his cheek. It is an instinctive mechanism that encourages eating. Babies lose this primitive reflex by three to six months of age.

Sacral dimple. This is a tiny divet, or dimple in the lower portion of the back. These can be associated with a minor abnormality of neural tube development called spina bifida occulta. The L5-S1 vertebrae bone is slightly abnormal but the spinal cord (nerve) is formed normally. Most babies with sacral dimples are unaffected and do not need evaluation or treatment.

Seborrhea. (Also known as dandruff, cradle cap) A skin problem that causes greasy, flaky, and sometimes red skin in areas where 'sebaceous glands' reside—typically the scalp, ears, beside the nose, eyebrows. Many babies are afflicted with this and outgrow it. Teenagers can also get seborrhea and have it for a lifetime. Treatment includes anti-dandruff shampoos, low potency steroid creams/lotions, and vegetable oil to loosen up the flakes in the scalp.

Sensory Integration Disorder. A constellation of behaviors stemming from an inability to process and adapt to stimuli of the five senses. Children with this disorder have trouble with activities of daily living and social encounters (aversion to textured foods, dislike of socks and tags on clothing, avoidance of messy activities, avoidance of being touched...) Diagnosis occurs most frequently in pre-school or school aged children.

Serous otitis media. Fluid in the middle ear space. This fluid can be present several weeks to months after an acute infection (i.e. ACUTE otitis media). This fluid is sterile (free of bugs), but has the potential to get re-infected. Antibiotics are not usually necessary or helpful to clear the fluid.

Shoulder dystocia. This refers to a difficult delivery where the shoulders are forcefully pulled to get the baby out. This happens to a mom with a small pelvis or a big baby. Occasionally, the collar bone (clavicle) breaks during delivery. It heals nicely without any residual problems.

Sickle cell anemia. A hereditary abnormality of the red blood cell structure, causing impaired oxygen carrying capacity and increased destruction of the red blood cells.

Sinusitis. (see Appendix D, Infections)

Skin tags. These are tiny pieces of raised skin that can occur anywhere on the body. In the newborn, they are most frequently found in front of the ear (**preauricular tag**) or on the vagina. They are not problematic and require no intervention.

Spina Bifida. A congenital abnormality of the spinal cord development. There is a spectrum of severity of the defect. Most severe defects cause paralysis of the legs and body parts supplied by the affected nerves (bowel, bladder function). The incidence of spina bifida is decreasing as more women are taking pre-natal vitamins (folic acid) during pregnancy. See **neural tube defects.**

Stevens-Johnson Syndrome. A serious allergic reaction that can be fatal.

Strawberry Hemangioma. A birthmark made of a collection of blood vessels. The vessels grow and enlarge for the first few years of life. So, the birthmark gets bigger. The good news—the vessels shrink up and disappear, usually by age five years. Surgery is usually not done to remove these.

Stridor. A squeaky, high pitched noise with breathing in that can be heard without a stethoscope. In newborns, it is usually caused by **laryngomalacia**. In any other situation, it is a sign of respiratory distress at the level of the throat. Children with severe **croup** infection have a very swollen airway if they have stridor. If your child has stridor, call your doctor immediately.

glossary

Stork Bites see Nevus Flammeus

Sturge Weber syndrome. A serious disorder that includes brain abnormalities in combination with a port wine stain on the face. Brain atrophy, seizures, and paralysis can occur.

Supranumerary nipple (accessory nipple). These are extra, nonfunctional nipples found along the same vertical line as the nipples themselves. They are not problematic. They can be removed for cosmetic reasons.

Syndactyly. Two or more fingers or toes are fused either partially or fully together. The severity of the defect determines whether treatment is required.

Thrush. (see Appendix D, infections)

Tongue-tied (see ankyloglossia)

TORCH infections. This is an acronym for the standard tests that are done in Mom's prenatal evaluation. They include: Toxoplasmosis, Syphilis, Rubella, Cytomegalovirus (CMV), Hepatitis B, HIV, and Herpes. In certain situations, Varicella (chickenpox) and Parvovirus are also tested. If Mom has been infected, or is a carrier of the Hepatitis B virus, her baby receives not only the Hepatitis B vaccine at birth, but also a shot of medicine to prevent passage of infection.

Torticollis. A stiffening of the neck muscles that occurs in newborns and young infants. If the neck muscle gets stiff, a baby will preferentially turn his head only one direction. Occasionally, the muscle is so tight that you can see the muscle spasm (a knot in the neck). Treatment includes muscle stretching exercises and encouraging the baby turn his head in the opposite direction. Untreated torticollis can result in facial asymmetry (one side is flatter than the other).

Transient Tachypnea of the Newborn (TTN). A common cause of mild respiratory distress in the newborn. Fetuses swallow amniotic fluid while in the womb. When a baby is born vaginally, that fluid gets squeezed out as the baby passes through the birth canal and cries for the first time. Rarely, some of that fluid remains in babies delivered vaginally. More commonly, babies delivered by C-section have this problem. The good news is that the babies all do just fine. They breath faster than normal and may need a little oxygen for the first hour of life.

Transitional heart murmur. The term for a benign, flow murmur heard in the first 24 hours of life. As a baby is born, the fetal heart circulation changes over to the newborn circulation. There are a series of valves that close off the fetal blood pathways and open pathways to the lungs. We often hear the turbulence of blood flow as this is happening. It's nothing to worry about. If a murmur is heard after 24 hours of life, or has a different quality or location that it is heard, your doctor will evaluate it further.

Transmitted upper airway noise. Noise that comes from the nose that is heard and felt in the lungs. When there is a moderate amount of nasal congestion (snot) in the nose, the air going through it makes a loud noise as it passes through. Since babies and young children don't know how to blow their noses, this is often a unique occurrence in this age group.

Tuberculosis. (Known as TB. Previously known as "consumption"). Infectious lung disease that causes nodules in the lungs, but can spread to the lymph nodes and brain. The scary part of the disease is that people can be infected or be "carriers" of the infection without showing symptoms. People with active infection classically have fever, cough, weight loss, night sweats, and blood in the mucus they cough up. Although TB is less common than it used to be, it occurs in urban populations and immigrants from Asia, Africa, and Latin America. Recommendations for TB screening (PPD) varies among communities, but is usually required for public school entry.

Umbilical hernia. See **hernia.** These are very common in newborns, particularly African American babies. The size of the hernia can be quite large, but the intestine almost never (I've had one patient) gets stuck (incarcerated). These are caused by weak abdominal muscles which will get stronger as the baby starts using them. Most of these hernias resolve on their own. If the hernia is still present by age two, I'll refer a child to a pediatric surgeon for repair. Old Wives Tale: You do not need to bandage the hernia or place a coin on it to make it go away. Your baby will fix the problem himself when he starts doing Ab crunches.

Undescended testes. Failure of the male sex organs to descend into the scrotum in the newborn male. (In fetal development, they grow in the pelvic area, then travel down to the scrotum.) Often, the testes will come down on their own by six months of life. If they don't, a surgical procedure is performed to affix the testes in the scrotum. Testes in the pelvis are at slightly higher risk for testicular cancer, and make it awfully difficult to perform a monthly self-testicular exam in that location.

Uric acid crystals. A waste product found in the urine. When the urine is concentrated (low water volume), the uric acid will pull itself out of the urine solution and can be found in crystal form in the diaper. It looks like brick dust and tends to alarm parents who think it is blood. It is an indication of mild dehydration—so aggressive feeding is the only treatment.

Urinary tract infections (UTI). An infection in the urinary bladder. It is difficult to diagnose a bladder infection in babies because they do not complain that it burns when they urinate. Sometimes fever and irritability are the only symptoms. It is a good idea to obtain a urine specimen on babies who have a fever with no obvious source of infection.

Vaginal discharge. Newborn girls often have vaginal discharge due to fluctuating hormone levels. Older girls who have vaginal discharge prior to puberty need to be evaluated for infection.

Ventricular Septal Defect (VSD). The most common type of congenital heart defect (abnormal formation of the heart in the fetus). In this defect, a hole is present in either the muscle wall or tissue between the two large chambers (ventricles) of the heart. A murmur is detected due to the blood flow that crosses between the chambers. Most of these holes close on their own with no medical intervention. Children with VSD's are followed by pediatric cardiologists until the hole closes.

Vernix. A cheesy, greasy white coating found on the skin of newborns. The nursery nurses will wash it off nicely at your baby's first bath.

Vesicles. Pinpoint, fluid filled blisters seen classically with chickenpox, shingles, and herpes infections. In chickenpox, these lesions appear in crops over a period of a few days.

Vesicoureteral reflux (VUR). An abnormality in the urinary tract system that causes urine to track backwards towards the bladder and kidneys. This urine is not sterile, thus these children are predisposed to bladder and kidney infections. Any boy and any pre-pubertal girl with a bladder infection for the first time needs to be tested for this disorder. Many children outgrow this disorder, but it can take several years (up to age seven). Children with severe reflux (Grades 3-4) may need surgical repair to prevent scarring and permanent kidney damage. Children with milder forms (Grades 1-2) remain on preventative doses of antibiotics until they outgrow it. There is a hereditary predisposition to this disorder. If a parent has VUR, their children should be tested. Some doctors will test siblings of affected individuals as well.

von Willebrand Disease. A genetically inherited bleeding disorder that affects both the platelets and the blood clotting chain reaction. People with this disorder have frequent, excessive nosebleeds, easy bruising, and heavy periods.

Whooping Cough. (see pertussis in Chapter 12)

Yeast infection. (see thrush, yeast diaper rash in Appendix D)

References for this section are footnoted in Appendix G.

Q. How do I know if an Internet site has reliable medical information?

Here are a few thoughts:

1. Find out who has created the website. Is there contact information?
2. What is the purpose of the website?
3. Who are the experts giving the advice?
4. What references are cited? Citations should be listed from scientific journals.
5. Be suspicious of information that is opinionated or seems biased.
6. Be suspicious of products that are touted as cure-alls or miracles.

Source: ImmunizationInfo.org

Good books to have in the house

Alternative Therapies
Kemper, K. *The Holistic Pediatrician*. New York: HarperCollins, 2002.

Breastfeeding
Hale, I. *Medications and Mother's Milk*. 10th Edition. Amarillo: Pharmasoft Publishing, 2002.
Huggins, K. *The Nursing Mother's Companion*. Boston: Harvard Common Press, 1990.

Child Development/Behavior
Brazelton, T. *Touchpoints*. Reading: Addison-Wesley, 1992.

Medical Information
Woolf, A. *Children's Hospital Guide to Your Child's Health and Development*. Persens 2002.

Multiples
Luke, B. *When You're Expecting Twins, Triplets, or Quads*. New York: Harper Perennial, 1999.

Prematurity
Garcia-Prats, J. *What To Do When Your Baby is Premature*. New York: Three Rivers Press, 2000

Sleep
Ferber, R. *Solve Your Child's Sleep Problems*. New York: Simon and Schuster, 1985.
Weissbluth, M. *Healthy Sleep Habits, Happy Child*. New York: Fawcett Books, 2003.

Vaccinations
Humiston, S. *Vaccinating Your Child. Questions and Answers for the Concerned Parent*. Atlanta: Peachtree, 2000.
Offit, P. *What Every Parent Should Know About Vaccinations*. New York: Macmillan, 1998.

Reliable web sites

Adoption

University of Minnesota, Adoption Clinic	peds.umn.edu/IAC/
International Adoption Alliance	i-a-a.org
Association for Research in International Adoption	adoption-research.org
Centers for Disease Control	cdc.gov/ncidod/dq/
U.S. Dept. of State	travel.state.gov/adopt.html

Allergies

American Academy of Allergy, Asthma, and Immunology	aaaai.org
Allergy, Asthma, And immunology Online	allergy.mcg.edu
Food Allergy Network	foodallergy.org
Allergy and Asthma Network	aanma.org
Allergy Center	onlineallergycenter.com
Asthma and Allergy Foundation of America	aafa.org
The Allergy Group	immunecom/allergy/index

Alternative Therapies/Herbal remedies

National Institutes of Health	http://odp.od.nih.gov
	ods.od.nih/gov/databases/ibids.html
Longwood Herbal Task Force	mcp.edu/herbal/default.htm

Breastfeeding

iBreastfeeding Bookstore	ibreastfeeding.com
Breastfeeding.com	breastfeeding.com

Cancer

National Cancer Institute	cancer.gov/cancer_information/
Johns Hopkins	hopkinscancercenter.org

Carseats

National Highway Traffic Safety Administration	nhtsa.gov
American Academy of Pediatrics	aap.org
National Safe Kids Campaign	safekids.org

Childcare

National Association for the Education of Young Children	NAEYC.org
Child Care Aware	childcareaware.org

Child Development

Reach Out and Read	reachoutandread.org
Zero to Three	zerotothree.org
National Institute of Health (cerebral palsy)	ninds.nih.gov
Learning Disabilities Association of America	ldanatl.org
Easter Seals	easter-seals.org

Cord blood banking

General info	parentsguidecordblood.com
National Marrow Donor	programmarrow.org/NMDP/cord.blood.bank.list.html
Lifebank	lifebankusa.com
CBR	cordblood.com
New England Cord Blood Bank	cordbloodbank.com
California Cryobank, Inc.	cryobank.com

Diabetes

American Diabetes Association	diabetes.org
Juvenile Diabetes Research Foundation International	jdrf.org

Emergency Care

Emergency Medical Services for Children	ems-c.org

Gastrointestinal problems (stomach/intestine)

North American Society for Pediatric Gastroenterology and Nutrition	naspgn.org

General medical information

American Academy of Pediatrics	aap.org
Keep Kids Healthy	keepkidshealthy.com
Kids Health	kidshealth.org
WebMD	webmd.com
Mayo Clinic	mayohealth.org
National Institutes of Health	ncbi.nlm.nih.gov
Medscape	medscape.com
Centers for Disease Control	cdc.gov

references

Heart defects

American Heart Association   americanheart.org
Cincinnati Children's Hospital   cincinnatichildrens.org/heartcenter/encyclopedia/

HIV in children

U.S. Dept. of Health and Human Services   aidsinfo.nih.gov/

Lung Problems

American Lung Association   lungusa.org
Cystic Fibrosis Foundation   cff.org
Stanford University CF Center   cfcenter.stanford.edu
American Academy of Allergy, Asthma, and Immunology   aaaai.org

Nervous System/Seizure disorders

American Academy of Neurology   aan.com
Epilepsy Foundation   epilepsyfoundation.org

Nutrition

Centers for Disease Control   cdc.gov
American Dietetic Association   eatright.org
Mead Johnson   meadjohnson.com
Nestle   nestle.com
Ross   rosspediatrics.com

Parenting

Baby Center   babycenter.com
Baby Corner   thebabycorner.com
Baby Zone   babyzone.com
Parenthood.com   parenthood.com

Sickle Cell Disease

Sickle Cell Disease Association of America, Inc.   sicklecelldisease.org

Skin Disorders

Johns Hopkins Hospital   med.jhu.edu/peds/dermatlas
National Eczema Association   nationaleczema.org

Supplemental Newborn Screening

Baylor   Baylorhealth.com/newbornscreening
March of Dimes   Marchofdimes.com
Mayo   mayoclinic.com
National Newborn Screen   genes-r-us.uthscsa.edu
Neogen   neogenscreening.com
Save The Babies   savethebabies.org
CBR   newscreentest.com

National Coalition for PKU and Allied health   pku-allieddisorders.org
disorders

Travel Health

Centers for Disease Control   cdc.gov/travel/index.htm

Vaccinations

Johns Hopkins: vaccinesafety.edu
World Health Organization   who.int/gpv
Immunofacts   immunofacts.com
Immunization Action Coalition   immunize.org
National Network for immunization info   immunizationinfo.org
Vaccine Adverse Event Reporting System   fda.gov/cber/vaers/vaers.htm
Centers for Disease Control   cdc.gov/nip
Children's Hospital of Philadelphia   vaccine.chop.edu

National Organizations

*There is a support group for virtually every medical disease and syn-
drome. The organizations below should be able to link you to a specific
organization to meet your particular needs.*

American Academy of Pediatrics
141 Northwest Point Blvd., Elk Grove Village, IL 60007
Phone: (847) 434-4000; Web: www.aap.org

Centers for Disease Control and Prevention
1600 Clifton Road, Atlanta, GA 30333
Phone: (800) 311-3435; Web: www.cdc.gov

Easter Seals
230 West Monroe St., Suite 1800, Chicago, IL 60606
Phone: (800) 221-6027 x7153; Web: www.easter-seals.org

March of Dimes Birth Defects Foundation
1275 Mamroneck Ave., White Plains, NY 10605
Phone: (888) 663-4637; Web: www.modimes.org

National Center on Birth Defects and Developmental Disabilities
4770 Buford Highway, N.E., Atlanta, GA 30341
Phone: (770) 488-7150; Web: www.cdc.gov/ncbddd

ZERO to THREE: National Center for Infants, Toddlers, and Families
2000 M Street NW, Suite 200, Washington, DC 20036
Phone: (202) 638-0851; Web: www.zerotothree.org

references

Growth Chart: Boys (Birth to 36 months)

Birth to 36 months: Boys
Length-for-age and Weight-for-age percentiles

NAME _____

RECORD # _____

Published May 30, 2000 (modified 4/20/01).
SOURCE: Developed by the National Center for Health Statistics in collaboration with
the National Center for Chronic Disease Prevention and Health Promotion (2000).
http://www.cdc.gov/growthcharts

Growth Chart: Girls (Birth to 36 months)

Head Circumference (Boys, Girls)

Appendix G

Footnotes

Chapter 1: Decisions

1. Castellsague, X., et al: Male circumcision, penile human papillo-mavirus, and cervical cancer in female patients. *New England Journal of Medicine* 2002 Apr 11; 346 (15): 1105-12.
2. American Academy of Pediatrics policy statement. *Pediatrics* 1999 July; 104 (1): 116.
3. Celedon, et al: Day care attendance, respiratory tract illnesses, wheezing, asthma, and total serum IgE level in early childhood. *Archives of Pediatric and Adolescent Medicine* 2002; 156: 241-245.
4. Martinez, F: The "coming of age" of the hygiene hypothesis. Respiratory Sciences Center, University of Arizona, Respiratory Research, April 2001.
5. American Academy of Pediatrics Policy Statement: Initial medical evaluation of an adopted child. *Pediatrics* 1991; 88(3): 642-44.

Chapter 3: You &Your Baby's Doc

1. American Academy of Pediatrics Policy Statement: Newborn and Infant Hearing Loss: Detection and Intervention. *Pediatrics* 1999; 103(2): 527-530.
2. American Academy of Pediatrics, American College of Obstetrics and Gynecology, and the Centers for Disease Control as of 2002.

Chapter 4: Hygiene

1. Fradin, MS: Comparative efficacy of insect repellant against mos-quito bites. *New England Journal of Medicine* 2002; 347: 13-18.
2. Wall Street Journal May 20, 2003. PD8.
3. American Academy of Pediatrics Policy Statement: Oral Hygiene. *Pediatrics* 2003; 111(5): 1113-1116.

Chapter 5: Nutrition &Growth

1. Behrman, RE. Editor: *Nelson Essentials of Pediatrics*. Philadelphia: WB Saunders, 1990.
2. Bernbaum, J.C: *Primary Care of the Preterm Infant*. St. Louis: Mosby,1993.

3. Behrman, RE. See footnote 1.
4. Behrman, RE. See footnote 1.
5. American Academy of Pediatrics Committee on Nutrition: *Pediatric Nutrition Handbook*, 4th Ed. Elk Grove Village, IL, 1999.
6. *American Academy of Pediatrics News*, April 1998.
7. Gartner, LM, et al: American Academy of Pediatrics. Prevention of rickets and Vitamin D deficiency. New guidelines for Vitamin D intake. *Pediatrics* 2003; 111(4): 908-910.

Chapter 6: Liquids

1. Mortensen, EL, etal: The association between duration of breast-feeding and adult intelligence. *JAMA* 2002; 287: 2365-2371.
2. Danner, SC, Cerutti ER: *Nursing your neurologically impaired baby.* Waco, TX: Childbirth Graphics.
3. Barnes, GR, Lethin, AN, Jackson EB et al: Management of breast-feeding. *JAMA* 1953; 151:192.
4. Huggins, K: *The Nursing Mother's Companion.* Third Revised Ed. Boston: The Harvard Common Press, 1995.
5. Huggins, K. See footnote 4.
6. Lawrence, RA: *Breastfeeding: A Guide for the Medical Profession*, 5th ed. St. Louis: Mosby, 1999.
7. Riordan, J, Auerbach, KG: *Breastfeeding and Human Lactation.* Sudbury: Jones and Bartlett Publishers, 1999.
8. (1) Suitor CW: Nutrition care during pregnancy and lactation: new guidelines from the IOM. *J Am Diet Assoc* 1993; 93: 478.
9. FDA, Press release Jan 12, 2001
10. Sampson, HA: Food Allergy, Part 1. Immunopathogenesis and clinical disorders. *J Allergy Clin Immunol* 1999; 103: 717-28.
11. Lawrence, RA. See footnote 6.
12. Lawrence, RA. See footnote 6.
13. Lawrence, RA. See footnote 6.
14. Lawrence, RA. See footnote 6.
15. Schuman, AJ: A concise history of infant formula (twists and turns included). *Contemporary Pediatrics* 2003; 20 (2): 91-103.
16. Chandran, L: Is there a role for long-chain polyunsaturated fatty acids in infant nutrition? *Contemporary Pediatrics* 2003; 20 (2): 107-124.
17. American Academy of Pediatrics Committee on Nutrition: Soy protein-based formulas: recommendations for use in infant feeding. *Pediatrics* 1998;101:148-153.
18. Wall St. Journal, June 24, 2003 p. D4
19. Tran TT, et al: Effect of high dietary manganese intake of neonatal rats on tissue mineral accumulation, striatal dopamine levels, and neurodevelopmental status. *Neurotoxicology* 2002; 23: 635-643.
20. American Academy of Pediatrics Committee on Nutrition: Iron-fortified infant formulas. *Pediatrics.* 1989; 84 (6): 1114-1115.
21. AAP. See footnote 20.
22. Georgieff, M. Taking a rational approach to the choice of formula. *Contemporary Pediatrics* 2001; 18(8):112-130.

Chapter 7: Solids

1. Sampson, HA: Food allergy. *J Allergy Clin Immunol* 2003; 111(12): 540-547.
2. Eigenmann, PA, et al: Prevalence of IgE mediated food allergy among children with atopic dermatitis. *Pediatrics* 1998;101(3): E8.
3. Mofidi, S: Nutritional management of pediatric food hypersensitivities. *Pediatrics* 2003; 111(6): 1645-1653.
4. American Academy of Pediatrics, Committee on Nutrition: Hypoallergenic infant formulas. *Pediatrics* 2000; 106(2): 346-349.
5. Sampson, HA. See footnote 1.
6. Wood, RA: The natural history of food allergy. *Pediatrics* 2003; 111(6): 1631-1637.

Chapter 8: The Other End

1. McClung HJ, et al: Constipation and dietary fiber intake in children. *Pediatrics* 1995; 96: 999-1001.
2. American Urological Association: Pediatric VUR Clinical Practice Guidelines Panel. Report on the Management of VUR in Children. 1996.
3. See footnote 2.

Chapter 9: Sleep

1. Kleitman, N.: *Sleep and Wakefulness*, 2nd Ed. Chicago: University of Chicago Press,1963.
2. Hunt, CE, etal: Infant sleep position and associated health outcomes. *Arch Pediatr Adolesc Med* 2003; 157: 469-474.
3. Fleming, PJ, etal: Mattresses, microenvironments, and multivariate analyses. *British Medical Journal* 2002: 325: 981-82, 1007-1009
4. Data from McKenna, JJ. Mother-Baby Behavioral Sleep Laboratory, University of Notre Dame.
5. Willinger, M, etal: Trends in infant bed sharing in the United States, 1993-2000: the National Infant Sleep Position study. *Arch Ped Adol Med* 2003; 157(1): 43-49.
6. Okami, P, et al: Outcome correlates of parent-child bed sharing: an eighteen-year longitudinal study. *Dev and Behav Pediatrics* 2002; (23) 4: 244-253.
7. Touchette, E: Annual meeting of the Associated Professional Sleep Societies, 2003.
8. Ferber, R: *Solve Your Child's Sleep Problems*. New York: Simon &Schuster, 1985.
9. Ferber, R. See footnote 8.

Chapter 10: Development

1. Brainerd, C: *Piaget's Theory of Intelligence*. Englewood, NJ: Prentice-Hall, 1978.
2. psychology.about.com

Chapter 11: Discipline & Temperament

1. Adapted from Thomas A, Chess S: *Temperament and Development*. New York, Brunner/Mazel 1977.
2. High, P: Data compiled at Infant Development Center, Brown University, 2003.
3. www.msn.com, April, 17, 2003.

Chapter 12: Vaccinations

1. http://www.library.ucla.edu/libraries/biomed/smallpox/
2. Fenn, EA: Biological warfare in eighteenth century North America: beyond Jeffrey Amherst. *Journal of American History* 2000; (86) 4: 1552-1580.
3. O'Connell, RL: *Of Arms and Men: A History of War, Weapons, and Aggression*. NewYork: NY and Oxford University Press, 1989.
4. (1) Atkinson, et al: CDC: Impact of vaccines universally recommended for children in the United States 1900-1998. (2) MMWR 1999: 44-243. (3) MMWR 1999; 44: 243. (4) MMWR 2002;50:1174. (5) MMWR 2002;51:549.
5. Reis EC, et al: Taking the sting out of shots: control of vaccination-associated pain and adverse reactions. *Pediatric Annals* 1998; 27(6): 375-386.
6. Schuval, S: Avoiding allergic reactions to childhood vaccines (and what to do when they occur). *Contemporary Pediatrics* 2003; 20(4): 29-53.
7. Pickering, LK, editor: *Red Book: 2003 Report of the Committee of Infectious Diseases*. 26th ed. Elk Grove Village, IL: American Academy of Pediatrics, 2003.
8. See footnote 7.
9. www.immunizeinfo.org
10. National Public Radio news service.
11. Zeiger, RS. Current issues with influenza vaccine in egg allergy. *Journal Allergy Clin Immunol* 2002; 110; 834.
12. Gershon, A: Varicella vaccine- are two doses better than one? *New England Journal of Medicine* 2002; 347(24): 1692-3.
13. Data from Centers for Disease Control.
14. Wakefield, A.J., et al: Ileal-lymphoid-nodular hyperplasia, non-specific colitis, and pervasive developmental disorder in children. *Lancet* 1998; 351: 637-641.
15. Taylor, B. et al: Autism and measles, mumps, and rubella vaccine: no epidemiological evidence for a causal association. *Lancet* 1999; 353: 2026-2029.
16. Dales, L. et al: Time trends in autism and in MMR immunization coverage in California. *JAMA* 2001; 285:1183-1185.
17. American Academy of Pediatrics Technical Report: Mercury in the environment: implications for pediatricians. *Pediatrics* 2001; 108 (1): 197-205.

Chapter 13: Infections

1. Dowell, SF: Seasonal variations in host susceptibility and cycles of certain infectious diseases. *Emerg Infect Dis* 2001; 7 (3): 369-74.
2. Peter, G: Bacterial resistance in office practice: the need for judicious antimicrobial therapy. Lecture at 25th Annual Pediatric Postgraduate Symposium, Houston, 2003.
3. Mangione-Smith, RM, et al: The relationship between perceived parental expectations and pediatrician antimicrobial prescribing behavior. *Pediatrics* 1999;103: 711-718.
4. Donowitz, L: Infection control in the office: keeping germs at bay. *Contemporary Pediatrics* 2000; 17(9): 47.
5. Rosenfeld, RM, etal: Clinical efficacy of antimicrobial drugs for acute otitis media: metaanalysis of 5400 children from thirty-three randomized trials. *Journal of Pediatrics* 1994; 124: 355-67.
6. Baker, RB: Is ear pulling associated with ear infection? *Pediatrics* 1992; 90: 1006-7.
7. Peter, G. See footnote 2.
8. Post JC, et al: Is pacifier use a risk factor for otitis media? *Lancet* 2001; 357: 823-4.

Chapter 14: Diseases

1. Expert Panel Report II: *Guidelines of the Diagnosis and Management of Asthma*. 1997.
2. Behrman, RE. Editor: *Nelson Essentials of Pediatrics*. Philadelphia: WB Saunders, 1990.
3. Behrman. RE. See footnote 2.
4. Behrman. RE. See footnote 2.
5. Behrman. RE. See footnote 2.
6. Behrman. RE. See footnote 2.
7. Behrman. RE. See footnote 2.
8. Behrman. RE. See footnote 2.
9. Ownby, D. et al: Exposure to dogs and cats in the first year of life and risk of allergic sensitization at six or seven years of age. *JAMA* 2002; 288(8): 963-972.
10. Fleisher, G., Ludwig, S, editors: *Pediatric Emergency Medicine*, 3rd Ed. Baltimore: Williams and Wilkins, 1993.

Chapter 15: First Aid

1. Gunn, VL, Nechyba, C, editors: *The Harriet Lane Handbook: A Manual for Pediatric House Officers*,16th ed. Philadelphia: Mosby, 2002.
2. American Academy of Pediatrics: The management of acute gastroenteritis in young children. *Pediatrics* 1996; 97 (3): 424-35.
3. Chowdhury HR, et al: The efficacy of bismuth salicylate in the treatment of acute diarrhea and the prevention of persistent diarrhea. *Acta Pediatrica* 2001: 90 (6): 605-610.
4. Crocetti, M: Fever phobia revisited: have parental misconceptions about fever changed in 20 years? *Pediatrics* 2001;107 (6): 1241-6.

5. Fleisher, G., Ludwig, S, editors: *Pediatric Emergency Medicine*, 3rd Ed. Baltimore: Williams and Wilkins, 1993.

Appendix A: Medications

1. Murphy JL, editor: *Prescribing Reference for Pediatricians: Spring-Summer 2002*. New York: Prescribing Reference, Inc., 2002.
2. American Academy of Pediatrics Committee on Nutrition: *Pediatric Nutrition Handbook*, 4th ed. Elk Grove Village, IL: American Academy of Pediatrics, 1998.
3. AAP Committee on Nutrition. See footnote 2.
4. AAP Committee on Nutrition. See footnote 2.
5. (1) Hale, T: Medications and Mother's Milk. *A Manual of Lactational Pharmacology*, 10th ed. Amarillo: Pharmasoft Publishing, 2002. (2) AAP Committee on Nutrition. See footnote 2.
6. Shared PJ, Berfman DA: The effect of inhaled steroids on the linear growth of children with asthma: A meta-analysis. *Pediatrics* 2000;106 (1): E8.

Appendix B: Alternative Medicines

1. Kemper, KJ: *The Holistic Pediatrician. A pediatrician's comprehensive guide to safe and effective therapies for the 25 most common ailments of infants, children, and adolescents*, 2nd ed. New York: HarperCollins, 2002.
2. Gilroy CM, Steiner, JF, Byers T, Shapiro H, Georgian W: Echinacea and truth in labeling. *Archives of Internal Medicine* 2003;163: 699-704.
3. Politics and lobbying in the US nutritional and dietary supplements industry. National Public Radio, All Things Considered, June 23, 2003.
4. Rodriguez-Bigas, M: A comparative evaluation of aloe vera in the management of burn wounds in guinea pigs. *Plastic Reconst Surg* 1988; 81: 386-9.
5. Kemper, KJ. See footnote 1.
6. Weizman Z. et al: Efficacy of herbal tea preparation in infantile colic. *Journal of Pediatrics* 1993; 122: 650-2.
7. (1)Barrett, BP, et al: Treatment of the common cold with unrefined Echinacea. A randomized, double blind, placebo-controlled trial. *Annals of Int Medicine* 2002;137(12): 939-46. (2) Kemper, KJ. See footnote 1.
8. (1) Horrobin, DF: Essential fatty acid metabolism and its modification in atopic eczema. *American Journal Clin Nutrition* 2000; 71 (supp): 367s-372. (2) Hederos, C. Berg, A: Epogram evening primrose oil treatment in atopic dermatitis and asthma. *Archives of Dz in Childhood* 1996; 75: 494-7.
9. Weizman, Z. See footnote 6.
10. Gardiner P, Kemper KJ: Herbs in pediatric and adolescent medicine. *Peds Review* 2000; 21 (2): 44-57.
11. (1) Schmid, R. et al: Comparison of seven commonly used agents for prophylaxis of seasickness. *Jnl Travel Med* 1994; 1; 203-6. (2)

Motion sickness, ginger, and psychophysics. *Lancet* 1982; 91: 655-7. (3) Gardiner P. See footnote 10.

12. (1) Iwasa K: Structure activity relationships of protoberberines having antimicrobial activity. *Planta Med* 1998; 64(8): 748-51. (2) Gardiner P. See footnote 10.

13. (1) Das SK, et al: Deglycyrrhizinated liquorice in aphthous ulcers. *J Assoc Physicians India* 1989; 37(10): 647. (2) Teelucksingh S: Potentiation of hydrocortisone activity in skin by glycyrrhetinic acid. *Lancet* 1990; 335 (8697): 1060-3. (3) Gardiner P. See footnote 10.

14. (1) Fox N: Effect of camphor, eucalyptol, and menthol on the vascular state of the mucous membrane. *Arch Oto HNS* ; 1027 (6):112-122. (2) Eeles R: The effect of menthol on nasal resistance to airflow. *J Laryng Otol* 1983; 97: 705-9. (3) Gardiner, P. Longwood Herbal Task Force website: www.mcp.edu/herbal/

15. (1) Fox N. See footnote 14. (2) Eeles R. See footnote 14. (3) Gardiner, P. See footnote 14.

Appendix C: Lab Tests

1. Gunn, VL, Nechyba, C, editors: *The Harriet Lane Handbook: A Manual for Pediatric House Officers*,16th ed. Philadelphia: Mosby, 2002.

2. Loeb, S., editor: *Clinical Laboratory Tests: Values and Implications*. Springhouse, Pennsylvania: Spring House, 1991.

Appendix D: Infections

1. Pickering, LK, editor. *Red Book: 2003 Report of the Committee of Infectious Diseases,* 26th ed. Elk Grove Village, IL: American Academy of Pediatrics, 2003.

2. Pickering, LK. See footnote 1.
3. Pickering, LK. See footnote 1.
4. Pickering, LK. See footnote 1.
5. Pickering, LK. See footnote 1.
6. Pickering, LK. See footnote 1.
7. Pickering, LK. See footnote 1.
8. Pickering, LK. See footnote 1.
9. Pickering, LK. See footnote 1.
10. Pickering, LK. See footnote 1.
11. Data from Centers for Disease Control. www.cdc.gov.

Appendix E: Glossary

1. Behrman RE, Kliegman R. *Nelson Essentials of Pediatrics*. W.B. Saunders, 1990, Philadelphia.
   Urdang Associates. *The Bantam Medical Dictionary*. Bantam, 1981, New York.
   Cloherty JP, Stark AR. *Manual of Neonatal Care*, 3rd ed. Little Brown, 1992, Boston.
   Shelov, SP. *Your Baby's First Year.* Bantam, 1998, New York

INDEX

Coagulation tests, 383
Coarctation of aorta, 44
Coffee grounds, vomiting, 147, 300, 314
Cognitive skills, 185, 188, 194, 195
Colace, 353, 355
Cold/flu season, 8
    on-call doctors and, 292
    scheduling during, 37
Cold medicines, 256, 363-64
    breastfeeding and, 364
Colds. See Common colds
Colic, 145, 206, 210-11
    chamomile tea and, 374
    gas and, 151
    heartburn and, 208
    soy formula and, 114
    treating, 209, 211, 212, 356, 374
Colitis, 301
Colostrum, 54, 92, 93, 95
Columbia School of Nursing, soap
study by, 252
Comfort objects, 171, 179, 212-13
Committee on Nutrition (AAP), 118
Common colds, 254, 259, 260, 263,
        273, 304, 307, 377
    antibiotics and, 257, 262
    breastfeeding and, 105
    contagiousness of, 257
    ear infections and, 265
    exposure to, 53
    treating, 256-57, 375
    vaccines and, 229
    vomiting and, 313
Communication, problems with, 197, 202
Community programs, 202
Complementary therapies, 374
Complete blood count (CBC), 382
Comprehensive metabolic panels, 381,
382-83
Computer Tomography (CT), 337, 380
Comvax, 238
Concrete operational, 189
Concussions, 336
Confidence, instilling, 198
Conflicts, 190, 215
Congestion, 71, 307-9
Conjunctivitis
    bacterial, 263, 315, 392-93
    viral, 389
Consciousness, loss of, 337
Consequences, 214, 217
Constipation, 139, 151, 295
    abdominal pain and, 296
    crying and, 208
    iron and, 117, 140
    relieving, 140-41, 355
    solid foods and, 301
Consumer Product Safety Commission
(CPSC), 162, 195
    recalls and, 200
    toy guide by, 203
Consumer Reports, on sunscreen, 67
Contact dermatitis, 297
Convulsions, 232, 325, 333
Cooking, 23
Coombs test, 383
CorCell, 19

Cord blood, 4, 17-20
cordbloodbank.com, 18
Cord Blood Registry Systems, 19
Cord shorteners, 201
Corneal abrasions, 316, 338
Cortaid, 366
Co-sleeping, 165, 175
    advantages of, 164, 176
    photo of, 165
Couch potatoes, 83, 202
Coughing, 53, 71, 253, 256, 299, 306,
315, 319, 320, 328
    breathing and, 309
    common cold and, 257
    congestion and, 308
    fevers and, 309
    mucus and, 304
    nighttime, 305
    problems with, 237, 299, 307-9, 364
    vomiting and, 313
Cough medicines, 256, 308, 363-64
Cowpox virus, 224, 226, 244
Cow's milk
    allergy to, 125, 131
    hypersensitivity to, 103
    switching to, 122, 281
Coxsackievirus, 254, 273, 388-89
    rashes with, 330-31 (table)
CPR, 133, 200, 293, 333
CPSC. See Consumer Product Safety
Commission
Cradle cap, 61, 65-66, 375
Cradle hold, 96
Craniosynotosis, 42, 75
Crawling, 184, 195
Creams, 283
    acne and, 64
    anesthetic, 229
    antibiotic, 47, 293, 303, 334, 364, 365
    antifungal, 70, 106, 364, 365
    diaper rash, 365, 367-68
    numbing, 16
Creamy Vaseline, 283
Cribs, sharing, 181
Cross eyes, 42, 192, 275
Croup, 254, 263, 273, 304, 305, 388
    treating, 375
Crutches, 173, 175, 210
Crying, 306
    curbing, 208, 209
    guilty parents and, 174, 179
    listening to, 179
    as self-expression, 212
Cryogenic techniques, 18
Cryptosporidium, 310
CSF. See Cerebrospinal fluid
CT. See Computerized Tomography
Cuddling, 186
Cultures, 377, 386
Cups, sippy, 120, 121, 197, 219
Cushingoid features, 362
Cystic fibrosis, 44, 278

Dactylitis, 281
Dairy products, 78, 88, 123
    alternative, 122
    calcium in, 86

index

index

index

index

index

How to Reach the Authors

Have a question about

Baby 411?

Want to make a suggestion?

Discovered a great tip you'd like to share?

Contact the authors, Denise Fields and Ari Brown in one of four flavorful ways:

1. By email: authors@Baby411.com

2. On our web page: www.Baby411.com

3. By phone: (303) 442-8792

4. By mail: 436 Pine Street, Suite 600, Boulder, CO 80302

If this address isn't active, try one of our other URL's:
www.WindsorPeak.com or www.BabyBargainsBook.com
Or call our office at 1-800-888-0385
if you're having problems accessing the page.

What's on our web page?

◆ *Updates on this book between editions.*
◆ *THE LATEST NEWS on medical research for babies.*
◆ *MESSAGE BOARDS with in-depth reader feedback.*
◆ *CORRECTIONS and clarifications.*
◆ *Sign up for a FREE E-NEWSLETTER!*